Sophia Peabody Hawthorne

Sophia Peabody Hawthorne

A Life, Volume 2, 1848–1871

—————— Patricia Dunlavy Valenti ——————

University of Missouri Press
Columbia

Copyright © 2015 by
The Curators of the University of Missouri
University of Missouri Press, Columbia, Missouri 65201

Printed and bound in the United States of America

5 4 3 2 1   19 18 17 16 15

Cataloging-in-Publication data available from the Library of Congress
ISBN 978-0-8262-2047-9

This paper meets the requirements of the
American National Standard for Permanence of Paper
for Printed Library Materials, Z39.48, 1984.

Typefaces: Caslon, Palatino, and Pristina

 *To Christine and Marco*

Contents

Preface

A biographer decides to write about a particular woman for various reasons. She may have been a trailblazer, or, conversely, an index to her time and place. Perhaps she was neglected or misrepresented. Or perhaps her story is simply so interesting it begs to be told. All of these reasons have impelled me to write this two-volume biography of Sophia Peabody Hawthorne.

Sophia was among the first professional women artists in America to earn income from original oil paintings as well as from her copies, illustrations, and decorative art. She was also among the first American women to write about travel abroad. In the early 1830s, her *Cuba Journal* juxtaposed whimsical accounts of local mores against transcendental insight into nature. She simultaneously revealed herself to be a sensuous, vibrant woman, infatuated with her charming Cuban suitor, and gladly flouting propriety. After she returned to New England and the practice of art, the widely circulated *Cuba Journal* introduced her to Nathaniel Hawthorne, who was smitten with the "Queen of Journalizers" as he dubbed her, and immediately began to emulate her detailed recording of the real world in his own journals. Drawn to her though he was, she augmented his profound insecurities. He, therefore, invented a less threatening version of Sophia, the frail "dove" (as he called her) requiring his protection, a fantasy that was accepted and perpetuated by his biographers. Sophia believed marriage to Nathaniel would be a union of equal creative partners: she would paint; he would write. As newlyweds, they began keeping a journal together, their separate entries exposing fundamentally divergent attitudes. Sophia's otherness ignited Nathaniel's imagination, resulting in some of his most textured, enduring female characters. He earned little money from his publications, however, and Sophia hoped to bolster her family's finances by painting an oil canvas which John Louis O'Sullivan, Nathaniel's editor at the time, offered to broker. But Nathaniel squelched O'Sullivan's offer, and Sophia's career.

When the Hawthornes faced eviction from The Old Manse, Sophia negotiated her family's removal to the Salem house where her husband had lived with his mother and sisters. He would return to his bachelor quarters; Sophia and baby Una would occupy a room beneath the parlor. *Sophia Peabody Hawthorne, A Life, Volume 1, 1809–1847* concludes amid humiliating circumstances that Sophia greeted with indefatigable optimism. Ralph Waldo Emerson had praised her talent as a painter who transformed the real world into an ideal one. She could "read poetry out of dull prose," he told her. She had a "beauty making eye."[1] And henceforth she focused her talent upon her family, a creation she sought to perfect as if it were a work of art.

The decade since the publication of volume one of this biography bore witness to increased interest in Sophia and the need for this second volume. In *The Peabody Sisters: The Three Women Who Ignited American Romanticism* (Houghton Mifflin, 2005), Megan Marshall concludes her collective biography of Elizabeth, Mary, and Sophia at the moment of the Hawthornes' marriage, leaving three decades of Sophia's life yet to be told. *Reinventing the Peabody Sisters*, edited by Monika Elbert, Julie Hall, and Katherine Rodier (Iowa, 2006), addresses the sisters' various literary and pedagogical contributions; four of its fourteen articles examine Sophia's travel writing. Judy Smith's novel *Yellowbird* (Lewis-Clark Press, 2007) invents the eroticized lives of Sophia Hawthorne and Lizzie Melville. Each of these publications considers Sophia's actual or fictional life and accomplishments in conjunction with those of others, but she became the exclusive focus of scholarly attention in a 2009 session of the Modern Language Association and in the 2011 fall issue of *The Nathaniel Hawthorne Review*.

Sophia Peabody Hawthorne, A Life, Volume 2, 1848–1871 explores the largely uncharted territory following Sophia's departure from The Old Manse. Nathaniel moved temporarily to the Herbert Street house, but Sophia did not. She preferred the more congenial atmosphere of her parents' or sister Mary Mann's home in Boston. There, during Sophia's second pregnancy, she obtained advice from a homeopathic physician. Several patterns in her life were now established: persistent financial hardship driving a somewhat nomadic existence; the quest for medical expertise to assure her own and her family's physical well-being; and recurring separations from her husband. Although Sophia unfailingly announced that she was married to an exceptional man with whom she had borne equally exceptional children, her family did not satisfy her voracious appetite for intense, personal relationships. Increasingly, she turned to friends—prominent abolitionists, major political figures, as well as some of the country's wealthiest people—who serve to illuminate her character during this period of national conflict and emerging class divisions. Her attachments to men and women other than her husband expand or upend (depending on one's point of view) the notion of the Hawthornes' storied bliss.

Sophia tells the story of this bliss, as well as its countervailing narrative, in her voluminous journals and letters. For her, and later for her husband, writing about life was tantamount to living it. The years before the Hawthornes sailed for England were the most productive of Nathaniel's career; three novels and other fiction reveal the indelible mark of Sophia's presence and demonstrate how literature is produced in a domestic context charged with gender politics. But when the flame of Nathaniel's imagination began to flicker, he used his pen to record the sights and sounds of the real world. After Nathaniel's death, Sophia discovered the abysmal state of her finances, the result of her husband's feckless behavior. Transgressing norms of propriety, she converted his personal notebooks into a commodity. Poverty also legitimated a dormant desire to bring her own writing beyond the scope of family and friends, and she published *Notes in England and Italy* the year before she died. Her delightful, at times idiosyncratic, descriptions of Cuba, Portugal, and Germany still await publication.

Sophia's prolific writing is as much a topic in her biography as it was a resource for it. Quotations from letters and journals allow the reader to distinguish her voice from the voices of her husband, her sisters, her children, their governess Ada Shepard, and others who produced their own copious records of their time together. They confirm and, at times, challenge Sophia's perceptions, just as the narrative of her life challenges entrenched ideas about the man she married. Presenting her perspective in this biography often shines an unflattering light on Nathaniel Hawthorne—one that Sophia herself may not have seen. What she saw reveals much about her; what she did not see reveals more. Her "beauty making eye" was her triumph and her tragedy.

This volume owes its existence to the preservation of thousands of pages of Sophia's holograph journals and letters. Her children were the first curators of these manuscripts now housed in numerous collections throughout the United States where I have been graciously assisted in my research. I am particularly grateful to Isaac Gewirtz, curator of The Henry W. and

Albert A. Berg Collection of English and American Manuscripts at the New York Public Library for his encouragement and for selecting Sophia's manuscripts to be part of the Polonsky digitalization project thereby making them available online at the New York Public Library's website. At the Berg, staff members Neil Mann, who oversaw this digitalization, Anne Garner, and Stephen Crook were unfailingly cordial and helpful. I also thank Christine Nelson, the Drue Heinz Curator of American Manuscripts at the Morgan Library, who has long recognized the power of Sophia's writing and placed it prominently in "The Diary: Three Centuries of Private Lives," a 2011 exhibition. With the vast majority of Sophia's "treasures," as she called them, located at the Berg and the Morgan collections only seven New York City blocks apart, I savored a remarkable opportunity for research. At the Boston Public Library, I am grateful for the generous assistance of Kimberly Reynolds, curator of manuscripts in the Rare Books and Manuscripts department. I also thank the following persons for their help locating archival material and making it available to me: Elizabeth Frengel, research services librarian at the Beinecke Rare Book and Manuscript Library of Yale University; Cheryl Gunselman, manuscripts librarian at Washington State University; John Mustain, rare book librarian at The Green Library of Stanford University; and Scott Sanders, archivist of Antiochiana at the Antioch College Library. Megan Marshall was most helpful in locating the image of Sophia Hawthorne used on the cover of this volume. The Servants of Relief for Incurable Cancer, the order of nuns founded by Rose Hawthorne Lathrop, have generously assisted me over many years with material from their archives that I have used in three books. Sister Mary Joseph and Sister DePaul have been particularly helpful to me with this present volume.

I thank many friends and colleagues for their interest in the progress of my work. Samuel Chase Coale, David Grevin, Julie Hall, Sandra Harbert Petrulionis, Rollin Shaw, Martha Tournas, and Sandy Waterkotte read and critiqued various chapters. Joel Myerson and Larry J. Reynolds provided me with detailed comments on the entire draft. Members of Women Writing Women's Lives, in particular Betty Boyd Caroli, provided continuing encouragement, as did William L. Andrews, Monika Elbert, Rita Gollin, Claudia Durst Johnson, and Melinda Ponder. I owe a special debt of gratitude to John L. Idol for his long-standing support of my work. Thomas Woodson deserves major recognition for his scrutiny of Hawthorne manuscripts and prescient observations about Sophia's influence upon her husband. And I thank Clair Willcox, editor-in-chief at the University of Missouri Press, who has traveled with me on the long, sometimes bumpy road between the first and second volumes of Sophia's biography. Finally, I thank my husband, Peter L. Valenti. His admiration of Nathaniel Hawthorne's fiction predated my own. This book has benefited immeasurably from conversations during our morning walks.

Editing Practices

Throughout this volume, italics replace the underlines used for emphasis in holograph letters and journals. Sophia's habitual reversal of the letters "i" and "e" has been corrected silently as have other spellings that do not conform to contemporary usage, unless these convey particular value in a quoted text.

Sophia Peabody Hawthorne

— Chapter 1 —

Carefulness of Living

Sophia Peabody Hawthorne was the "happiest of women," her happiness now exceeding anything she had imagined on the glorious day of her wedding to Nathaniel. Three years of marriage brought her to the summer of 1845, when she rejoiced in the "rich music" of his amorous declarations and in "the living expression of [her] happiness," her daughter Una. But Sophia's exuberant, if redundant, proclamations were due less to her domestic circumstances than to her "beauty making eye." Ralph Waldo Emerson had coined that phrase to describe Sophia's talent as an artist who could transform her surroundings into objects of wonder, who could "read poetry out of dull prose."[1] And in the fall of 1845, Sophia looked at her life with this "beauty making eye," even as she and her family were being evicted from The Old Manse.

Those who knew about the Hawthornes' financial problems had proffered various solutions to them. Though Nathaniel's friend John Louis O'Sullivan had finally paid the one hundred dollars long-owed for stories published in the *Democratics*, that sum was insufficient to cover the Hawthornes' rent, which was months in arrears. Nathaniel needed more than sporadic income from his fiction, O'Sullivan realized, so he floated Nathaniel's name before those who might grant him a consulship in France, or Italy, or Spain— or even China. Was O'Sullivan serious when he suggested that Una, his goddaughter, "would be delighted to play with Chinese pigtails for a few years"? O'Sullivan's more reasonable suggestion involved "manufacturing"

Nathaniel into a "Personage" by having his daguerreotype made or having Sophia sketch his likeness. His face might thereby accompany his name when he was suggested for a political appointment to the newly inaugurated president of the United States, James K. Polk.[2]

Nathaniel's friends from his days at Bowdoin College also rallied around him. Naval officer Horatio Bridge had arranged for him to edit his *Journal of an African Cruiser* and to receive the royalties from that book. This money, to Nathaniel's great humiliation, did not prevent his request for a $150 loan from Bridge, who gave it readily; but Bridge, like O'Sullivan, knew that some kind of government job would be of more lasting value. So Bridge attempted, but failed, to have George Bancroft secure the position of Salem postmaster for Nathaniel. Then Bridge joined forces with another Bowdoin alumnus, Franklin Pierce, a former United States senator from New Hampshire. In May of 1845 the two men had visited The Old Manse where Sophia met Pierce for the first time, and she immediately took to him. She understood that, as a politician, he was an advocate who might succeed with Bancroft on behalf of her husband, though Pierce's efforts at this moment also availed nothing.[3]

Then Bridge, who had become a supervisor of the Portsmouth, New Hampshire, naval yard, asked some friends, including the Hawthornes, to vacation at his home. Nathaniel thought that he and Sophia were too poor to travel. Sophia persuaded him that they were too poor *not* to accept an invitation to join "into social relations," as Bridge later explained, with some of his most "influential friends and their wives." In addition to Franklin and Jane Pierce, Senator and Mrs. Atherton from New Hampshire, and Senator John Fairfield from Maine were to be Bridge's guests. Sophia foresaw problems accommodating Una's routine for meals and naps in Bridge's bachelor "establishment," so she made an extraordinary decision: Una would stay with Sophia's sister Mary Mann while she and her son Horace briefly boarded with the Hawthornes' Concord neighbors, the Prescotts. Sophia had prided herself on being Una's sole caregiver and had not parted with her for one instant since her birth a year and a half before. Enduring a separation from Una now signaled the profundity of Sophia's desperation, and hope. Being with powerful friends might enable her husband to secure employment. But such was not the case, at least not immediately.[4]

After their interlude in Portsmouth, the Hawthornes returned briefly to The Old Manse before quitting it in September. Louisa Hawthorne helped Sophia negotiate her family's removal to the Herbert Street house where Nathaniel's mother and sisters lived, a house owned by their cousin William Manning. For a pittance in rent to Manning, Nathaniel could reclaim his bachelor quarters; Sophia and Una could occupy a room beneath the parlor. Had it come to this? Nathaniel was again an inhabitant of that "dismal and squalid chamber," the place of his decade-long emotional incarceration after college. "Here I am," he frankly admitted shortly after landing there, "where I wasted so many good years of my youth." But he was no longer a youth but a forty-one-year-old married man with a wife and a child, and another child on the way, for shortly after the Hawthornes' departure from Concord, Sophia became pregnant. The prospect of having another child to love gladdened her. She quickly announced the good news to her mother-in-law in the guise of a letter from Una. But Nathaniel greeted Sophia's revelation with near despair: "I read Una's note, addressed to 'Madame Hawthorne,' then sealed it up and threw it down stairs." This letter rendered him "shamefaced" about how he might provide for a second child when he could not provide for the first, or for his wife, or for himself.[5]

Though some of Sophia's furnishings had been deposited in the Herbert Street house, and she did visit her husband there from time to time, she spent the first six months of her pregnancy—from October 1845 through March of 1846—in Boston with friends, or with the Manns or the Peabodys. Travel between Boston and Salem had to be carefully calculated because of the cost, and although Nathaniel worried about Sophia being jostled or finding a seat when she traveled in crowded cars, he worried more about the expense of traveling to Boston to escort her and Una back to Salem. On one occasion, he regretfully announced that he would not fetch her: "as we are miserably poor, methinks the dollar should be reserved for indispensables."[6]

During this nomadic period, Sophia's aversion to the Herbert Street house grew. "Castle Dismal," as she called it, was the site of Mrs. Hawthorne's "mysterious chamber" which admitted no one to its "penetralia," except on that rare occasion when her grandchild was permitted to enter. Even when Mrs. Hawthorne granted access to her room, Sophia was reluctant to allow Una to crawl on its cold, uncarpeted floor. Sophia deemed the house on Herbert Street to be an unwelcoming, unhealthy environment. By the beginning of 1846, she was steadfast in her decision to remain in Boston near the esteemed homeopathic physician, Dr. William Wesselhoeft, her pregnancy the ostensible reason, and she increasingly relied on his advice. Thus, despite the plan so deliberately negotiated barely a year before, Sophia informed her sister-in-law Louisa that she would "*never* go back to Herbert St. . . . under any circumstances."

The lack of money, home, and profession had chipped away at Nathaniel's identity as a man who could be wage-earner, husband, father, and author. These circumstances must have taken an incalculable psychic toll as his humiliations multiplied. "Dismal"—his word for his "chamber" and Sophia's word for the Herbert Street house—aptly described his life as the fall of 1845 yielded to the winter of 1846. Then came the spring, and with it good news. Senators Pierce, Atherton, and Fairfield had persisted in their efforts on Nathaniel's behalf, as had Bridge, O'Sullivan, and Bancroft who were then joined by the powerful Charles Sumner. Finally on March 23, 1846, Sophia was able to write her mother: "we have authentic intelligence that my husband is nominated by the President himself as Surveyor of the Custom House." Nathaniel's salary would be $1,200 a year; he was sworn in on April 9. And in another stroke of good fortune, the home the Manns had been building was near completion; they were ready to vacate their rented house at 77 Carver Street in Boston. Having spent many weeks there with them, Sophia knew it would make an ideal home for her family, if only they could afford the rent.[7]

Once again the Hawthornes became the beneficiaries of their friends' largesse when Sarah Sturgis Shaw gently intervened. Sarah's family wealth derived from maritime ventures; her husband, Frank, a member of a wealthy family of bankers, had resigned from business in his late thirties to support various utopian and reform movements. He was an advocate of Fourier and Brook Farm as well as abolition and women's rights. The Shaws were well-known philanthropists, but Sarah sought ways to give Sophia what she needed without the appearance of charity. Indeed, Sarah made it appear she was the one who was receiving a gift rather than giving it. She had once thanked Sophia for indicating that she would like the clothes that Shaw children had outgrown. As if she were requesting a favor, Sarah asked Sophia's permission to enlist that "group [at Brook Farm] set apart as excellent makers of baby linens." She asked Sophia to reply quickly, for these women were "ready to begin." And when Sarah discovered that the Hawthornes needed money to rent the house on Carver Street, she and her husband supplied it, saying that they were "thankful for the privilege of having been able to chase one shadow from the brow of him you love so well."[8] The next month Sophia, her husband, and her daughter were living together, at last. Nathaniel commuted by train to his job in Salem, leaving early each morning and returning at night.

On June 22, 1846, a "small troglodyte . . . made his appearance" at 77 Carver Street. Thus did Nathaniel announce the birth of his son in a postscript to the long, chatty letter Sophia had written her sister-in-law the previous day. Sophia had thanked Louisa for a visit, then requested her return "to have an eye upon Una" after the new baby was born. If Louisa could not come, Sophia would ask the eldest Alcott girl, fifteen-year-old Anna, for help; but Sophia preferred Aunt Louisa Hawthorne, who gladly complied for she was as fond of Una as the child was of her: "Aunties are always in requisition at such emergencies."[9] Well, perhaps not all aunties in every emergency. Nathaniel's other sister, Elizabeth, kept her distance along with his mother. Sophia did not deem them to be salutary influences. Restrictions were also applied upon visits with her own sisters, Elizabeth and Mary. Sophia scrutinized every person and every practice that might affect her children's health and character.

Sophia's reliance upon Dr. Wesselhoeft and homeopathy became, therefore, near obsessions. The German-born doctor adhered strictly to theories described by Samuel Hahnemann in his *Organon of the Art of Healing*. Deducing that "like cures like," he administered infinitesimal doses of drugs that produced symptoms like those of the afflicting disease. Allopathic physicians such as Oliver Wendell Holmes were among the dominant group of medical professionals who scorned homeopaths. But homeopathy offered more humane and enlightened methods of treating disease than did bleeding, lancing, cupping, blistering, or purging which were performed without benefit of antiseptics or analgesics. Sophia had endured some of these potentially lethal, standard treatments before her marriage. Now, minuscule homeopathic doses, coupled with the homeopath's advice about fresh air, exercise, and diet provided a reasonable and salutary alternative to contemporary medical practice. As Taylor Stoehr points out, "this combination of material means and transcendental ends" made homeopathy (and other pseudosciences) very popular in the United States: "Nothing could have suited the national temperament better."[10] And nothing could have suited Sophia's temperament better.

Sophia's advocacy of homeopathy with her relatives was at times solicitous, at times strident. She was confident that minuscule dilutions of homeopathic medicine would truncate any disease, citing the cure of her illness in November 1846 as proof. More ill then than at any time since her marriage, Sophia claimed a dose of byronica eliminated headache and nausea and that a dose of aconite cooled her fever. During another indisposition, Sophia credited the reduction of fever to homeopathy, not to the cold cloths that had also been administered. Sophia's mother, who was showing the first signs of failing health, had forsworn cough-suppressing opium and the "irritability of nerves and stupifying headach [sic]" it caused in favor of homeopathic remedies. Sophia also tried to persuade Horace Mann to use homeopathy just as she unsuccessfully urged it upon Mrs. Hawthorne when her mother-in-law became gravely ill.[11]

Proper diet, Sophia had come to believe, was also essential to preventing illness. Nathaniel reported that her lectures to Louisa about nutrition and a daily regimen had had a positive effect upon his sister. Some of Sophia's preaching produced unintended salutary effects, for during the cholera epidemic of 1849, she avoided fruits and vegetables, having heard the disease was transmitted by them. Inaccurate though her understanding was about the etiology of cholera, which is actually spread by contaminated water, Sophia nonetheless avoided food potentially exposed to pollution. And her attitude toward cholera was more scientific than others that prevailed, for many of her contemporaries still believed that divine retribution for sin caused this epidemic, an idea that prompted President Zachary Taylor to call for a national day of prayer and fasting.[12]

Beyond preventing disease, the right food would foster good character, Sophia claimed. The Hawthorne children were strong, she insisted, because they drank water and milk and ate potatoes and rice. Julian's voracious appetite would regulate itself with rice as his staple, for no one, she asserted, would eat plain rice "longer than he need" to slake hunger. Sophia "rejoice[d] to think that not a sweetmeat, not the simplest cake . . . not a particle of butter or any kind of fatness, not any flesh of beast has defiled [her children's] little temples of spirit," as she wrote to Mary Mann, who had her own ideas about what to feed children. Woe to the auntie who countermanded Sophia's dietary injunctions. Aunt Lizzy's suggestion that a little bit of meat could do no harm was rejected outright. Aunt Ebe had the temerity to offer more than advice. She gave candy to Una and worse, encouraged the child to dissimulate about eating it: "'Oh, never mind; your mother will never know!'" Because Una's conscience, as well as her diet, had been contaminated, she confessed to her mother: "'Auntie Ebe makes me naughty.'" Julian later recalled that this transgression led for a time to "'the total disappearance from mortal view of Aunt Ebe.'"[13]

Sophia also followed Dr. Wesselhoeft's recommendation that Una should have more "air." This "plan of nakedness & air bathing" was urged upon Mary Mann's son, whose improved health Sophia credited to herself. Cleanliness was an important component of Sophia's healthful regimen. Her children were bathed more frequently than was common at the time, and Una's baths in ice water stimulated the child to such a degree that Sophia had difficulty holding her. Clean clothes and bed sheets that required weekly washing—another uncommon practice—were part of Sophia's routine, and she demanded that her children have their own rooms in which to sleep so that they might "never breathe [. . .] any but their own sweet atmosphere."[14]

These hygienic practices multiplied Sophia's household chores, requiring the assistance of hired help. And while laundering clothing or bed linens might be willingly relegated to servants, Sophia refused to abdicate her babies' care to anyone. Aside from that one extraordinary occasion when she went to Portsmouth, leaving Una with Mary, "[h]er father & I are her sole nursery maids," Sophia wrote her mother. Sophia had no leisure, therefore, and would not even attend church, refusing to entrust her children to "hired people for anything whatever." Nathaniel commiserated with Sophia that a mother could "find rest in Heaven, but nowhere else." But Sophia knew that while she was recovering from the birth of her second child, she could not manage Una's "constant watching."[15] That Aunt Louisa was the only candidate for the job testifies to Sophia's affection for her and the comfortable relationship these sisters-in-law enjoyed.

As the mother of two children, Sophia grew increasingly confident in her maternal judgments and was quick to dispense advice, often displaying the Hawthorne tots as specimens of good health. She was concerned that her little nephew Horace had difficulty nursing and failed to gain weight, but boasted to Mrs. Peabody that Una was as strong as a "lion" nourished on Sophia's breast milk—thanks, of course, to her wise choice of diet. After the birth of each sister's second baby, Sophia continued an apparent competition over whose child flourished more robustly. Julian was bigger at eight weeks than was Mary's baby George at six months. Julian's size and health were, Sophia insisted, a result of her "carefulness of living." And when Mary announced her third pregnancy, Sophia bluntly questioned her ability to "bear the burden" of another child. Ever since Julian was seven months old, Sophia explained, she could have become "*enceinte*," but she and Nathaniel did "not conceive it wise to go on quite as fast as you do," as oblivious to her pun as she was to a similar charge of ill-timed pregnancy which might have been leveled against the Hawthornes two years earlier. After Mary gave birth to her last child, Benjamin, she did not observe a sufficient period of rest, according to Sophia, who charged Mary's doctor with a lack of wisdom for allowing her to be up and active too soon. Invoking the authority of Dr. Combe (none other than George Combe, the educational reformer and good friend of the Manns after whom they had named their second son!), Sophia chastised Mary for subjecting Benji to loud noises, which Dr. Combe would prevent an infant from hearing during the first weeks of life. Because a home with young children was a place where illnesses might also reside, particularly if a mother subscribed to different child care or hygienic practices, Sophia announced that she and her children would come to Mary's newly constructed home in West Newton only if Una and Julian could have their own sleeping quarters. There would be no visit at all if the Mann children had scarlet fever. The next year Sophia again refused to visit if Mary's children might have chicken pox. As Sophia explained, she would not put her children "in a danger that could be averted by mortal means."[16]

Threats of illness and death were everywhere. Child mortality was the rule rather than the exception for nineteenth-century mothers, and the pain of losing a child might not be assuaged for Sophia as it was for her evangelical contemporaries. For them, bringing children into the world had one purpose: to prepare them to depart for the next. To that end, literature for children was saturated with books like the widely popular *Memoir of Mary Gosner of Philadelphia*, a didactic story of one girl's patient and pious acceptance of sickness and death.[17] But Sophia did not raise *her* children to excel in *ars moriendi*. Rejecting the waning belief that illness was divine punishment for sin, she strove diligently to cultivate her own health and that of all her family, facts that lay to rest the long-held, erroneous notion that Sophia was a woman who cherished invalidism.

On the contrary, Sophia was a new breed of mother, the kind of mid-century American woman who, according to Charles Rosenberg, believed she could shape "her child's hereditary endowment during gestation and nursing." She must, therefore, avoid volatile, angry, or envious emotions and passionate, sexual desire which could transform her milk into a noxious brew, capable of producing anything from "colic to congenital criminality." This belief would have infused Sophia's judgment that Mary's domestic turmoil (certainly less than the turmoil in Sophia's own life, though she could not see that) affected her ability to nurse Horace successfully. Conversely, Sophia's ability to nurse Ellery and Ellen Channings' baby, Greta, in addition to her own infant, Una, would have been proof of her personal equilibrium and domestic stability. That the Channings asked Sophia to nurse Greta suggests that they subscribed to the notion that a wet nurse from the lower class might impart "seeds of sensuality, alchoholism, and criminality." Amid this emphasis upon maternal influence, the father's importance shrank, believed as it was to be "limited to the moment of conception." The mother's responsibilities grew to "all inclusive" proportions, demanding her "early and thoughtful prophylaxis," because "the physician's timely counsel," Rosenberg writes, "might make the difference between sickness and health," life and death.[18] Hence Sophia's near fanatical devotion to Dr. Wesselhoeft: his word became her gospel, homeopathy became *her* evangelical cause, and those who dared to doubt its efficacy were, to her mind, lost.

Assiduous adherence to homeopathy, deliberate control of diet and hygiene, avoidance of unhealthy circumstances and persons also chimed with Sophia's optimism about human potential. Like other transcendentalists, she believed that reforming one's daily practices would assure personal well-being. Like other transcendentalists, she assumed a connection between the material and the immaterial, the physical and the spiritual.

Nurturing the body was a first step in developing a child's good disposition, which, in turn, would become the foundation of good character. But when a child fell ill or demonstrated bad temper, the mother must be at fault for her lack of enlightenment or diligence. And despite the fact that Sophia did not "relax [her] superintendence,"[19] Una and Julian got sick and had temper tantrums. Sophia defended her practices and her children against Mary's implied or expressed criticisms in exchanges that drew heat from several fires.

Though married within the same twelve-month period and bearing their first children only a week apart, these sisters experienced courtship, then marriage, and now motherhood very differently. Horace and Mary were undeceived about the nature of their love for each other, having met in 1832 soon after the death of Horace's first wife, Charlotte Messer Mann. In the words of Mann's biographer Jonathan Messerli, Charlotte was a woman much younger than Horace whom he could "pamper, protect, and idolize." Mary immediately admired then fell in love with a man in the throes of grief. Unwilling or incapable of abandoning his sadness, Horace mourned to the point of depression, which then grew into despair. Elizabeth Peabody had attempted to rescue him from his emotional and religious vacuum by demonstrating the value of the Christian faith and reliance upon Providence during adversity; she simultaneously hoped to win Horace's affections, all to no avail. But what did avail Horace, then and thereafter, was his unwavering commitment to action that resulted in communal good. He believed that the individual could find true happiness only through public service, just as he believed that only public institutions could assure the well-being of individuals; hence his career in law evolved as he became a champion for reform and an innovator in public education. Though morose, depressive, humorless, and often monomaniacal about causes he espoused, Horace was exceedingly attractive to Mary; he was, after all, "the first strong male in her life," according to one contemporary observer.[20]

As a decisive man of action and a leader in the public sphere, Horace was unlike the diffident men in Mary's immediate family, and Mary was unlike Horace's first wife. A far more durable woman than had been Charlotte, Mary's fortitude and patience would stand her in good stead. As Horace's helpmeet and companion, she accepted, Messerli concludes, that she would "dwell with him within the shadow of brighter times."[21] Mary would never be to Horace what Sophia was to Nathaniel, a soul mate or ideal embodiment of womanhood. Those roles had been ascribed to Charlotte, who died before she could disappoint. But Sophia would occupy an unenviable position on the pedestal of Nathaniel's imagination, his ardor as a Victorian lover revealed in love letters, the likes of which Mary never received from Horace.

The Manns were, however, a prominent couple. Mary's husband, a recognized authority on educational theories and a leader in public education, was lauded by Mrs. Peabody as "perfectly identified with the interest of the common schools, . . . believing as he does that the republic can have no secure future except through diffusion of knowledge through the whole population." Among his closest friends was George Combe, a source of comfort to Horace during his protracted mourning, namesake to his second son, and renowned educator whose theories incorporated the science of phrenology adduced by Johann Caspar Spurzheim. The mind, Combe believed, was composed of more than thirty "propensities" some of which—combativeness and benevolence, for example, would result in radically different behavior. Because each propensity was purportedly housed in a specific area of the cranium, a trained observer might determine an individual's proclivity for certain behavior based upon the relative size of different portions of the head. Horace seized upon the implications of Combe's theories for the educator, whether teacher or a parent. Examination of the head would yield an assessment of a child's propensities. These could be cultivated or repressed, according to their social usefulness. Horace was enthralled with Combe's theories, believing them to be "the only practical basis for education."[22]

Thus Mary's approach to raising her children was fortified by various authorities: her husband, his friend, and her own experience as a teacher. She had, after all, conducted schools with Elizabeth for many years, and as a governess in Cuba, she had full responsibility for the Morrell children. Now, as a married woman and mother, she functioned among men who were highly respected for their understanding of how children learn and develop. Sophia wryly commented that in such an environment, Mary's first baby undoubtedly "pronounced a School Report" at the moment of his birth. Sophia claimed, however, that she herself knew nothing of "an unfolding intelligence" before Una was born, a somewhat inaccurate statement for she had spent time with Bronson Alcott at the Temple School, where she had recorded his conversations with children after her sister Elizabeth abandoned that task. Sophia had also read and admired Combe's educational theories.[23]

Absent reliance on any specific theory, Sophia's maternal attitudes derived from her experiences as a child, recorded in narrative form decades after they occurred. When she was but four or five years old, she had dropped a squealing puppy, thereby incurring the wrath of an aunt who shook Sophia violently, making her feel like a "criminal." The incident rendered her confused, ashamed, and mute, for how could she—or any child—"find language to express its inward emotions?" As an adult, Sophia realized that a child was mistaken to believe "that a grown person could do no wrong." She also recalled that in the home of her grandmother, a "severe disciplinarian," Sophia was punished for an error in spelling by being put in a dark room. These and other instances of cruelty led Sophia to confide to her own mother, who was as tender as her relatives were harsh, that "[n]o one, I think, has the right to break the will of a child, but GOD," and God, Sophia believed, only "invites and suggests." Sophia determined never to impose harsh discipline, guilt-inducing threats, or "unenlightened religious zeal" upon her children, because, she concluded, "I am not aware of having derived any benefit from that Spartan severity."[24]

Sophia did not look, as Mary might have, to educational theorists or her husband for guidance. But Horace Mann's educational expertise, which he energetically invested in public institutions, earned him Mary's respect, public acclaim, and more. By 1846, he could provide his rapidly growing family with a comfortable house built to their specifications in West Newton. Modern plumbing and ventilation were among the marvels of a home that Mary proudly described to Sophia; more marvelous still was the conspicuous upward trajectory of Horace's career and income—conditions that eluded the Hawthornes. Nathaniel's career had taken a detour into the Salem Custom House, and although some of his publications had been greeted with critical praise, he was not making his living from writing. And despite his salary from employment as a government servant, the Hawthornes continued to rely upon the beneficence of friends. The Shaws again supplied money for rent after the Hawthornes moved from Carver to Chestnut Street, and when Nathaniel was dunned for back rent at the Old Manse (nearly a year and a half after he and his family had left it), he requested help from Frank Shaw to pay this overdue obligation.[25]

The authority Mary brought to bear in an argument over child rearing was far more impressive than anything Sophia mustered, as was Mary's entire domestic situation, if anyone were judging the apparent relative merits of each household. Sophia, now as the mother of a two-year-old and an infant, enjoyed none of the trappings of established married life, none of the comforts attendant upon being married to a respected public figure such as those her sister experienced. Thus the vehemence with which Sophia sought to win moral victories for herself and her children in skirmishes with Mary may have originated in Sophia's need to vindicate herself, her children, her marriage, and her judgment in each area where the sisters differed. Whatever Sophia's conscious or unconscious motives, her shrill remarks to Mary evinced an ungenerous, previously dormant, near vicious facet of Sophia's personality.

Early in 1848, Sophia's relationship with Mary reached its nadir. Sophia penned a twelve-sheet diatribe against Mary for her decision to admit Chloe Lee into the Mann home. This free black young woman had, late in 1847, been accepted into a school in West Newton. Although Mary's fellow citizens set aside their prejudices to educate a black person, they would not allow her to board with white students. Mary, therefore, invited her to stay with the Manns in their newly completed house. Sophia was among those who found Miss Lee's presence in the Manns' home intolerable. Sophia claimed the young woman's odor was so offensive that no one should have to sit near her at meals, an allegation that extended to generalizations about the "intolerable atmosphere of black skin," which Sophia deemed to be "one natural barrier between the races, for no neatness can overcome it." But Sophia could not "mourn over Miss Lee's skin . . . because GOD made it so," and Sophia continued to invoke a divine necessity as the basis of her cruel judgments: "I never disturb my faith or repose by questioning the Phenomena of GOD'S creation. . . . I should feel impious to doubt it. . . . I should suspect myself of too much zeal, if I found myself doubting." Thus impugning Mary for an excess of zeal and a deficiency of faith, Sophia also insinuated that Mary lacked judgment about Miss Lee's intelligence, for Sophia doubted the young woman's capacity to learn. Without her color to distinguish her, Sophia wrote, Miss Lee would be "perfectly ordinary" for she had not the "mind or the manners to command good society."[26]

The intensity with which Sophia expressed ignoble sentiments about race was replicated in her shrill remarks about little Horace later that year, when, after an early July visit to West Newton, her son contracted scarlet fever from his cousins. Sophia returned to Boston and Dr. Wesselhoeft, to seek treatment for him, but she herself had become infected during her visit to Mary's home with a malaise born of her defensiveness over Una's behavior toward her cousin Horace. Sophia vented her spleen during two hours spent penning another voluminous—nineteen-page—letter to Mary in which Sophia exonerated Una and blamed Horace for their childish fights. Mary must stop repeating that Una had "slapped his distorted little phiz," Sophia exclaimed, because Una "could not bear to see it." *He* had precipitated Una's behavior by making an ugly face; *he* had "outraged" Una's "sense of beauty." Una had innocently excited her cousin, which made him "grotesque." While Sophia acknowledged Una's moodiness and faults (as did the two-and-a-half-year-old Una herself!), Sophia's "imp & angel" had the sense not to promise to be good when she knew she was incapable of keeping such a promise. And Sophia refused to bribe her children into acceptable behavior, convinced that "[w]ith bad management, stern treatment . . . base inducements . . . I think [Una] would become wholly intolerable . . . . But with generous trust, the most tender love, & the highest motives always held out, I have hope she will prove a noble woman." Not content with merely defending her child and her child-rearing practices, Sophia then went on the offensive, charging her sister with being willfully ignorant that little Horace was "violent in his temper," notwithstanding Mary's avoidance of all that might incite this propensity in her son. With barely contained glee, Sophia pointed out that her sister's refusal to read Horace classical poetry, one of her several means to prevent his exposure to violence, had not, evidently produced its intended result.[27]

Mary did not need her sister to alert her to what her husband had already observed, his son's "paroxysms of passion." These were all the more frightening to Horace Mann, who saw a phrenological basis for his child's disposition. An examination of little Horace's skull caused his father to identify a combative propensity that required redirection through the "conscience and reason." Neither Horace nor Mary Mann would employ corporal punishment, the method of disciplining children so prevalent during the nineteenth century; Horace, therefore, devised a system of withholding affection when his child misbehaved. But turning his back on little Horace's sobs only resulted in the child's crying all the more. Although Mary conceded in principle to her husband's methods, her heart was torn by her son's outbursts. When Mary would relent with demonstrations of affection, her husband had a convenient excuse for the failure of his disciplinary strategy—its inconsistent application by his wife. But withholding affection may have been prompted by Horace's psychic afflictions more than by his educational theory. The experience of lost love hovered over all human interaction, even with his own children, convinced, as Messerli says Horace Mann was, that "so few things were now predictable since an inscrutable and amoral fate, neither providential nor benign, seemed to be governing men's lives."[28]

Una Hawthorne and her cousin Horace Mann were high-strung children who engendered passionate defenses from their mothers. The sisters' shared belief in the magnitude of their maternal task made tempered assessment of their first-born children impossible. Sophia's words on Una's behalf might have delivered a death blow to sisterly relations with Mary, but their bonds were too strong to be destroyed by Sophia's hostile outburst. Perhaps Mary realized that her sister's anger emanated from personal frustrations as much as from genuine criticism of little Horace's character or Mary's practices as a mother. Unable to sustain a grudge,

Sophia subsequently burned those letters from Mary she considered "unloving." And Sophia sought to build bridges even while she might have been tearing them down, for in the same letter chronicling little Horace's faults, she acknowledged that it would indeed be a "pity if two loving sisters cannot speak of their children without bitterness or acrimony. . . . We ought to have the benefit of each other's experience in so momentous a task as educating immortal beings."[29]

Chapter 2

Imp and Angel

Dramas of maternal affection in conflict with paternal distance were performed in both the Hawthorne and Mann households, but on each stage, the characters acted from very different motives. Sophia's love for her children was instinctive and immediate. Una and Julian were the products of her careful living and emblems of an extraordinary, transcendent marital love. Sophia saw her children's faults in the most positive light. Or perhaps she was simply blind to them. She maintained, for example, that Una took "pleasure" in being compliant. Una did not disobey; she simply "chooses another way," which was preferable to the behavior of a child who seemed "docile & less trouble . . . & what people call 'good.'" Una's "heated" temperament demonstrated that, like her father, she possessed a "genius" that was "finer & more susceptible" than that of ordinary mortals. The Doctors Sawyer, Cummings, and Wesselhoeft each assured Sophia that Una's moods could be managed by the avoidance of meat. And so Sophia did not worry about Una's "infinite ennui" or repeated refrain, "'I am tired . . . I am *tired!*'" With a childish lisp, she declared, "'I am so tired I wish I could slip into GOD! I am tired of all sings. . . . I am tired of little Julian & I am tired of Una Hawsorne.'"[1]

Her mercurial behavior and depressive comments were more than off-set by expressions of precocious moral wisdom. "Oh GOD, *Wrongness never reigns*" the child would chant over and over. What greater proof could exist that Una possessed (to an exceptional degree, of course) what

all children were born with: an instinctive affinity for virtue that flourished in the absence of adult restraints or disciplinary structures. Sophia's
own education had been grounded in similar optimism. Her principal
instructor, Elizabeth, had assigned books on various theological contro-
versies confident that Sophia would arrive at the correct (that is, Elizabeth's)
conclusion. Bronson Alcott's philosophy at the Temple School also assumed
that children's unfettered conversation elicited their inborn understanding
of Gospel truths. Sophia allowed Una similar freedom in her development,
as one particular event aptly illustrates. When Una began to walk, Sophia
decided against hemming her in with chairs. The folly of such restraints,
when Sophia briefly attempted them, had only resulted in Una's repeating
over and over, "'Damn'." Sophia refused to destroy this "spontaneity" of
language. The "comicalness of hearing this baby utter that naughty oath"
amused Sophia, notwithstanding its constituting evidence of the "corruption of Adam" in her one-year-old daughter. Una was "steering through
an infinitude of space on her own responsibility."[2] A mother could not
demonstrate greater confidence in her daughter's innate ability to negotiate
the perils of life, both physical and moral.

Julian's arrival in the Hawthorne household gave Sophia new opportunities to praise Una's character. Sophia saw no signs of jealousy in Una, who
never complained, even when her baby brother pulled her hair. Sophia
also insisted that Una, when barely five years old, understood how "a soft
answer turns away wrath," an attitude, Sophia believed, that governed her
daughter's responses to her younger brother. In this display of virtue (if
such it was), Una seemed to resemble her literary prototype, particularly
as Edmund Spenser's Una had been re-interpreted by Mrs. Peabody in her
1836 publication, *Holiness; or the Legend of St. George: A Tale from Spencer's
Faerie Queene.* In that story, when Duessa is exposed as an evil being,
the Red Cross Knight relinquishes her fate to Una, who saves her from
execution, saying, "It were revenge to kill her." Sophia had been closely involved with the production of her mother's book, having been enlisted to
sketch its illustrations (though none appeared in the final publication).
Before Una's birth, Sophia had deliberately chosen her daughter's name
laden with these allusions. When John Louis O'Sullivan gave his goddaughter a dog, Sophia just as deliberately chose its name too: Leo, Latin
for "lion," the very beast that protected Una in the *Faerie Queene.* Referring
to her baby as "lady Una," Sophia wrote that she "already has her Lion to
guard her from all peril,"[3] furthering the fantasy connection between her
flesh-and-blood child and this literary character. No surprise to Sophia, if
Una Hawthorne possessed the attitudes of her namesake—that repository
of virtue who was long-suffering, faithful, pure, gentle, humble, trusting,

and most of all, forgiving. Mrs. Peabody's rendition of the *Faerie Queene* emphasized the very themes that were the basis of Sophia's moral instruction. Just as the literary Una repels retribution, so did the real-life Una, according to her mother, refrain from vengeful or violent responses to her brother's rough treatment.

Sophia's son had come into the world without the excessive expectations that had burdened his older sister's arrival. His name, for example, did not harken to any literary prototype of virtue, nor had it been selected before his birth. Indeed, during the entire first year of his life, his parents referred to him variously as Theodore, Gerald, Bundlebreech, Hercules, or the Black Prince. Several months after his birth, Sophia wrote to her mother that it would be strange if Mrs. Peabody "could love the Black Prince as well as you do Una. We [Sophia and Nathaniel] do not know how any mortal mixture can be to us what Una is."[4] Although parents' comparisons of their children seem odious, particularly when a second child does not appear to reach the heights achieved by the first, the Hawthornes' son was, nonetheless, allowed to fashion his own identity as a robust, powerful, independent being before he was finally assigned a name that bore no familial or mythical freight: Julian.

Just as Sophia had put the most positive interpretation on Una's moods and actions, so did she spin Julian's personality traits into a beautiful cloth of superior virtue and character. Although his boyish games horrified his grandmother, Sophia claimed his "shouting" and "exhibition of force" emanated from his self-proclaimed realization: "Why—I'm a boy!" So confident in his person was this child that his first prayer contained a list of those people for whom he was grateful, notably himself, an exclamation Sophia described as "a wonderful recognition of individuality."[5]

Both parents' appraisal of their son was tinged with expectations that a boy's behavior would differ from a girl's, even though Sophia allowed Una (with her exclamation of a "naughty oath") far more latitude with regard to feminine decorum than did her husband. Sophia saw her son as a paragon of size and strength: "The little boy is so independent & powerful that he seems sufficient to himself." He grew into an "infant Hercules" with "vast thighs" and "an endless series of chins," and he soon "lost all appearance of a neck." Nathaniel wrote Horatio Bridge when Julian was barely six months old that the "boy is thought by most people to excel his sister in all admirable qualities . . . ; but such is by no means my opinion." Sophia followed this letter to Bridge with one of her own, announcing that her son was a "Titan in strength & size . . . . His father declares he does not care any thing about him, because he is a boy, & so I am obliged to love him twice as much as I otherwise should."[6]

Whether Sophia actually believed what she wrote or accurately expressed her husband's emotions, Nathaniel was the parent more likely to measure affection while Sophia dispensed it liberally. Nathaniel had greeted Una's birth with the restraint that had characterized the "troglodyte's" arrival. Referring to his *first*-born child, Nathaniel had informed Louisa that "it" was "*lovely*," "pretty" and "fine," according to mother-in-law, maid, and mid-wife respectively, but he, of his own "personal knowledge . . . can say nothing." While the infants Una and Julian grew into toddlers, Nathaniel kept a detached, pensive record of his offspring in the journal where Sophia recorded unfailing admiration for their daily antics and sayings. In his first substantial entry about the children, Nathaniel adopted the role of a spectator taking notes on someone else's family, at times referring to himself in the passive voice or in the third person as "the father." He identified Julian as "the little boy" and Sophia as "their mother." As if he were merely a witness to, rather than a participant in, this domestic drama, Nathaniel inserted Sophia into his record with the words "enter Mamma," and often referred to the lives of his children as a history, one which warranted periodic clarification of their ages. Highlighting his removal from family activities, Nathaniel used the present tense to create a moment-by-moment account: "Now Una offers . . . Now Una proposes . . . ." And so accustomed did Una become to her father's role as writer that when she asked, "'Where is little Julian?'" she was not inquiring about her flesh-and-blood brother but about her literary sibling: "'where is the place of little Julian, that you've been writing about him'."[7]

Nathaniel also cataloged Una's words and actions that he deemed un-pleasant, annoying, and possible evidence of a split at the very core of her nature. Her appearance was "cloudy; her aspect . . . ominous"; her talk was "babble," her requests "exceedingly ungracious," her objections the "harsh and [ill-bred] little croak of a voice." Although he was troubled by her perceived lethargy and laziness, he also disparaged her animated movements as "sudden jerks, and . . . extravagant postures; . . . she is never graceful or beautiful, except when perfectly quiet. Violence—exhibitions of passion—strong expressions of any kind—destroy her beauty." Even when Nathaniel conceded to Una's moments of good disposition, he still found her "as troublesome as a little fly, buzzing round people." He greeted her quieting at bedtime as "the blessedness and kindliness of a euthanasia." Occasional praise of his daughter was tainted by oxymoron or under-statement as when, for example, Nathaniel found Una in a "strangely complaisant mood" or when she looked "not altogether unpretty." Occasionally and oddly, he expressed delight in her "praiseworthy" legs. Yet when Una attempted to make "her leg . . . a *standing* joke," he noted without enthusiasm: "she is rather apt to repeat a witticism that has once been successful."[8]

But the very behavior Nathaniel found offensive in his daughter, he found appealing in his son. Una's "extravagant postures" and volatility paralleled Julian's admirable, "sturdy and elastic life . . . expressive of childish force and physical well-being." When Una complained of being warm and "open[ed] her breast," Nathaniel interpreted her gesture as "the physical manifestation of the evil spirit," but when Julian ran about nude, Nathaniel applauded his son's "felicity of utter nakedness." Sophia's attempts to dress Julian, according to Nathaniel's brief report, were greeted with the boy's "cries of remonstrance." When Nathaniel sought to dress his naked girl, he elaborated about her "terrible struggle—and she gets almost into a frenzy; which is now gradually subsiding and sobbing itself away, in her mother's arms." Although Nathaniel judged his son to be "a little outlaw or pirate—fonder, I think, of mischief than Una, and yet, more easily kept within rules," these rules cast a wider circumference around the boy than the girl. Nathaniel was not disturbed by Julian's "disposition to make use of weapons," but he condemned Una's "[v]iolence [and] exhibitions of passion." Elsewhere Nathaniel wrote, "[w]hen Una is mischievous—which is not often—" (a curious remark considering his unremittingly negative accounts of his daughter), "there seems to me a little spice of ill-nature in it," though he added, "I suppose her mother will not agree to this."[9] Indeed, she did not.

Nathaniel's love for Una and Julian developed slowly, cultivated by their absence rather than by their presence. "I am happy," he wrote his "dearest Phoebe," "a truth that is not so evident to me, until I stand aside from our daily life. . . . Indeed, it does not require absence and distance to make an angel of thee; but the divine qualities of the children do become somewhat more apparent by occasionally getting beyond the reach of their clamor."[10] Sophia penned her response to Nathaniel the day after she received this letter. Beginning diplomatically, she expressed her pleasure in his correspondence, then chastised him—albeit gently—for requiring separation from the children to appreciate them. The second sentence of her letter begins with a thrice-underscored "I": "I do not need to stand apart from our daily life to see how fair & blest is our lot, . . . & the little cares make no account by the side of the great blisses." Resuming the stance of a diplomat, Sophia credited Nathaniel with her ability to endure the tribulations of motherhood: "indeed no other mother has such a father of her children, & such a husband to herself, so that my cares forever kick the beam in the balance. This I tell thee all the time, but thou canst not believe it." She offered proof of her happiness in being "eminently well and sound, & rubicund" in the midst of "simultaneous screams from both darling little throats." Sophia recognized, however, that her husband did not hear "dulcet sounds" in the children's noise, and she did not blame him for that inability. "Thou, belovedest, oughtest not be obliged to undergo the wear & tear of the nursery," she continued. "It is contrary to thy nature & to thy mood—Thou wast born to muse & to be silent." The day would come, she promised her husband, "[w]hen I can once shut thee away in thy study, & shew thee our jewels only when they are shining—."[11]

This exchange of letters occurred in July of 1847. Sophia had absconded with the children to Boston where she passed the summer in her parents' home, for the Hawthornes had moved from Boston to Salem the previous summer. The decision to return to a city they despised could not have been easy, but more abhorrent was the strain of maintaining a home in Boston while Nathaniel traveled back and forth to work at the Salem Custom House. So they moved, first to one, then another house on Chestnut Street, rented with the help of money supplied by the Shaws. The unfortunate patterns in the Hawthornes' lives continued to repeat themselves: the forced separations because they could not afford a suitable house in which to live together; the reliance on friends to supply the money to rent a home, however unsuitable; the lack of a separate room where Nathaniel might write and the presence, therefore, of squabbling children. In order to find an affordable house in Salem that would accommodate Nathaniel's "nature" and "mood," the Hawthornes struck upon a surprising plan.

By September of 1847, Sophia, Nathaniel, Una, and Julian Hawthorne were living at 14 Mall Street together with Nathaniel's mother and both sisters.[12] Although a three-generation household was not unusual in mid-nineteenth-century New England, for the Hawthornes, it was extraordinary. But advantages to every party erased any resistance to such an arrangement. The economic benefits were obvious, for together all Hawthornes could afford to live in this sunny, three-story house with its yard and garden. The house was large enough to contain a "suite" of rooms for the Hawthorne women as well as a room for Nathaniel to use as a study. With each branch of the Hawthorne family occupying separate quarters, neither Una nor Julian was "forced to be in the constant presence of unhealthy persons," as Sophia explained to her own mother: "we only meet when we choose to do so." Thus were Mrs. Hawthorne, Elizabeth, and Louisa enticed away from "Castle Dismal," to an arrangement which might suit that "invisible Entity," Nathaniel's sister Elizabeth, whom Sophia had seen only once in two years. The degree to which the Elizabeths Hawthorne—both mother and daughter—had avoided contact with Nathaniel's wife made all the more remarkable Sophia's generous desire to have her mother-in-law near her son and grandchildren "during her remaining years."[13]

And less than two years remained. By July of 1849, day after sweltering day, Mrs. Hawthorne clung to life. During her dying moments, Nathaniel's misery was exacerbated by Una's fascination with her grandmother's agony, her "strong and strange interest in poor mother's condition." In fact, Nathaniel's journal record of his mother's protracted dying is framed by his account of Una's reaction to it. Una, he wrote, "can hardly be kept out of the chamber—endeavoring to thrust herself into the door, whenever it is opened." The little girl experienced this mortal struggle variously—sometimes in terms of the neglect of her childish needs; sometimes as the opportunity to exercise her superiority as the older sister; and sometimes as the stuff of a childish drama. She irritated her father with "infinite complaint, and whining, and teazing [sic] about her hair, which has not been combed and put in order . . . everybody being busy with grand-mamma." But the child occasionally rose above her own inconveniences to flaunt personal knowledge about illness, explaining to Julian that their grandmother was "sick as I was, when I had the scarlet-fever in Boston," a comment Nathaniel dismissed as a "contrast between that childish disease, and these last heavy throbbings—this funeral march—of my mother's heart." Una relished opportunities to administer comfort; she fanned flies from her grandmother's face, the performance of such tasks signaling her status as the elder sibling, for she judged that attending to his grandmother "would be very painful for little Julian." This role of real-life, child nurse often yielded to that of make-believe nurse, played opposite Julian's enactment of their dying grandmother, a drama which Una herself directed: "'No; grandmamma lies still,'" she informed Julian. "'You must not move your lips so hard'." When dissatisfied with Julian's acting, Una would periodically recast the players, giving herself the lead, and Nathaniel recorded what seemed to be his daughter's macabre echo of his mother's death throes: "[Una] groans, and speaks with difficulty, and moves herself feebly and wearisomely—then lies perfectly still, as if in an insensible state. Then rouses herself, and calls for wine. Then lies on her back, with clasped hands—then puts them to her head."[14]

Una's unflappable attitude toward death and whatever might follow it intensified Nathaniel's anxiety about mortality and his doubts about immortality: "I know not what she supposes to be the final result to which grandmamma is approaching. She talks of her being soon to go to God, and probably thinks that she will be taken away bodily. Would to God it were to be so! Faith and trust would be far easier than they are now." So at odds with his own perspective was Una's that Nathaniel concluded:

> [T]here is something that almost frightens me about the child—I know not whether elfish or angelic, but, at all events, supernatural. She steps so boldly into the midst of everything, shrinks from nothing, has such a comprehension of everything, seems at times to have but little delicacy, and anon shows that she possesses the finest essence of it; now so hard, now so tender; now so perfectly unreasonable, soon again so wise.[15]

Sophia's Una was "imp & angel"; to Nathaniel, the child was "elfish *or* angelic." How much is revealed by a conjunction! *Sophia's daughter* was "Una," one and indivisible; the "corruption of Adam" could coexist in this child who also possessed a "delicacy of soul." Sophia's daughter could "utter a naughty oath" and still recall the mythical "lady Una." *Nathaniel's daughter* was "Duessa," riven in her very nature. So profoundly disquieting was this awareness of good and evil in his own little girl that Nathaniel questioned his paternity: "I cannot believe her to be my own human child, but a spirit strangely mingled with good and evil, haunting the house where I dwell. The little boy is always the same child, and never varies in his relation to me."[16]

Una bore the enormous burden of each parent's very different beliefs about the nature of humans and the world they inhabit. The child was the living embodiment of their differing responses to the Concord River: for Nathaniel the troubling evidence that a fragrant, white pond lily could emerge from "the black mud over which the river sleeps"; for Sophia a "golden river" that "turned all the plants that grow in its bed to gold." Nathaniel feared signs that nature—and now his daughter—mingled good and evil; Sophia celebrated the dynamic "power of counter-forces" in her young body.[17]

Chapter 3

The Gods Prefer Integrity to Charity

A brief interval of domestic conventionality had commenced in the fall of 1847. Nathaniel was *pater familias* with three generations of Hawthornes living together under the same roof. But barely two months after their arrival on Mall Street, Sophia confided to Mary that Nathaniel's income was "wretchedly small" and that she was overwhelmed by household tasks, "that vast overplus of things to be done that do not get done."[1] So despite financial constraints, a maid was deemed an essential rather than an extravagant expenditure, one that would assist Sophia with the implementation of time- and labor-intensive hygienic practices.

Dora Golden had been hired when Julian was an infant and quickly became an exception to Sophia's rule that Irish maids must be incompetent and dishonest. She was trusted to care for Una and Julian while Sophia enjoyed a rare evening out with her husband. Bonds of affection were not sundered when Dora eventually left the Hawthornes' employ to follow a path trod by so many Irish immigrants who renounced domestic work for the promise of more lucrative positions in factories. Sophia would then commiserate with Dora over being ridiculed for her honesty and decency. But notwithstanding Dora's helpfulness when she was with the Hawthornes, Sophia's obligations consumed her time. As she wrote so euphemistically to Mary, she devoted many patient hours attending to Julian while "he performs little ceremonies on his chair (one of a serious nature & multitudinous of a less important character)."[2]

None of Sophia's domestic duties compared with the one she had assumed at her mother-in-law's deathbed. For varying reasons, Mrs. Hawthorne's blood relatives were unable or unwilling to nurse her. Her sister Priscilla Dike was a "marble fiend," according to Sophia: "I hope GOD will forgive her but I do not see how he can." Elizabeth, Louisa, and Nathaniel were overwhelmed by the sound of their mother gasping to breathe during the last five days of her life. Her ordeal, so gruesome to witness, had initially forced Sophia from Mrs. Hawthorne's room, but Sophia determined to "brave" the spectacle because others could not, "torn with anguish" as they were. Thus while Mrs. Hawthorne hovered between life and death, it was not her sister, not her daughters, not her son but her daughter-in-law, Sophia, who functioned as nurse and comforter. Sophia brushed away flies (as did Una) and held Mrs. Hawthorne in her arms. Suppressing her own emotions in an "agony of sympathy" for Elizabeth and Louisa, Sophia remained strong and vigilant "every second." She was gratified to think that her mother-in-law passed her most tranquil dying moments in her embrace.[3]

The days immediately following Mrs. Hawthorne's death afforded Sophia little opportunity for relief. She contained her emotions in the presence of her children, who were in "transports of sorrow." The magnitude of her husband's grief frightened her. This was, as Sophia wrote to Mary, Nathaniel's first actual experience of bereavement, his father's death having been remote physically and emotionally from the then four-year-old boy. Sophia explained that although Nathaniel and his mother rarely communicated with each other, they experienced the "deepest sentiment of love & reverence on both sides." Her death, so painfully proximate, brought Nathaniel to the brink of "brain fever," a nineteenth-century term signifying illnesses of cerebellum, but more generally referring to mental and emotional derangement following a great shock.[4]

Nathaniel was truly bereft during this summer of 1849, the Hawthornes' losses compounded because Nathaniel had been fired from the Custom House shortly before his mother's death. His dismissal should not have come as a surprise. Zachary Taylor, a Whig, had been inaugurated the twelfth president of the United States in March. Nathaniel was a Democratic political appointee, but he reasoned, somewhat naively, that because he had not deposed a Whig, he would not be replaced by one. He enlisted George Hillard's influence with Rufus Choate, one of the founders of the Whig party, and put his case before Henry Wadsworth Longfellow, claiming no inclination toward vengeance—"political or literary"—against those who might conspire to dismiss him. But despite everything Nathaniel mustered in his defense, on June 7, 1849, Taylor announced his removal from office.[5]

The next day, Nathaniel wrote Hillard with the news he had thus far withheld from his wife: "I am turned out of office! . . . The intelligence has just reached me; and Sophia has not yet heard it. She will bear it like a woman—that is to say, better than a man." Nathaniel correctly predicted his wife's resilience. Optimism dominated her response to this new setback, which she announced to Mary as a "condition of unexpected freedom," adding, "I am an india rubber ball, bounding up from the hardest fall." But in this same letter, Sophia also expressed regret that Nathaniel had not sought Horace Mann's intervention with President Taylor. As a Whig who had been elected to Congress in 1848, Horace occupied a position of influence in that party, but Nathaniel "had infinite repugnance to request the favor," Sophia wrote, knowing full well that her husband had overcome such repugnance to request similar favors of others. By the end of July, when the announcement of Nathaniel's dismissal had become public, Horace proffered his unrequested help, writing Nathaniel to express "interest towards reinstating [him] in the office of Surveyor." Nathaniel deflected this overture, however, by referring to discussions with Elizabeth Peabody and claiming, somewhat equivocally, that he was "unwilling" to involve Horace *and* that he would "feel truly obliged" to him if he interceded.[6]

Why such equivocation about his brother-in-law's intercession? Was Nathaniel resisting chronic pressures brought to bear by Sophia's relatives? Did Horace's access to the president demonstrate yet again who was the more powerful and savvy man, further diminishing Nathaniel's stature, at least in his own eyes? No longer a Hawthorne living among Hawthornes, supporting his family (barely, briefly) in a style that permitted his wife to have a maid, Nathaniel had lost more than his position in the Custom House. Must he now be grateful to Sophia's family and their friends? Though he might benefit from Horace's intervention, receiving it would have galled Nathaniel mightily. And there was another reason to resist Horace's assistance, for Nathaniel would be "bound to accept the re-instatement, if offered." The drudgery of a government sinecure had inhibited his imaginative life. Sophia's characterization of his dismissal as "condition of unexpected freedom" conveyed more than her habitual optimism, for, according to Julian's later account, she "buoyantly" added, "Oh, then, . . . you can write your book!"[7]

Nathaniel avoided Horace, but he and Sophia could no longer escape the formidable Elizabeth Peabody. Though she had been kept at bay for the better part of a decade, she had formerly exerted tremendous influence upon her youngest sister. As a child, Sophia had been Elizabeth's pupil; as a young woman, Sophia had profited when Elizabeth negotiated buyers for her paintings. Elizabeth had also coerced Sophia into producing lithographic illustrations, thereby precipitating her crisis of near-breakdown proportions and a nightmare that Elizabeth lay dead in a coffin. Elizabeth's beneficence exacted its toll. In the years immediately following Sophia's return from Cuba, she distanced herself from Elizabeth when Elizabeth presumed intimate, possessive identification with Sophia. Having been informed by none other than Charles Poyen, an authority on magnetism, that she—Elizabeth—was "a highly magnetized body," she decided to magnetize Sophia and thereby cure her headaches. "[T]ell Sophia to be prepared," Elizabeth had written Mary in June of 1836,[8] when it was most unlikely that Sophia would have submitted to Elizabeth's self-proclaimed power to enter her mind. That summer Sophia had declared her independence from Elizabeth, allying herself with the Alcotts just as Elizabeth severed ties with them, an allegiance implying more than the younger sister's approval of Alcott's "conversations" which so discomforted the older sister.

Notwithstanding their burgeoning differences, Elizabeth's influence continued to affect Sophia, never more profoundly than by introducing her to Nathaniel. In 1838, while Nathaniel was transforming himself from Sophia's acquaintance into her suitor, Sophia attempted to assure Elizabeth that she would not be abandoned. To that end, Sophia wrote her a series of long, detailed journal-letters, comparing them to those she had written to their mother while in Cuba. Sophia claimed to reveal all her activities, thoughts, and emotions to Elizabeth: "you are a part of me." But Elizabeth's doubt that her sister did, indeed, reveal *all* prompted Sophia's bemused reply: "I am diverted at the idea of cutting *you* out," for "Mr H's" visits to Sophia were "one sure way of keeping you in mind."[9] So did Sophia hope to lessen Elizabeth's anxiety about the position she held in Sophia's life by announcing Nathaniel's conspicuous place in it.

Awkwardness between these sisters turned into animosity, as a pair of letters reveals. Both sisters took the text "the gods prefer integrity to charity" as the basis for charges and countercharges. Elizabeth claimed that Sophia had willfully misunderstood her, agonizing that Sophia insisted "on *words of your own* & . . . sometimes interrupting my remarks with corrections calculated to give other people the idea that I was not veracious . . . . An exaggeration in words sometimes conveys an idea much more completely than literal exactness." Anticipating their friend Ralph Waldo Emerson's words, "a foolish consistency is the hobgoblin of little minds," Elizabeth averred: "I always speak the truth as it appears to me—and with no regard to consistency." If Sophia did not understand Elizabeth's "truth," she should blame her own limited insights: "Exercise a little of your generous imagination in this department & you will find that I am all the truer for all my exaggeration . . . . [T]o be true to one's self is the first thing . . . to sacrifice the perfect culture of my mind to social duties is not the thing."[10] Elizabeth outdid Waldo in her Emersonian proclamations!

Sophia was not swayed. She could no longer respect Elizabeth "if truth in detail *expressed* & *implied* is not there . . . . I have known for a fact, that you have not considered truth in every contingency in every conceivable point as infinitely momentous." Sophia "knew that no human soul, especially such a high far reaching one as yours could be happy under such a mistake." Sophia delivered the *coup de grâce*, telling Elizabeth that her lack of veracity "destroyed your influence over me." Both sisters were battered, one by the charge that she lacked integrity, the other by the claim that this realization "tortured" her.[11]

But what, according to Sophia, had Elizabeth exaggerated to the point of falsehood? And what did Elizabeth assert as a truth that superseded fact? The answer to these questions may be found in the timing of this rift. When Nathaniel ceased to be merely Sophia's friend and became her lover, Elizabeth's prior claim on him vanished. That Elizabeth had known him first meant nothing. That she had lavished upon him the emotional energy she had expended upon other male protégés—Horace Mann among them—was also for nought. Horace had similarly been the object of her intense attraction and equally intense disappointment when he chose her other sister, Mary, as his intended mate. Elizabeth's feelings for Nathaniel may have clouded her already blurry vision, feelings she perceived to be reciprocated, when they were not. Thus she may have conveyed hopes as if they were facts.[12] A misrepresentation of this magnitude—that Nathaniel wished to marry her, that she rather than Sophia was the object of his ardor—could have caused a shift of seismic proportions in an already strained relation between sisters. Sophia's ire over "such a mistake" and her announcement that Elizabeth had destroyed her capacity for influence: these were far more than words spoken in the heat of anger. Sophia had drawn a line that Elizabeth dare not cross, as subsequent letters, and then, all the more poignantly, the absence of letters and the lack of contact, attest.

When the Peabodys learned that Sophia and Nathaniel were engaged, Sophia wrote bluntly to Elizabeth that her "happiness" was "rebuked by your sick looks." Soon thereafter Sophia wrote to Elizabeth again, now chiding her about "naughtiness for imagining that you are not loved." But this letter could not have lifted Elizabeth's gloom, for Sophia practically flaunted her status as a beloved, betrothed woman: *"Now* I am indeed made deeply conscious of what it is to be loved." Nor would Sophia's remarks about Elizabeth's want of "cheerfulness & serenity"[13] have dissipated her sister's mood, which may be attributed to her perception that she had lost—once again and to yet another sister—a man who might have become her own husband. But Elizabeth's loss need not be interpreted so specifically, for losing the admiration and the adulation of her youngest sister and one-time pupil could have generated a sense of isolation equal to any derived from rejection by a potential mate.[14]

This 1838–1839 correspondence signaled a rupture of bonds that persisted for more than a decade as evidenced by the lacuna in extant letters from Sophia to Elizabeth.[15] Sophia chose as her wedding attendants her artist-friend, Sarah Clarke, and Connie Park, the woman Sophia allowed to mesmerize her before the ceremony. While Sophia and Nathaniel were newlyweds at The Old Manse, their journal accounts make no mention of Elizabeth, although they entertained numerous other visitors there. Indeed, Elizabeth *Peabody* deserved the epithet "invisible entity" that Sophia had applied to the other Elizabeth—Elizabeth *Hawthorne*. And Elizabeth Peabody's exclusion from the Hawthornes' household is made painfully obvious by a remark made by Mary, when she wrote to Sophia about plans to stay in Concord during the summer of 1845. She assured Sophia she was not hinting for an invitation to stay with the Hawthornes. Mary and infant Horace would board with the Prescotts, because, as Mary wrote, "I do not wish to be situated anywhere where E. will not feel free & happy to come to me."[16]

Nathaniel would hardly have encouraged Sophia's reconciliation with Elizabeth Peabody—he, who possessed his own list of differences with her, though early in their acquaintance, they had been of mutual assistance. Nathaniel had interceded with John O'Sullivan more than once on Elizabeth's behalf, resulting in her anonymous publication of "Claims of the Beautiful Arts" in the *Democratic Review*. Writing about another potential publication, Nathaniel indulgently dismissed Elizabeth's demurral about being paid for an article "forced upon" O'Sullivan: "She is a good old soul, and would give away her only petticoat, I do believe, to anybody that she thought needed it more than herself." Nathaniel tolerated Elizabeth's eccentricities and "accepted assistance from Elizabeth when it served his ends," as E. Haviland Miller puts it, for in addition to promoting Nathaniel as the writer of tales, she had published his *Grandfather's Chair, Famous Old People, Liberty Tree* in the early 1840s, and finally *Biographical Stories for Children*.[17]

But sales of these books had been slow, and when Elizabeth was about to move her press from West Street to Washington Street, she wished to remainder these first editions. She also initiated, to Nathaniel's chagrin, negotiations with James Munroe to reprint his books. When Nathaniel learned of Elizabeth's maneuvers, he shot her a testy letter, coldly referring to both himself and to her in the third person. "Mr. Hawthorne has been somewhat misunderstood," the letter began. He then explained his assumption that Elizabeth had approached Munroe, ignoring or refusing "to accede to" the terms offered by the publisher, Tappan and Dennet. Nathaniel concluded with his hope that "Miss Peabody would see the justice, to both parties, of taking to herself the publisher's share of the profits. . . . He [referring to himself] *now* recommends that [his books] should be got rid of on *any* terms." Elizabeth would recall this letter as having been "written during a very temporary quarrel" between herself and Nathaniel.[18]

But the pattern of Elizabeth's behavior and the response it provoked had been firmly established. Believing herself to be helpful and practical, she would attempt to promote a career—now Nathaniel's, formerly Sophia's. Too often, however, Elizabeth undertook such actions without the knowledge or consent or desire of the person directly affected. And often Elizabeth's intervention was not met with gratitude. After Nathaniel was a married man, he dreamed Sophia announced with "perfect composure and *sang froid*" she was no longer his wife; then Elizabeth "informed the company, that, in this state of affairs, having ceased to be thy husband, I of course became her's [sic]." Even in a dream, this circumstance caused Nathaniel "infinite agony," "unspeakable injury and outrage . . . ."[19]

Poor Elizabeth! She had become the stuff of nightmares for both Sophia and Nathaniel. But circumstances during the fall of 1849 permitted her to reinsert herself into their lives.

Chapter 4

An Art That Sufficed

Throughout the fall of 1849 and into the winter of 1850, the Hawthornes depended more than ever upon others to meet their expenses. So empty were their coffers that Sophia borrowed, rather than bought, mourning attire after Mrs. Hawthorne's death. Ann Hooper sent some money she had set aside for "a friend in need," as did Henry Wadsworth Longfellow, James Russell Lowell, and Evert Duyckinck. John Louis O'Sullivan, typically late with payments to contributors, now sent Nathaniel an overdue $100 and promised to advance another $100. Other friends sent testaments of their love and esteem which were valued more highly than tangible gifts. George Hillard graciously claimed that he was merely "paying in very imperfect measure the debt we owe you for what you have done for American literature." Moved to tears by this friend's support, Nathaniel vowed to regain his self-respect through hard work that would prevent ever again having to rely upon such generosity. And Sarah Shaw sent "a check from Frank, which he hopes Mr. Hawthorne will accept as it is offered, and as *he* would do if the fate had been reversed . . . so pay it back when you don't want it, here or hereafter, or never."[1]

The Hawthornes also managed during this period because of Sophia's shrewdness. Poor as they were, she scrimped together money from two sources. She had providently laid aside some of the wages Nathaniel brought home while he was working at the Custom House. These savings hardly constituted the "large pile of gold" that Julian would later recall.

But just as he surely exaggerated the size of this "unsuspected treasure," so did he fail to acknowledge another, significant source of money that sustained the Hawthorne household while Nathaniel wrote *The Scarlet Letter*. Sophia supplied her family's "bread & butter & rent," as she explained to Mary,[2] through the production and sale of decorative arts.

Sophia's customers comprised a veritable "Who's Who" of Salem society, giving Elizabeth Peabody the occasion to resume her role as intermediary between her artist-sister and the marketplace. After nearly a ten-year lacuna in extant correspondence, Sophia wrote to her on November 11, 1849, this letter detailing her purchases of heat-resistant, transparent paper to make lampshades and pieces of ivory and ebony to inlay hand screens. Sophia would turn these materials into a shade depicting the Dream of Menelaus for Lucy Howes, another depicting Pandora for Mrs. Alexander Pope, and four more shades embellished with separate scenes based on Penelope's story in the *Odyssey* for Mrs. William Pope. After completing this set, Sophia intended to begin work on yet another to satisfy an order from Mrs. George Russell. These painted lampshades, hand screens, and illustrated books fetched between five and ten dollars each and were so popular that Sophia had difficulty keeping up with the demand for them. As she explained to Elizabeth, caring for her children in the absence of any help from her husband, who was consumed by his writing, had prevented her from filling promptly Miss Allen's order for an illustrated book of classical drawings, its intricacy making it worth twice the price Sophia obtained for a lampshade—twice the five dollars for which she had agreed to sell it. Miss Rawlins Pickman, Sophia's tireless patron, confirmed Sophia's judgment, saying that this book demanded a higher price because it would "last beautiful forever." Sophia decided never again to produce a book for less than ten dollars and cautioned Elizabeth against stipulating prices "beforehand." Sophia was learning about compensation for labor, wearily realizing that everything—even sewing—lacked "adequate return."[3]

For a time, this lucrative work satisfied Sophia's long-dormant aesthetic and creative desires, for she aspired to meet "the demand for beauty." Deeming Penelope a fitting subject for a book given as a wedding gift, Sophia took orders from Octavius Frothingham and Anne Saltonstall. Sophia began a book for Miss Allen on "The Ideal Life," promising to complete it in ten days even though she had not yet completed a second book for *Mrs.* Allen on the nativity of Christ. Did Mrs. Allen prefer an "angel to Mary mother" for a scene to be titled "The Birth"? Sophia's preference, which was shared by her husband, was for a picture of "the Mother of Christ folding her hands in silent prayer over every new born babe." And about Mrs. Allen's order for a lampshade, should its style be "Classic or Dantesque"?[4]

The need for such clarifications, made via Elizabeth, tinctured Sophia's creative joys as did unrelenting pressure to earn income. She strained her eyes; her neck and head ached from sore muscles, a point she made clear to Elizabeth who attributed these symptoms to "neuralgia." Sophia insisted that she did not now have—nor had she ever had—neuralgia. Rather, she candidly identified "a nervous pain" as the nature of her ailment. And indeed, she had reason to be nervous. She was tending to her children and working feverishly on her art in order to support the Hawthorne household, while her husband, just as feverishly, wrote his novel, claiming it had been delayed due to his wife's indisposition. Sophia's pain would have to subside if she were to fill six new orders, as well as the one for Mrs. Russell, who had already paid a five-dollar advance for a lampshade. Sophia would be forced to repay this money if she could not complete the job, and, as she explained to Elizabeth, "five dollars are more needed now than they may be henceforth."[5]

But by the beginning of 1850, the market for Sophia's books had been saturated, and she commissioned Elizabeth to sell her "Life of a Poet" for seven—*not* six dollars—because no buyers appeared ready to pay ten. Working diligently for Mrs. Frothingham on a shade that illustrated "The Kissing Pleaides," Sophia further informed Elizabeth that she could not make presents for her benefactors "for my time is literally bread & butter." Miss Rawlins, Miss Burley, Sarah Shaw, and Caroline Sturgis (now married to William Aspinwall Tappan) would be "embarrass[ed]" to receive a gift from Sophia in her desperate financial circumstances. Sophia also chaffed at Elizabeth's assertion that she was "inventing" her art. Sophia insisted that she was merely a "mortal woman, not a bit of a goddess." Sophia's further remark that men and women "must not try to do every thing at once" suggests as much about current stresses as Elizabeth's offenses. In her efforts to be mother, wife, and breadwinner, Sophia extended herself to the limit of her resources and grew intolerant of Elizabeth's remarks, whatever their motives.[6] The interlude of easy relations had expired. Elizabeth was the overbearing meddler rather than the helpful agent. Sophia was the aggrieved rather than grateful younger sister.

Elizabeth then provoked Sophia's further resentment by suggesting how she should educate her children. Though her most lasting contributions to pedagogy would not occur until the 1860s, Elizabeth was becoming a formidable presence in the educational arena, having already acquired enormous practical experience. Whether in Mrs. Peabody's, Alcott's, or her own schools, Elizabeth had taught the children from some of New England's most educated and influential families. She also drew conclusions about the development of young children from her observations of Foster Haven, when that child had been relegated to the Peabody sisters' care fifteen years earlier. His mother, Lydia Sears Haven, had been their friend, and her lingering death from tuberculosis was only one factor in her inability to nurture Foster. Withholding her affection, refusing to read to him, and restricting his diet had produced a "fretted" boy lacking, in Elizabeth's words, "childish joyousness." She hoped to fill his emotional vacuum with a rich array of experiences, both intellectual and playful.[7]

Elizabeth's positions on education also proceeded from her serial patronage of innovative educational theorists. Her enthusiasm for William Russell in the early 1830s had been diminished by the time she began working with Alcott, whose ideas she abandoned when she became interested in Charles Kraitsir. His theory, that sounds were fundamentally connected to universal human emotion or experience, was generally unpopular though highly congenial to transcendentalists who were prepared to see the unity of all reality. As so often happened, Elizabeth's enthusiasm for a man's theories led to her involvement in his personal affairs. She intervened on Kraitsir's behalf when he attempted to wrest custody of his child from his mentally unfit wife. Mrs. Peabody compared her to Rochester's wife in *Jane Eyre,* but efforts to commit Mrs. Kraitsir to an asylum generated unsavory reports in the press. Then Elizabeth shifted her attentions to Joseph Bem. He advocated teaching history in chronological fashion using enormous color-coded charts which Julian would later judge a failure, at least in his case. "I was always most inapt and grievous, in dates and in matters mathematical especially," he recalled more than a half-century after his aunt's lessons, "so that I gave her inexhaustible patience many a sad hour."[8]

Sophia employed a less mechanical more visual, tactile, and kinesthetic style of teaching her children, as her November 11, 1849 notebook account of a "regular lesson" reveals. A story about Sophia's "hero" Columbus occasioned a lesson in history and geography. Una located Genoa and Madrid on a map and recounted his voyage to America in vivid detail before turning to sketching. When she and Julian became "weary" of that activity, they and Sophia enacted the characters Pandora, Minerva, and Mercury. Then Una was instructed to take two sea shells, divide them, and determine how "many ones made two." This arithmetic lesson continued with four shells, separated into equal parts, followed a demonstration of the number required "to make four & so on to how many sixes make twelve." The beautiful shells were placed in the form of a triangle, and here Sophia interrupted her written account to sketch a pyramid of dots on the page, rendering through this visual structure the multiplied progression of numbers.[9]

As an artist, Sophia instinctively relied upon visual representation to convey information. She engaged her children's natural proclivity for movement and manipulation, eschewing the most common nineteenth-century practices of rote memorization, to engender genuine comprehension and abstract thinking. She enlisted imagination so that Una and Julian could better grasp history and myth. And she permitted Una and Julian to dictate the rhythm of their lesson, governed by their mutable interests rather than by an authoritarian notion of what they should address during a morning's instruction. Sophia's pedagogy derived from her confidence that (even though the imp might coexist with the angel!) the child's nature would lead her toward what was correct and good. Neither as parent nor as a teacher did Sophia impose constraints.

Sophia's principles were anathema to mainstream mid-nineteenth-century American classrooms where rigid academic and physical discipline dominated instruction. These classrooms were organized around very different assumptions about the nature of children and the duties of adults in educating them. According to one commentator, "Evangelical parents did not share the optimism of romantic Transcendentalists . . . [and] had no use for educational reformers, like Bronson Alcott . . . . Evangelicals of all denominations continued to believe that children still had much of the old Adam in them." Such educators would have been appalled by Sophia's sanguine awareness of the "corruption of Adam" in her little girl who uttered a "naughty oath." They would have been horrified that Sophia's maternal duties did not include subduing her child's spontaneity, even when it was expressed by running about naked! Sophia would have been judged a very bad mother indeed by those who believed, in the words of a prominent evangelical leader: "There can be no greater cruelty than to suffer a child to grow up with an unsubdued temper."[10] An abyss separated those who espoused this harsh evangelical didacticism from the practices of Sophia and her sisters, but smaller fissures separated even those enlightened educational leaders and their adherents. Philosophical and practical differences ignited debates among Alcott, Combe, Bem, Kraitsir, and Mann himself. These differences infiltrated the domestic spaces inhabited by Mary, Elizabeth, and Sophia, exacerbating existing sisterly stresses.

While Sophia juggled her children's regular lessons with her "usual liabilities" (as she described all manner of household chores), earned wages through the sale of decorative arts, and scrimped for money to pay bills, her family mourned Mrs. Hawthorne's death and reeled from the affront of Nathaniel's dismissal from the Custom House. In this atmosphere

Nathaniel was writing *The Scarlet Letter*. As summer turned to autumn, he nearly became ill working in a cold room because there was no money to purchase wood or coal. Money was but one motive for Nathaniel to write; catharsis was another. "In the process of writing, all political and official turmoil has subsided within me," Nathaniel claimed to his publisher. But Sophia confided to her mother that her husband "writes immensely I am almost frightened about it."[11] He was in the grip of forces greater than his anger over being sacked.

Nathaniel was exorcising his personal demons—his failures as a writer who had not earned a living in his chosen profession and as a husband and a father who had not fulfilled his duties as such. Autobiographical material surfaces transparently in "The Custom-House," the novella's satirical, introductory portrait of Nathaniel's unproductive government coworkers. These criticisms rebound ironically, however, upon Nathaniel who identifies himself as an "idler" chastised by his imagined Puritan ancestors: "'A writer of story-books! What kind of business in life, . . . may that be?'" Their disapproval is matched by the disregard of coworkers, none of whom had "ever read a page of my inditing." However disreputable or irrelevant his imaginative faculty may be, he fears he can no longer summon it. Fictional characters resist and mock him: "'The little power you might once have possessed over the tribe of unrealities is gone! . . . Go, then, and earn your wages!'" Linking impotence as a writer with the injunction to earn money is so painful that Nathaniel utters these thoughts in the third person, as if speaking of someone else. "Conscious of his own infirmity," he writes of himself, "his tempered steel and elasticity are lost." This phallic metaphor conspicuously associates sexual with professional and economic inadequacy, an association that typified a man's understanding of his masculinity in the nineteenth century. How sadly confessional, then, is Nathaniel's admission that he "looks wistfully about him in quest of support external to himself"! Was he thinking of his dependence upon George Hillard, Ann Hooper, Sarah and Frank Shaw, and others as he penned these recriminations? Dependence upon his wife's sale of decorative arts to pay for "bread & butter & rent" must have been a particularly emasculating "infirmity."[12]

The Hawthornes' domestic tensions saturate the very fabric of the novella. Nathaniel's vexed ruminations about his "elfish or angelic" Una infuse the precocious, almost preternatural Pearl, as scholars have observed.[13] But if the fictional child owes existence to his daughter, how much more does Hester derive from his wife? An outsider embraced as comforter to the dying; a mother justifying how she raises her child; an artist earning wages by producing ornaments for the wealthy—Nathaniel observed all this in Sophia while he composed his most famous character, Hester Prynne. Sophia had assumed the role of "ministering angel" to Mrs. Hawthorne, whose room, like her heart, had been impenetrable until she lay upon her deathbed. Hester, like Sophia, becomes a "self-ordained . . . Sister of Mercy," a comforter to sick and dying persons through her "power to do, and power to sympathize." Hester, too, attains the status of a "rightful inmate" in the homes of people who had formerly shunned her. Like Sophia, she asserts her authority against those who presume "wiser and better guardianship" of her daughter. Governor Bellingham and the Reverend Wilson, representing the combined weight of state and church, accuse Hester of jeopardizing her child's "temporal and eternal welfare," a situation that mimics the virulent arguments among nineteenth-century evangelical teachers as well as those of Alcott's stripe. And Hester, like Sophia, possesses an "art that sufficed" to produce desperately needed income. Hester's "handiwork" of "[d]eep ruffs, painfully wrought bands, and gorgeously embroidered gloves" is enormously popular among Boston's "individuals dignified by rank and wealth"; she "had ready and fairly requited employment for as many hours as she saw fit to occupy," as did Sophia with her decorative arts and the money they earned.[14]

Yet the very strengths of character Nathaniel found in his wife and depicted in Hester pointed simultaneously to weaknesses in himself. These he reflected in the minister Arthur Dimmesdale and the elderly physician Roger Chillingworth,[15] male characters that depict the male character as the author experienced it. The narrative of *The Scarlet Letter* is propelled by the efforts of Puritan authorities to discover and punish the father of Hester's illegitimate child, Pearl. These same officials assume that Hester is a widow, though her husband actually lives in their midst. Chillingworth had abandoned his young bride to research native tribes, and his identity is revealed in the third chapter, as is the identity of Hester's lover, Dimmesdale. He has remained single despite Puritan cultural pressures to marry. Both husband and lover enjoin Hester's silence about the true nature of their relation to her; she never reveals Arthur's secret, though she reveals belatedly, and only to Arthur, the truth about Roger. With their secrets thus protected, both men eschew conventional heterosexual relationships.[16] Both men embody a kind of impotence, Roger because of his age and removal from Hester, Arthur because of his lack of moral force. His fear prevents him from acknowledging that Pearl is his daughter, an anguish over paternity that magnifies and dramatizes Nathaniel's incredulity over his relation to Una: "I cannot believe her to be my own human child," he had penned in his journal.[17]

Thus, by imagining Dimmesdale to be unmarried, Nathaniel imposed psychological and emotional constraints upon this character's exercise of sexuality reminiscent of the author's own self-imposed, protracted celibacy in his "dismal and squalid chamber." Dimmesdale's refusal to acknowledge publicly his love for Hester recalls Nathaniel's courtship of Sophia when he had encumbered her with a burden of secrecy like that placed upon Hester. Though Nathaniel had repeatedly, but privately, protested his love in letters to Sophia, he had demanded that she keep that love and their engagement a secret: "I have an inexpressible and unconquerable reluctance to speak of thee to almost anybody. It seems a sin," he wrote her, even though she had yearned for an "external pledge of one eternal and infinite union." She had insisted that "man should marry us," all the while Nathaniel had cautiously, obsessively hidden his feelings even from his immediate family until barely two months before the wedding.[18]

The woman who would proclaim her love, the man who would have her remain silent: in *The Scarlet Letter*, this silence finds its narrative rationale by setting adultery in a Puritan society where illicit love survives through secrecy. Hester's exhorting Dimmesdale to public speech and action emerge, nonetheless, from profoundly held historical and cultural expectations about manhood and a man's place in the public sphere. Hester charges Dimmesdale to "'Preach!'" and to "'Act!'" But her demand that he "'Write!'" suggests a charge not to this character but to its author who had, in "The Custom-House" chapter, clearly expressed his fear that he could no longer do so. There, Nathaniel's imagined creatures had challenged him: "'Go then, and earn your wages'."[19]

And he did. Speaking the unspoken, he fashioned a magnificent statement about the power of woman, and *The Scarlet Letter* turned the tide of his literary career. He admitted that this, his first full-length work of fiction, was a "positively h-ll-fired story." His treatment of it, he hoped, would provoke "no objections on that score," but when Nathaniel read his conclusion aloud to Sophia, she reacted with violent emotions. Nathaniel was pleased that *The Scarlet Letter* "broke her heart and sent her to bed with a grievous headache-which I look upon as a triumphant success!" But what, exactly, broke her heart? What gave her a headache? Did Sophia recognize herself in Hester's strength, talent, and assertiveness? Did she recognize in Dimmesdale her husband's publicly mute courtship that had encumbered her like Hester, with secrecy? "[L]ightning writing" she wrote to her sister Elizabeth; "I really thought an ocean was trying to pour out of my heart & eyes."[20]

Chapter 5

Keep Thee Like a Lady

Sophia reported to her sister that James T. Fields had "exploded & gone off like a sky-rocket" after reading *The Scarlet Letter*. This junior member of the publishing house Ticknor, Reed & Fields credited himself with the discovery—and success—of that novella. He had suspected that Nathaniel was writing a story and "charged him vehemently" to produce it. Nonplussed, Nathaniel obliged, and the rest is literary history. Fields may have overstated his responsibility for *The Scarlet Letter*, but he was undoubtedly prescient about books and authors. His skill had permitted him to rise from humble beginnings in the world of publishing after moving to Boston from Portsmouth, New Hampshire, in the early 1830s. Barely more than a boy, he went to work for William D. Ticknor, who was then in business with John Allen. Over the next two decades, Fields demonstrated an uncanny ability to predict literary trends and to cultivate people whose taste mattered to a publisher. He became indispensable first as an office boy, next as a junior clerk, then as a senior clerk, until finally he obtained the position of partner.[1] And he was to become an integral part of the Hawthornes' lives.

With the publishing house of Ticknor and Fields (as the firm became known), Nathaniel found himself among the most marketable authors on both sides of the Atlantic. The firm's British authors included Charles Dickens, William Makepeace Thackeray, and Alfred Lord Tennyson. In the United States, many in the Hawthornes' circle—Henry David Thoreau,

Henry Wadsworth Longfellow, Oliver Wendell Holmes, and Ralph Waldo Emerson—were published by Ticknor and Fields. The firm also published works by Julia Ward Howe and Harriet Beecher Stowe, members of Nathaniel's so-called "d——d mob of scribbling women," as he labeled them in a letter to Ticknor, who were immensely popular and whose earnings far exceeded any money Nathaniel made. As he observed, "[m]y writings do . . . not attain a very wide popularity. Some like them very much. Others care nothing for them, and see nothing in them." Or despise them, and see something quite terrible in them. In fact, many of his contemporaries thought that *The Scarlet Letter* was a dirty book about a story that should never have been told. Orestes Brownson declared the subject itself "not fit . . . for popular literature," and Arthur Cleveland Coxe's comment echoed complaints about *The Scarlet Letter's* "undertide of filth."[2]

Whatever might be thought about *The Scarlet Letter*, its author was no longer a man to be ignored. But notoriety, fame, and even acclaim—the novella garnered as much praise as it did condemnation—did not equal good income, and after Mrs. Hawthorne's death, the living arrangements on Mall Street had unraveled. The Hawthorne sisters were forced to live apart for the first time in their lives. Louisa moved into the Salem home of her Aunt Priscilla and Uncle John Manning Dike, and Elizabeth boarded at a farm north of Salem, at Montserrat in the town of Beverly. The remnants of the immediate family of Hawthornes were thus scattered, and the Peabodys were in Boston, a city far more congenial culturally and intellectually to Sophia. Because some of Salem's most prominent citizens had been the object of Nathaniel's contempt in "The Custom-House," he had alienated those who might have helped him find another position. Reasons multiplied for the Hawthornes to despise Salem, and Nathaniel was impatient to "bid farewell forever to this abominable city."[3]

Sophia and Nathaniel contacted friends who might help them find a house—at the shore, in the mountains, anywhere but Salem, some place they could afford. Portsmouth, New Hampshire, near Nathaniel's old friend, Horatio Bridge, might be an option, but Sophia's correspondence with her friends suggested better possibilities, particularly because of a pleasant visit the previous spring with her friend Caroline Sturgis Tappan, now living in Lenox, Massachusetts. The Tappans were leasing Highwood, the estate owned by Sam Ward; there Sophia's children were in "raptures." So during the fall of 1849, Sophia suspended her labors over decorative arts to travel again to Lenox where she espied a Tappan property, an old red farmhouse. In the early months of 1850, Sophia obliquely inquired if it might be rented, first asking her sister Mary whether Caroline had "disposed" of the house and then asking her mother to determine

Caroline's intentions with it. When Caroline learned of the Hawthornes' interest, she offered the house gratis, but, as Sophia wrote to Elizabeth, "Mr. Hawthorne will not be under an obligation if he can help it."[4] Thus the Hawthornes purchased their autonomy and self-respect with a token annual rent of $50.

While preparations were made to "remove our household gods from this infernal locality" (Nathaniel's description of imminent departure from Salem), he escaped to Portsmouth and a vacation with Horatio Bridge. Sophia and the children took harbor with her parents in their boarding house at 13 West Street in Boston. While in Portsmouth, Nathaniel resisted joining them, for he reasoned, somewhat disingenuously, "it seems a sin to add another human being to the multitudinous chaos of that house." No matter what the circumstance, Nathaniel considered living with boarders to be abhorrent and "unnatural." At The Old Manse, he—not Sophia—had rejected taking boarders when income from resident-friends such as Caroline Sturgis or Ellery and Ellen Channing might have eased their financial burdens. And Nathaniel had an additional reason—in the person of boarding-house proprietress, Mrs. Peabody—to avoid his in-laws' "caravanserai" even for relatively brief visits; he had confided to Bridge, now himself a married man: "[Y]ou have very kindly feelings for your mother-in-law. You were always more amiable than I—but this is between ourselves."[5]

But Sophia returned happily and often to the bustling confines of the Peabody household. She was not averse, nor had she ever been, to life in a boarding house—her parents' or those run by others. The Peabodys were among the large number of city-dwellers (between one-third to one-half the urban population, according to social historians) who lived in boarding houses or who took in boarders during the nineteenth century. Sophia herself had boarded at Mrs. Clarke's in Boston amid the intellectual stimulation of other artists during the 1830s, and at the present moment of her life, she thought such an arrangement could provide welcome respite from the drudgery of housework, as Mary also observed when Horace left for Washington to assume his position in Congress.[6] Anticipating Charlotte Perkins Gilman's advocacy of "kitchenless homes" that would permit mothers the freedom to focus upon the important work of nurturing children, Sophia's attitudes demonstrate more than pragmatism. She was not overly attached to the cultivation of a "home," the private domestic space that was becoming so important to middle-class, mid-century Americans. Neither was she perturbed by the notion that traditional "women's work" might have economic value. It was she, after all, who had turned decorative arts into commodities that were sold expressly to support her family. The work of proprietress, cook, or cleaning woman similarly transferred women's labor from the private sphere, where it was performed for love or duty, to the public sphere. In a boarding house, housework became a commodity that earned wages. Peabody women—in this matter Sophia Hawthorne and Mary Mann remained *Peabody* women—did not believe, as Wendy Gamber has explained, that "[p]laying cash for house-keeping services (and accepting cash for providing them) defied the social logic of the domestic ideal."[7]

But as Americans began to cultivate the notion of the home as a sanctuary of virtue, many assumed that boarding houses fostered an inappropriate mingling of the sexes under one roof. For some people—Nathaniel Hawthorne among them—the ubiquity of boarding houses did not elevate their status or cancel their association with poor hygiene or poor morals. And at this moment of the Hawthornes' transition and turmoil, staying in a boarding house, for whatever duration, would only have augmented Nathaniel's sense of being déclassé. People who lived in boarding houses were factory girls in Lowell, farm boys relocating to cities for employment, immigrants recently arrived from foreign soil, and yes, artists gathered under the perfectly respectable supervision of Mrs. Clarke. But noted authors who were married men with means, *they* did not take up residence with their families in boarding houses. Noted authors ought to provide their families with homes that were full of comfort and luxury. Lamenting his situation, Nathaniel reverted to his courtship rhetoric of "thees" and "thous" to express regret and indulge fantasy: "Thou must never here-after do any work whatever; thou wast not made strong," he wrote his wife. "Thou didst much amiss, to marry a husband who cannot keep thee like a lady, ... I should so delight to keep thee doing only beautiful things, and reposing in luxurious chairs, and with servants to go and come." Had he forgotten that Sophia was strong enough to earn their "bread & butter & rent" after his dismissal from the Custom House? That her resourcefulness landed them a house in Lenox? No, he had not forgotten, and he continued this letter with an unhappy realization: "Thou hast a hard lot in life; and so I have to witness it, and can do little or nothing to help thee."[8]

Sophia, Una, and Julian remained at the Peabodys as April turned to May. When Nathaniel left Portsmouth, he also took up residence in a boarding house on West Street in Boston, *not* the Peabodys' boarding house to be sure. During his three-weeks existence as a boarder, he scrutinized fellow inmates and recorded lively impressions of an artist, a French youth, and a middle-aged bank clerk. The cacophony of communal dining, where napkins were "unrecognizable as one's own," signaled the "general absence of beautiful behavior." And many other nineteenth-century writers similarly characterized boarding houses as undesirable living arrangements even though they provided respectable, relatively clean, and comfortable situations. Although some people (Nathaniel at this moment, his sister Elizabeth for the remaining thirty-three years of her life) were forced to reside in a boarding house, others elected to live in one as a perfectly acceptable alternative to "keeping house."[9] Far more than the clattering of plates was causing the dissonance in Nathaniel's life. The man who wished "beautiful things" for his *"lady,"* was living as if he were a bachelor amid the "general absence of beautiful behavior."

Then, on May 23, the Hawthornes moved from boarding house to estate. They arrived in Lenox, and, because their cottage still required repair, they stayed for nearly a week at Highwood with the Tappans. Caroline graciously invited them to remain and "mingle households," but only the "threat of starvation" would permit Sophia to accept this offer, despite Caroline's warning about the deficiencies of their soon-to-be new home. Caroline knew firsthand of problems in the little red house, having lived in it briefly before moving into Highwood. The farm-house was very small; its floors were warped, and drafts blew through the clapboard walls, making the winters frigid—, and doubly so in the second-floor bedrooms, which lacked fireplaces. The only warmth in the house emanated from a lone stove in the entry. But there was a bonus in the form of an adjacent orchard.[10]

Sophia ignored minor discomforts by transforming the house into the semblance of a proper home. Some of the Hawthornes' possessions had been "abused" in transit; the bust of Apollo, a wedding gift from Caroline, had a broken neck (an omen, perhaps?), but other objects of art made the transition successfully. Sophia decorated the walls with reproductions (possibly her own) of work by Claude Lorrain and Salvatore Rosa, painters who had so inspired her early career. She arranged sundry heirlooms from the Hawthorne-Manning side of the family. She laid a red carpet in Nathaniel's study, that long-coveted place where he could write without the distraction of children clamoring about. A sofa upholstered in red cloth was positioned to take advantage of views of the meadow and Stockbridge Bowl. A red couch and a red carpet in "an old red farmhouse, (as red as the Scarlet Letter)," Nathaniel remarked parenthetically to Zack Burchmore. No wonder Sophia dubbed their home "La Maison Rouge."[11]

In Lenox, homes had names and some very grand homes they were. Highwood and Tanglewood. The Hive. The Perch. Highlawn. Nestledown. Woodcliff. The Elms. Beecher Hill. Vent Fort. But these mansions were called "cottages" by their owners, who fled to them, escaping the summer heat of New York or Boston. And many of these owners—the

Wards and the Tappans in particular—had been Sophia's longtime friends. Her regular visits to Caroline Tappan at the Wards' Highwood estate must have evoked happy memories of their past associations and entwined, sometimes highly charged, connection to Margaret Fuller.

The Wards are credited with discovering that the Berkshires could be a playground for the rich. Samuel G. and Anna Hazard Barker Ward were each born to wealthy banking families, though Sam aspired to a life of Emersonian transcendentalism and contributed articles on art and architecture to the principal journal of the transcendentalists, the *Dial*. Sam had been the object of Margaret Fuller's considerable emotional energies though he could not return her amorous feelings. These he reserved for Anna, whose great beauty compelled Emerson's admiration as well as that of the sculptor Hiram Powers, who cast her likeness in marble as a Roman figure. Margaret had also been attracted to Anna's charms. According to Fuller's biographer, Charles Capper, Margaret's letters to her were "laden with, not only ethereal passion, but homoerotic passion as well." Like Sam, Anna did not reciprocate Margaret's sentiments. In September of 1842, a couple of years after the Wards married and a couple of months after the Hawthornes' wedding, Sam and Margaret visited The Old Manse. He was delighted by the Hawthornes' rural home and modest parlor, claiming it demonstrated better taste than anything he had seen in Boston. He also spoke of enjoying a delicious idleness with Anna in the months immediately following their marriage. On the banks of the Concord River, Sam and Margaret passed a lazy, late-September afternoon with the Hawthornes. Eventually, at Margaret's suggestion, Sophia led Sam back to The Old Manse, while Margaret remained for some time with Nathaniel.[12]

When Sam commissioned his home in Lenox, he put to use his European travels and interest in architecture by asking Richard Upjohn, famous for Trinity Church in lower Manhattan, to design Highwood in the Italianate style. This estate commanded views of Lake Mahkeenac, situated as it was on some of the most desirable acreage in the Berkshires, and Sam secured enormous tracts of land during visits to longtime Lenox resident, Charles Sedgwick, brother of novelist Catharine Maria Sedgwick, at their home, the Hive. The Wards moved into Highwood in 1844, but they had departed by 1850 because Sam could never fully reconcile the split in his personality between the lord of leisure on a country estate and the productive urban man of business. By the time the Hawthornes arrived in Lenox, Sam had concluded a pastoral interval at Highwood, allowing the Tappans to lease it while they made plans to build their own estate. But even in her absence, Anna continued to reign, at least in Sophia's mind, as "Queen of the Berkshires."[13]

Sophia's history with Caroline Sturgis Tappan had been long and reward-ing. Caroline was the daughter of William Sturgis, a sea captain turned maritime merchant who made a fortune trading with China. The vast Sturgis wealth notwithstanding, Caroline was something of a bohemian and transcendental poet, who, like Sam, published in the *Dial*. She had been one of those "diamonds" in Margaret Fuller's necklace of intense feelings before Margaret had turned to Anna Barker and Sam Ward. The denouement of the Margaret–Caroline drama resembled the resolution of Margaret's relationship with each of the Wards. Friendship prevailed over anything else Margaret might have sought. During Margaret's busy four years abroad as the first female correspondent for the *New York Tribune*, she maintained a vigorous correspondence with Caroline.[14]

After her marriage to William Aspinwall Tappan in 1847, Caroline and he purchased a tract of land adjacent to the Wards' property. The Tappans' land boasted only "La Maison Rouge" where they planned to live until the completion of their own estate, similar in design and grandeur to High-wood. With the Wards' departure from Highwood, the Tappans now had the opportunity to live in more accustomed conditions. The Tappans had also hired Richard Upjohn to draft plans which came under criticism from Caroline's father, who stepped in to supervise. The project stalled and was finally abandoned. At a much later period of her life, when Caroline and William were living separately, she built her own home on the land and called it Tanglewood, and William returned to the cottage to live amid his books.[15]

The marriage between Caroline and William was not to be a happy one, but it brought Caroline into the orbit of powerful abolitionists. William's father was Lewis Tappan, founder of the Mercantile, an agency that pre-dated the Wall Street firm of Dun and Bradstreet. But Lewis Tappan's place in history is assured not because of his significant business acumen but because of his role during the *Amistad* case. In 1839, Africans who were being transported into slavery on that Spanish ship rebelled. The hapless rebels were apprehended by the United States Navy in waters off Long Island and eventually tried before the Supreme Court. Lewis Tappan, a staunch abolitionist, took the lead in securing legal representation for the escaping slaves, whose victory was won in the landmark case *United States v. Libellants and Claimants of the Schooner Amistad*. With his brother Arthur, Lewis Tappan founded the American Anti-Slavery Society, and contributed considerable time and money to the notable reform movements of mid-nineteenth-century America.

Common threads of wealth and liberal thought wove together the lives of these friends who came to Lenox. They had known each other for years and at various stages of their lives. They belonged to families whose wealth reached back at least a generation. So wealthy were the Wards and Tappans that they could forsake, to quote Wordsworth, "getting and spending" in order to pursue poetry, philosophy, and noble causes while they appreciated the wonders of nature in the Berkshires. Thus Lenox became a magnet for a conscientious, art-loving upper class. Philanthropists and abolitionists, Frank and Sarah Shaw, for example, would travel from their home in Staten Island to be frequent visitors at Vent Fort, the estate built by Ogden Haggerty, financier of international cargo and patron of the arts. His daughter would later marry the Shaws' son, Robert. The flamboyant abolitionist preacher, Henry Ward Beecher (brother to Harriet Beecher Stowe), would also leave the sweltering summers of Staten Island and his congregation at the Plymouth Church, for Lenox and his estate, the eponymous Beecher Hill. The Sedgwicks' Hive was a hub of literary conversation, as was William Cullen Bryant's Homestead and Oliver Wendell Holmes's Canoe Meadows. As one visitor to the Sedgwicks remarked, "There are many things which sound commonplace in Lenox, which are radical in Boston."[16] But high-minded pursuits did not oblige the wealthy businessman, or preacher, or author to forsake living in the opulent houses whose grandeur was guaranteed to endure for generations.

The Hawthornes lived at the opposite end of the residential spectrum, renting a decrepit little farmhouse that, nonetheless, represented an improvement over the boarding houses they had recently left. Soon their days settled into a routine that permitted Nathaniel to write, and by the first week of August, he was at work on *The House of the Seven Gables*, its first chapter an apparent comment on the mammoth Lenox estates surrounding him: "There is something so massive, stable, and almost irresistibly imposing, in the exterior presentment of established rank and great possessions that their very existence seems to give them the right to exist; at least, so excellent a counterfeit of right, that few poor and humble men have moral force enough to question it."[17] But the "poor and humble" author did, through this novel, interrogate rank and class, as well as the iniquities of inheritance, and the distinction between moral and legal rights to property.

Though set in Hawthorne's contemporary New England, the novel begins by tracing the convoluted, two-century history of the "house" in its dual meaning of "structure" and "dynasty." The "great house" of the title, "a specimen of the best and stateliest architecture," is built on land that had been owned by Matthew Maule, reputed to be a wizard. His rights to this land signify nothing against the demands of a man with the status of Colonel Pyncheon, who accuses Maule of witchcraft. After Maule's execution,

Pyncheon acquires the land he coveted and, with the help of Maule's carpenter-son Thomas, builds his mansion. Like the estates surrounding Nathaniel in Lenox, Pyncheon's mansion was destined to "assume its rank among the habitations of mankind"; but its "grotesqueness of a Gothic fancy" and "gables pointed sharply towards the sky" recall the Turner-Ingersoll House Nathaniel visited as a boy. Whether in the Lenox of Nathaniel's present or the Salem of his past, houses like these signal a man's "highest prosperity attained, —his race and future generations fixed on a stable basis, and with a stately roof to shelter them, for centuries to come . . . ." But at the moment Colonel Pyncheon should have celebrated the completion of his grand house, he is found dead beneath his own portrait, fixing forever the "stern features of a Puritan-looking personage." The seven-gabled house remains in the Pyncheon family, although thirty years before the action of the novel commences, one descendant, believing that Matthew Maule had been "foully wronged out of his homestead, if not his life," considers returning the property to Maule's heirs. Before this conscientious bachelor can act on his ethical intentions, he is murdered. The property is inherited by one nephew—the apparently upstanding Judge Pyncheon—while another nephew, Clifford Pyncheon, is convicted and imprisoned for their uncle's murder. Clifford's sister Hepzibah now lives in the house by virtue of her uncle's will, which grants her a "life-estate."[18] Judge Pyncheon lives in his country home, bidding his time until he can claim the Pyncheon property.

Nathaniel was at pains to establish the Pyncheons' tenuous hold upon their house. Treachery obtained the land upon which it was built, and violent crime permits its continuance in the Pyncheon family. Its current residents lack the resources—in the broadest sense of that word—to maintain the house. Now at the age of sixty, Hepzibah, whose squinting vision pinches her face into a permanent scowl, must "earn her own food, or starve!" But how? Poor eyesight prevents her from producing "orna-mental needlework" as did the fictional Hester, or decorative arts as did Sophia. Instructing children in her home for pay, as had the Peabody women (both Elizabeths and Mary), would require more "intimate acquaintance" with children than she could "tolerate," and teaching had become a "science, greatly too abstruse" for her.[19]

So Hepzibah reopens a cent shop which "an unworthy ancestor" had "fitted up" in the house, and she takes in a boarder. Despite these attempts to overcome her aristocratic aversions, Hepzibah is "wretchedly poor, and seemed to make it her choice to remain so." She resists taking money for a biscuit from her first customer, "for her old gentility was contumaciously squeamish at the sight of the copper-coin." Finally touching it produces an imagined "sordid stain." Transacting business and making money are like sins whose indelible marks irrevocably change Hepzibah's status without, unfortunately, changing her finances. As for being a proprietress of a boarding house, the identity of the boarder cancels her success in that endeavor, for Thomas Holgrave, the reader discovers, is the moral if not legal heir to the House of the Seven Gables rather than one who lives in it by right of rent. As a daguerreotypist, he is an artist in a modern medium, cheerful and spry, both bourgeois and gentlemanly in a "summer sack of cheap and ordinary material" that simultaneously reveals a "rather remarkable whiteness and nicety of his clean linen."[20]

Clifford's release from wrongful incarceration coincides with Hepzibah's attempt to become a shopkeeper and her fond examination of his representation in a miniature. This likeness of Clifford's face sets him apart from both his Pyncheon ancestor of the massive portrait and the vigorous boarder. Clifford's "tender lips, and beautiful eyes" belie "gentle and voluptuous emotion," and Hepzibah's lingering glance prompts the narrator's question, "Can it be an early lover of Miss Hepzibah?" The answer is, of course, no. It is Hepzibah's brother, who now, after thirty years in prison, retreats to the gabled house, as if imprisoned again, idly spending day after day gazing out the window of his second-floor chamber at the passing spectacle of life. This "wasted, gray, and melancholy figure—a substantial emptiness, a material ghost"[21] is more emasculated than any of the creatures imagined in "The Custom House" or The Scarlet Letter.

Coming to the rescue of this pathetic brother–sister pair is their young country cousin, Phoebe, whose competence results from having escaped being brought up with the affectations of a lady. "'You know,'" she tells Hepzibah, "'I have not been brought up a Pyncheon.'" Quite so, for she brings to these gloomy precincts the resourcefulness and resilience needed to succeed in the world of commerce, which exists in microcosm in the decrepit mansion. Phoebe has the knack for acquiring merchandise "without a hazardous outlay of capital." She pleases customers with her attention and smile. While she exhibits "vastly superior gifts as a shopkeeper," she also transforms the Gables into a cozy home with her decorative touches and welcoming table. With her gift of "practical arrangement," Phoebe possesses Sophia's "beauty making eye," permitting her to "bring out hidden capabilities of things around them; and particularly to give a look of comfort and habitableness to any place which, for however brief a period, may happen to be their home."[22]

Phoebe and Hepzibah are, according to the narrator, "a fair parallel between new Plebianism and old Gentility." They represent the alternatives available to mid-nineteenth-century women when circumstances—widowhood or spinsterhood, feckless husbands or evaporating status—create their need for income. Women like Hepzibah clung to the "overpoweringly ridiculous" illusion that their inability to succeed in the market place announced virtue and superior status. Cringing at the thought of exposure in the public sphere, they retreat behind a metaphorical or actual curtain. Hepzibah, a "forlorn old maid in her rustling rusty silks"[23] recalls Nathaniel's sister Elizabeth. Rose later described her aunt, never concerned with aesthetics, in a stiff mohair dress and fearful of leaving her home: "the excitement of change and crowds, and danger from steam and horse, made her extremely tremulous and wretched." This "invisible entity," as Sophia called her, had finished her days in a boarding house and without the disposition to contribute to her own support.[24] But women like Phoebe—they were another breed entirely. And Sophia *was* "Phoebe," as Nathaniel would sometimes fondly call her. The "Phoebes" of the world were working-class women whose hands were not sullied by the coins they earned. And no person with "any fair and healthy mind" would assume that transacting business disqualified "Phoebe" from being a "lady." In the words of the narrator of *The House of the Seven Gables*, "it would be preferable to regard Phoebe as the example of feminine grace and availability combined, in a state of society, if there were any such, where ladies did not exist. There, it should be woman's office to move in the midst of practical affairs, and to gild them all."[25]

Determined to conclude this novel on a cheerful note, for many criticisms of *The Scarlet Letter* decried its intractable darkness, Nathaniel ends *The House of the Seven Gables* with a very Victorian, though somewhat contrived and melodramatic happy ending. Judge Pyncheon is found dead beneath his ancestor's portrait. Clifford fears again being falsely accused of murder and persuades Hepzibah to flee with him. But Hepzibah's "mind was too unmalleable to take new impressions so readily as Clifford's," who is "startled into manhood and intellectual vigor" by this dramatic experience of the outside world: "Thus it happened, that the relation heretofore existing between her brother and herself was changed." If Hepzibah and Clifford are uncomfortably reminiscent of the too-close relationship between Elizabeth Hawthorne and her brother during his years of bachelorhood, now Nathaniel—the married man, father, and author—creates a character that escapes unproductive isolation.[26] And Clifford can savor his freedom because Judge Pyncheon's death, it turns out, was due to natural causes, possibly the hereditary illness that killed their ancestor. Phoebe Pyncheon marries Thomas Holgrave, and as a Pyncheon, she has legal rights to the inherited property. As a Maule,

Holgrave possesses moral rights to it. But as a couple, they reject the "house"—the edifice and symbol of class status—to live in an iteration of the red cottage, the judge's rural home, albeit one which they inherit as a consequence of his death. Thus does marriage celebrate the union of a woman, who does not need to be a "lady," with a man whose place in society is secured by public recognition of his right to it.

Chapter 6

The Paradise of Children

Caroline Tappan shattered the mid-summer calm with terrible news. Margaret Fuller was dead. Her child was dead; the child's father was dead. On July 19, 1850, all three perished when the ship bringing them from Italy to the United States foundered off Fire Island.

Margaret's departure from Italy had been burdened by misgivings and forebodings. She dreamed that she visited Anna Ward and others in Lenox, only to be excluded from their conversation or to have Anna reply "carelessly" to her. "You must not be so indifferent when I *do* come," Margaret implored. Indifference, downright hostility, or even harsh judgments about the man in her life might indeed have greeted her. Who exactly was this Giovanni Ossoli? And was Margaret actually married to him? Her evasive answers to these questions prompted Sarah Clarke's candid disclosure of what many felt: "[W]e were placed in a most unpleasant position—because the world said injurious things of you which we were not authorized to deny," Sarah had written Margaret in March: "This was annoying."[1]

Uncertainty about her reception in New England perhaps intensified fears about the dangers of a trans-Atlantic voyage made more treacherous because she could not afford passage on a safer steamer. The family of three had, therefore, boarded the sailing ship *Elizabeth*, despite a fortune-teller having warned Ossoli: "Beware of the Sea." Shortly after departing from Leghorn, Captain Seth Hasty took ill with smallpox, as did Margaret's son, Angelino. The two-year-old boy survived, the captain did not. The *Elizabeth* was then commanded by the less experienced first mate, Henry P. Bangs. His error in calculating the ship's position was a fatal one that led to the death of seven of the twenty-two persons on board.[2]

These tragic events, originally reported in the *New York Tribune*, became painfully real to residents in the Berkshires who, like Sophia and Caroline, were Margaret's longtime friends. Vent Fort owner, Ogden Haggerty, had gone to New York Harbor to meet the *Elizabeth,* which bore a cargo of marble statuary that he was importing. The merchant grimly asked Sam Ward for the correct spelling of the Italian names should bodies surface and tombstones be needed. But Margaret and Ossoli, and the sculptures by Lorenzo Bartolini, Hiram Powers, and Joseph Mozier, would forever lie unrecovered in the waters of Long Island Sound, though Angelino's body did wash to shore. Before the ship broke apart, he had been wrested from his mother's arms by a steward, who flung both himself and Angelino into the sea in a futile effort at survival. Those who did survive as well as spectators on the shore would recount that Ossoli seemed unable or unwilling to move, as if accepting the fate dealt him by fortune. A huge wave washed him away, leaving only Margaret who sat as if paralyzed. "I see nothing but death before me—I shall never reach the shore" were the last words she was heard to speak. Others had grasped at survival, however they might, grabbing planks from the wrecked ship, hoping to stay afloat or, better still, to make their way to shore. Why did Margaret refuse her chance, slim as it might have been, to live? According to Fuller biographer, Charles Capper, Margaret's lifelong fear of turbulent waters disabled her. More than that, Capper suggests, Margaret might have despaired of surviving without Ossoli and Angelino. Analyzing her final moments, Capper cites a letter she had written to Caroline after the death of Maria Lowell's child: "I could not, I think, survive the loss of *my* child. I wonder daily how it can be done."[3]

Shock over the terrible manner of her death and sadness over the loss of her boundless potential mingled with discomfort about the perceived irregularity of her relationship with Ossoli and resentment about her lack of candor. Grieving for Margaret was a complicated process for many of her friends, but Sophia's mourning focused only upon the loss of a woman who loved, who was loved, and who was now a mother. Sophia imagined Margaret's terror: "Oh was anything ever so tragical, so dreary so unspeakably agonizing as the image of Margaret upon that wreck, alone, sitting with her hands upon her knees—& tempestuous waves breaking over her." "Margaret is such a loss," Sophia wrote her mother, but because the joys of marital love and motherhood dominated Sophia's life, she rejoiced that Margaret "had the bliss of being a mother" and took comfort, however oddly expressed, that Margaret and Ossoli died together, particularly if, as rumor had it, he was "a person so wanting in force & availability." "I am glad they died together," Sophia repeated: "How infinitely sad about Margaret—I am really glad she died—."[4]

Sophia did not judge the legitimacy of Margaret's relationship to Ossoli, although questions about his suitability as a mate quickly became the stuff of correspondence. Mary Mann, wrote to Sophia reporting information that came via Lydia Child who claimed Sarah Shaw had received letters from Margaret in which she was "always apologetic" about her "husband" (Mary's designation, although Ossoli's status was still undetermined) because he was "uneducated." Margaret feared, according to this chain of sources, that her New England friends would think ill of him. And Mary also reported that Margaret had confided to the widow of the *Elizabeth's* captain her worry that this "match" was unsuitable. But according to Mary's report of Lydia's assessment, whatever the discrepancies between this mismatched woman and man, "longing to be loved as [Margaret] did, his affection prevailed over other considerations. But he was wholly unfit to be her husband."[5]

Margaret would have been more acutely aware than her friends of Ossoli's limitations as a mate. In "The Great Lawsuit," her signature tract on the status of women and men, she had adduced four categories of marriage: "household partnership," "mutual idolatry," "intellectual companionship," and "pilgrimage towards a common shrine." The fourth and "highest grade of marriage union" subsumed all others and assumed an "intellectual communion"; "how sad it would be on such a journey," she had written, "to have a companion to whom you could not communicate your thoughts and aspirations as they sprang to life." Margaret's own words, published six years before her death, indicted her union with Ossoli, while Sophia's union with Nathaniel appeared to fulfill—or exceed—this definition of an ideal marriage, particularly at this moment of Sophia's life. She reveled in her love for Nathaniel, which had increased during twelve years of "intimate union," beginning with their secret engagement in 1838. But she was defensive when discussing her perfect marriage and her perfect husband with the Peabody women. "I am not deluded nor mistaken as the angels know now," she wrote to her mother. Sophia confronted Mary about her recent "unfounded aspersions" against Nathaniel, that "Ideal being whom I call my husband" whose "love first awoke in me *consciousness*." Sophia insisted that "misery" would ensue if she were "deprived of the power of loving."[6]

Sophia's emotions were particularly expansive at this moment. She addressed Mary, as "the beautifullest, the wittiest, the most enchanting of mortals" and praised Elizabeth, but without superlatives, as an "intimate friend." Mrs. Peabody had, of course, been the lifelong recipient of Sophia's ardent affection; a "peculiar sympathy," Sophia claimed, caused her to share her mother's "bodily pains." Now her declining health provoked Sophia's emotional upheavals as well as her resolve to accept the inevitable "without convulsive grief." The Peabody sisters discussed with one another their concerns about their mother's slow journey toward death, and Elizabeth assumed primary responsibility for her parents. She moved with them into the West Newton home of her brother Nat and his wife, Elizabeth ("E. Nat" as she was sometimes called to distinguish her from all the other Elizabeths), and their daughters, Ellen Elizabeth and Mary. Nathaniel Hawthorne was determined, however, to control any news Sophia received about her mother. Writing secretly to Elizabeth, he insisted that she not convey anything that would "agitate" his wife and directed Elizabeth to send reports about Mrs. Peabody to the Sedgwicks, who could then keep him informed; *he* would judge what to tell Sophia.[7]

While Nathaniel attempted to protect his wife from disturbing news, she shielded her mother from news of another kind. At the age of forty-one, Sophia was pregnant again and feared that her condition might be a source of more anxiety than joy for the overprotective and now very frail Mrs. Peabody. Sophia wanted to wait until the child was born and then announce that she "had multiplied [her] powers of loving . . . by a whole new soul in a new form." But in April, Mrs. Peabody responded "serenely" to learning that Sophia was expecting her "little flower."[8] Even before this baby's birth, Sophia referred to the child in her womb as "Rose," an application of the flower metaphor that would shape both parents' reception of their last child. But Sophia was largely reticent about this pregnancy in journal entries and letters to her sisters, for she seemed to take her condition as a matter of course that demanded no detailed documentation. Sophia's father, Dr. Nathaniel Peabody, was present for "the momentous hour" on May 20, 1851. He was "self possessed, gentle, firm, & patient" as her attendant during labor, although he required his son-in-law's help, for the nurse assistant had failed to arrive on time. Sophia ruefully remarked to Mary, "I meant my husband should never be present at such a time." But with the help of father and husband, Sophia delivered a baby girl whom they immediately called Rose, a name free from heavy literary symbolism or lengthy deliberation.[9]

Nathaniel announced his new daughter's arrival with characteristic detachment. "You have another niece," he wrote to Louisa, before quickly turning to *The House of the Seven Gables* and chiding his sister for her silence about it. Several days later in a long letter to his sister-in-law Elizabeth,

Nathaniel ruminated about the financial implications of being a man now with a third child. He decided to forgo life insurance, leaving his family's financial future to the "dispensation of Providence" and the value of his copyrights. About Rose, he had not "discovered the *first* beauty" in his "autumnal flower." Sophia, of course, compensated for her husband's impartial views, for Rose demonstrated anew the wonders of "love for which there is no mortal expression."[10]

Claiming that she was in the midst of "[u]nbroken, immortal love [that] surrounds & pervades me," Sophia elevated mundane domestic occurrences into the realm of high rhetoric: the view from their windows, "opaline mists on the mountain"; her children awakening, "such dewy sleep, such joyful uprisings, . . . 'Bon-jour, mamma! Bon-jour, papa!' "; her husband reading aloud from Dickens or De Quincey, "better than any acting or opera"; and her husband reading aloud from *his* work, the "Poet sing[s] his own song." Sophia's accounts of her life now displayed a previously unseen, self-conscious artifice: "Mamma seizes Julian (for Una attends to her own toilet) to brush his wet hair; but it is hard enough to keep him still, for who can hold a fountain!" Thus using the present tense and referring to herself in the third person, she adopted her husband's style of journalizing, when, three years earlier, he had constructed such vignettes around Sophia's interactions with the children: "Now their mother has taken the German picture-book, and is sitting on the floor, with a child on either side, displaying the pictures. . . . [T]he book, between the two children, appears to be in some peril. 'No, little boy must not pull—No, no!' cries papa, so loudly that Julian begins to cry."[11] Both spouses were compelled to record the life they lived. They lived life by writing about it. But how different were their narratives! For Nathaniel, household melodramas might foreshadow tragedy. For Sophia, marriage and motherhood was a story of constant domestic bliss; characters were perfect, even in their imperfections; endings were always happy.

And Sophia's first ten months in Lenox were particularly blissful, notwithstanding the shadows cast by Margaret's death and Mrs. Peabody's lingering illness. Sophia was buoyed by unassailable, nearly delirious optimism, and myriad distractions from worry. While she supervised her children's daily regimen, she was assisted with housekeeping and cooking by an Irish (and Catholic) maid whom Sophia quickly dispatched in favor of a superior helper, the free black and *Protestant!* Mrs. Peters. Her first name remains unrecorded because Sophia always used the honorific "Mrs." when referring to her. Sophia complied with her request to install a "wide bedstead" so that when her "man" visited, he might stay the night. Mrs. Peters also requested that Sophia teach her to read. Caroline was teaching her maid to read, and Mrs. Peters wanted the same opportunity. Considering it a "duty to teach" her—and anyone else—to read, Mrs. Peters and Sophia developed a relationship that was mutually respectful and beneficial.[12]

Sophia also continued to be her children's only teacher, providing instruction in arithmetic and reading which typically occurred in tandem with some other instructional agenda. Rejecting the kinds of didactic, moralistic, evangelical, and pseudoscientific children's books marketed to the vast majority of literate households in mid-nineteenth-century America, Sophia brought into her home juvenile literature written by authors in the Hawthornes' immediate circle. Mary Mann's enormously popular *The Flower People: Being the Account of the Flowers by Themselves* yoked transcendentalism to botanical information specifically for the enlightenment of young girls. Such content was far tamer than that found in classical poetry which Mary refused to read to her children. Caroline Tappan was the author of *Rainbows for Children,* a book of particular interest for (and hence source of dispute between) Julian and Una. Grace Greenwood (the pen name for Sarah Jane Clarke Lippincott) became acquainted with the Hawthornes through Ticknor and Fields, the publisher of her *History of My Pets.* Sophia wrote Greenwood that Nathaniel believed it to be "the best children's book he has ever seen." But the very popular evangelical literature, which coupled instruction in reading with hell-fired religious education, never found its way into Sophia's home. She hoped to instill in her children the "blessedness of goodness" for its own sake, never coercing them through fear of eternal or temporal punishment. Sophia even considered a bribe to be coercive, hence her negative assessment of one of Laetitia Barbauld's stories where a child was offered cake for good behavior.[13]

Sophia also withheld from her children the so-called facts and pseudo-science found in *Peter Parley's Universal History on the Basis of Geography,* which had sold nearly seven million copies by midcentury. Peter Parley was the pseudonym of author and publisher Samuel Griswold Goodrich, who sought to inspire young people with honesty, duty, and hard work— traits of character that would cultivate good citizens in a developing nation. To further his ends, Goodrich used carelessly researched biographies of stalwarts in American history such as Benjamin Franklin and George Washington. For a short time in the 1830s, Nathaniel made money by contributing anonymously to *Peter Parley's,* hack work so inimical to his creative nature that he quickly abandoned it. Goodrich, for his part, deplored creativity and imagination in children's literature, and he particularly abhorred fairy tales and nursery rhymes, claiming that as a child, the story of Little Red Riding Hood had "excited . . . the most painful impressions." For him, fairy tales were full of "falsehoods"; nursery rhymes "like 'hei-diddle diddle' in Mother Goose" were "nonsense," all so "very shocking to the mind."[14]

Sophia found nothing shocking at all in fairy tales. The Hawthorne children delighted in that "German picture-book" and in "The Bear and the Skrattel" from Eliza Lee Follen's edition of *Gammer Grethel; or German Fairy Tales*. Sophia would enact the Skrattel's voice, "squeaking as sharply as occasion required" and provoking Una's fearful cries. Sometimes Julian would make up his own stories, such as one about a wolf and a little lamb to which Una, with great *sangfroid*, supplied a gruesome ending: the wolf tore the lamb "all to pieces, and ate him up." The children were also familiar with "Little Red Riding Hood" in all its frightening power. But frightening to what purpose? Child psychologists continue to debate why fairy tales fascinate and how they affect developing psyches. Sophia had her own thoughts about the matter: fairy tales conveyed "wisdom & goodness" without "heavy saws."[15]

Sophia also introduced her children to the pantheon of mythical figures, among them Pandora, whose curiosity unleashed vice upon the world. This legend became a great favorite with Hawthorne children. Una enacted Pandora; a "jaunty cap," and Julian was transformed into Mercury with "as good a caduceus" as Sophia as could fashion.[16] Firmly believing her children possessed an innate moral compass to steer them aright, Sophia was unfazed by the prospect that they might imitate the mischief or belligerence presented in these myths. So, unlike their Mann cousins, Una and Julian learned about Juno, the protector and chief goddess of Rome; Minerva, the goddess of warriors; and Menelaus, who fought bravely in the Trojan Wars. "Doesn't God's archangel fight evil?" Sophia asked Mary rhetorically, hoping to enlighten her sister that the natural tendency toward aggression could serve divine purposes. Grandmother Peabody "shuddered," however, when contemplating Julian's "military outbursts." She hoped that the boy's "energies [would]be turned to objects promotive of love and Peace!" This discussion of Julian's behavior allowed Sophia's mother to express disapproval of her son-in-law's friend Franklin Pierce, who had led troops into battle during the unpopular Mexican War. How could the General "enjoy the horrors of battle—the groans of his murdered fellows," Mrs. Peabody lamented. Could it be that as a child he was allowed to play soldier, to "mimic warfare"? Defending her husband's friend, Sophia countered that war might be waged "conscientiously" if other ways of "adjusting differences" failed. Then, bringing their discussion back to the domestic realm, Sophia assured her mother that Julian did not exhibit "military tendencies." But Julian certainly enjoyed translating mythical conflicts into an imaginary "warfare with the thistles—which we called hydras, chimaera, dragons, and Gorgons." Nathaniel recorded these playful battles in July of 1851, the very month he published *A Wonder Book for Girls and Boys*, with its own renditions of these characters for children.[17]

Sophia's deliberate choices about suitable stories for Una and Julian had fostered the perfect environment for Nathaniel's return to the juvenile market, now for a third time and under his own banner. Despite his frustrations working with Samuel Goodrich years earlier, Nathaniel had taken a second stab at children's literature shortly after meeting the Peabody sisters. Mary had delighted in his stories about innocent children in "Little Annie's Ramble" and "The Gentle Boy," and believed that Nathaniel might be "creating a new literature for the young." For his part, Nathaniel had wanted to "make a great hit, and entirely revolutionize the whole system of juvenile literature," as he wrote to Longfellow. Nathaniel also wanted to make money with a series of biographies for children that Elizabeth published in 1841. "[H]ow much depends on those little books!" he wrote to his fiancée, Sophia, when these stories were reissued by Tappan and Dennet (with an illustration supplied by Sophia) in 1842.[18]

Nathaniel had adhered to contemporary conventions for juvenile literature. He did, after all, want these books to sell, and his depiction of the boy Samuel Johnson was so aligned with guilt-inducing evangelical stories that the Sunday School Society obtained his permission to reprint it. But his collection of stories, structured around a kindly father or grandfather spinning yarns to groups of children, subtly took unconventional directions. These children, like those in Alcott's Temple School and like Nathaniel's own children now, learn their history from a teacher whom they interrupt and question. More revolutionary still were Nathaniel's vindications of the imagination. Samuel Johnson *regrets* rather than repents his mistakes because his "vivid imagination," not the fear of damnation, "tormented him." Nathaniel had also warned his readers that he "sometimes assumed the license of filling up the outline of history with the details, for which he has none but imaginative authority." And in that 1842 publication titled *The Whole History of Grandfather's Chair*, a chair spoke![19] Goodrich must have cringed. But Nathaniel no longer needed to have his writing for children published by Goodrich; he had the Peabody sisters as his champions.

After the success of *The Scarlet Letter*, Nathaniel had become a recognized author and an asset to his publisher. Fields capitalized upon Nathaniel's acclaim by reissuing his separate volumes of previously published juvenile literature together under the title *True Stories for History and Biography*, which appeared in November of 1850. Six months later, Nathaniel wrote to Fields proposing an entirely new book for children. He had already hatched the title, "A Wonder-Book for Girls and Boys," as well as the book's structure and content. A college-age student would entertain young children with the stories of Pandora, the Gorgon, and the Chimaera, among other classical mythical figures. Una and Julian had responded so enthusiastically to Sophia's telling and retelling of these stories that Nathaniel knew they would "work up admirably." Now an author with considerable clout, he would give these myths "a tone in some degree Gothic or romantic, or any such tone as may best please myself."[20]

Nathaniel also adjusted these myths in ways he deemed proper for youth. In "The Gorgon's Head," Polydectes was motivated by jealousy, rather than lust; in "The Miraculous Pitcher," the guests drink milk, rather than wine. In "The Paradise of Children," Epimetheus and Pandora are no longer the classical version of Adam and Eve but playmates. Nathaniel did not, however, shy away from presenting gory details like those his children had themselves invented. His Chimaera devoured "people and animals alive," and cooked "them afterwards in the burning oven of its stomach" only to be vanquished by Bellerophon's sword and then to fall "from that vast height, downward; while the fire within its bosom, instead of being put out, burned fiercer than ever and quickly began to consume the dead carcass." This story was a favorite with Una and Julian, who asked to have it read repeatedly. The boy was "powerfully affected," Sophia recorded, and "was thrilled & stirred by every sentence—...." She concluded this notebook account with her apostrophe: "Oh my husband! Thy pen surely is inspired with the divinest fire—." Yes, at home and in the marketplace Nathaniel had finally made "a great hit."[21]

Sophia was more than a predictably flattering audience for her husband's writing. Both *A Wonder Book for Girls and Boys* and the 1853 *Tanglewood Tales* were composed around her selection of stories for their children and her conviction that myths might inspire morality without those "heavy saws" so common in popular contemporary literature for children. Yet Nathaniel's renditions of these myths reflect some skepticism about his wife's carefully conceived and executed domestic plans. In "The Golden Touch," for example, Nathaniel created a daughter for Midas named Marygold, a name persistently associated with this myth as if it had originated in the ancient source.[22] This fictional little girl, who is turned into gold, suggests how a parent might endow a child with tremendous, perhaps excessive, or even inappropriate value. Was this how Nathaniel perceived

Sophia's enormous philosophical and practical investment in raising their children? Perhaps so, as two of these stories particularly demonstrate.

Protective mothers and the consequences of their choices are the focus of "The Pomegranate-seeds," Nathaniel's refashioning of the rape of Proserpina. This young girl obtains her mother's permission to play with sea nymphs, but Ceres cautions her about "wandering about the fields by yourself. Young girls, without their mothers to take care of them, are very apt to get into mischief." Proserpina ignores her mother's counsel. Like Little Red Riding Hood who disobediently wanders into the forest, she runs into the fields to gather flowers. As her mother predicted, harm comes to her; she is abducted by Pluto who tempts Proserpina with "rich pastry, . . . highly seasoned meat, . . . spiced sweet-cakes," delights such as those that had never passed Una's or Julian's lips under Sophia's watchful eye. Proserpina refuses these appetizing delicacies because their aroma—contrary to all expectations—"quite took away her appetite, instead of sharpening it." She is, however, tempted by a "wizened" pomegranate, "something that suited her taste . . . ." One whiff and "being in such close neighborhood to her mouth, the fruit found its way into that little red cave." The mother had so controlled her daughter's diet, so suppressed her daughter's normal appetites that the girl succumbs to abnormal cravings for unpalatable fruit. Sophia would certainly have denied being the source of this maternal dietary dictatorship. The very day Nathaniel sent *Wonder Book* to Fields in July of 1851, Sophia wrote her mother that she had "no inflexible theory" regarding Una's diet: "I *hate* [she underscored that word six times!] theories."[23]

Sophia might have titled her euphoric entries about daily life at La Maison Rouge "The Paradise of Children," but this is the title Nathaniel gave to a story about Pandora, ironically underscoring the absence of paradise in the presence of children. In Nathaniel's rendition, before Pandora's arrival, "children never quarrelled among themselves; neither had they any crying fits; nor, since the first time began, had a single one of these little mortals ever gone apart into a corner, and sulked!" "Oh," Nathaniel wrote, "what a good time was that to be alive in!" Enter Pandora (or a child like Una) who pesters, vexes, and questions Epimetheus about his box; and "if she chanced to be ill-tempered, she could give it a push, or kick with her naughty little foot." Echoes of Nathaniel's journal jottings about Una continue. When Epimetheus chides Pandora for having loosed a swarm of "Troubles" upon the world, she protests: "'You might speak a little more kindly!'" Although Pandora eventually sets Hope free, she had unleashed "evil Passions," "many species of Cares," "fifty Sorrows,"

"Diseases," "and more kinds of Naughtiness, than it would be of any use to talk about." This litany of woes constitutes a spectrum of "Troubles" from the petty to the tragic. A "wrong act" committed in the domestic sphere of childish squabbles might very well precipitate "calamity to the whole world."[24]

And "Troubles" were now to descend upon the Hawthornes, blighting their experience in Lenox and Sophia's relationship with Caroline. The women had maintained their long-standing friendship through this present interval of social calls and help with each other's children. Una was often entertained at Highwood, and Caroline would drop by the "shanty" (Sophia's alternate, less exalted name for the red cottage) to enjoy a glass of champagne foam with beaten egg. In February of 1851, three months before Rose was born, Caroline gave birth to her second child, a girl, and Sophia planned to dispatch Una and Julian to Caroline's care at the first "intimation" she was in labor. Both mothers occupied their days caring for their children (although Caroline was assisted by four "reliable women in service") and teaching their maids to read.[25] In important ways, they lived parallel lives. But similar domestic circumstances and years of friendship could not bridge the economic divide between Caroline, the daughter and wife of enormously wealthy men, and Sophia, the daughter of struggling parents and wife of a man only now earning a living suffi-cient to pay his family's basic expenses.

Late in the second summer of the Hawthornes' residence in Lenox, Caroline ceased to be Sophia's friend and became only her irate landlady. She wrote Sophia "a note of remonstrance," as Nathaniel would put it, about fruit taken from the orchard surrounding La Maison Rouge. The Hawthornes had no right to this fruit, and worse yet, Caroline insinuated that their maid was collecting fruit for distribution or sale to others. Caroline's implications that Sophia, in cahoots with her maid, was dis-honest, a petty thief, and a huckster were so hurtful, so humiliating that Sophia could not respond.

Nathaniel therefore penned a lengthy letter to "Mrs. Tappan," outlining his understanding that their rent entitled the Hawthornes to fruit from the trees adjacent to the cottage. While his letter affected "a spirit of undisturbed good humor," it mounted considerable evidence of Caroline's capricious exercise of "manorial privileges." She had not previously objected to their taking fruit from these trees. And what if they considered a "parallel case, that Mrs. Ward should take it upon herself to pursue the same course in regard to the fruit of Highwood"? In other words, must Caroline refrain from the use of fruit growing upon the trees of the Highwood estate which the Tappans were leasing from the Wards? Before moving to Lenox,

Nathaniel had understood the need to declare independence from the bounty of Sophia's rich friends by paying at least nominal rent. "I had *bought* my rights," he reminded Caroline, whose letter demonstrated that she regarded the Hawthornes "as having no right here whatever." He nonetheless gallantly ceded rights to the fruit, offering with feigned levity to return it. "[S]light acidity of sentiment, between friends of some years' standing, may impart a pleasant and spirited flavor to the preserves and jams" made of the contested plums, he concluded.[26]

Despite Nathaniel's efforts at diplomacy, Caroline remained "silent— incommunicative & solemn" toward Sophia who was determined not to quarrel: "I have no quarrel in me & she cannot very well—I am only sorry, & not angry." As summer lapsed into fall, Caroline became "hugely disagreeable" for a person with "Christian sentiment." Then Sophia caught herself: "(but I believe she despises Christ)."[27] The rift would not be mended.

Chapter 7

Shock of Recognition

Even before the unpleasantness with Caroline, the Hawthornes had wanted to move. By mid-July 1851, La Maison Rouge felt like the shanty it really was. "[T]he most inconvenient and wretched little hovel that I have ever put my head in" was how Nathaniel described his home. Confined within its precincts were three children, two parents, household help, and occasional visiting friends and relatives. Una had been "out of tune" after Sophia's confinement, and Nathaniel was out of sorts because his father-in-law, Dr. Peabody, had overstayed his usefulness. Nathaniel's feeling about the cottage, Lenox, and the Berkshires was firm: "I detest it! I detest it!! I de-test!!! I hate Berkshire with my whole soul, and would joyfully see its mountains laid flat."[1]

So the Hawthornes discarded the possibility of moving to Fanny Kemble's more spacious cottage, and Nathaniel asked friends about houses for sale in the range of $1,500 to $2,000, something on the coast or near it, surrounded by land—a spacious house that would not need repair. He was confident that he could now afford a home, if his prosperity in "the literary line" continued.[2] And there was every indication that it would, for he was in the midst of the most prolific period of his life. In slightly more than three years, he composed and would publish three novels, two volumes of stories for children, and a campaign biography for Franklin Pierce. Nathaniel would issue a second edition of *The Twice Told Tales* and publish another collection of short stories titled *The Snow Image*. He would write eight prefaces or introductions in addition to reprinting the prefaces in the 1851 publication of *True Stories*. Having earned the fame, recognition, and respect that had eluded him for decades, he proclaimed his ideas on authorship and the theoretical basis of imaginative literature.

Good reviews and a regular flow of income were but two of the rewards of authorship. Nathaniel basked in the attention of those who valued his opinion and influence. Budding writers requested his advice; at times too busy to respond, Nathaniel commissioned Sophia to assume secretarial duties. On one occasion, she conveyed her husband's opinion to L. W. Mansfield that his manuscript was "not too intimate to publish."[3] The Hawthornes also enjoyed visits from prominent American authors such as James Russell Lowell, the husband of Sophia's friend, Maria White Lowell. Sophia and Nathaniel socialized with the physician–author Oliver Wendell Holmes and with the Sedgwicks. Catharine Maria Sedgwick, the author of the popular, avant-garde historical novel *Hope Leslie*, remained steadfastly single throughout her life. While visiting her brother's home, The Hive, she came to La Maison Rouge, where she presided over a "baby tea party" with Sophia and her children. Sophia was disappointed when Nathaniel declined the Sedgwicks' Christmas Day invitation to The Hive, opining to her mother: "Our intercourse with society is very small now."[4]

But Sophia's assertion appears to contradict the facts. Not since their two-and-a-half-year residence at The Old Manse had they entertained so many guests. In Concord, Sophia's friends and family members, famous writers, and even some utopian experimenters had visited the Hawthornes, sometimes to Nathaniel's chagrin. Now in Lenox, Sophia hosted a different but equally numerous array of people, some of them strangers who wished to meet her now famous husband. Fredrika Bremer of Sweden was on a two-year tour of the United States when she visited the Hawthornes in September of 1851. An advocate for the rights of women, prisoners, and members of the working class, Bremer had been horrified to observe the realities of slavery during her trip across America. Sophia fêted her with an "elegant table" set by Mrs. Peters and prepared a bedroom for Bremer, though she did not spend the night. Bremer's accented English was hard for Sophia to understand, but on one topic Bremer was clearly understood: She was unsympathetic with Sophia's refusal to leave her baby to accompany the group into the village.[5]

Bremer shared her visit with another writer, one whom the Hawthornes had met at a gathering shortly after their arrival in Lenox nearly a year earlier. James T. Fields and his young wife, Eliza, had invited Sophia and Nathaniel to picnic on Monument Mountain with Oliver Wendell Holmes, editors Evert and George Duyckinck, Cornelius Matthews (who referred to Nathaniel as "Mr. Noble Melancholy" in his recollection of this outing), and "Mr. Typee," as Sophia called Herman Melville. "Mr Omoo" was her name for Melville when he called a month later with two others. These three men "devoured" Nathaniel "with their eyes," according to Sophia, who wondered if Melville was "a very great man," for his eyes were "small" and "undistinguished." Although he seemed "brave & manly," she characterized his expressions as sometimes "indrawn, dim."[6]

Sophia did not realize that she had already reached her conclusion about Melville the previous week when she praised the author of "Hawthorne and His Mosses," a recent review in Evert Duyckinck's *The Literary World*. The reviewer, identified only as "The Virginian," was "the first person who has ever in *print* apprehended Mr Hawthorne," Sophia wrote with delighted emphasis to Duyckinck: "There is such a generous, noble enthusiasm as I have not before found in any critic of any writer. . . . Who can he be, so fearless, so rich in heart, of such fine intuition? Is his name altogether hidden?" Hidden in plain sight, for her very next sentence mentioned Herman Melville and thanked Duyckinck for sending Melville's books, which "very much interested" both of the Hawthornes. In Nathaniel's postscript to Sophia's letter, he, too, expressed pleasure in the accolades from a man with "a truly generous heart," adding that "next to deserving his praise, it is good to have beguiled or bewitched such a man into praising me more than I deserve."[7]

The Hawthornes must be excused for not guessing the identity of the reviewer—if review it may be called. A "love letter and a confession" are the genres Hawthorne biographer E. Haviland Miller assigns to this remarkable tribute. Melville had taken great pains to disguise himself as a vacationer in Vermont, a "Virginian" who had read several stories in Nathaniel's 1846 *Mosses from an Old Manse*, put the book aside, and then returned to it "charged more and more with love and admiration of Hawthorne." He wondered: "To what infinite heights of loving wonder and admiration I may yet be bourne, when repeatedly banqueting on these Mosses"? And, the "Virginian" continues, "I feel that this Hawthorne has dropped germinous seeds into my soul." Referring to Nathaniel as a "wizard," the reviewer is possessed; "the soft ravishments of the man spun me round in a web of dreams." Melville commended to his "countrymen . . . an unimitating, and, perhaps, in his way, an inimitable man." By applauding Nathaniel Hawthorne, Herman Melville also celebrated of his own opportunities for a truly national literature with international implications: "For genius, all over the world, stands hand in hand, and one shock of recognition runs the whole circle round."[8]

Melville's comments proclaimed publicly what Sophia had recorded privately for years. Here was a man who could match her hyperbole and enthusiasm. Subtly comparing Nathaniel to Shakespeare, Melville echoed Sophia's opinion that her husband's "universal power" was akin to that of the "Great Swan of Avon." Nathaniel's fiction produced similar effects upon both Sophia and Melville, transporting them into dreamlike states which they described using the vocabulary of mesmerism and the current vogue of spiritualism. When Nathaniel read aloud the legend of Alice Pyncheon from his draft of *The House of the Seven Gables*, Sophia claimed that its "grace & witchery" put her "in a trance." This story exposed "so dark yet so clear a law—such roundness of line—such complete spherical harmony." But Sophia rarely considered the "dark" element of her husband's fiction. She therefore ignored Melville's insistent exploration of Nathaniel's "power of darkness," with its origins in "that Calvinistic sense of Innate Depravity and Original Sin, from whose visitations" Melville asserted, "no deeply thinking mind is . . . wholly free."[9]

Although Sophia did not believe in this "power of darkness," Melville exempted her from the ranks of shallow thinkers, for, as his biographer Hershel Parker points out, he "admired Sophia Peabody Hawthorne uncritically and admired her relationship with her husband." Perhaps Sophia's unprudish, prescient appreciation of Melville and his writing prevented him from disparaging her relentless optimism. She "identified," quoting Parker again, "with the exotic eroticism of *Typee*—to the point of visualizing the naked Fayaway when she first looked upon Melville." "I see Fayaway in his face," Sophia wrote to Elizabeth, decorously referring to a perfectly proper aspect of Melville's anatomy while perhaps indecorously feminizing him though allusion to a female character whose nudity signified innocent sexuality. Sophia appreciated the "freshness of primeval nature" and "true Promethean fire" that blazed in Melville. Nathaniel also appreciated having discovered a kindred author, and he embarked with uncharacteristic speed upon a new friendship. Two short days after meeting Melville, even before he was known to be the adulatory "Virginian," Nathaniel declared: "I met Melville, the other day, and liked him so much that I have asked him to spend a few days with me."[10]

Sophia Hawthorne, Nathaniel Hawthorne, Herman Melville: Each experienced a shock of recognition in the other as if a mirror had reflected inner sensitivities and perceptions. But the outer Herman Melville was conspicuously unlike Nathaniel Hawthorne. Melville was fifteen years younger and came from a prominent though bankrupt New York family. At the age of twenty-two, he had set sail on a whaler. Two years in the South Pacific provided material for novels that immediately earned him good notices as a writer of adventure stories. Experiences with native people, including a dalliance with the young woman who inspired Fayaway, had opened his mind to sexual relations beyond those between a woman and a man, married or otherwise. By the time he entered the Hawthornes' lives, his popularity had dissolved; his writing baffled the public. Even though Herman Melville and Nathaniel Hawthorne both posed troubling questions about the nature of good and evil, their experiences and their fiction were very different. Melville's life as a sailor produced capacious novels set on the high seas and in strange lands. Nathaniel's decade-long sequestration in his mother's home yielded tightly woven stories set in New England and sometimes based on colonial history.

In fact, Sophia's life before marriage had more in common with Melville's earlier "ocean-experiences," as she called them, than anything in her husband's past. Shortly after her twenty-fourth birthday, she had set sail for an eighteen-month sojourn in Cuba, a trip that permitted her to appreciate the "sea-room to [Melville's] intellect."[11] She, too, had been swayed by the charms of tropical romance and the pleasures of an exotic island, all documented in her *Cuba Journal*. Her nonchalant reference to Fayaway suggests ease with sexuality, though her expressions of it in her paintings "Isola," "Menaggio," and "Endymion" had been symbolic rather than representational.

If Sophia Hawthorne, Nathaniel Hawthorne, and Herman Melville did not vibrate to precisely the same chords, they nonetheless created a most harmonious trio. These facts adjust speculation about the nature of Melville's attraction to Nathaniel. In "Hawthorne and His Mosses," Melville's praise for the writing had morphed into his longing for the writer. The "eroticism is unmistakable," claims Hawthorne biographer Brenda Wineapple. An "epiphany" of "erotic-aesthetic union" is E. Haviland Miller's assessment. But Melville was attracted to both Hawthornes, and they were both attracted to him.[12] That Sophia welcomed Melville so readily suggests her expansive, perhaps expanding, sense of the marital relationship. Overjoyed to discover someone who perceived Nathaniel's work as she did, she happily offered her home, her heart, and her husband to a new friend. Thus did Melville gain unprecedented access to the inner recesses of the Hawthornes' domestic life.

Over the next fifteen months, friendship flourished between the two authors who were married men with growing families. Sophia surely basked in Melville's assumption that her marriage was the epitome of bliss; his to Elizabeth Shaw, the daughter of Massachusetts Supreme Court

Chief Justice Lemuel Shaw, was not. But both the Hawthornes and the Melvilles added a child to their households in 1851, and Melville certainly enjoyed being in the presence of children. Julian would later remember that Melville made the red cottage "a paradise for the small people" with his playful antics. One night Melville treated Sophia, Nathaniel, Una, and Julian to a dramatic rendition of a fight between "savages," one of them wielding a "heavy club." So "graphic" was Melville's account that, after he departed, the Hawthornes searched for the club he had used to illustrate this story. Had he left it in a corner? Had he taken it with him? No, Melville explained at his next visit; he had left it on the Pacific island of his story. On another occasion, in the guise of a "cavalier on horseback," Melville accosted Nathaniel and Julian, saluted them in Spanish, and hoisted "little man" into the saddle where he sat, according to his father's report, "with the freedom and fearlessness of an old equestrian." Herman Melville thus became inextricably woven into the fabric of Julian's earliest memories of his father, forever pairing Nathaniel with his jovial, fun-loving companion. And as an adult, Julian would claim that he and Una had no recollection of a prior period "when their father was not their playmate, or when they ever desired or imagined any other playmate than he." Unless that playmate might have been the "familiar and welcome" guest Julian recalled so fondly.[13]

In late July, Sophia took her daughters to West Newton. She wanted her mother, who was too infirm to travel, to meet baby Rose. Sophia also wanted to give her husband some respite from his growing family, and this interlude with Julian is captured in Nathaniel's charming, sometimes perplexed account of these twenty-eight days with the little boy. Nathaniel seized an opportunity to create "A Paradise of Bachelors" (as the title of one of Melville's stories would have it). Now Nathaniel might finally imbibe that brandy Melville had promised him when the two conversed about "ontological heroics" and smoked cigars. Now, Julian accompanied his father, Melville, and others to enjoy a picnic with a "considerable quantity" of gingerbread, nuts, and raisins. And after this illicit repast (for Sophia would not have condoned Julian's stuffing himself with sweets), the group toured the Hancock Shaker community in Pittsfield.[14]

Known as "Shakers," because their worship sometimes included gyrations and dancing, the United Society of Believers in Christ's Second Appearing is remembered today through their legacy of unornamented, handcrafted furniture and homes. Though these aesthetic contributions survive, the group is nearly extinct owing to its requirement that every member practice celibacy. The Shakers' eighteenth-century English founder Ann Lee had endured the death of her four children in infancy, an emotional trauma that could explain forswearing sexual relations and their inevitable, sorrow-filled consequences. Lee also believed that God was both female and male, granting Shaker women considerably more equality than their counterparts in other religions or society at large. Shakers organized themselves into groups they called "families" and clustered into self-sufficient villages segregated by sex for the purposes of sleeping and working.

On that August day in 1851, Nathaniel and his companions observed firsthand a Shaker establishment. Although he noted the convenience, cleanliness, and neatness of the Shakers' arrangements, he excoriated them as "the most singular and bedeviled set of people." Nathaniel recoiled at their lack of privacy and the one-person beds that were shared by two men, perhaps an uncomfortable reminder of his childhood experience when he had been forced to share a bed with his detested Uncle Robert Manning. The "little man hopping and dancing," Nathaniel noted, remained innocently unaware of the peculiarities of this sect and his father's disparagements. Upon returning to Lenox with his exhausted son, the "full, rich, cloudless moonlight" made Nathaniel wish he had instead ridden "the six miles to Pittsfield," and to Melville. Happy thoughts filled Julian's head when he awoke the next day declaring to his father that "he loved Mr. Melville as well as me, and as mamma, and as Una."[15] And Mr. Melville loved them too.

In the fall of 1851, Melville published *Moby-Dick* with its stunning dedication: "IN TOKEN / of my admiration for his genius / This work is inscribed / To / NATHANIEL HAWTHORNE." Nathaniel expressed his gratitude in a letter (now lost) that Melville called "joy-breeding and exultation-giving." On November 17, Melville responded with his own admittedly "long letter." Nearly manic, he poured his emotion into several vessels of allusion. "I feel that the Godhead is broken up like the bread at the Supper. Hence this infinite fraternity of feeling." Conflating Christian theology and ritual with an intense "fraternity," Melville perhaps hinted at male attachments and unconventional arrangements. Signing himself simply, intimately "Herman," he galloped to a postscript: "The divine magnet is on you, and my magnet responds. Which is biggest? A foolish question—they are *One*."[16]

Melville had announced that he would continue his visits until he was told that they were "both supererogatory and superfluous." And that is what they now became. Why? Nathaniel's correspondence for this period does not survive to tell us, a lacuna that provokes, rather than prevents, speculation among Hawthorne biographers. Had Nathaniel's habitual reserve overtaken his fleeting openness? Had the intensity of Melville's affections become disquieting to Nathaniel? Was the visit to the Shaker community in Melville's company too uncomfortably linked with relationships that appalled Nathaniel? E. Haviland Miller claims that Nathaniel was "viscerally repelled" by the Shakers, quoting as evidence Nathaniel's notebook account of their lack of privacy and the "close junction of man with man, and supervision of one man over another—it is hateful and disgusting to think of." Nathaniel's animus, according to Miller, "appears to originate in unconscious fears perhaps exacerbated by Melville's exuberant, seductive behavior and erotic language."[17] And that business of the magnet! Did Melville use the rhetoric of mesmerism as metaphor to describe kindred artistic spirits or to imply that he and Nathaniel were powerless to resist attraction to one another?

Whatever cooled Nathaniel's relationship with Melville was imperceptible to Sophia. She remained warm toward Melville, the only man, besides John Louis O'Sullivan, with whom she had developed a genuine and mutual friendship since her wedding. "He is an incalculable person," she wrote to her mother. But her praise for *Moby-Dick*, in a letter to Melville (also lost), can only be calculated by his response to her on January 8, 1852. Sophia was "the only *woman*" who had expressed pleasure in his novel, "for as a general thing, women have a small taste for the sea. But . . . you," Melville continued, "with your spiritualizing nature, see more things than other people, and by the same process, refine all you see, so that they are not the same things that other people see . . . ."[18] Melville extolled in Sophia precisely the trait Emerson had lauded.

Sophia Hawthorne and Herman Melville shared an appreciation for each other's androgynous qualities. She had likened his appearance to that of a woman (Fayaway); he now likened her taste to that of men. And Sophia would have applauded Melville's nod to mesmerism, she who herself had been mesmerized time and again before her marriage to Nathaniel, despite his "invincible repugnance" that her "holy name" would be "bruited about in conjunction with these magnetic phenomena." He was appalled to think that she had relinquished her will, and worse, that an "intruder" had gained access to her "holy of holies."[19] But because Sophia's debilitating headaches were relieved by mesmerism, she had repeatedly defied her fiancé. Nathaniel would have found Melville's mention of a trance-inducing magnet as abhorrent as the possibility that he might succumb to its powers.

Many of the valuable (from Sophia's perspective) or objectionable (from Nathaniel's perspective) aspects of mesmerism had recently surfaced in "spiritualism," a phenomenon that began in 1848 with Kate and Margaret Fox, then twelve and fourteen years old respectively. These upstate-New

York sisters claimed to interpret communications from the dead through otherwise unexplained rapping or knocking noises in their home. After these girls convinced their much older sister, Leah, that they were genuine mediums, she assumed a role somewhere between chaperone and manager. When the Fox girls moved to Rochester, they resided with Quakers, whose home was a gathering place for abolitionists. There, Kate and Margaret immediately gained acceptance and credibility. By 1850, they had become a *cause célèbre*, attracting the attention of James Fennimore Cooper and William Cullen Bryant as well as Horace Greeley, William Lloyd Garrison, and Sojourner Truth. The Fox sisters and a fast-growing number of other mediums thus became associated with abolitionism and liberal causes, such as women's rights.[20]

Like persons who were mesmerized, the so-called "rappers" or "knockers" entered into a trance-like state. While mesmerists claimed to heal by placing another individual in a trance, spiritualists claimed that "trance mediums" were vehicles through which the spirits of the dead communicated with the living. Sophia's sister Elizabeth was among those fascinated by rappers just as she had enthusiastically endorsed mesmerism two decades earlier. Her mother had "disbelieved" though Sophia reported that it cured her. "[H]umbuggery" was what Mrs. Peabody now called the carnival atmosphere surrounding the rappers. But she was perplexed if not actually open-minded about "Katy Fox" because of Elizabeth's encounters with her in Boston. With the Fox girl as her medium, Elizabeth claimed she had twice conversed with William Ellery Channing, who had died in 1842. Mrs. Peabody found it "unaccountable" that "Katy Fox should be able to talk or cause her spirits to talk to Elizabeth, a perfect stranger, in the very language of Dr W E Channing."[21]

But then Elizabeth struck upon an idea that might confirm the capacity of mediums to communicate with the spirits of the dead. Like many others, she assumed that child-mediums would be unlikely to perpetrate fraud because "there is less ability, as well as less desire, to practice trickery and deception in the child than in the adult." Such was the opinion voiced in a spiritualist publication, *Banner of Light*, in response to the powers of the golden-haired, eleven-year-old medium, Laura Ellis. If Laura Ellis, why not Una Hawthorne? So Elizabeth proposed that rappers meet her barely six-year-old niece and enlist her in their cause. The "purity of the medium," Elizabeth wrote to Sophia about Una, "would create a fine chance for observation," thus testing the validity of the rappers' claims.[22]

Elizabeth's hasty acceptance of one after another novel idea or eccentric person was nothing new to the Peabodys, but Mrs. Peabody was "astonished" that Elizabeth wanted to subject her niece to people who might be frauds or worse, demonic practitioners of occult. She had beseeched Elizabeth to abandon this idea and never to mention it to Sophia. But Elizabeth's audacity could not be subdued. She ignored her mother's advice, and the response from the Hawthornes was emphatic. Invoking her husband, Sophia wrote to her sister in February of 1851: "Mr. Hawthorne says he never [underscored seven times!] will consent to Una's being made a medium of communication, & that he will defy all Hell rather, so that he will have to disprove the testimony of the spirits, if it comes to that." Sophia forbade Elizabeth to visit Lenox with the rappers; "it would injure Una physically & spiritually to be subjected to such influence." Sophia was, nevertheless, curious about the circumstances that prompted Elizabeth's injudicious idea. Had Elizabeth volunteered her niece or had the rappers requested Una? Discussion of the matter persisted for another month, and in March, Sophia drew the line: "Mr. Hawthorne thinks it would destroy Una body & soul to become a medium."[23]

Sophia, it should be noted, did not use her own authority to rebuff her sister's request, which by its insistence had become a demand. Rather, Sophia became, as it were, the medium for her husband by communicating *his* denunciations of rappers. Indeed, Sophia did not entirely reject spiritualism. She could more easily reject the idea that loved ones who died (or were about to die) would become forever silent. Mid-century Americans, Sophia among them, stood on the threshold of a more scientific, rational era. Comforting beliefs in the afterlife were disappearing to be replaced by—well, nothing. That void might be filled by those who claimed communication between the dead and the living. Such was perhaps the emotional and psychological source of Horace and Molly Greeley's belief in the Fox sisters' messages. The Greeleys frequently invited the girls for séances in their Rochester home, convinced that they thus communicated with their five-year-old son who had recently died.[24]

Of course, not everyone considered spiritualism benign. The vast majority of mediums were girls or very young women bearing a perilous resemblance to another group from New England's past. The history of witchcraft in Salem suggested that young women—deemed hysterical or possessed—were at risk for becoming objects of fear and persecution. Given Nathaniel's family history and his lifelong shame over his ancestors' role in the Salem witch trials, he had more reason than many of his contemporaries to beware of mediums and to reject the thought that his daughter might be used as one. For Nathaniel, as Samuel Chase Coale has astutely observed, mesmerism was "a modern form of witchcraft."[25]

In so many ways, Sophia and Nathaniel perceived the world, and now the world beyond, differently. She continued to see brightness and light, goodness and happiness. He could never escape the specter of shadow and darkness. Differences such as these would surely stress a marriage. And slowly microscopic fissures in their relationship appeared. During Sophia's stay in West Newton, Nathaniel wrote brief letters to his "Phoebe." In one note, he dissimulated, "as to enjoyment, I don't remember to have had any, during thy absence. It has been all doing & suffering." When Sophia returned to Lenox, she was disappointed that her husband failed to greet her at the train station. He had sent someone else to "fetch" her home. Two exhausting hours later, Sophia with her daughters arrived at La Maison Rouge.[26]

Chapter 8

The Deeper Her Cry

First Concord, then Salem, now Lenox and another exodus.

On a bleak late November day, the Hawthornes crammed their possessions into a farmer's wagon and left the little red cottage, Lenox, the Berkshires, and their erstwhile friends. Much to Sophia's disappointment, Mrs. Peters also remained behind. The Hawthornes' five cats "scampered . . . despairingly after the rapidly receding vehicle," as Julian would later recall. His memory of arrival at their temporary home in a "dismal and unlovely little suburb" was equally unhappy.[1]

Once again the Hawthornes deferred their dream of purchasing a home. They moved instead into the Manns' West Newton house, recently vacated because Mary and her children had joined Horace, now a congressman, in Washington. While Sophia relished the opportunity to be near her ailing mother in West Newton, Nathaniel was determined to evade the duty that Sophia had readily assumed for *his* mother. As he bluntly wrote Sophia, he would not "have the care and responsibility" of her father and mother. They were to be kept at a safe distance with Elizabeth, Nat, and his family. Sophia, therefore, announced to her relatives that no one would be permitted to visit Greenwood, as she dubbed the Manns' home, without a specific invitation.[2]

Because of the unpleasantness with the Tappans, Nathaniel had resolved "in all future cases to have my rights more sharply defined." Thus the Hawthornes negotiated carefully with their new landlords for rent that would not exceed $350 should the Hawthornes remain in West Newton for the duration of Horace's congressional term. During this period, Ticknor and Fields would advance money needed to buy a house, when the right one came along. The very day Nathaniel announced these arrangements to Sophia, she quizzed Mary about her furnishings and requested an inventory "fair & whole" so that the Manns' items could be separated from the Hawthornes'. To avoid any confusion, the sisters determined that Mary had better store her kitchen goods. And Sophia promised they would take no boarders, unless they were at the point of "starvation," a criterion that had governed Sophia's previous financial decisions.[3] The Hawthornes had learned the cost of inadequately delineated boundaries with friends and would avoid paying that price with Sophia's relatives.

"Greenwood," a house that bespoke Horace's success, had been built to the Manns' specifications. Contemporary conveniences permitted the most advanced hygienic practices. Cleanliness was made easy in a "bathing room" fitted with pumps for hot water, and a water closet was located near Nathaniel's study.[4] Ah, that study! Sophia was relieved that her husband would not be disquieted by the children when he sequestered himself to write. Nathaniel was delighted to have space that he might share only with his imagination—his imagination and the inescapable presence of the owner of the house, his brother-in-law Horace, as well as a host of other friends, family, and his current circumstances.

Within five months' time—the duration of the Hawthornes' residence in Greenwood—Nathaniel wrote and published *The Blithedale Romance*, a novel that pits a voyeuristic writer against a monomaniacal reformer. Set in an experimental utopian community, Blithedale's resemblance to Brook Farm prompted Nathaniel's disingenuous disavowal of connection between the two. He insisted that the major characters (two female and two male—a foursome that had come to structure his full-length fiction) "never made their appearance there." Indeed, these characters are not drawn from that "most romantic episode." Hollingsworth, in his relentless dedication to prison reform, resembles the humorless Horace Mann. But Hollingsworth's intense desire to enlist the allegiances and affections of Miles Coverdale owes much to the pressures for intimacy exerted upon Nathaniel by Herman Melville. The mysterious and sensuous Zenobia, a renowned advocate for her sex and writer of popular works, derives from both Margaret Fuller and the mid-century "d——d scribbling women."[5] The mysterious and ethereal Priscilla foretells who Una might become in the hands of spiritualists. The bachelor writer, narrator (and author-surrogate), Coverdale, presents these characters through a combination of memory and sometimes flawed inferences that rebound to his discredit.

The Blithedale Romance lays bare Nathaniel's discomfort among people whose causes and ideas he viewed with skepticism and disdain—people Sophia had introduced to him and made an inextricable part of his life.

The novel begins by undermining any optimism that might ground a utopian community, be it the Blithedale of Nathaniel's imagination, the Brook Farm of his past experience, or the Hancock Shakers of his recent observation. Coverdale quickly determines that Blithedale members "looked rather like a gang of beggars or banditti," unconsciously contradicting his own descriptions of Blithedale's most conspicuous member. Zenobia's association with a combination of images and allusions forces the reader to see her as anything but a beggar. She has "as much native pride as any queen," a word repeatedly applied to her. Her opulent manner of dress reveals her wealth, a discovery Coverdale makes by spying on her through a boarding house window when they both take respite from Blithedale in town. But when enacting egalitarian life, Zenobia wears homespun clothes and a bandanna, adopting a costume more exotic than rustic thanks to the hothouse flower perpetually adorning her hair. Despite such detailed description of Zenobia's attire, Coverdale imagines her without any clothing as a "perfectly developed figure, in Eve's earliest garment." Several Edenic allusions (those harbingers of inevitable fall from grace) do not absolve him from prurience, for he would penetrate the core of Zenobia's sexuality. Is she a virgin? Was she ever married? "If the great event of a woman's life had been consummated, the world knew nothing of it," but could she really "have given herself away so privately"?[6]

While Nathaniel was penning these words, such questions swirled around the recently drowned "Queen Margaret," as Sophia had often fondly referred to her. In this and other ways, Sophia's rhetoric and imagery suffuses Zenobia's depiction. Nathaniel knew well Sophia's *Cuba Journal* in which she writes of herself as newly made on that Edenic island, her hair "dressed" with flowers. "Spanish Ladies" she had written, "always wear natural flowers in their hair." Nathaniel had previously used just this adornment to construct another doomed female character, Beatrice Rappaccini, whose "magnificent" flowers, like Zenobia's, become "languid." Coverdale parenthetically attributes Zenobia's wilting blossom to "(the fervency of the kitchen-fire)," but Zenobia, or Beatrice, or any woman who would step beyond prescribed gender boundaries (Sophia in Cuba, Margaret Fuller in Italy) risks destroying the natural order. A woman like this, for all her sensuality, is not really a woman, as Zenobia unwittingly reveals by referring to herself as "an auditor—auditress, I mean—."[7]

Neither is Hollingsworth, despite his burly attributes, a representative of full manhood: "There was something of the woman moulded into the great stalwart frame." Coverdale's description of this thirty-year-old man with his "great shaggy head, his heavy brow, his dark complexion, his abundant beard" might be a verbal portrait of Herman Melville. For all Melville's appearance of rough masculinity, Sophia's first impression of him had evoked a mental image of one of his female characters—and a naked one at that! When Coverdale falls ill upon arrival at Blithedale, he initially responds to Hollingsworth's "more than brotherly attendance" only to recoil from the intensity of his friendship and "stern and dreadful peculiarity." Men like Hollingsworth—men like Horace Mann—"will keep no friend, unless he make himself a mirror of their purpose." Nathaniel shared no common purpose with his brother-in-law, a man who demanded what Hollingsworth demands of Coverdale: "a purpose in life, worthy of the extremest self-devotion—worthy of martyrdom, should God so order it!" But Coverdale can maintain, he discovers to his dismay, ideological distance more easily than emotional detachment. An "almost irresistible force" tugs at his "heart." Coverdale knows, "[h]ad I but touched his hand, Hollingsworth's magnetism would perhaps have penetrated me with his own conception of all these matters. But I stood aloof." So, too, had Nathaniel resisted when Melville declared: "The divine magnet is on you, and my magnet responds." For Nathaniel then, and for his character Coverdale now, "the bands, that were silken" turned into "iron fetters."[8]

Coverdale withstands Hollingsworth's magnetism, but he fears that the waif Priscilla cannot. Originally mistaken for one of Hollingsworth's "guilty patients," Priscilla is childlike, "wan, almost sickly," lame, and insubstantial, yet she appears to possess preternatural abilities. In Priscilla, Nathaniel's readers would have recognized Kate or Maggy Fox or Laura Ellis or any number of contemporary female mediums. Closer to the Hawthorne home, however, Priscilla resembles Una with her "large, brown melancholy eyes" and "brown hair" that fell "not in curls, but with a slight wave." Una's unruliness and mercurial temperament are reflected in Priscilla's pivots between "wildness . . . scrambling up trees like a squirrel" and moments when "animation seemed entirely to desert her." For Priscilla, this transition is associated with "her gift of hearing," as Coverdale speculates, a gift or curse or sorcery controlled first by Moodie, then by Westervelt, and lastly by Hollingsworth.[9]

Why Priscilla has been deposited in Blithedale under Zenobia's reluctant care is revealed in the last third of the novel. A "colorless and torpid" old man called Moodie confides to Coverdale that Priscilla is his second daughter by his second wife, now deceased. During his first marriage, Moodie—then a wealthy man known as Fauntleroy—fathered his first daughter, Zenobia as she is now called, but "he had no just sense of her immortal value. . . . If he loved her, it was because she shone." Then Fauntleroy committed "the sort of crime . . . which society . . . neither could nor ought to pardon. More safely might it pardon murder," and his wife dies, shamed by her "alliance with a being so ignoble." The unspeakable nature of this offense parallels the unspoken sexual status of Zenobia. Married? Single? Virgin? Or had she "given herself away"?[10] Worse, had Moodie taken from her that which she alone had the right to give, but never to her father?

Whatever blights Zenobia, she has become an independent writer, a proponent of women's rights, and the heir to her wealthy uncle; she, therefore, appears to possess everything her dependent sister lacks. But these women share more than biological sisterhood; they are both objects of violation as well as agents of transgression. Just as Coverdale penetrates Zenobia's life through his imagination and spying, so does he indulge his prurient "impulse to take just one peep beneath [Priscilla's] folded petals." He and contemporary observers of her trance-like behavior would have wondered if purity really existed beneath her innocent façade, for the mediums of the 1850s, like the women who were mesmerized a decade or two earlier, were *ipso facto* contaminated in the public eye.[11]

Zenobia, like Leah Fox who acted as chaperone to her much younger sisters, informs Priscilla, "'you absolutely need a duenna.'" Priscilla's response, "'I am afraid you are angry with me,'" suggests the burden of perceived transgressions, but she retains, Coverdale tells us, "a persistency to her own ideas, as stubborn as it was gentle." These words might have been written about Alice Pyncheon in *The House of the Seven Gables*, another "gentle and proud" girl whose father submits her to a hypnotist or sorcerer (whatever term applies) to obtain title to property. Pyncheon convinces himself (as Elizabeth Peabody had convinced herself about Una) that the girl's "own purity would be her safe-guard" while functioning as a "telescopic medium . . . with the departed personages." Alice does not, however, survive her trance unsullied. She becomes the object of "ungenerous scorn. . . . [S]o lost from self-control, she would have deemed it sin to marry."[12]

In two novels, Nathaniel exposed his horror over what might occur should he (like the fathers Moodie or Pyncheon) permit his own daughter to fall prey to the rappers, or to his sister-in-law, or even perhaps to his wife, who was, from his perspective, insufficiently resistant to the spiritualist phenomenon. And his horror derived from seemingly opposing possibilities: that a woman is too weak to survive—chastity intact—the infiltration of her psyche; that a woman is too strong to submit to male supervision of her sexuality. Such, in fact, were paradoxes that colored perceptions of

Kate and Maggie Fox and their cohorts, women who appeared demure yet might be unchaste, women whose public position was more conspicuous than that of reformers such as Margaret Fuller and Elizabeth Peabody. Possessing voices that could not be silenced, the reformer and the medium were truly sisters.[13]

But *The Blithedale Romance* does not deal these women an equal concluding fate because of their unequal relationship to Hollingsworth. He rejects Zenobia, and all her erotic allure, for Priscilla, but his feelings for this girl had "differed little from those of an elder brother." Zenobia, for all her independence, cannot bear rejection and drowns herself. This dramatic denouement echoes Nathaniel's record of the night that he and Ellery Channing (Margaret Fuller's brother-in-law) searched for the corpse of a melancholy young teacher in the Concord River. Martha Hunt's suicide by drowning resonated with Margaret's recent watery death, by some accounts a suicide because she appeared to refuse attempts at survival. In the end, a common woman like Martha, who "died for want of sympathy," differs not a whit from the queenly Zenobia. That she could be fatally affected by romantic rejection justifies the narrator's musing on the unhappy lot of any woman capable of unquestioning devotion to man:

> when a woman wrecks herself on such a being, she ultimately finds that the real womanhood, within her, has no corresponding part in him. Her deepest voice lacks response; the deeper her cry, the more dead his silence. The fault may be none of his; he cannot give her what never lived within his soul.

When the inevitable tragedy occurs, who is at fault? The larger-than-life man who demands fealty from everyone around him, who inspires selfless devotion from women and men alike? Or is the woman to blame for expecting this man to reciprocate the intensity of her feeling? Sophia might have answered these questions by comparing her sister Mary to the fictional Priscilla, each so deferential to a charismatic husband. But would Sophia have recognized in the narrator's words an indictment of her own worshipful posture toward the "Ideal being whom I call my husband"?[14]

One can only guess what she saw reflected in *The Blithedale Romance* for she was atypically reticent about it. Although Sophia was the first person to read the novel, she leaves no record of her impressions, no hint if she had been entranced by its "spell" or if *The Blithedale Romance* contained the "strain of grace & witchery" that she had found in *The House of the Seven Gables*. Then her words of praise, like Melville's, cast Nathaniel in the role of persons he so mistrusted. The writer of fiction—particularly the fictional writer Miles Coverdale—possesses many of the unsavory characteristics of the mesmerist or sorcerer. He stands apart, penetrates, manipulates, and perhaps violates with his imagination those who are the objects of his observation and display. Just as Coverdale had spied on Zenobia with impunity through the boarding house window, he "never once dreamed of questioning" the propriety of observing her most distraught moments after Hollingsworth tosses her aside. Zenobia recognizes disdainfully that Coverdale "'is turning this whole affair into a ballad.'"[15] Had Sophia looked steadily into the mirror of *The Blithedale Romance*, she might have drawn the same conclusion.

Some reviewers thought *The Blithedale Romance* superior to Nathaniel's previous full-length works of fiction. That opinion of the novel was squeezed into Sophia's letter to Louisa among other newsy tidbits, among them that the sale of its copyright to Chapman and Brown in London earned some two hundred pounds. This "windfall" permitted Nathaniel to act on what he had learned: "The right of purchase is the only safe one." Early in June, he bought a "horrible old house" (Sophia's words) in Concord, Massachusetts, from the dreamy philosopher Bronson Alcott. A far cry from the efficiency, comfort, and convenience of the home built to politician and reformer Horace Mann's specifications, Alcott's house had "no suggestiveness about it, and no venerableness" (Nathaniel's words). Its exterior "olive rusty hue" was unappealing; its terraces and arbors had fallen into disrepair. But there were enticing patios—the Hawthornes referred to them as piazzas—at each end, and Sophia was pleased with her "excellent" stove and a "good, easy pump." She willingly undertook the challenge of supervising "magical" transformations, hiring painters, carpenters, and paperers as well as people to clean. She had furniture upholstered and bought carpets. She adorned the walls of every room with pictures. A copy of Da Vinci's "Holy Family" was hung in the dining room, and she displayed her own art. With great pleasure, she placed "Endymion where I always wanted it—in my husband's study, and it occupies one whole division of the wall." Art, she believed, would cultivate aesthetic sentiments in her children, and Julian perhaps proved her point by requesting that a picture of the infant Christ be hung in his room. Despite its need for interior renovations, which would be deferred, the house had a marvelous location. A "quiet retreat," Mrs. Peabody called it, finding ways to mitigate her loss of proximity to Sophia. Never mind, Mrs. Peabody counseled, that water leaked into the cellar. Situated upon lush wooded acreage, this "hollow among the hills," as Rose would later describe it, showed to great advantage as summer approached. Abundant elms, oaks, and pines formed a canopy of cooling shade. Sophia counted a "mosaic of flowers" and "music" from birds and insects among her numerous blessings. "GOD is so bountiful," she proclaimed.[16]

The Alcotts' "Hillside" was thus transformed into the Hawthornes' "Wayside." Sophia's cousin, George Palmer Putnam, planned to feature it in *The Homes of America* and wanted to have the article accompanied by a sketch, which he asked Sophia to provide. Although she began work on it immediately, so pressing were all other tasks, that she was forced to abandon the effort.[17] She may have been disappointed to forgo this opportunity to return to art, but she was nonetheless deeply satisfied to be in her own home, the only home the Hawthornes would ever own.

Chapter 9

The Revulsion of Joy

Barely two years had passed since Caroline Tappan had brought the news of Margaret Fuller's death when another friend announced yet another tragic drowning. Louisa Hawthorne had been sailing down the Hudson River on the *Henry Clay*. That ship's reckless crew had decided to race the *Armenia*, also on its way to New York City. The ensuing collision and explosion left passengers with a grim choice: stay on board and certainly burn, or jump overboard and possibly drown. Louisa gambled against death by water, and lost. She was among the sixty men, women, and children who died that day, but her uncle John Dike, with whom she had been traveling, survived.[1] He commissioned William Pike to convey the news to the Hawthornes.

Before breakfast on July 30, 1852, Sophia looked out her window and saw Pike. He had been at the Wayside, the Hawthornes' new Concord home, just a few days before, and his return so early in the morning, so soon after his last visit, boded ill. His demeanor was serious, pained; he could not buffer the announcement of Louisa's horrible death. Nathaniel responded by stoically retreating to his study. Sophia wept and attempted to console the children with the notion that Aunt Louisa was now with her mother: "Let us think of her spirit in another world!"[2]

Sophia's shock and grief were undoubtedly tinged with "what if"? What if she had not encouraged Louisa to delay her planned visit? What if, only days before the fatal accident, Sophia had not written Louisa, who was then with Uncle Dike at a spa in Saratoga Springs: "pray do not fail to go down the Hudson & see the great Gotham. I am really glad your visit to us will be after such a fine airing"? This little voyage was but one of the many benefits that life with the Dikes afforded Louisa, and Sophia derived peace of mind knowing that her sister-in-law was so comfortably situated. Louisa's death would deprive Sophia of the affectionate sisterly relationship she lacked with her other sister-in-law or, at times, with her own sisters, whose love was freighted with bouts of contention and competition. Louisa "had such a genuine joy in the children," Sophia realized, having counted on her to "observe & rejoice in their developments." Julian would remember his aunt fondly, as "a lady of sociable and gentle disposition, and a great favorite." Happy memories were Louisa's legacy, as was a brooch that cousin Robert Manning had recovered from her corpse and given to Una.[3]

Sophia stayed with the children in Concord when Nathaniel left for Louisa's funeral in Salem on August 3. But he arrived too late; the funeral was over. He was, therefore, thankfully spared from hearing all the "Calvinistic talk," the "most hopeless ingredient in whatever thing," according to Sophia. Her habitual philosophical optimism explained even Louisa's death: "no event can occur which is not the best for each & for all & forever." But such belief would not—should not—cancel expressions of deepest sorrow: "Tears that will flow do not drown faith & hope, but only relieve the loving heart. It is unnatural to be stoic."[4] Were these comments an oblique criticism of her husband's method of mourning? His study became his refuge, and he was able to deliver the presidential campaign biography of his friend Franklin Pierce to Ticknor and Fields by the 30th of August. The same day, Nathaniel left Concord for his reunion at Bowdoin, after which, at Pierce's invitation, he went directly to Appledore, the largest among the Isles of Shoals, situated six miles off the eastern coast of New Hampshire in the Gulf of Maine. He stayed on Appledore at the Laighton Hotel for nearly three weeks.

With other vacationers, among them Pierce, Nathaniel thoroughly enjoyed himself. By day, he fished, explored rugged terrain, sailed to an adjacent island, or simply relaxed on the verandah. At night, he smoked cigars, drank "hot gin-and-water . . . excellent stuff," or played cards; his whist-partner was "an agreeable young lady from Portsmouth." Conversations with the hotel's proprietor and his recently married daughter, Celia Thaxter—who would later become a spiritualist—turned to tales of island ghosts. All this fun quickly depleted Nathaniel's cash. He wrote Ticknor requesting ten dollars and, in the extensive journal Nathaniel kept during this vacation, he noted when Ticknor's letter arrived, presumably with money enclosed. That day, Nathaniel remarked that he longed for a letter from home with good news; this was his only mention of his family in the journal while on Appledore. His planned departure on September 14 was delayed by inclement weather, and that evening, he imbibed "*two*," as he recorded with emphasis, "glasses of hot gin-and-water." He was in "the breeziest and comfortablest place in the world," he realized; "here one may sit or walk, and enjoy life, while all other mortals are suffering."[5]

And other mortals were suffering. At the Wayside, Sophia endured extreme, late summer heat and became exhausted to the point of prostration while caring for quarrelsome, restless children. Not even the presence of Ellen Herne, Sophia's extraordinarily competent new maid, eased the burdens of motherhood that currently outnumbered its joys. During his absence, she too kept an extensive journal where she lamented that Una threw burrs into Julian's hair, tangling his curls; that Julian screamed when Sophia forbade him to play outside during the "red hot" noon; that Rose interfered with Julian, whom he called an "'ugly thing'"—then worse, claimed it was not he who called names "'but the dragon'"! Even Julian's pet turtle added to Sophia's woes. "'Beloved'," as Julian curiously called it, was the object of his constant solicitude and chatter. He queried his mother: "'[D]o you wish I had never known what a turtle was? [D]o you wish Papa had never given me a first one?'" Sophia responded: "'Why I do not know if you would be happier if he had not.'" Of course it was Sophia who would have been happier without the turtle, which was tormented by the Hawthornes' cat, and the cat, in turn, was tormented by Rose, who pulled "pussy's tail terribly."[6]

When she was not annoying cat or brother, Rose nursed fitfully (Sophia was in the process of weaning her) and slept poorly. Sophia repeatedly rued her "rather heavy responsibility with these three children alone," but she also claimed that eight-year-old Una, six-year-old Julian, and Rose, at barely sixteen months of age, "feel a responsibility about me which is beautiful to see." A paradoxical comment follows: "[T]here never were such divine children, far diviner than if more spotless of blame—I cannot explain this remark now." Cannot or would not? On several occasions, Sophia merely hinted at behavior that she found too disturbing to record. This was no "Paradise of Children." Nor was it Nathaniel's twenty-day, carefree interlude of bemused observation of Julian and his little bunny in Lenox the year before. Sophia's nineteen days with Julian and little turtle, and screaming Rose, and burr-throwing Una were "dreary, dreary." She suffered headaches and despaired that her journal was "good for nothing," a glum admission from the Queen of Journalizers.[7]

Never before as wife and mother had she recorded such feelings, but why this unhappy turn? Why now? Certainly the specter of Louisa's recent death by water clung to her thoughts and to the children's, lacing Nathaniel's sea-travel with their anxiety. Uncertainty about the date of her husband's return, coupled with little news from him, exacerbated fears that he might have come to harm. Julian besieged Sophia wanting "to know if I expect him this morning, this afternoon, tomorrow—to night— & every other assignable hour." Sophia was unable to answer these questions or, better yet, to produce Papa, so Julian voiced what the others would not say: Papa was "probably *drowned* which was the reason he wrote no letter nor came." Una objected: "'Why *no* Julian, I know he is not, for he does not go near any water'," to which her brother countered, "'the Isle of Shoals—& what is an Island?'" Una could only respond dolefully, "'Oh—'." Sophia then segued into the source of their fears— poor, drowned Aunt Louisa and Julian's claim to have seen her: "'I see her now just as well as I see you, Mamma, & she is perfectly beautiful—'."[8] Sophia made no comment about this declaration, apparently unwilling to dislodge Julian's comforting vision.

Sorrow and anxiety do not account, however, for the depth of Sophia's emotional upheaval and self-deprecation. "One would think that *I* must weep only for an offset to my blessedness in having such a husband & such children," she wrote about her flow of tears, "& it is probably some thing of this—but yet it is also because I am not better, more beautiful, more worthy to be his wife & to sun in his love." Her self-recriminations continue: "It should be a celestial angel to deserve him—& I am not. I wish I were—But I will not write any more of this here." What was the source of Sophia's misery? Was it that "Mr. Hawthorne's passions were under his feet"? That was how Elizabeth Peabody, late in her life, explained to Julian how his parents managed to space the birth of their children at deliberate intervals—a little over two years between the first and second child, five years between the second and third, and then, no more children, facts that lead E. Haviland Miller to assert that Nathaniel forswore sexual relations with Sophia after Rose's birth.[9] How Elizabeth would have obtained information about "Mr. Hawthorne's passions," she did not reveal to Julian. Surely Nathaniel himself would not have been her source, and Sophia leaves no record of the matter, whether in letters to Elizabeth or in journals that Elizabeth might have seen. Sophia would not likely confide directly in her busybody sister about intimate sexual matters. Such surmises would, however, suggest the source of Sophia's profound anguish in the late summer of 1852. She was not a "celestial angel" but a forty-three-year-old, flesh-and-blood woman with bodily appetites who feared having lost her physical attractiveness.

For all Nathaniel's recent literary productivity, he was no longer in the bloom of youth; he had observed the inescapable specter of aging at his Bowdoin reunion where his "cotemporaries" appeared to be the "funniest old men in the world. Am I a funny old man?" he queried.[10] This question followed upon his publication of *The Blithedale Romance*, a novel that undermines the notion of marital sexuality by cynically coupling Priscilla and Hollingsworth, whose asexual affection for each other seems more like that of siblings than spouses. The communal premise behind Blithedale and utopian communities in general does not lead to heterosexual domesticity. Perhaps observing the Shakers, or knowing Melville, or witnessing the instinctive, mutual affinity between Sophia and Melville turned Nathaniel's imagination upon a new axis. Sophia's uncharacteristic reticence about *The Blithedale Romance* perhaps further suggests a wedge between the stand-offish writer and those with faith in mesmerism or reform.

While Nathaniel vacationed at the Laighton Hotel, Sophia sequestered herself in his study. Lying upon that lapis rug she had so carefully chosen and stretched over the floor, she could gaze at her painting, "Endymion," her "record" of "happy, hopeful days" when the Hawthornes had made their first home in Concord nearly a decade before. There she would wait for her husband's so infrequent letters, becoming "faint & weary" with worry. By the time Nathaniel returned from his vacation on the Isles of Shoals, he had penned only a very brief note to "Ownest Phoebe," announcing his arrival in Portsmouth prior to leaving for Appledore, a short note to Una, whom he greeted as "My dear old lady," and a third letter, this to Sophia, which does not survive. On September 13, exhausted from anticipation and disappointment, the hoped-for missive from her husband caused a "revulsion of joy," a reaction "so immense that my head almost burst asunder," Sophia wrote in her journal, "& all the rest of the day it ached so desperately that I had to hold it together, while my heart was dancing for joy."[11] Sophia's violent reversal of emotion was as painful as it was welcome. Clearly something was out of sync in her married life.

And something in Sophia was out of sync with the prevailing mood in Concord. The *Life of Franklin Pierce* had been rushed through the press and appeared while Nathaniel was still away. Sophia daily encountered people, like Dr. Sawyer, who were eager for a book that she had not laid eyes upon. She was miffed: "[T]oo bad that all the world should read it before I do," she wrote. When twelve copies were finally delivered to the Wayside, Sophia immediately carved out a day for reading. She then began her own campaign, praising and justifying Nathaniel's "new Romance," as *The Register* dubbed it. Elizabeth Hawthorne conveyed this disparagement and also reported Uncle John Dike's judgment that Nathaniel had not told the "precise truth." Not so, Sophia insisted. The newspapers were the source of "falsehoods" about Pierce, not Nathaniel, who "would put down whatever he did not like in [Pierce]—as well as what he did—were it the truth." On September 19, Sophia defended Nathaniel's veracity to her mother by defending Pierce against "fabricated" stories that he was "a gambler & also pusillanimous." Sophia's letter then turned to domestic matters, specifically her husband's return from vacation that day: "You may be sure . . . I might have made myself miserable very easily [while he was away]; but I did not. And now we are happiest."[12] Nathaniel was not the only fabricator of romances in the Hawthorne household.

Readers of the *Life of Franklin Pierce* who were familiar with Nathaniel's earlier "true" histories and biographies for children would have known that he did not aim to produce "precise truth." Now, Nathaniel thought he had struck a discreet balance while also satisfying "Frank" with this campaign biography; "it puts him in as good a light as circumstances would admit," Nathaniel explained to his old friend, Horatio Bridge, and "though the story is true, it took a romancer to do it." Surely any biographer's ingenuity would have been taxed by the circumstances of Pierce's military career, which lacked evidence of leadership commensurate with his aspirations to the nation's highest office. He had not distinguished himself in command of troops during the Mexican War, when he had been sidelined by severe diarrhea and injuries from an unruly horse. Consequent absence from battle sparked rumors of cowardice that Nathaniel hoped to dispel by quoting copiously from Pierce's wartime journal and reminding readers that he was the son of *Benjamin* Pierce, a veritable hero of the Revolutionary War.[13] If this strategy of heroism by heredity convinced some, it would not have swayed the extended Peabody family and Sophia's Concord neighbors who believed Franklin Pierce had taken part in an unjust war.

The seeds of the Mexican War had been sown in 1845 when the United States annexed Texas from Mexico. The same year the Hawthornes' good friend John Louis O'Sullivan coined the term "manifest destiny" in "Annexation," his article published in his own *Democratic Review*. O'Sullivan voiced the inchoate belief of many Americans that westward expansion from the Atlantic to the Pacific was somehow a self-evident, even "divine destiny." While he did not endorse the use of force to acquire new territories, "manifest destiny" justified the Mexican War and led to problems O'Sullivan did not foresee, the increased hostilities between slave and free states.[14]

Abolitionists deplored that the acquisition of southern territories would expand the power of slave states. Henry David Thoreau famously went to jail rather than pay the poll tax that supported the Mexican War, and out of this experience, he wrote a seminal tract on passive resistance, "Civil Disobedience." This article originally appeared under the title "Resistance to Civil Government" in *Aesthetic Papers*, Thoreau's editor and publisher none other than Elizabeth Peabody.

Pierce's role in this war was quite different. However limited his actual time in battle, he earned Horace Mann's condemnation as an "unmitigated, irredeemable, pro-slavery" scoundrel. Mann's voluble denunciation of Pierce implicated Nathaniel, who, according to Horace, would have penned his "greatest work of fiction" if he should cast Pierce in a good light. If Sophia's brother-in-law found him contemptible, her mother's displeasure with Pierce was even more profound. Not only did she condemn his involvement in the Mexican War, she deplored his military profession altogether. As a confirmed and consistent pacifist, Mrs. Peabody opposed all forms of violence, whatever the motive. Unbeknownst to her, Pierce's abhorrence of the atrocities of war matched her own, and he vented his anguish in a private wartime diary: "I hate war in all its aspects, I deem it unworthy of the age in which we live & of the Govt of which I have borne some part."[15] These sentiments, had they been widely known, might have earned him yet another term of opprobrium: hypocrite.

Defending her husband's friend was indeed a formidable task that required Sophia to muster the theory of just war. One might engage in conscientious combat as a last resort, she claimed, when other means of settling disputes had failed. Sophia did not, however, elaborate upon how this theory applied to the Mexican War or its causes—a war being prosecuted by one friend (Pierce, however lackluster his military skills) under the rallying cry of another (O'Sullivan, who did not espouse the use of force). And although she could propound a just war in theory, she would never consider the abolition of slavery sufficient cause for the use of force. About abolition, she advocated patience and trust in divine Providence, a position that Nathaniel ascribed to Pierce in words that might easily have been Sophia's. Slavery was "one of those evils, which Divine Providence does not leave to be remedied by human contrivances."[16]

Positions such as these became increasingly difficult to profess during Sophia's second period of residence in Concord. She could no longer shove abolition to the corners of her awareness as she had when she was a bride and new mother living at The Old Manse from 1842 to 1846. Then, many Concordians—Josiah Bartlett, Maria and Timothy Prescott, the

Thoreau women, Lidian Emerson and her mother-in-law Ruth Haskins Emerson, Elizabeth Hoar, and Abba Alcott—had subscribed to the anti-slavery publication, *The Liberator*. These women also belonged to the Concord Female Antislavery Society at the very moment William Lloyd Garrison proclaimed: "[T]he destiny of the slaves is in the hands of the American women."[17]

But Sophia could not be counted among them. Her journals and letters barely mentioned the cause that so absorbed her friends. She had noted that the "ladies of the antislavery society take sewing . . . and do it very cheaply," and she planned to pay them "as little as possible" without "scruple" for their help making baby clothes. Otherwise, she wrote Mrs. Peabody, she would have paid "full and ample price" for this service "to a poor person, or a seamstress by profession." Out of tune with efforts to free slaves, Sophia nonetheless understood the merit of fair compensation to poor and working-class women. And she may well have identified with such women, particularly at that moment. While she was calculating the cheapest way to obtain a layette, she was painting "Endymion" with the hope of earning a "small bit of gold" for the Hawthorne household.[18] Domestic allegiances—for good and ill—always took precedence over public causes.

Positions on abolition were complicated and influenced by many factors. While abolitionists concurred that slavery was an abomination, not all believed that African Americans were equal to Caucasians, or that freed slaves should remain in the United States, or that the Union should be preserved, particularly if violence were required to do so. Disunionists advocated dividing the country into separate, sovereign nations—one prohibiting, the other permitting slavery. The embarrassing "peculiar institution" might thereby be eliminated from their nation, without improving the lot of slaves one whit. But those who would preserve the Union sometimes had alloyed motives, not all of them serving the interests of abolition. The North's economy thrived upon cotton trade, tempering just how righteous an individual might be about the current plight and future circumstance of the slave. Nathaniel thus claimed that Pierce's legislative efforts to preserve the Union, a position he held with "unbroken consistency," justified his refusal to ruffle the South over abolition. Pierce wanted only to "redeem the pledges of the Constitution, and to preserve and renew the old love and harmony among the sisterhood of the states."[19]

But by 1852, when Sophia returned to live in Concord, annexation of slave territories and the strengthening of the Fugitive Slave Law had galvanized abolitionists' sentiments. This law, originally enacted in 1794 mandating the return of runaway slaves, had generally been ignored in

Northern states until 1850, when it was expanded to require prosecution and fines of federal marshals and others who failed to enforce the rendition of slaves. In April of 1851, Thomas Sims, a runaway slave who had lived in Massachusetts for several years, was dragged to a waiting ship in Boston Harbor and retuned to South Carolina where he was flogged. Sims's rendition located the slavery issue right on the doorstep of New Englanders.

In this climate of controversy, Sophia's exchanges with Mary grew increasingly heated. Mary's position on abolition had been grounded in firsthand observations of Cuban slaves under heinous conditions that Sophia herself had observed. But Sophia's passive expression of sympathy for slaves contrasted sharply with Mary and Horace's commitment to personal and political action on behalf of those who were enslaved, or who had escaped slavery, or who were free blacks seeking a better life in the North. When Mary had taken Chloe Lee into the Mann home so that she might attend school in West Newton, Sophia's outraged and outrageous response revealed a vein of racism beneath her reliance on Providence and detachment from the Concord Female Anti-Slavery Society.

But the Manns exerted no influence upon Sophia, who claimed that her brother-in-law "stoop[ed]" when he hurled "invectives" at Franklin Pierce and "trample[d]" on Daniel Webster, whom she continued to admire although he had become a pariah in his own state. Webster was among those who feared the prospects of disunion more than he disapproved of slavery, and throughout his long legislative career, he had used his legendary oratorical powers to promote strong federal government, at this moment, by placating the South and endorsing the 1850 Fugitive Slave Law. During his infamous "Seventh of March Speech," Webster proclaimed before the senate that he spoke not as a man from a particular state or region but as an American. Claiming that "inferiority of the black or colored race to the white" legitimated slavery, he predicted horrific consequences should disunion occur. With these words, Webster irrevocably destroyed his reputation among many prominent New Englanders and became for Horace Mann "a fallen star." The abolitionist minister, Theodore Parker, compared Webster to Benedict Arnold, and Ralph Waldo Emerson charged Webster with treachery. He died shortly after this "final act of apostasy from his New England faith," as one of his detractors called it. Sophia took the unpopular position, however, that Webster's career should not be defined by "a *speech*." Barely a week after his death, she matched Webster's rhetorical prowess in a eulogistic letter to her mother, recalling the man who had been revered for distinguished accomplishments. Despite her "utmost abhorrence of his *habits*" (she was undoubtedly referring to his reputation as a womanizer and drinker), she believed he was a man of "pith & moment." His mistake was that he "did evil that good might come of it."[20]

For Sophia, the ends could never justify the means, a principle she applied in the political and domestic spheres. Shifting the focus of her letter from Webster to her children, she reminded her mother that they were taught to "do what is right because it is right." They must learn never to retaliate but to exercise forbearance and be "longsuffering"; if a child (in this case, Julian) did not return a harsh word or a poke or a slap, the aggressor (at this moment, Una) would "forget how to be provoking." And in this same letter, Sophia included her reaction to a novel she had just completed. She might have mentioned, but did not, that the title character of "Mrs. Stowe's book" was the paradigm of "longsuffering" and forbearance Sophia wished to instill in her children. Nevertheless, she dismissed *Uncle Tom's Cabin* as "overrated" and "too much addressed the moveable passions—not to the deeper soul." She was convinced that "it would do no good to the slave. Time will show."[21] In a great miscalculation of literary power, Sophia did not foresee that the passions stirred by this novel would win hundreds of thousands of readers to the abolitionists' cause and ultimately serve the slaves' interest.

Sophia understood how literature might move an individual, as her on-going arguments with Mary over their children's reading attest. About those gory, violent myths that Mary withheld from her children, Sophia reasoned that a child already possessed an instinct toward aggression that could be restrained through cultivation of virtue, or, in exceptional cases, be channeled to righteous purposes. But Sophia began to back away from these theoretical positions as tensions over abolition increased fears that violence would inevitably follow too much advocacy of the slave, resulting in too much confrontation with the South. Sophia observed that increasingly heated efforts of abolitionists triggered stricter proslavery measures, such as the 1850 strengthening of the Fugitive Slave Law, which worsened the lot of slaves. This reality permitted her to concur with General Pierce that, should abolitionists push the South to secede, "severance of the Union would be the worst thing for the slave."[22]

While Sophia speculated about the tenuous bond between states, she was forced to acknowledge that her older children, now eight and six, periodically engaged in their own civil wars. Her New Year's Eve 1852 request of her eldest child was that she remember that a "soft answer turneth away wrath." Sophia recognized, however, that at any moment her darlings could be "returning to savagery."[23]

Chapter 10

All Partings in This World Are Final

The dreaded moment arrived without a fierce "struggle between her tenacious life and the death angel" according to Elizabeth Peabody's account of events on January 11, 1853, when her mother quietly drew her final breaths. Her pain and cough lessened by morphine, she was surrounded by her husband and her daughters Mary and Elizabeth. But Sophia was not present. Mrs. Peabody had encouraged her to remain in Concord with her children. Shortly after their mother's "life went out into free spaces," Elizabeth declared that they were "all at peace—peace—peace." Sophia also felt "peace & happiness" that her mother had "ceased forever from suffering." Mourning had, to some extent, preceded her death, the Peabodys having begun their goodbyes while the possibility of recovery faded over the course of two years. As Dr. Peabody frankly acknowledged, "I had buried her in my mind long before the final crisis."[1]

Thus did the Peabody sisters face dying and death. That inevitable human transition had provoked very different reactions among the Hawthorne siblings four-and-a-half years earlier. The filial trauma experienced by Elizabeth, Nathaniel, and Louisa Hawthorne was not replicated among the Peabody sisters. Elizabeth, Mary, and Sophia were not threatened by "brain fever," as was Nathaniel over his maternal loss. Neither did "hopeless," "Calvinistic talk" prevent the calm departure of a woman who had just as calmly seen death approach and given her family instructions about what to do with her body. Mrs. Peabody wished to be "examined" in order to prevent being "buried alive" (her desires emphasized by under-scoring those words four times) and to "have it known of what disease I have suffered so long."[2]

Such information about pulmonary disorders might prove invaluable to Sophia, who ten days after Mrs. Peabody's "wracking cough" had ceased forever, developed her own "hard cough"—a harbinger of her future ill-nesses. Despite wearing a woolen breastplate, as Mary had advised, and seeking the indispensable Dr. Wesselhoeft's counsel, Sophia's influenza persisted during the period of raw emotion after her mother's death. Her grief was assuaged, however, as was her sisters' by an amalgam of attitudes and beliefs. Christian narratives, stripped of their hell-fired tones, were becoming increasingly part of Sophia's philosophical repertoire, but religion did not displace confidence that science might uncover the nature of illness and provide a cure. Elizabeth consoled Sophia with the thought that their mother would be present "more intimately than ever; for the spirit must be where the heart's affections are." That the "spirit"—however that word might be defined—would endure and remain accessible to loved ones was a belief promoted by spiritualists and gaining traction in all segments of society. The sisters rested in the reality of their mother's profound, oft-expressed love for each of them. Mrs. Peabody had been "the only being in the wide world whose affection for me had no limit," Elizabeth declared.[3] Sophia might well have said the same.

If Sophia's life had been a novel, her mother would have performed the function of a ficelle, a character who does not figure directly in the plot but occasions the protagonist's self-disclosure. As such, Mrs. Peabody had allowed Sophia to indulge the "impulse . . . to put as much of myself as possible on paper" thereby obliterating physical and emotional distances, particularly while Sophia was in Cuba. Soon after her mother's death, Sophia wanted to reclaim all the letters she had written to her and espe-cially the magnificent verbal artifact of her more than eight hundred closely written journal-letters, the Cuba Journal. Sophia hoped to read them to Una, who delighted in hearing stories about that period of her mother's life. Sophia was also frankly worried about preserving the Cuba Journal for it had "been lent a great deal." It might be in the hands of a stranger, or perhaps in Elizabeth's possession, a thought that did not lessen Sophia's concern, which grew urgent, while she prepared for yet another move.[4]

Even before the Life of Franklin Pierce had been published, rumors swirled that it would earn Nathaniel something more than the sum he had been paid to write it. Both he and Sophia were defensive at the hint that Pierce would offer Nathaniel a plum position, such as the Liverpool consulship. But the Hawthornes' finances did not allow them to ignore monetary

rewards. Nathaniel had "consented . . . somewhat reluctantly," he wrote
Fields, to write Pierce's biography at a moment of heavy expenditures "in
consequence of having bought an estate!!! and fitting up my house." Writing
to Bridge, Nathaniel was blunt. He might indeed accept "the consulship at
Liverpool" because Pierce "certainly owes me something; for the biography
has cost me hundreds of friends." Despite Nathaniel's understanding of
quid pro quo, Sophia maintained that her husband's motives in writing the
biography had been entirely disinterested, as well as objective. That book
had actually hindered his prospects for an appointment, for Pierce had
hesitated to nominate his friend and biographer, she wrote her father, for
fear that the "book" might cause people to "impugne" Pierce's motives.
So "wholly superior to the matter" was Nathaniel and "so large-handed"
with regard to money, he might not accept an appointment, if offered. She,
however, would "be glad enough to have the pinch and strain taken off
his mind after such a long discipline of poverty and effort." She no longer
wanted to "debate" about every penny they spent.[5] Pierce did nominate
her husband United States consul to Liverpool, the Senate approved, and
Nathaniel accepted.

The lives of Nathaniel Hawthorne and Frank Pierce had grown increasingly intertwined. These college friends were now positioned to advance
one another's careers and to comfort each other at moments of crisis and
suffering, and by March 4, 1853, when Pierce took the oath of office as
fourteenth president of the United States, he and his wife had experienced
the extremity of domestic tragedy. Jane Pierce's Calvinistic upbringing
had prepared her to despise Washington with its social demands and the
evenings of smoking and drinking that Frank enjoyed entirely too much.
So she retreated into a home that was saddened by the death of their
first two sons and insisted upon returning briefly to New Hampshire
after Frank's stint in the Senate. When he was nominated as Democratic
candidate for the presidency, a position he eagerly sought, he falsely
claimed to Jane that—honor-bound—he had merely accepted a call to
duty. When his lie was exposed, their marriage was strained even further.
Then, two months after his election on January 6, 1853, they were plunged
into unfathomable grief. They were traveling with their third son and only
remaining child, eleven-year-old Benjamin, by train from Boston to New
Hampshire when their car broke loose and careened over an embankment.
Jane and Frank sustained minor injuries, but Benny died gruesomely,
instantly before their eyes. Jane interpreted this horrific accident as
punishment for her husband's ambition.[6]

Franklin Pierce's inaugural address began with mention of his son's
death, casting a pall over his political victory. Although Sophia asserted

that this speech won him praise from "all quarters," such was not the case. Those who were at odds with Pierce over abolition and states' rights interpreted his personal disclosure as an attempt to curry sympathy. Others considered the intrusion of his grief unseemly, even unmanly. Jane took no part in the inaugural ceremonies. She absented herself from them and from the duties incumbent upon a first lady, sequestering herself in her bedroom where she wrote letters to her dead Benny.[7] Franklin Pierce's tenure in office was filled with contention not to be mitigated by a happy home and solicitous wife. Having lost his three sons to death, he lost Jane to grief and depression. And he was about to lose any proximity to his closest friend who could not then comprehend the Pierces' losses.

The Hawthornes were moving to England. The money spent purchasing and furnishing the Wayside became the compelling reason to leave it for the Liverpool consulship, reputed to be the most lucrative post of its kind. In addition to his base salary, the consul earned a portion of the fee charged for signing, and thereby certifying, invoices for those goods exported to the United States. After expenses paid to his staff, he could expect to pocket between $5,000 and $7,000 a year. An additional $3,000 a year would come from the emoluments of the Manchester consulship, now also available to Nathaniel. Surely the Hawthornes would no longer have to scrutinize ordinary expenditures. Surely Nathaniel's earnings would secure a comfortable future for themselves and their children. And surely they would have money to spend in extra-ordinary ways. Sophia would finally realize her dream of traveling again. And once Nathaniel had fulfilled his four-year term of office, the Hawthornes would spend a year in Italy.[8] There, Sophia could immerse herself in art that had captured her imagination as a young woman. Her prospects were so very bright.

But departure for England was nonetheless laced with small regrets and large responsibilities. Winter had melted into spring; the peach and cherry trees surrounding the Wayside were laden with glorious blooms. Leaving her home and parting from Hawthorne and Peabody relatives would be difficult. Elizabeth Hawthorne relied on Nathaniel for financial support, so he requested that his publishers, who held his money on account, draw as much as two hundred dollars a year for her. Nat Peabody, always a concern for his three sisters, had not been blessed with the attention Mrs. Peabody had lavished upon her talented daughters, nor had life favored him with good health or success in business. Now Sophia's brother and his family could live at the Wayside, lessening their financial burdens, and supplying family members to care for the Hawthornes' home. And Dr. Peabody, at seventy-nine years of age, was approaching the end of his life. Sophia dutifully promised him that his children and grandchildren would "love and honor" him forever, but her affection and respect were tempered with negative judgments. Something was amiss in the old man's character, as signaled by Rose, who did her best to avoid him. Even a glance at him provoked her "expression of pain . . . as if she were hit with an arrow." More disturbing to Sophia was her father's "savage anger." He had railed at Nat for wishing to "seek his fortune" and at Ellen for taking wood for the fire. "He was perfectly insane," Sophia reported to Mary, and his "want of self-control"—perhaps a sign of incipient senility— seemed to be increasing. Sophia announced flatly: "He should not live where there is a child."⁹ But he did move in with Nat and his family at the Wayside, until Elizabeth, with neither child nor husband, provided a home for her father.

Amid these preparations to leave for England, Sophia maintained a "real school" each morning by inviting neighbor children to join Una and Julian for their lessons. Sophia's four "scholars" studied English grammar, French, Latin and Greek, as well as some classical and Biblical literature. Among the children's books was some contemporary and popular fiction including Nathaniel's just published *Tanglewood Tales*, Robert Louis Stevenson's "rich & racy" *The Adventures of Robinson Crusoe*, and a novel by one of the verboten "d——d mob of scribbling women." Susan Warner's *The Wide, Wide World* "deeply interested" Una, and no wonder. That novel's focal character, Ellen Montgomery, was a young girl like Una who strug- gled to control her emotions and obtain her elders' approval. Una was among thousands of readers who were devoted to this quintessential nineteenth-century Christian coming-of-age novel. Its sentimentality tugged at the heart, its moral certitude salved the conscience. *The Wide, Wide World* became America's first best seller and, much to Nathaniel's chagrin, reaped far greater financial rewards for its author than did *The Scarlet Letter*.¹⁰

Sophia once again enjoyed motherhood and her husband's love. Domes- tic life was paradise regained. "I feel as if I had just begun to know that there is nothing else for me but thou," he wrote her, "I want thee in my arms." As for Una, Julian, and Rose, these "children, too, I know how to love, at last." Sophia was "animated" by these declarations in letters from her "lord," this correspondence occasioned by Nathaniel's trip to Washington, D.C., in the spring of 1853. But he saw little of Pierce, whose presidency, begun in the shadow of personal tragedy, had already been darkened by another death, that of his vice president, William King. Never mind that Pierce was absorbed by an increasingly fractious nation. Nathaniel was miffed that others were "made much of" while Pierce's attentions to him "were few and by no means distinguished." When Jane

Pierce ventured to Mount Vernon, Nathaniel joined her, later regretting that "the nation should be compelled to see such a death's head in the pre-eminent place among American women." Better Frank had no wife than a wife like this, Nathaniel complained. He could not grasp the magnitude of his friends' political responsibilities or their personal woes.[11]

The weeks immediately preceding the Hawthornes' departure for England were busy ones. Sophia determined that Cunard Steamers would best accommodate her family during their transatlantic voyage. The *Niagara* was her choice, and Nathaniel concurred. He, meanwhile, was occupied with his own preparations, burning "great heaps of old letters and other papers, a little while ago . . . Among them were hundreds of Sophia's maiden letters—the world has no more such; and now they are all ashes."[12] Concerned though Sophia had been about securing her letters from Cuba, there is no evidence that she had worried about her love letters to Nathaniel. Knowing her husband's penchant for privacy, she would not have feared they might fall into strangers' hands while they were abroad. But had Sophia feared—did she *know*—that her husband would destroy almost every letter she had written him during their courtship? If she did, she was mute about her loss.

On July 6, Sophia boarded the *Niagara* with her husband who would be sailing on the Atlantic for the first time in his life. They were accompanied by their children, Ellen Herne and her sister Mary, and William D. Ticknor, the business associate who was fast becoming a good friend. Ticknor was well known and well respected on both sides of the Atlantic. While other editors readily pirated foreign publications, he was credited with making the first international copyright payment of $150 for the right to publish Alfred Lord Tennyson's *Poems* in 1842. He more than merited his reputation as a fair and honest man. According to Warren S. Tyron, the biographer of Ticknor's partner, James T. Fields, "in money matters, in the actual details of costs, expenses, and possible profits and losses," Ticknor was in every way "superior" to the shrewd, sometimes flamboyant Fields. But Ticknor, appreciating his junior partner's talents, gave Fields "loose rein."[13]

And Fields, recently returned from his own trip abroad, was standing on the dock to bid farewell to Ticknor and the Hawthornes. Fields had gone to England, France, and Italy after the death of his young wife in 1851. Eliza Willard Fields had died of tuberculosis, as had her sister, to whom Fields had been engaged at the time of her death some six years earlier. His current bereavement was also to be brief, as Elizabeth Barrett Browning predicted when she met him in Paris: "widowhood is not likely, I should imagine . . . to last six months longer. Why, he seemed to me upon the whole, in incline to the 'jolly'." The *bon vivant* Fields had succeeded in shedding his grief in Europe, while he prepared a path for Nathaniel with anecdotes that placed Fields in the brightest possible light. Mary Russell Mitford spread his claims that the "great romancer" had been as needy as a "sick child," "in extreme penury," "starving," "literally starving," but Fields's "encouragement and liberality" had made the author "almost affluent."[14]

And on that dock with Fields that July morning were Sophia's brother and her father. They all watched as the *Niagara* sailed out of Boston Harbor on its way to Halifax before heading to Liverpool. To lessen the gloom of imminent separation, Sophia attempted nonchalance about the distance that would lie between her and Dr. Peabody. Although Una at nine years of age was saddened to leave friends, Julian, who had turned seven a few days earlier, was full of "delighted wonder & hope"; as for two-year-old Rose, "what matters it to her whether she stand on one hemisphere or the other, provided Mamma, Papa, 'Oona,' & 'Dulan' are within sight?" Sophia predicted that "Ericsson's caloric ship," a recent invention in steamship navigation, would make people as comfortable and "as safe as in a parlor." There was no danger, she insisted; their journey was "more like a pleasure excursion on a lake." She promised her father that he would not feel the distance between them, for she would send letters by every steamer.[15]

Sophia immediately made good on that promise by posting Dr. Peabody a letter from Halifax on July 7. She graced him with the kind of vivid description that always characterized her travel writing and made her so welcome a correspondent from Cuba some two decades earlier. Resuming her role as "Queen of Journalizers," she described the ship moving "magically over the sea like a vast pearl." A long cannonade "thundered" when the *Niagara* pulled out of Boston Harbor "because Mr. Hawthorne, the distinguished United States consul and author, was leaving the shore." The Hawthornes and their entourage were among 141 passengers who enjoyed a calm crossing. The ship's skilled Captain Leitch added to their pleasures at sea. Julian remembered him as "courtly" to his mother and "pranksome" with the children. With them under the Herne sisters' supervision, Sophia was free to enjoy lively dinner conversations at the captain's table among affluent, prominent people. She realized that she could not enforce restrictions upon her children's diet in the middle of the Atlantic, but she did seek their advantage in one matter. The ship's cow produced milk that became an unsavory concoction when mixed with water for the passengers' consumption. Rose did not like it, and when Sophia complained, the child was given undiluted milk. Sophia took note: "It is very convenient to have rank with these English people. It commands good service."[16]

Later in his life, Julian reflected upon his family's departure from the United States: "[A]ll partings in this world are final: we never find on our return the same thing or person we left; at any rate, we never bring the same person back."[17]

Chapter 11

Sick to Death

When Hawthornes landed in Liverpool on July 17, 1853, they went immediately to the Waterloo Hotel where they experienced luxury and service befitting the United States consul and his family. In the dining room, Mr. Lynn, the head of the hotel, held the bowls while Sophia ladled soup from a tureen. This venerable-looking person was Sophia's very "idea of an ancient duke." But such attention came at the cost £16 a day, so after ten days, Sophia was relieved that accommodations became available at Mrs. Blodget's boarding house at 153 Duke Street; the total cost of the Hawthornes' nine days' stay there amounted to slightly more than £12. Mrs. Blodget, the widow of an American, had lived in Boston during her youth, and she knew how to maintain a welcoming, comfortable, clean establishment. The food was excellent and abundant, and Julian, whose appetite was becoming a significant aspect of his character, would later recall that he had never before "consumed so much." After dinner, women repaired to one parlor to converse, while men conversed and smoked in another. For very good reasons, Mrs. Blodget's had become the Liverpool gathering-place for affluent Americans—sea captains and their wives in particular.[1] Nathaniel's aversion to boarding houses as "unnatural" arrangements did not cross the Atlantic with him.

On August 1, Nathaniel's official duties as consul began. By the time he gave his "maiden speech," Sophia had enjoyed the hospitality of several members of the British upper class, and she turned these experiences into entertaining letters to her father. The "cordial and excellent" Mrs. William Rathbone sent her carriage to transport her to Green Bank, where an Indian gong announced that tea was served at an enormous table. Another day, another invitation, this one to Poulton Hall. Mr. Barber, president of the Chamber of Commerce, sent his "carriage—a chariot it was—with a coachman as straight as a lightning rod" to fetch Sophia. In a drawing room that looked like "a brilliant apartment in Versailles," bejeweled women in black velvet recounted tales of ghosts and torture in attic chambers; these same women spoke "with admiration and wonder about *The Scarlet Letter.*" And Henry Bright—the bewildered Mary Herne believed him to be the incarnation of Eustace Bright, the teller of *Tanglewood Tales*—proffered many invitations. The "tall, slender, good-humored, laughing, voluble" *Henry* Bright who had met the Hawthornes in Concord through Emerson, now escorted them to the theater and on a tour of his company's enormous steamship, the *Great Britain* (a thoroughly appropriate name for the product of a quintessentially British family). Sophia and the children all took tea at the Bright's Sandheys, West Derby estate with its swans and lush green grass in a garden so manicured that no weed dared appear.[2]

Sophia visited these mansions while deliberating about her own, far less luxurious home. It would not be in Liverpool. There, the children had taken ill with colds, and Sophia began to cough, the fog insinuating its dampness into her lungs. With every breath, she inhaled contamination and the soot of the industrial city; "this atmosphere takes the enterprise out of me," she wrote to her father barely two-and-a-half weeks after arriving in Liverpool. The next day Nathaniel confided to Ticknor, "I really doubt whether she will be able to bear this abominable climate." The Hawthornes therefore decided to move to Rock Ferry, on the western side of the Mersey Estuary, where, Sophia believed, the "the air is pure and healthy." A twenty-minute ride on the ferry would allow Nathaniel to commute to work. Sophia ignored her awareness that thick fog frequently made crossings rather unsafe, particularly during the winter. But because the ferry's last nightly departure from Liverpool was at ten o'clock, Nathaniel had a ready-made reason to decline social engagements.[3] On August 6 the Hawthornes moved from Mrs. Blodget's to the Rock Ferry Hotel and then found the house where they would reside for nearly two years.

Though hardly an estate on the order of Green Bank or Poulton Hall or Sandheys, 26 Rock Park was a roomy, three-story house built for the comfort of wealthy professionals and merchants who wished to live quietly, and to have their comfort and quiet assured by a gate and gatekeeper at the top of the road. The agent for the property agreed to lower the rent to

£160 a year when she learned that the United States Consul would be living there "instead of Mr. Nobody. . . . So much influence has rank and title in dear old England," Sophia explained to her father. But like the family of "Mr. Nobody," the Hawthornes haggled over the money they paid for rent. And just like the wife of "Mr. Nobody," Sophia was forced to spend ten days cleaning the house. Although it had been leased fully furnished, she immediately purchased silverware, a complete tea and dinner service, table linens as well as bed linens, slipcovers, and more. Whether impelled by her sense of hygiene or desire to entertain in the manner befitting a consul's wife, Sophia settled in at some cost. And the costs multiplied with salaries for the staff required to maintain such a household. Mary and Ellen were paid to perform housekeeping chores, and Ellen also cared for Rose who was too young to accompany her mother and older siblings on their outings. Sophia employed a cook, a gardener who doubled as a butler at infrequent dinner parties, and a laundress, but Sophia hired no housekeeper, as would have been typical of the mistress of such a home in Victorian England.[4]

Diligently recording all expenditures, Sophia quickly, painfully realized that life at Rock Park was far more expensive than life at the Wayside had been. That unpleasant discovery occurred in tandem with another: Nathaniel's income would be significantly less than they had anticipated. Sophia was riled by Elizabeth's notion that ten thousand American ships arrived in Liverpool annually and that Nathaniel's yearly income would therefore be around $40,000. "So far is this from the truth that it is really *funny* & melancholy at the same time," Sophia emphasized to her father. The ships numbered barely seven hundred, and her husband earned accordingly.[5]

Nathaniel's less-than-expected salary was further eroded by having to pay his three clerks their annual wages totaling £430. Yet another portion of his pay went to Americans with all manner of problems who approached him in his official capacity. His clerks, who had "seen a thousand such cases," warned him that his generosity would "never be repaid," as he explained in a December 1853 letter to his friend and publisher-cum-banker, Ticknor. Nonetheless, Nathaniel enclosed in that letter "a small draft" for an elderly man "whose funds failed him here, and whom I have had to assist and send home—as I am compelled to do in many other cases, at my own risk." And Nathaniel continued giving money to his impoverished and improvident countrymen such as a minister—and an orthodox one at that!—who had gone broke in a brothel and needed to be shipped back to New Orleans. "It is," Nathaniel concluded, "a very disagreeable office; but some amusing incidents happen occasionally."[6]

This largesse as consul replicated his openhandedness while he was measurer in the Boston Custom House from 1839 to 1841. Although he had taken that position ostensibly to acquire the money he needed to marry Sophia, he lent substantial sums to his editor at the *Salem Gazette*, Caleb Foote, and to men who had been dismissed from the Custom House, William Loring and John Muzzy. These loans became difficult to collect, to Nathaniel's chagrin, when he had become a married man, himself short of cash. Then he also sought to recoup another loan, this to George Ripley and Charles Dana made during his days at Brook Farm. Though Hillard sued them on Nathaniel's behalf, and won, this legal victory did not result in the recovery of his money. And yet in the spring of 1854, after repaying a $500 debt to Horatio Bridge, Nathaniel lent him $3,000, happy to do so "even," he boasted to Ticknor, "if I were certain of never getting it again."[7]

During the same period, however, when John Louis O'Sullivan requested a loan in the same amount, Nathaniel exercised a caution lacking during his period of extreme liberality in the early 1840s, for then Nathaniel's generosity toward O'Sullivan had exceeded any that he currently lavished upon Bridge. While Nathaniel was claiming to Sophia that his poverty prevented their marriage, he had bragged to O'Sullivan that he was "in no present need of the money" and did not require "additional security" on O'Sullivan's loan of over $550. Nathaniel basked in "the pleasant feeling" of his own beneficence and concluded the matter with a grandiose promise: "[If] you will borrow as a friend you may command every cent that I can spare." Such generosity may suggest Nathaniel's indebtedness of another kind entirely to this friend, publisher, and erstwhile rival. Nathaniel may have owed his very life to this man who had purportedly deflected his challenge to duel over the conniving Mary Silsbee, now married to Jared Sparks. Mary had just suffered a miscarriage, as Nathaniel noted in that very letter to O'Sullivan promising an interest-free loan lasting for an indefinite period. But three years after making this offer, when the Hawthornes were struggling at The Old Manse, Nathaniel acknowledged that O'Sullivan's "faith and honor" coexisted with careless "very unkind—at least, inconsiderate" business practices, a discomforting realization about the man whom Sophia believed was "dearer" to her husband than any of his other friends at that time.[8]

This friendship persisted in spite of O'Sullivan's financial and political missteps. Having wed the wealthy Susan Kearney Rogers in 1846, he was drawn into Cuban affairs via Cristobal Madan, the husband of Susan's sister. This wealthy planter and merchant convinced O'Sullivan that if Cuba were annexed by the United States, the institution of slavery—which was the foundation of Madan's wealth—would be protected. Knowing that the annexation of another slave territory would be unpopular, O'Sullivan furtively attempted to convince President James Polk to offer Spain one hundred million dollars to purchase Cuba.[9] This proposal failed, but Sullivan's meddling in Cuban politics did not end. Without the authority of the United States government, he assisted Narisco Lopez, mistakenly assuming that this Cuban revolutionary sought annexation to the United States rather than independence from Spain. Because American citizens are forbidden to engage in aggression against peaceful foreign nations, O'Sullivan was charged with violating the Neutrality Act of 1818, an indictment he accepted with "a perfect non-chalance." Though he was clearly guilty of breaking international law, his trial ended with a hung jury in 1852. O'Sullivan's tarnished reputation did not prevent Franklin Pierce from relying upon his help to dole out positions among New York supporters. Out of gratitude for his assistance and with some prodding from Nathaniel Hawthorne, Pierce rewarded O'Sullivan with the position of chargé d'affaires in Portugal. O'Sullivan requested the immediate advance of a year's salary, for he was nearly bankrupt.[10]

And so it was that he appealed to Nathaniel for yet another loan. Understandably chary about lending money to O'Sullivan, Nathaniel nonetheless entered into a convoluted arrangement by buying from him property in upstate New York. "I must either buy this property, or lend $3,000 to O'Sullivan, who would never be able to pay me back," he wrote Ticknor, from whom he drew cash for this purchase because business at the Consul's office was "very bad": "Friends and strangers settle on my poor little pile of gold, like flies on a lump of sugar. You must save what you can for me." But the circumstances of this transaction gnawed at Nathaniel even after he obtained the deed to this to property in March of 1855. O'Sullivan requested secrecy about their deal for the property had been inherited by his wife, and he hoped to "redeem it" before anything about its sale leaked out. There is no evidence that Nathaniel confided in his own wife the details of this arrangement, which would have lasting effects upon the Hawthornes' finances. Once again Nathaniel sought Ticknor's confidential advice, sending him the deed, asking him to scrutinize it, and questioning if it could be recorded "without interfering" with O'Sullivan's desire for secrecy. Regarding the promised $300 in annual earnings on this investment, that too must be handled clandestinely. The agent for the property would continue to collect rent and hand it over to O'Sullivan who would then "account to me," Nathaniel explained, adding somewhat uneasily: "There is no fear of another conveyance, nor, I suppose, of an attachment, it having been his wife's property." Still worried in October of

1855, Nathaniel again requested that Ticknor investigate "(without giving rise to any scandal)" to determine if there had been any "legal impediment" to the sale. Indeed there was no legal impediment—a nineteenth-century husband having all rights over marital assets. But Nathaniel admitted "little confidence in O'Sullivan's business-qualifications" before segueing to yet another parenthetical thought: "(though entire confidence in his honor)."[11] These hesitant queries suggest Nathaniel knew this transaction with O'Sullivan was somewhat less than honorable, perhaps because Nathaniel, like his friend, kept his wife in the dark.

All the while Nathaniel gave, repaid, lent, and invested thousands of dollars, he groaned about the shortfall in his income that grew worse as the year progressed. Congress passed a bill in March of 1855, effective three months later, that eliminated emoluments for consuls and paid them only a flat salary. Months before this dire news—or to put it another way, during the months he was buying land for $3,000 from O'Sullivan and the month after he lent Bridge $3,000—Nathaniel complained about his financial predicament to none other than Bridge. How was a consul to provide a home—a *bona fide* home—for his family? His predecessor consul, a younger man married but without children, had lived at Mrs. Blodget's, but Nathaniel recoiled from living there for the duration of his tenure in office. How was a diplomat to mingle with people in "highest society" if his entire income amounted to less than they spent on "entertainments and other trimmings and embroidery of their lives"?[12]

Rubbing elbows with members of the British upper crust augmented Sophia's perception of financial limitations as never before. Although she had been inserted into the luxurious life of her hosts in Cuba, her status there, as sister to the governess of the Morrell children, had absolved her need to reciprocate hospitality. And although many of Sophia's friends were among American's richest people, they were also bohemians or philanthropists whom she might easily entertain at The Old Manse or La Maison Rouge, however modest or shabby those homes. Now in England, the Hawthornes lacked by an enormous measure the financial resources to move in the same circles as the Rathbones, the Barbers, the Brights, and others. Sophia was increasingly aware that she must save money or be "ruined." She confided to Mary that she had "no freedom of purse" and to Elizabeth that she regretted having expected a life of ease, even having hoped for a life of affluence in England. Her calculation of expenses and income did not, however, fully explain why they were so short of funds, further evidence of her ignorance about Nathaniel's dispersal of thousands of dollars to his friends. Despite the good sales of *Tanglewood Tales*, which quickly went into second and third printings, she believed that the publishing house of Ticknor and Fields made mistakes with their accounts. More precisely, she believed that although Ticknor himself made "no blunders," when he was absent from the firm, "those whom he left behind may not be so exemplary. Mr Fields probably takes poetic licenses [sic]."[13]

Thus did the "pinch and strain," the "long discipline of poverty and effort" follow Sophia from America to England. To their ordinary expenses (the repair of the roof at the Wayside, which remained their responsibility) were added extraordinary ones (loans that Nathaniel made to sailors, which he assured Sophia would be repaid even though experience demonstrated they would not). And for the first time, Sophia incurred the cost of lessons for Una and Julian. Within days of arrival at the Rock Ferry Hotel, she had attempted to establish a regular schedule of classes, just as she had in Salem, Lenox, and Concord. But any routine was sabotaged by the chaos of settling into the Rock Park house and the flow of visitors such as the Hoopers, Sturgises, and Ticknor, who, after a brief trip to London, stayed with the Hawthornes for several days before returning to America in October of 1853. He had become a great favorite with the children, who "all miss you more than they would their father," Nathaniel wrote him.[14]

It was just as well that Sophia could not maintain a schedule of classes for her children. The older two needed more than the intellectual nourishment their mother supplied. The study of Latin was no antidote to Una's homesickness, Sophia's label for the malaise that enveloped her. Dr. John James Drysdale, a prominent homeopath, determined that she was in a "very delicate & critical state," a diagnosis Sophia reported to Elizabeth. Una was "depressed," her growth spurt having taxed her mental capacity. So, accompanied by her mother, she began biweekly music lessons in the Liverpool home of her instructor, Mme. Husson. After several months, Dr. Drysdale advised against exposing Una, "in her pale sad condition" to the inevitably foggy ferry rides to and from Liverpool. In order to eliminate these regular crossings and continue her music lessons, Una boarded with her teacher. Sophia reasoned that Monsieur Husson would pose no threat to Una's innocence, for he was Swiss, not French, "or I would not put her into the same house with him." Brightening Una's mood evidently required drastic measures, among them the loosening of ties that bound Sophia so closely to her. As for Julian, his sphere too must widen; Nathaniel knew he needed the company of other boys. Sophia therefore enrolled Julian and Una in dance lessons at Monsieur Duget's school, although Nathaniel thought fencing would be a more appropriate skill for his son.[15]

While Sophia adjusted to this necessary, albeit temporary, separation from her older daughter, she contended with the consequences of separation from her father. A contentious situation arose with Elizabeth, who bore nearly exclusive responsibility for his care. Dr. Peabody left Nat at the Wayside to join Elizabeth in New Jersey once she had accepted a teaching position in Eagleswood at Theodore Dwight Weld's Raritan Bay Union school. Among Weld's staff of ardent abolitionists were his wife, Angelina Grimké Weld, and her sister, Sarah. Nathaniel initially offered to pay the expenses for Dr. Peabody's "removal," but the old man demurred. He did accept the small drafts that his son-in-law authorized from England. More than that, the Hawthornes could not do. Sophia informed Elizabeth that "people" (those who came through the door of the consulate) looked to her husband for help; there was no money to spare for her family. "Friends and strangers" might "settle on" Nathaniel's "poor little pile of gold, like flies on a lump of sugar," but he was adept at brushing family members away.[16]

And had there been money to spare, Sophia would not have dipped into her husband's income for her family. This she made clear to Elizabeth. "We," writing of herself and Mary, "have always both said that whatever money we might earn from the sweat of our brows should go to Father, but that we should never feel authorized to *ask* our husbands for one penny for him or for any of our relations." Herein lay the paradox of the Peabody sisters' economic situation. As married women, Sophia and Mary (in widely varying degrees) experienced some financial security unavailable to their single sister. But Elizabeth, burdened by debts that had amounted to nearly $3,000 in 1853,[17] enjoyed financial freedom that her sisters lacked. Whatever she earned, she could spend as she pleased.

But Sophia quibbled with Elizabeth over her reports of their father's immanent death, charging her sister with "taking the darkest view" and exaggerating. Sophia's reflexive optimism was no less distorting, according to Elizabeth. These sisters were gnawing old bones of contention, but Sophia's rose-colored glasses may, in this instance, have signaled guilt about her absence from her dying father. Early in January of 1855, Sophia wrote him a typically newsy letter, enclosing a £10 New Year's gift to be added to earlier drafts from her husband so that her father might hire a nurse. But Dr. Peabody never received this gift, nor did he read the letter, for he had died on the first day of 1855. News of his death and the mourning that followed did not, however, prevent Sophia's niggling questions about the money Nathaniel had sent for her father's care. Why was Elizabeth unable to pay for any of his final expenses? Elizabeth's retort was intercepted by Nathaniel, who responded to it with considerable venom. He refused to let Sophia see Elizabeth's letter and would not dignify "accusations of neglecting her father and family" with the unnecessary effort to "vindicate" his wife. He did, however, feel called upon to attack Elizabeth and her criticism of Sophia's marriage: "[T]his conjugal relation is one which God never meant you to share, and which therefore He apparently did not give you the instinct to understand."[18]

Sophia's quarrels with her sister, her worry about money—these were genteel inconveniences compared to the problems Sophia observed on the streets of Liverpool. Rose-colored glasses could not blind her to the suffering of homeless Irish men, women, and children who fled famine in their own country only to starve in England. The poor lived in "holes and stifled hovels" or in fetid almshouses that were as horrific as the jails. Social conditions were at the root of these inequities, Sophia began to realize, when she encountered a group of girls from an industrial school; "ages of misery, ages of wickedness were inscribed" on their faces. Sophia's attention extended to striking workers, though she wondered if their methods would do them more harm than good. Commending their fate to "the providence of God," she also reasoned that a "political economist" might find a solution to their problems by examining the "powerful arguments on both sides." For the first time in her life, Sophia's descriptions of human suffering prompted her analyses of economic and social structures.[19]

While she occasionally speculated upon the ravages and causes of poverty, Nathaniel daily confronted the degradation of humanity, and his position forced him to deal with deceptive, degenerate, even violent people. "I am sick to death of my office," he wrote a mere two weeks into it; "beggars, cheats, simpletons, unfortunates, so mixed up that it is impossible to distinguish one from another, and so, in self-defense, the consul distrusts them all." Nathaniel also became aware of the miserable lives led by sailors. He was, after all, the son of a sailor, and the lot of sailors was, he believed, far worse than that of American slaves. And the poor! They were inescapable. A ramble down a Liverpool street pressed him against "[p]eople as numerous as maggots in cheese." On an official visit to an almshouse, he encountered a "little, sickly, humor-eaten fright" of a child who demanded physical contact by "taking hold of my skirts, following at my heels; and at last held up its hands, smiled in my face, and . . . insisted on my taking it up!"[20] Nathaniel became adept at describing the world around him with a vivid intensity never before found in his journals. As consul, he could not bring imaginative literature to fruition, but he had not put away his pen.

Observing these noxious extremes of wealth and poverty exacerbated the Hawthornes' private discomforts. And the very atmosphere of Liverpool was noxious; fog and damp "searches into one's marrow so piteously," lamented Sophia, and she was continuously ill. What had begun for her as a cold and cough worsened into chronic bronchitis. Then in April and

May of 1854, she was exhausted by an eagerly awaited but protracted visit from the O'Sullivans. She succumbed first to a severe stomach ailment and then to whooping cough, as did most of the household then consisting of fifteen people. John and Susan O'Sullivan, John's sister Ellie, his invalid mother with her maid and three additional servants were passing through Liverpool on their way to Lisbon. Their plan to depart immediately on the *Lusitania* was foiled when that ship, like others sailing under the British flag, was commandeered to transport troops upon the outbreak of the Crimean War. In order that the financially strapped O'Sullivan might avoid the cost of several hundred pounds for lodging, he, his family, and entourage remained with the Hawthornes for seven weeks. This interlude afforded O'Sullivan the opportunity—his near escape from conviction for violating the Neutrality Act notwithstanding—to take off for London where he met with Kossuth, Mazzini, and others to ascertain their sentiments about Cuba. Meanwhile at Rock Park, Ellen Herne's disposition was so adversely affected by the O'Sullivans' intrusion that Nathaniel dismissed her. Sophia accepted her husband's decision by heaping opprobrium on Ellen while claiming she herself had been at fault for having "petted" and thereby "spoilt" her.[21]

Despite the unpleasant departure of a formerly trusted helper and despite increasingly poor health, Sophia thoroughly enjoyed the O'Sullivans' visit. Dinner table conversations were enlivened by topics suggestive of short stories that Nathaniel might have written, or might still write. A particularly macabre tale was told by Mary Blackburn Rowly O'Sullivan, or "Madam O'Sullivan" as the Hawthornes referred to John's mother. Now confined to a wheelchair, she was nonetheless capable of regaling her host family with stories of adventures in exotic locales. She had lived in Africa and Europe, as well as the United States, and as a young woman on the Barbary Coast had suffered an illness that mimicked death. Her devoted husband, then consul general there, wished to gaze upon her face one last time before her burial. Pulling aside her shroud, he observed the very faintest wisp of breath, and she was "restored to life." For years she believed the episode to have been the product of delirium, and when her husband eventually told her that she had nearly been buried alive, "she fainted away."[22]

And John Louis O'Sullivan provided a fund of entertainment simply by being himself. "Mr O'Sullivan is an exceedingly good friend, & we could not well have enough of him," Sophia declared. For Nathaniel, this man who had "first lisped in Arabic" and had "hereditary claims to Spanish countship" (hence the Hawthornes' sometimes calling him Count Louis) was an intriguing paradox, an "unsettled and wandering character," an

honorable man though a secret partner in high-dollar, questionable investments. For Una, "Uncle John," as she affectionately called her "god-father"
(another title he bore within the family though without benefit of any
baptismal ceremony), was a source of "boundless" enjoyment. His presence at Rock Ferry banished her gloom. And for Sophia, he was much
more than a dashing figure and a diverting presence. After the O'Sullivans
had departed for Portugal, she portrayed John in a July 1854 letter as a
man who inhabited the elevated spheres usually reserved for her husband
and, on one occasion, occupied by Herman Melville:

> Mr O'Sullivan comes as near perfection of goodness as any mortal I ever
> knew. His character is ideal. Not a particle of worldly selfishness in his
> composition . . . [,] he acts after GOD's law, not man's. His magnanimity,
> Christian charity, gentleness & sweetness, his power of self sacrifice, his
> performance of duty are all without blemish.[23]

Sophia was obviously indifferent to O'Sullivan's widely publicized
political machinations and ignorant of his shenanigans with his wife's
property and the resulting drain upon her own income. But his public
stance against capital punishment—a practice permitted by human law
but prohibited by the divine commandment "Thou Shalt Not Kill"—
would unreservedly merit her highest praise. When O'Sullivan had been
a New York State legislator in 1841, he presented his "Report in Favor of
the Abolition of the Punishment of Death by Law," a measure that failed
amid the overwhelming majority support for a state's right to exact lethal
justice. Sophia and O'Sullivan were in the minority of Americans who
professed to abhor violence even when justified by self-defense or sanctioned by government.

Sophia's comments about O'Sullivan's "Christian charity, gentleness
& sweetness" gloss others she made in that July 1854 letter about abolitionists, their use of force, and the "great slave case in Boston." Anthony
Burns, a runaway slave, had been seized and then held in the courthouse,
awaiting the judge's decision about his fate. An outraged crowd gathered
to protest Burns's seizure at the hands of Southerners who dared to
impose their will in a Northern state. The fiery eloquence of the abolitionist ministers Theodore Parker and Thomas Wentworth Higginson
turned the crowd into a mob that stormed the courthouse, killing a guard.
All for naught, as far as Burns was concerned, for Judge Edward Greely
Loring ordered his rendition to Virginia where he was severely beaten
and died from his injuries. This event perfectly illustrated Sophia's belief
that good could never come from violence, and she had harsh words for

abolitionists. They were cowards who hid behind incendiary speeches: "I should like to see one dying for his cause." Parker was "the murderer of that officer far more than the man who shot him." It was abolitionists who caused Burns's death: "Oh how much harm to the wretched slave do those men do!"[24]

But had Sophia wished to find other remote causes for the increasing violence in her homeland, she needed to look no further than Rock Park and her beloved houseguest, John Louis O'Sullivan, with his powerful rhetoric of "manifest destiny" and westward migration. Burns's capture occurred but two days after the House of Representatives approved the Kansas-Nebraska Act, promoted by O'Sullivan out of gratitude to Pierce. This act abrogated the Missouri Compromise of 1820; settlers themselves could now vote to permit or prohibit slavery. In a contentious letter to Mary, Sophia defended the act and the president whose administration oversaw its passage. Sophia did not regard Pierce—as did those (Mary among them) who deplored his refusal to stand firm against slave-owning and slave-hunting Southerners—as an agent of increasing violence. Claiming that the constitutional rights of each state were at issue, Sophia agreed with "advocates of this bill" and not, she insisted, because "it promotes the extension of slavery—of course not."[25] No matter the distance between England and the United States, Sophia was forced to contemplate her country hurtling itself toward sectional strife, disunion, and worse.

When the O'Sullivans departed for Portugal, the Hawthorne home became a quieter place once more. But Sophia's whooping cough lingered, and when it ceased, bronchitis weakened her, so Dr. Drysdale prescribed a change of air. She went to the Isle of Man for a couple of weeks, then returned to Liverpool, and soon departed with the children for Rhyl. There she was joined by her husband and O'Sullivan, who had left Portugal to sightsee with the Hawthornes. O'Sullivan then invited them to join his family in their palatial Lisbon residence. A more temperate climate would surely improve Sophia's health, and quitting the Rock Park house would improve the Hawthornes' finances. Leaving Liverpool, and more particularly leaving the consulate, was appealing for yet another reason. Despite expending tremendous energy on the detestable position of consul, Nathaniel had been accused of negligence. It had occurred to him that he might resign and travel with his family in Italy for two years, even if this meant forfeiting the less-than-hoped-for income as consul. He confided to Bridge that he had enough saved to pay for Julian's education and "portion off the girls in a moderate way," and, he concluded, "if I die, or am brain stricken, my family will not be beggars;—the dread of which has often troubled me in times past."[26]

O'Sullivan now suggested an alternative. Nathaniel could retain his position and temporarily accompany Sophia and the children to Lisbon. But, when—to his chagrin—his request for a leave of absence from the consulate was denied, another plan was devised. He would fulfill his term as consul, and the Hawthornes would quit the Rock Park house. So in May of 1855, several months before their lease expired and to the consternation of their landlady who was, according to Una, "very mean," Sophia prepared to move. Personal possessions were packed and stored. Mary Herne was dispatched to America, her passage arranged in exchange for work as a stewardess aboard ship. All other servants, save for Fanny Wrigley who had joined the household after Ellen left it, were dismissed. And by June, the Hawthornes were again installed at Mrs. Blodget's.[27]

During the summer of 1855, Sophia made frequent trips to tourist destinations—Leamington, Litchfield, Uttoxeter, the Lake District, and London—never finding better health with a "change of air." Nathaniel continued his work at the consulate and joined her from time to time. Did the Hawthornes notice their departure from the Rock Park house resembled their circumstances precisely a decade earlier when they had left The Old Manse? Then, as an impecunious couple, they lived separately; Sophia, infant in tow, stayed with relatives or friends while Nathaniel returned to his bachelor chamber on Herbert Street. Certainly Sophia's vagabond life was grander now. The cachet of Mrs. Blodget's establishment might obscure its status as a boarding house such as the ones that Nathaniel had deplored in America. But the Hawthornes still lacked a place to call "home." Did they recognize that their lives were dogged by a pattern of insufficient income, financial miscalculation, and "ramblings,"[28] as they referred to their current mode of itinerant life?

Throughout the summer of 1855, Sophia coughed "portentously," as she described her ailment to Elizabeth. Una's letters to her Aunt Lizzy drew a more alarming portrait; her mother was too weak to sightsee and (more tellingly) too tired to write in her journal. Elizabeth sent cough syrup from the United States and was ready to come to England to nurse her sister, but the Hawthornes chose a more agreeable path toward healing. Sophia would accept O'Sullivan's invitation to go to Lisbon with her daughters, for Dr. Wilkinson warned that another winter in England would be dangerous for her. Sophia accepted his advice with melancholy eagerness: "It is only because thou art the soul of my life," she wrote her husband while visiting in Kensington, "that I do not look forward with delight to a winter in Lisbon with the O'Sullivans."[29]

On October 8, Sophia, Una, and Rose, along with Fanny Wrigley, boarded the *Madrid* for Portugal.

Chapter 12

At the Turning Tide

Una was "at the turning tide." She was "budding into womanhood with the loveliest forms you can imagine," Sophia explained in a letter to Mary:

> I think if there is anything in nature enchanting and touchingly beautiful, it is the gently budding bosom of a pure young girl. When one thinks how it may one day heave with emotion, with wifely love & maternal tenderness—how it may also swell with sorrow—it seems the chief scene of tender humanity—so quiet now & so innocent! henceforth possibly so tumultuous & disturbed.[1]

Sturm und drang was an inevitable, essential, and even desirable aspect of womanhood, Sophia seemed to say. Storm and stress had always characterized the disposition of this "imp & angel." Una's melodramatic inclinations were now coupled with rebellions of the mild and feminine sort. During the Hawthornes' Atlantic crossing on the *Niagara*, while others were below deck and seasick, she had reveled in the rough sea. "I liked it better than anything in the world, to see the great waves dashing over the sides and to have the ship go down in a deep pit and then rise onto another great wave," she wrote her beloved Aunt Lizzy. And of all the distractions her Uncle John would provide in Portugal, Una took greatest pleasure in a "vicious" horse, one of his "magnificent black Andalusians." As she declared to her Aunt Mary, "I like to ride horses that take a good deal of management."[2]

But her mood could also be melancholy, anxious. She was "too fine a harp string," according to her mother, who sought to manage Una's expectations and aspirations to prevent frustration or disappointment. No longer was Una entirely trusted to steer her own course "on her own responsibility" as she had been when she was a child, when Sophia was so sanguinely optimistic about the consequences of Una's independence. Precautions now rose to the level of restrictions. Elizabeth must not send Latin books because the challenge of that language discouraged Una. Elizabeth must not ask to see Una's poems and stories. Such encouragement might make her "unduly" excited or prone to consider herself "uncommon" (though Sophia often touted her daughter's superiority to other children). Both parents claimed Una's stories were "not perfect enough to send across the Atlantic," so Una burned many of them. Sophia hoped to quash desires—fastened deep in Una's "sinews"—to become a romance writer. Professing "an unmitigated horror of precocious female storytellers & poets," Sophia informed Elizabeth, "that in every way I pass over with indifference what she does in this way." While in England, Sophia had acquired her husband's level of distaste for Mrs. Stowe and "Miss Wetherell," the pseudonym Susan Warner used when she published *The Wide, Wide World*, the book Una loved so. Sophia also reversed her opinion of Grace Greenwood, whose *Haps and Mishaps* she now pronounced "quite disgusting," the epitome of "bad taste."[3]

If Una wanted to write, she might emulate her mother and become a worthy correspondent. At the age of ten, Una had begun acquiring epistolary skills. Over a year's time, she was capable of finishing a letter, happily flaunting superiority over her "shameful" brother who had written no letters at all while in England. Her penmanship matured, her vocabulary increased, but her spelling lagged a bit. She reported that Mamma had to care for "fractious & irritable" Rose, while the entire family suffered from "hooping" cough. Conveying her impression accurately sometimes required striking through a word; the drawing room at Rock Park, for example, was "warmer & ~~snugger~~ pleasanter" than the dining room. Rather than commending her child's search for the *mot juste*, Sophia criticized Una for having written "so carelessly," this comment cross-written at the end of Una's letter to her grandfather. Herself an inveterate cross-writer, Sophia oddly rebuked her daughter for using that nineteenth-century practice. Una persisted, however, in filling a page with her writing, then turning that page and filling it again with a second set of sentences written at right angles over the first. Her ideas flowed better when she did so, Una claimed.[4]

Rejection of Sophia's advice amounted to liberation from Sophia's control. Small demonstrations of independence, notwithstanding her mother's petty criticisms, Una had developed a "saddening sense of duty," as Sophia explained to Mary. No wonder Una said that she was "ashamed" of her "empty letters." No wonder she was sometimes timid about tackling complex subjects. She could not honor her Aunt Lizzy's request to summarize a magnificent sermon delivered by Unitarian minister, radical reformer, and Peabody family friend, the Reverend William Henry Channing. He had assumed the pastorate of the Renshaw Street Chapel in Liverpool shortly after Hawthornes moved to that city, and Una attended his service without her mother, who was then too ill to leave the house. Sophia informed Elizabeth that Una's demand for perfection—the very perfection as a letter-writer Sophia herself demanded—prevented the girl from attempting anything which "cannot reach the climax." Una feared that Elizabeth might consider her dull, that Elizabeth might not write to her, "so I will not ask you to."[5]

Una nonetheless provided a remarkable picture of life in Portugal in many letters to her aunts Lizzy and Mary. At the "turning tide," no longer a child but not yet an adult, Una became adept at handling language and subject matter, and her letters augment her mother's surviving account of their sojourn. Sophia's extant letters are relatively few, and although the originals of many letters to Nathaniel have disappeared, portions of them were saved from oblivion in copies made by Una upon her return to England. She undertook this transcription for her Aunt Lizzy, Sophia having rebuffed her sister's request to see her "Lisbon Journal." It never existed, Sophia insisted, protesting too much. But a series of "journal letters" to Nathaniel, reminiscent of those Sophia wrote her mother while in Cuba, had existed and Una's transcriptions of them became a treasured artifact that she guarded into adulthood. Rose called what eventually fell into her possession the *Madeira Journal*, but it was Una years earlier at the age of twelve who had acted as the precocious first conservator and curator of her mother's letters from Portugal. Una implored Aunt Lizzy to take special care of those portions she copied and sent to America.[6] Sophia's writing was regarded as "perfect enough to send across the Atlantic" by this daughter with a "saddening sense of duty."

Sophia's *Madeira Journal* (something of a misnomer for it contains letters from Lisbon as well as Madeira) rivals her *Cuba Journal* as a vivid, engaging record of a foreign land and cements Sophia's position among the first American women to document travel abroad. Both trips were taken to recover from illness in a warmer, sunnier climate; both trips immersed her in a pleasurable life of ease, elegance, and excitement. And both trips occasioned her keen, sometimes whimsical and irreverent observations of

nature and society. Her analyses of cultural and religious practices pivot
between the constraints of prejudice and an astonishing freedom of appreciation. Together with Una's letters, Sophia's loving, sometimes worshipful
descriptions supply, according to O'Sullivan's biographer, Sheldon Howard
Harris, "the best glimpse into the social life the O'Sullivans led in Portugal" and at the court of King Pedro V.[7] Missing Nathaniel and Julian did
not prevent Sophia from thoroughly enjoying herself.

Her pleasures began on the deck of the *Madrid*; ever the discerning lover
of nature, she noted shore, sky, and sea: "Grand, bold crags on the sunset
side rose up, making several gates into an azure, purple & golden world
of waters." But her initial impressions of Lisbon were not so glorious. The
city's unkempt gardens and buildings fell short of those she had praised
in England. Grottoes particularly offended her, their "artificialness so disgusting." She was similarly displeased by the old part of Lisbon, "defaced
& ragged & bare looking" with neither trees, nor grass, nor any kind of
shrub—the lasting destruction of the great earthquake of 1755. That natural
disaster with its ensuing tsunami and fires killed tens of thousands of
people and nearly leveled Lisbon. One hundred years latter, its rubble
oddly suggested "the aspect of a cat walking out without a bonnet & shawl,
with its ears cut, its tail stripped of hair, its body shaven in patches." Sophia
observed customs like those she had encountered in Cuba. Ladies in
public were accompanied by a servant or chaperone. The death of a family
member was followed by a prescribed period of mourning, the obligatory
black attire standing out like a "crow on a gala day" against the backdrop
of buildings colorfully painted scarlet, blue, and yellow. Such images
caused Sophia to mitigate her initial harsh judgment of the city, for its
newer portions contained "tall & stately" homes, even if they lacked
"order and fashion." And she found the Portuguese to be "heartily polite
and self-possessed," instinctively honorable and trustworthy, "so perfectly
at ease, so finished are the manners of all."[8]

Sophia made these assessments from the vantage of one who resided
in a mansion rented by the O'Sullivans and owned by Count Graciosa
Geraldo on a street that bore his name. For the benefit of her husband and
son, Sophia described the opulently furnished seven suites that comprised
the house on Pateo de Geraldes. In the library, bookcases were lined with
crimson silk; windows were adorned with "curtains of crimson & gold-
color." The ceiling was "bordered with beautiful frescoes of flowers," the
chairs were upholstered with tapestries depicting the fables of La Fontaine.
Busts of Franklin, Calhoun, Clay, and Webster functioned as reminders
that this was actually the home of a United States diplomat. Adjacent to

the library was the drawing room with its "velvet-piled carpet," couches covered in "crimson satin damask & embroidered muslin," and chairs "inlaid with pearl." The many well-appointed rooms—the huge ballroom, the cozier tea room, the kitchen with its pantries, the bedrooms with their dressing rooms—were all managed by a staff of twelve servants including a page and footman whom Sophia described as being "courteous and genial" rather than "servile."[9]

In "his Excellency's position," she reasoned, "it is difficult to be economical. Balls, parties & dinners cannot be refused, & dress is very costly." But his "Excellency" made no attempt to economize—witness his installation of a pink marble fireplace. He spent far more than his $4,500 income as chargé d'affaires. Even with the additional annual allowance of $500 for expenses, and even when his promotion to minister to Portugal bumped his salary up to $7,500 per annum, O'Sullivan lived well beyond his means. He lacked, moreover, the anxieties of his friend the consul to Liverpool who agonized about the gap between his income and that of his associates. O'Sullivan lived flamboyantly as an equal among members of the Portuguese upper class and aristocracy, and he was quickly accepted by them despite a reputation for political meddling which had preceded him. But he was a talented linguist and immediately learned Portuguese, a language the multilingual Sophia found difficult to master: "Letters are also cruelly cut off, like the heads of persons from their trunks," she observed whimsically. The Portuguese were flattered that O'Sullivan spoke to them in their own tongue, while most other diplomats could not; he further impressed them by his hard work.[10]

Sophia was correct in her opinion that John and Susan O'Sullivan were the *"ne plus ultra"* of Portuguese society. With them as her hosts, she experienced a fairy tale existence of gala evenings at the opera and ballet, elegant parties, and presentation at the court of King Pedro V. Sophia regaled Nathaniel with an account of a grand ball at the residence of the Belgium minister who, she noted irreverently, was "so lame with rheumatism that he went hobbling about with his ministerial right leg stuck out straight like a stick." In another letter—this one addressed to her "Sunny Bunny" Julian—she described a night at the ballet where music sounded like "audible flowers, summer breezes, and bird songs all blended together in a bouquet." A "great Duchess" in the audience supplied additional entertainment; "her features, in the midst of an acre of cheeks and chin, look as if they had lost themselves on a vast plain." At only twenty-four years of age, this woman had already been married half her life to a nobleman who suffered from epilepsy. As if a moral to Sophia's story might justify her biting comments, she concluded: "So you see a noble

Duchess, the first noble in the land, with palaces and luxury, can be very uncomfortable and unhappy, as well as a poor beggar."[11]

Soirées were scheduled every second week in the O'Sullivans' grand house, but protocol prohibited Susan from inviting members of the royal family, for this "would be too great a liberty for any subject or person of lesser degree to take," Sophia explained to Nathaniel. Susan, therefore, merely dropped welcoming hints: "I could not presume to ask your Majesty, but my house, & all that is mine, is at your Majesty's disposal." The "Majesty" so coyly addressed and so often a visitor was the thirty-nine-year-old German prince also known to Sophia as Dom Ferdinando. He had borne the title of King by virtue of his marriage to Queen Maria II of Portugal. Upon her death in 1853, their eldest son Pedro V, the sixteen-year-old principe real and duke of Braganza, had ascended to the throne. Despite Pedro's youth, he was an enlightened monarch. Sophia found this boy-king to be "grave & serious & heavy in his contour,"[12] his appearance foretelling the tragic life that would be his. Without heirs, he died of cholera in 1861, three years after his wife, the princess Stephanie, died of diphtheria. Pedro's father survived him by more than two decades.

This Dom Ferdinando of the present may have called to mind—his name so similar—Don Fernando of Sophia's past in Cuba. The Ferdinando of the present was a lover of flowers, a good artist, and a wonderful singer who enriched the O'Sullivans' gatherings with his melodious voice. He was also physically attractive, a "magnificent athlete" with "buoyant, bounding step." One day in the Pateo Publico, Susan and Sophia alighted from their carriage the very moment Ferdinando descended from his equipage of "two open chariots with four horses to each, & grooms, & attendants." He "smiled radiantly" at the women, making a "motion of the head like that of a superb stag—a little thrown back." The very gait of this "extraordinary athlete" commanded Sophia's attention. She was also taken with his capacity for simple pleasures. By the standards of royalty (as Sophia had learned), soirées at Pateo de Geraldes would be considered simply pleasures that "signified his royal wish to be a private gentleman." The O'Sullivans were quite clearly Dom Ferdinando's particular "pets," for he accorded them "honors withheld from every one else." And more pleasing to Sophia than any of his other attributes was his fondness for Nathaniel's writing.[13]

She therefore requested that her husband's work be "royally bound" and sent to His Majesty as a present from the O'Sullivans. Sophia was emphatic that her host should not pay for these volumes; they were to be the Hawthornes' "small return" for John O'Sullivan's "bountiful hospitality & loving kindness to us here, which, however, never can be repaid."

Sophia, Una, and Rose all became increasingly fond of John—as Sophia was now wont to call him—while they resided in Portugal. For the girls, he was the source of many happy experiences. He arranged music classes for his goddaughter with the "patient" Cavalier Daddi, the pianist to the late queen, whom Una preferred as a teacher to Mme. Husson in Liverpool. O'Sullivan also insisted that Una be taught to manage those black Andalusians "artistically," and regular riding lessons made her a proficient, daring equestrian. On one occasion, according to her memoir of life in Portugal, she mounted a "very hard-mouthed animal" and "dashed off at such lightning speed" that the boy attending her was left standing in the stable; "though I had a lingering fear that I should presently find myself on the ground, I really enjoyed it very much, as my horse did."[14]

Una gratefully responded to O'Sullivan's "ministrations," and she was deeply affected by the death of his brother Tom in a railroad accident. Both Una and Sophia had learned of it in a November letter from Nathaniel, but they withheld the tragic news from the O'Sullivans. Perhaps they were unable to be the bearers of such terrible tidings, or perhaps Sophia abided by Nathaniel's implied request to avoid sharing with John the intimate moment that would follow a sorrowful disclosure. "Do not thou sympathize too much," Nathaniel cautioned her, "[t]hou art wholly mine, and must not overburden thyself with anybody's grief—not even that of thy dearest friend next to me." When a packet of letters for O'Sullivan finally arrived the following month, Una's "foreboding," she wrote Aunt Mary, was followed by Uncle John's "cry of agony" inside the privacy of his study. When he emerged, she saw "how changed was his face." Una struggled to utter wisdom and consolation, to find "perfect submission to Gods [sic] will" amid so much grief.[15]

Rose, not quite five years old, brought an entirely different dimension to the O'Sullivans' household. She was, according to her mother, "the pet and joy of all." Unlike Portuguese children, who "all look like little old men & women," Rose acted like a child, a mischievous one at that, as a visiting monsignor discovered when she took his hat—the very symbol of his ecclesiastical rank!—and ran around with it on her head. Rose was not intimidated by this church authority any more than she was by the idea of God; "if I knew God was naughty I would get someone to kill him," Rose declared, to her mother's amusement. John called Rose the "plenipotentiary" of the American diplomatic corps. Nathaniel called her "Pessima," and she was the object of his gently ironic reproaches: "I am sure you never get into a passion, and never scream, and never scratch and strike your dear Nurse or your dear sister Una." Nathaniel hoped that "if ever there was a little angel on earth, it is our little Rosebud!" And an angel she was for her Uncle John, whose "[m]oral influence" over her worked wonders.[16]

Sophia continued to believe that John could do no wrong, save for one mistake, a "pair of frightful moustachios" which hid "his upper lip . . . a distinguishing beauty of his face" and worse yet, made him "look like a foreigner"! But during a "social soiree" at the palace of Pedro V, O'Sullivan cut a commanding figure—his clothing signifying his status as an American diplomat, his rank announced by eagle-embossed buttons on his coat. While a mandatory period of mourning after Tom's death prevented the O'Sullivans from conducting their fortnightly parties at home, they nonetheless continued to attend elegant events elsewhere. Nathaniel had been wrong to "suppose this calamity of the O'Sullivan's [sic] will shut them up from the world, for the present."[17] John was, after all, a man who loved society, high society in particular. And Sophia, whose sociability had been curtailed by her husband's habit of refusing invitations, could now indulge her convivial instincts because she was the beloved guest of the American minister to Portugal. In January 1856, she penned a twenty-three page letter to Julian in which she described her pleasures at a palace soirée. In a décolleté, short-sleeved dress, the work of "a Parisian *modiste*," its color a subdued violet, she was bejeweled with a diamond pendant, jet bracelets, and a pearl brooch. Her hair, "rolled in coronet fashion," was adorned with feathers. This extravagant attire fulfilled her husband's directive to "live and dress and spend like a lady of station" while in Portugal. Susan O'Sullivan wore a black velvet dress as befit her deeper mourning. She, Sophia, and many ladies of the European aristocracy sat in chairs lined against the walls, as was the custom, while gentlemen circulated throughout the grand room. The ladies remained seated until King Pedro "should see fit to come and speak to us" or to "keep us in his presence all night." While others could not "bask long enough in the rays of a royal countenance," Sophia wearied of their adulation of the king, who was, after all, just a man and a very young one at that. When he finally dismissed the gathering, she happily stepped into the carriage of the American minister.[18]

Perhaps Sophia was having too much fun at those dazzling events, the likes of which she had never attended with her husband. In one letter, she interrupted a catalog of delightful experiences to recognize that he had been left behind in "the fog & mire of Liverpool." She had assured him (shortly after arrival in Lisbon) of her love with lines from a passionate poem—"Oh, come mine own, & take me to thy breast/And let me feel thy love's effectual fire." But Sophia's life was full of excitement that excluded Nathaniel. On February 7, he responded to her letter received the previous week, compelled by "the absolute necessity of expression. I must tell thee I love thee. I must be told that thou lovest me." Then he asked, "Oh, my wife, why did God give thee to poor unworthy me? Art thou sure that He made thee for me?" Nathaniel seemed uncertain of the answer, yet he knew how much Sophia cherished his letters. She would sequester herself in the tearoom to pore over them as well as his courtship correspondence, which she had carried to England, then brought with her to Portugal. About this ritual reading, Una had written her father in December: "It is really very funny." How the girl would have laughed to know that her father had performed a similar ritual during her parents' courtship, even washing his hands before repairing to a private room to read letters from Sophia.[19]

What was not funny, at least not to Nathaniel, was Sophia's somewhat too intense bond with "John." What had Nathaniel made of Una's awkward remark in her early February letter that Uncle John "is next to you to her she says . . . . She cannot pour out her heart to me as she does to" him. Was Nathaniel alarmed by these observations when on February 7, his protestations of love segued into protestations of another kind? "Did we not entirely agree on thinking 'John' an undue and undesirable familiarity?" Nathaniel asked his wife. Although he immediately conceded, "thou mayst call him 'John,' or 'Jack' either, as best suits thee," the balance of this very long letter gently warned Sophia about her relationship with O'Sullivan, who had "never been in such fortunate circumstances as during his present intercourse with thee; and I am willing to allow that thou bringest out his angelic part, and therefore canst not be expected to see anything but an angel in him." Claiming to prefer for Sophia to have O'Sullivan "for a friend than any other man I ever knew," parenthetically allowing that George Bradford "(who can hardly be reckoned a man at all)" might also qualify for that honor,[20] Nathaniel did not include on this very short list, Herman Melville.

Nathaniel continued his letter with caveats about his "genuine affection" for O'Sullivan who had kept his "integrity intact" despite "his defects in everything that concerns pecuniary matters." Here Nathaniel hinted at his own transactions with O'Sullivan without divulging their peculiar nature. And Nathaniel continued with another veiled remark: "If we had his whole life mapped out before us, I should probably forgive him some things which thy severer sense of right should condemn." Exactly what condemnable "things" did Nathaniel have in mind? O'Sullivan's imbroglio with Madan and Lopez in Cuba? That was public knowledge. Or the business with Mary Crowninshield Silsbee? If O'Sullivan had done— could do?—"some things" that might require a gentleman's defense of a lady's honor, Nathaniel surely had reason to worry even though he gave unstinting "heartfelt thanks" to O'Sullivan and his entire family for "affectionate care of Sophia." Whatever Nathaniel's fears and reservations, he eschewed contradicting Sophia outright in her opinion of John's "high principle." Rather, Nathaniel asserted that O'Sullivan was not a "man in whom I see my ideal of a friend." And that, surely, was another hint: neither should Sophia, who remained devoted to "John." Months after her husband's elaborate cautioning, she was still singing her friend's praises. "[I]n the absence of our sun," Sophia wrote Mary, "he was a light & joy for us, & took such tender care of us, that we each felt like a very precious thing."[21]

The "sun" had indeed been absent. Sophia's initial comparisons of Portugal's climate to Cuba's tropical warmth had proven overly optimistic, as had her confidence that she would be restored to "bounding life." Her cough persisted, and she was often short of breath in Lisbon. Although that city's climate was more temperate than Liverpool's, proximity to the ocean turned warm summers into cool autumns and colder winters. To Sophia's misfortune, she was in Lisbon during an unprecedented period of rain and floods of biblical proportions. "Within the memory of man, there has not been such a deluge on the Peninsula," she wrote Nathaniel, "I wonder it is not broken off the Continent, by dint of soaking, so as to set us afloat on the high seas." Mudslides destroyed buildings as well as the walls surrounding the city. Bodies floated down the Tagus River. Seeds were washed out of the ground; crops could not grow resulting in widespread starvation. The poor resorted to looting and were imprisoned by the hundreds. A musical soirée at the palace was canceled while "prayers besiege Heaven for a cessation of the rain."[22]

In search of good weather and better health, the ladies of Pateo de Geraldes—Sophia with her daughters and Fanny Wrigley, Madam O'Sullivan, Susan, and her sister Ellie Rogers—sailed for Madeira and its promise of sun and warmth. Almost three days long, the voyage was harrowing. The tempests that raged in Lisbon also churned the Atlantic. Although the women occupied "splendid accommodations," they were terribly seasick; Sophia was "in extremis" but "patient to think of my luxurious fate, in comparison" to the circumstances of Africans in the Middle Passage. "How man could be so fiendish as to put poor slaves, or poor people of any kind, in such holes as these," she wondered questioning further "whether the rest & bliss of eternity could ever wipe out the horrible suffering gone through, pent up without room or air." Neither her observations in Cuba nor her discussions with her friends and family in New England had ever given her such clear insight into the horrors of slavery. Even Sophia's relentless—sometimes admirable, sometimes foolish—optimism must admit that "rest & bliss of eternity" might not obliterate so much suffering.[23]

The perils of her own sea voyage did not end on February 11 when her ship arrived in the Bay of Funchal, the capital of Madeira. Roiling waters surged against the beach, and small boats conveyed passengers from the steamer to shore. On land at last, Sophia thought she had arrived in a "garden of Eden" and dutifully consoled her husband for having to toil in "grimy, foggy Liverpool." Madeira was reputed to have the best climate in the world, "heavenly weather" as Sophia called it. Funchal, serenely nestled at the base of mountains and facing the Atlantic, was situated on the southern sunnier and warmer side of the island. The city was abloom with flowers and verdant year-long gardens. The "tropical heat," Sophia immediately reported, was "delicious." But it was also fleeting. Although the view of a sugar plantation from her window looked "tropical enough," appearances differed from realities. Cold weather had followed Sophia from Liverpool to Lisbon and now, unfortunately, to Madeira. She could not find warmth and immediately took ill with a cold and suffered from a "heavy heart," realizing that her husband and son were more than twenty-three hundred miles away. She agreed with Nathaniel that "instead of the end of the world being a general conflagration, it will slowly freeze. I thus realize your conception of Hell as being very cold, & not too hot." And when the rains began, she again revised her opinion about how the world would end: "We shall neither burn, nor freeze, but soak!" Had she traveled so very far at such peril to herself and her daughters all for no purpose? She had not escaped pitilessly cold, damp weather, and Nathaniel feared her health had been "radically impaired." The longer she remained in Madeira, the more concerned he became: "[T]hou art blown about the world, in the midst of rain and whirlwind! It was a most foolish project of O'Sullivan's (as all his projects are) to send thee from his comfortable fireside, to that comfortless Madeira."[24]

But Sophia's health had not yet been "radically impaired," even if her cough continued to nag and the weather continued to disappoint. She was well enough to take full advantage of being a guest of O'Sullivan's friend John George Welsh, reportedly the wealthiest man in Portugal and "under great obligation" to the O'Sullivans. Sophia was taken with the "admirable & miraculous cleanliness of everybody & everything" in Welsh's home. Servants were immaculately dressed in white linen; garden paths were paved extravagantly in "mosaic patterns with fine oval stone." Sophia wondered how she might ever return his "magnificent hospitality." Perhaps realizing it could never be reciprocated, the Hawthorne and O'Sullivan women moved to other, less opulent accommodations. But not before many callers to Welsh's home had left their cards greeting Sophia and Susan, and on Washington's Birthday, Welsh gave a lavish dinner party where a particularly rare wine—a Madeira, of course—was served in honor of the first president. Sophia described, for Nathaniel's benefit, "a double-distilled American, a Mr. Hubbard of New York State; an inquisitive, slangish, rather ignorant & shrewd young man" who was among more cultured guests, such as the niece of the Archbishop of Canterbury and Mr. Rakeman, brother to the pianist whom the Hawthornes knew from their days in Lenox. And before Sophia left Welsh's estate, she reprised one of the pleasures of her youth. She mounted a horse for the first time since her marriage. Grooms guided her and Una to a "high promontory, from which we had a magnificent *coup d'oeil*." Though breathless from cantering, this "excursion was superb."[25]

Being in Madeira also introduced Sophia to new ways of thinking about Catholicism and Catholics. On the third Sunday in Lent, Sophia viewed a processional enactment of Christ carrying the cross. Her New England background should have disposed her to be repelled by "long lines of brethren, in purple silk cloaks; priests in black silk & white muslin; children as angels, & soldiers; & a band with muffled instruments, playing a death-march." Attitudes toward Catholicism had been influenced by transcendentalist philosophy, Unitarian associations, and contacts with Irish Catholic maids, and Sophia had not thought well of Catholics despite pleasant associations with them in Cuba. The *Cuba Journal* had been crowded with remarks about people who were nominally Catholic though not conspicuously religious. They did not engage in practices that seemed superstitious or idolatrous. They did not kowtow to Rome. Catholicism had not merited Sophia's analysis more than two decades ago, and just as well, for it would have been anathema to those who read her Cuban letters with such interest.[26]

But at this moment in her life, she was "completely overwhelmed" and "went into a convulsion of tears," she explained to Nathaniel; "all Christ's suffering & life of pain came to me with a reality it never had before." This experience of Catholicism was followed by another favorable one when she accompanied Mr. Welsh's sister to visit a woman who had temporarily "taken refuge" in a convent. The nuns seemed happy and bore no signs of the nefarious behavior attributed to them in popular novels or anti-Catholic tracts. Sophia took aesthetic pleasure in the convent's architecture and art as well as the music emanating from its chapel; "picturesque" was the word Sophia used more than once to describe what she saw that day.[27]

In June of 1856, when Sophia sailed from Portugal and returned to England, she was more open to people and ideas than she had been in America. She had acquired a deeper compassion for slaves. She had found value in a religion that so many New Englanders disdained. Yet there had been no change in Sophia's health. Her cough had not disappeared, and she was constantly tired, though she attributed her fatigue to "an excess of oxygen" in the air in Madeira rather than to her extraordinary activity. She never considered forgoing pleasurable outings for the sake of recuperating.[28]

Pencil sketch of a mother observing her baby crawling on the floor without restraints by Sophia Peabody Hawthorne. (Courtesy of the Department of Special Collections and Archives, Stanford University Libraries)

Pencil sketch of Colonel Pyncheon in *The House of the Seven Gables* by Sophia Peabody Hawthorne with a caption in her handwriting, "The Portrait, House of the Seven Gables, page 39." That page in the novel's first edition contains a verbal description of this portrait, though Sophia's sketch was not published there. (Courtesy of the Pierpont Morgan Library, New York, MA 3400 [SH 93] Gift of Mr. Lorenz Reich Jr., 1980)

Herman Melville, photograph by Rodney Dewey, 1861.
(Courtesy of the Berkshire Athenaeum, Pittsfield, MA)

Una and Julian Hawthorne, daguerreotype, ca.1850.
(Courtesy of the Boston Athenaeum)

John Louis O'Sullivan, etching.
(Courtesy of the House Divided Project,
Dickinson College, Carlisle, PA)

Sophia Peabody Hawthorne, photograph in Lisbon, 1855.
(Courtesy of the Department of Special Collections and Archives,
Stanford University Libraries)

Sketch of the Burns Bridge by Sophia Peabody Hawthorne in her letter to Una, June 27–29, 1857, p. 347, Sophia Hawthorne Collection of Autograph Letters. (Courtesy of the Pierpont Morgan Library, New York, MA 1220.9, purchased 1947)

Ada Shepard, ca. 1857. (Courtesy of Antiochiana, Antioch College, Antioch, OH)

Beatrice Cenci, by Harriet Hosmer, 1856. (Courtesy of the St. Louis Mercantile Library)

Sketch of an urn by Sophia Peabody Hawthorne in her Roman
sketchbook. (Courtesy of the Dominican Sisters of Hawthorne
Archives)

Bust of Nathaniel Hawthorne, by Louisa Lander, 1858. (Courtesy of the Concord Free Public Library)

Portrait of Rose Hawthorne, oil painting by Cephas Thompson, 1859.
(Courtesy of the Dominican Sisters of Hawthorne Archives)

General Ethan Allen Hitchcock, photograph, ca. 1865.
(Courtesy of Library of Congress, Prints & Photographs Division)

Annie Adams Fields, daguerreotype by Southworth and
Hawes, 1861. (Courtesy of The Metropolitan Museum of Art)

Nathaniel Hawthorne, photograph by Matthew Brady,
March 1862. (Courtesy of Library of Congress, Prints &
Photographs Division)

President Franklin Pierce, oil painting by Adna Tenney, 1852. (Courtesy of New Hampshire Historical Society)

WARREN.   289 Washington St.   HEALD.
Boston.

James T. Fields, ca. 1870. (Courtesy of the Peabody Essex Museum)

Chapter 13

The Most Perfect Pictures

When Sophia, the girls, and Fanny landed in Southport, they stayed briefly at Mrs. Blodget's. Nathaniel and Julian had been living there modestly and without adventure—save perhaps Julian's careening down banisters. Mrs. Blodget had warned him against it, fearing he would fall and break a bone, but the boy cheerfully defied her. Without the supervision of his more vigilant parent, Julian neglected his fingernails, ate as much as possible of Mrs. Blodget's good food, and avoided formal instruction but for classes in dancing and gymnastics. His physique developed in ways that made his father proud. But his father's life had not been so breezy during Sophia's absence, even though worries about expenses had been lessened. Living with Julian at Mrs. Blodget's was much more economical than maintaining his whole family in the Rock Park house, but Nathaniel had forfeited a home and intact family in the bargain. For a while he lost his appetite and became depressed; "like an uprooted plant, wilted and drooping," he rued the return of a "desolate, bachelor condition."[1]

Occasionally, acquaintances and new friends had interrupted Nathaniel's gloom. In March he took a three-week trip to London where he encountered Francis Bennoch, a very close friend of James T. Fields. Born into a family of merchants, Bennoch had published a volume of poems that brought him into the society of some minor, mid-century English writers and artists. Among these was Thomas Sibson, brother of the well-known allopathic physician Francis Sibson, who became Sophia's doctor upon her return to England, thanks to Bennoch. But the man had other, less salutary contacts. His reputation had been sullied by financial speculations and political controversy, about which the Hawthornes were apparently unaware. They gladly accepted his offer to stay with him at Blackheath, his home near London, where they moved in July. Nathaniel claimed to have had "some of the happiest hours that I have known since we left our American Home."[2]

But after two months in cramped quarters—Bennoch's generosity far larger than his home—the Hawthornes moved to 15 Brunswick Terrace in Southport. Sophia set about turning yet another temporary dwelling into a home, decorating a large sideboard with Julian's and Una's baby cups and adding other personal touches. Once established in Southport, Nathaniel commuted twenty miles to the consulate in Liverpool, while Sophia availed herself of the restorative advantages afforded by this seaside resort town. Dr. Sibson prescribed the rest cure, that classic Victorian treatment of any woman's malady, whatever its nature. Sophia was to limit walking to thirty minutes a day and to indulge in a nightly glass of wine and fattening foods. Above all, she was to be quiet and tranquil, just as John had advised his "Sofia" when he encouraged her to be "calma, majestosa." She welcomed this advice, confessing that she had been under "great stress" for twelve years, the period of her hypervigilant mothering. Sibson also prescribed bathing in the bracing waters of the Irish Sea, and Sophia complied with the help of "bathing machines." These contraptions, typically made of wood or canvas, combined the features of a hut with those of a carriage. A woman would don baggy swimming attire inside the bathing machine which was then pulled into the surf and doors flung open, thereby creating a screen to conceal her. Upon her signal, the attendant "bathing-man" (who somehow avoided looking at her) dipped her into waters that were cold even on the warmest days. Dr. Sibson ordered that dipping be immediately followed by rubbing, a task Fanny performed upon Sophia with a "patent friction mitten" until she was "aglow." This treatment "soothed and rested Mamma," according to Una.[3]

But according to Sophia, no lasting benefits resulted from dipping or rubbing. When her cough worsened, she discontinued Dr. Sibson's recommendations altogether. And she was no healthier after ten days of dosing herself with the Peruvian syrup Elizabeth had sent. Sophia briefly considered moving to Paris to improve her health, but Dr. Drysdale (a homeopathic physician) informed her this would be "deadly." She then followed the advice of Dr. James John Garth Wilkinson (another homeopath) to take iron daily. Nothing seemed to help. By the end of 1856, Una despaired that her mother would never recover sufficiently "to be able to read and talk as she used to do." She told her aunt Lizzy that Mamma caught cold easily and pegged hopes for her recovery upon sunny Italy, where the Hawthornes planned to travel the following year. Una's disclosures about Sophia's health were typically more candid than her mother's.[4]

Sophia had, in fact, withheld from Nathaniel the severity of her symptoms. She hadn't wanted to alarm him, she confided to Elizabeth. But during her first two years in England, and throughout her eight-month interval in Portugal, she had not been able to shake her cough. Back in England, her cough and resulting fatigue became all the more distressing by virtue of their persistence. These pulmonary problems may have signaled a recurrence of the same illness that had struck Sophia at the time of her mother's death from lung disease. Sophia did not, however, allow her current illness to interfere with the pleasures of friendship, and she made herself hoarse chatting with Melville during his visit, even though she knew that bouts of coughing resulted from lengthy conversations. And whatever the consequences, she would not forgo opportunities to travel throughout England and Scotland before departing for Italy, which, she claimed would restore her after a bout of influenza.[5]

Between April 10 and July 7, 1857, Sophia with her husband and son became *bona fide* tourists. The girls, however, remained with Fanny Wrigley, who had been hired to act as both governess and nursemaid. Rose, barely six years old, was too young for sightseeing, and thirteen-year-old Una preferred reading a book to looking at scenery through the window of a train, or so Sophia claimed. In fact, Una had simply wearied of the Hawthornes' itinerant life. She preferred predictable quiet moments and the routine of lessons. Even after moving into the Southport house, she still felt unsettled and opined to Aunt Lizzy, "Here I am writing to you from still another place; for, poor wanderers that we are, we cannot count where we will be for a day."[6]

Una's refusal to travel became Sophia's opportunity for another series of journal letters: "I want you to have a complete idea of what I am seeing and doing, or I shall not be contented without you. I will describe to you as well as I can, and I want you to read my letters quietly & alone and endeavor to see as pictures what I write, so as to travel with us." Once again Sophia sought to obliterate the distance between herself and a loved one. But her fifteen very long, carefully crafted and numbered letters to Una differ in significant ways from other journal-letters. When she asked, "My darling, how can I make you see with me these majestic sepulchers for the dead?" Sophia answered her own question with several drawings that are among the dozens illustrating these letters. She drew gargoyles and bits of lace, flowers and landscape—all rendered with exquisite precision. Less elaborate sketches are sometimes surrounded by sentences, indicating that her visual representations preceded the verbal descriptions. Some sketches—those of undulating hillsides, for example—look like faint watermarks behind sentences. Large, intricate drawings of an arched bridge over a stream or architectural facade occupy the entirety of one or two leaves and might easily stand alone as framed works of art. In an efflorescence of artistic creativity, Sophia yoked visual with verbal representation as never before.[7]

Touring Church of England churches further developed the aesthetic of religious art Sophia had begun in Portugal. Gothic architecture was the very "image of the soul," with its "frenzy" of "curves baffling geometric thought, setting unknown rules at defiance." She was displeased by Oliver Cromwell's tampering because he had "daubed" religious statues with white or yellow wash. Sophia announced that "while Love exists, let us have ruby red, heavenly blue and golden yellow & every intermediate hue." But at times, Sophia's displeasure had another source—"His Royal Highness," as she occasionally referred to Julian, who dared call the Queen of England "Old Vic" and had "pilfered frightfully" from the Lincoln Cathedral, somehow managing to grab bits of the Roman altar while Sophia was not looking. "He did not suppose it any harm," Sophia wrote, excusing her son's behavior while unburdening herself to her daughter.[8]

But such personal disclosures in these letters were relatively few; Sophia's writing was uncharacteristically cautious and reticent, her tone unexpectedly formal. Perhaps she anticipated Elizabeth's habitual request to see and circulate these letters. Sophia knew that her audience would likely be larger than her daughter, who was instructed to select portions of the letters before reading them aloud to Fanny or the governess, Miss Brown. Or perhaps Sophia was attempting to create an epistolary version of the calm she wished Una to experience while reading "quietly & alone." After all, the daughter writing to the mother from Cuba so many years ago was now herself a mother writing to her own daughter from the Bridge of Alain or Nottingham, Peterboro, or Dumbarton. Mrs. Peabody would have approved of Sophia's unemotional presentation of information. Sophia had adopted the tone of a tour guide or teacher whose letters lacked those "little bursts & enthusiasms & opinions & notions" that had invigorated the *Cuba Journal*.[9] Her idiosyncratic characterization of Portuguese as decapitated language was not matched in playful transcriptions of the Scottish burr. Sophia did not regale Una with metaphors about cats cavorting without their bonnets or crow-like mourners, quirky descriptions that graced letters to Nathaniel. Though Sophia analyzed the merits of the

English nose, she withheld from Una outrageous comments, such as those directed to her son about an outsized duchess.

Sophia had seen Portugal, as she had seen Cuba, with a virgin eye; her responses to those countries were largely free of preconceptions. But like so many other travelers, she had already *seen* England and Scotland by reading Burns, Byron, Wordsworth, Dickens, Scott, Ruskin, and others whose writing provided a yardstick for her perceptions. Although her drawings and sketches created an original form of expression, her thoughts were often adjusted to a template supplied by previous writers.[10]

And there may have been another, more compelling reason why Sophia omitted highly original or personal touches from these letters. She may have contemplated an audience wider than Una, and inevitably Lizzy, as well as other family, and friends. Each evening during their British travel, Sophia and her husband recorded their day's activities in separate journals. "Everything that I see in my travels goes down into my Journal," Nathaniel informed Ticknor in June of 1857: "I have now hundreds of pages which I would publish if the best of them were not too spicy. But Mrs. Hawthorne altogether excels me as a writer of travels. Her descriptions are the most perfect pictures that ever were put on paper." Nathaniel then hastened to avert misunderstanding: "[I]t is a pity [her letters] cannot be published; but neither she nor I would like to see her name on your list of female authors." A couple of months later, he toyed with the possibility of a joint publication with Sophia. In a letter to his sister-in-law and one-time publisher, Elizabeth, Nathaniel wrote that he and Sophia "might write an immense book of travels. . . . ; but I entirely yield the palm to Sophia on the score of fullness and accuracy of description." On this, he and Elizabeth agreed. His high praise of Sophia's journal-letters was not new; he had been infatuated with the *Cuba Journal*. More recently he had delighted in Sophia's "magically descriptive and narrative" letters from Portugal; "there never were such letters in the world as thine," he wrote his wife, praises he had made "over and over." Indeed, he had. Even so, less than two weeks before she returned to England, he burned many of her letters from Portugal just as he had burned her "maiden letters."[11]

Nathaniel had praised and destroyed Sophia's letters before, but now, however half-heartedly, he had opened the door to the possibility he abhorred—seeing his wife's name in print, and along with his. A book of travels by Nathaniel and Sophia Hawthorne! That might sell very well. And money was needed, now as ever. Nathaniel was planning to resign from the consulate and travel for an extended period. On February 13, 1857, he wrote to Horatio Bridge, "I expect to live beyond my income while on the Continent, but hope to bring myself up again after my return, both by literary labor, and by the economy of living in my own homestead." Exactly one month later, writing to Ticknor, Nathaniel made similar remarks. Though he was pleased with his publisher's accounting of finances, he would nevertheless need "a little more than" his income while living on the Continent, but he intended to make up these deficits "by subsequent industry and economy." And then Nathaniel recalled the financial albatross hanging over his head—the "New York property" which he had purchased from O'Sullivan who could surely buy it back; after all, he had been earning $7,500 a year as minister to Portugal.[12]

But, John, like Nathaniel, lived beyond his means, and Nathaniel had made that point vivid in his February 13 letter to Bridge. O'Sullivan had "spent more than his income" while in Lisbon and was "irremediably ruined," unless he could secure another government post, perhaps one in Spain. He had lapsed into "torpidity" after Sophia's departure, according to O'Sullivan biographer Sheldon Howard Harris, and craved the excitement of political intrigue. As minister to Spain, O'Sullivan hoped to function as negotiator or perhaps an unannounced agent to Cuba. But President James Buchanan ignored O'Sullivan, as well as those who tried to promote him, leaving him in his post as minister to Portugal until his term there expired. So O'Sullivan pursued another scheme. During a trip to Madrid, he had met the owner of an extensive collection of master works of art. Ever the visionary, O'Sullivan thought the time was ripe for New York City to have an art museum, and he attempted to attract American investors to purchase these nearly seven hundred paintings. Nothing came of it, however.[13]

John Louis O'Sullivan: publisher, promoter of literature, the arts, and American expansion; diplomat, bon vivant, and linguist; political and financial schemer. His contemporaries did not, and posterity does not, recognize him as the man who bewitched and delighted each of the Hawthornes in various ways. Julian, as an adult, recalled him as "a beautiful, innocent, brilliant child, grown up, . . . forever promising kingdoms," but he "never delivered the goods." To Una, as a girl struggling to become a woman, he was Uncle John, the godfather who remembered her thirteenth birthday when others had forgotten it. He arrived in Southport on March 3 with an extravagant gift: a cross of diamonds set in a locket containing a snippet of his hair. Her aunt Elizabeth Peabody, the recipient of so many letters in which she poured out her thoughts and feelings, had not marked the occasion, even though Una had reminded her that her special day was coming. And when it passed, Una wondered if Aunt Lizzy had remembered that she had "entered [her] teens."[14]

At five feet four inches and one hundred and twenty-two pounds, Una was taller and more robust than her mother. She was creating her own identity; her refusal to travel with her parents one very tangible sign of independence. Allowing her mother's voluminous correspondence to become lopsided was another. Sophia chided Una for not writing to her when Una was a frequent and formidable correspondent with Aunt Lizzy. Una initially rejected a journal her mother had given her, claiming it was "too stupendous an undertaking to keep a journal all the time," but she eventually embraced the task, to the benefit of anyone who wants a fuller picture of the Hawthornes' lives during this period. Una gave every indication that she might eventually match the epistolary prowess of the Queen of Journalizers, though she allowed for her mother's "state of perfection" as a recorder of travel.[15]

Subtle competition with her mother was not Una's only demonstration of independence. Her interest in religion was decidedly out of keeping with her Hawthorne forebears. Nathaniel was concerned. "The religious tone of her letters" from Portugal "startles me a little," he wrote to Sophia, the agent of some of Una's experiences in Anglican and Catholic churches. He worried his elder daughter would "follow Aunt Sue and Miss Rodgers into that musty old church of England." Or worse, what if Una emulated O'Sullivan's sister, who made the even more shocking journey into Catholicism and then to a cloistered convent in Spain? Nathaniel questioned the value of Una's experiences, which now inclined her to associate religion "with forms and ceremonials, and sanctified places of worship." He pressed Sophia on the matter. Would she allow their daughter to "compress the Deity into a narrow space, for the purpose of getting at him more easily?"[16]

These questions vexed Sophia not at all, but she and her husband concurred on one point. Religion was very important to Una who proudly announced to Aunt Lizzy that on the first day of January 1857, "Mr. Channing came, and baptized Baby, Julian, and me." Channing had been Una's spiritual advisor of sorts, passionately denouncing slavery when he visited the Hawthornes' home in Liverpool and writing to her while she was in Lisbon, exhorting her to "hope on, and not despair of performing" her life's work. Hold fast, he told her, to the "great Ideal," however shrouded in "mist," however flickering "alternately . . . dimmer and more distinct" this Ideal of "heavenly and human perfection might become." These heady words, which she conveyed verbatim to Lizzy, permeated Una's life. She went to church regularly on Sundays without her father, who had never been a churchgoer, and when other family members did not accompany her, she went alone or with one of the Brights, such good friends to all the Hawthornes. And Una was dismayed by a maid who thought the Bible "tiresome" and religion "troublesome"; "was that not sad to hear?" she asked Aunt Lizzy.[17]

It was this tendency to be sad, not Una's interest in religion, that worried Sophia. She thanked providence for removing her from the "morbid excitement" over slavery in her homeland. Even though the Hawthorne children desperately missed the Wayside, they were about to be "dragged over the continent," for America was in "sad condition," Sophia explained to Ticknor, and to Mary, she likened abolitionists to rabid dogs, stripping reason and civility from daily life.[18]

The Kansas-Nebraska Act had precipitated an epidemic of horrific violence. Freesoilers and slaveholders flooded these territories to cast votes for their cause, but these peaceable means of influence failed, neighbor now waging guerilla warfare against neighbor in "Bleeding Kansas." The Senate also became the scene of violence. On May 19, 1856, Massachusetts Senator Charles Sumner delivered a lengthy, incendiary speech titled "The Crime Against Kansas" in which he cast aspersions at Senator Andrew P. Butler from South Carolina. Butler's congressman nephew, Preston Brooks, avenged his uncle's honor by bludgeoning Sumner in full view of the assembled Senate. This violence inflicted by a slaveholding congressman against an abolitionist senator was exceeded five days later in Pottawatomie, Kansas, when John Brown, with a small band of followers, invaded a rural home under cover of darkness. These abolitionists dragged a proslavery father and his sons into the fields and hacked them to pieces, though they themselves owned no slaves.

More than ever, Sophia had evidence for her belief that violence begat violence, while peaceable behavior redressed all manner of injustice. God does not "reward us according to our just desserts," she counseled Julian when Rose wronged him, and Sophia applied this domestic philosophy, which was increasingly colored by Christian theology, to national politics. "GOD will educe good out of Evil," she insisted, but God will "rebuke" those who espouse "conscious action" and civil war. Even those who stole from the Hawthornes were exempted from their exercise of human justice. While Nathaniel and Julian had been living at Mrs. Blodget's, "almost every piece of plate we possess—all the spoons, forks, indeed every single bit!!!!!!!!" had been stolen from his trunk. Sophia may have been outraged, but her husband refused to have the thief, a boarding house servant, prosecuted. Several months later, those baby cups adorning the sideboard, and remnants of family silver were stolen by hardened criminals who broke into the Southport house while the Hawthornes slept. These brother-thieves were caught immediately, one with Nathaniel's boots on his feet. Despite this incontrovertible evidence of guilt, Nathaniel "rather wished them to escape." Whether prompted by philosophy, theology, compassion, or the temperamental disinclination to action, the Hawthornes were not to be the agents of justice.[19]

Sophia was an opponent of violence, not a proponent of slavery, she repeatedly insisted in letters to Mary and Elizabeth. But despite her recent, vividly imagined empathy for slaves in the Middle Passage, her argument continued to expose stereotypes and prejudices. Superior character in the Negro was the result of "awful tragedy," their "intellectual & moral refinements" a consequence of mixed blood. Enlisting Horatio Bridge as an authority, she noted he had abandoned his proabolition stance as a result of his tenure in Africa, claiming that the Negro in his natural state was "depraved." Sophia's argument with Mary and Elizabeth about slavery and abolition then detoured down the well-worn path of sibling animosities. *Sophia* would not compromise her "ideals." *Sophia* was objective about slavery because she viewed it from the distance of England. And Sophia was *angry* at sisters who "sneered" because she attempted to "judge justly—as if it were a disgusting weakness and venality."[20]

And one final volley in Mary's direction: "I am one of the happy wives who is not obliged to feel *above* her husband in moral rectitude and reach." Sophia was no longer arguing about slavery, and Mary had better not tread on the sacred territory of Sophia's marriage or criticize Nathaniel. Even the estimable Reverend Channing believed that Nathaniel possessed "the awful power of insight." And Elizabeth dare not usurp Sophia's maternal authority by writing to Una about slavery after Sophia explicitly forbade it, because keeping Una's "brain and heart *quiet* [underscored four times!] is my great aim, while this portentous growth is taxing her." Nathaniel had issued Elizabeth a parallel warning, when he returned her pamphlet on abolition to her and refused "to bother Sophia with it." He read only its first few lines before concluding that "like every other Abolitionist," Elizabeth viewed matters "with an awful squint." But Elizabeth was more determined than ever and again sent it to England. And Nathaniel again intercepted it. This time he read it before judging it "not worthy of being sent three times across the ocean." Grudgingly, he passed the pamphlet to Sophia while he informed his sister-in-law: "You agitate her nerves, without in the least affecting her mind."[21]

Perhaps it was Nathaniel whose nerves had been agitated by this correspondence with Elizabeth that transpired in August and October of 1857. In September, when he applied for passports, he claimed his age as fifty-one years, but he had turned fifty-three two months earlier. On the application for Sophia's passport, he recorded her age as forty-two, but her forty-eighth birthday had occurred merely two weeks before. Was he keeping their advancing years at bay through imagination, confusion, or falsehood? Mortality hovered over his preparations to leave England. Persistent nasty weather along with the children's illnesses infused leave-taking with gloom rather than pleasurable excitement. Entrusting six of his English notebooks to Henry Bright, Nathaniel charged his friend: "If unreclaimed by myself, or by my heirs or assigns, I consent to your breaking the seals in the year 1900—not a day sooner." Fields had already been the recipient of Nathaniel's somewhat different instructions; his "will," he claimed, would direct that the journals be "opened and published a century hence; and your firm shall have the refusal of them then."[22]

On January 5, 1858, the Hawthornes took a train to Folkstone and sailed across the English Channel.

Chapter 14

Like Sisters

When Sophia had ceased being her children's sole caretaker and educator, she hired a nursemaid and a governess to perform specific functions in the Hawthorne household. Fanny Wrigley had joined the Hawthornes in Rock Park, and she remained with them until shortly before their departure for the Continent, when her father died. He had been a wealthy cotton manufacturer before he lost his fortune, forcing her to seek employment. Fanny lacked prior experience as a domestic, but she had cared for her ailing stepmother and therefore knew how to soothe Sophia during episodes of coughing and fatigue or after dipping in the chilly Irish Sea. Fanny was also adept at practical tasks; she could go to market without being cheated by tradesmen; she kept busy "dusting furniture, boiling eggs, making church of England responses," as Julian later fondly recalled— trivial contributions to domestic order perhaps, but ones that made her a comforting, welcome presence. The children loved kindhearted if disheveled "Fancy," as they called her. Rose became especially attached to her after she assumed the responsibility of nursemaid that had, at times, been thrust upon Una. During a brief interval while Fanny was away, Sophia acknowledged that her elder daughter had "no idle moments," her time being occupied with care of "baby" and mending clothes. Una became her mother's echo on the subject of "little Bud." She "will bloom into a beautiful Rose with loving care and careful teaching. She can be perfectly managed with love," Una informed Aunt Lizzy, "but she will not be driven to do anything with threats or hard words."[1]

But the children needed more than sweet Fanny could give in the way of formal instruction, and by the end of 1856, the Hawthornes had added "a lady by birth and breeding" to their household. Though Miss Browne had been highly recommended, her deficiencies exceeded her virtues. She knew nothing of Spenser, and her command of French was weak. Clearly, she was not up to the task of being governess to the Hawthorne children. Sophia, therefore, put aside periodic bickering with Mary and appealed to her for help finding a young woman who would be thoroughly vetted as to character and credentials. And Mary was now ideally situated to perform that task. Shortly after the Hawthornes had rented their West Newton house—that is, shortly after Horace's stint in Congress and his unsuccessful campaign for governor of Massachusetts—he accepted the presidency of a newly founded college in Yellow Springs, Ohio. The Manns sold their house, and Mary, with the children, followed Horace to Antioch College. At this radically innovative institution of higher learning, women were among the students and faculty. Horace was determined to make this coeducational experiment succeed without scandal, so he instituted strict prohibitions: no drinking, gambling, or use of tobacco, and, above all, no dating between students. Antioch was not, after all, a place where young people went to find spouses.[2]

The Manns unreservedly recommended the talented Ada Shepard. She hailed from Dorcester, Massachusetts, had earned distinction for her studies at the Boston Grammar School, and was among Antioch's first graduates in the class of 1857. Ada was presently in France, though she planned to return to her alma mater to teach foreign languages. She also planned to marry Clay Badger, another Antioch alumnus. Their romance, which developed in violation of Antioch's cardinal rule for conduct, had been their secret while they were students. Now graduates, Clay and Ada had announced their engagement and plan to marry immediately upon her return from Europe. But if she prolonged her travels as governess to the Hawthorne children, she could acquire facility in Italian as well as French and German. So upon the Hawthornes' offer of a job, Ada left France immediately. Traveling on her own, she arrived at their doorstep, unannounced, on October 4, 1857.[3]

Ada enjoyed the liberties of study and travel and aspired to a profession, as any man might, but her emancipation was complicated by an underlying emotional instability and by an imagination fueled by erotic possibilities. She was passionately in love with Clay, the recipient of her frequent, voluminous letters laden with her longings and eagerness for their reunion. She also described her worshipful admiration for the Hawthorne household. Sophia and Nathaniel were "an instance of a true marriage," the paradigm of all she hoped for with Clay. "What can be so beautiful as a family circle such as this?" Ada mused, accurately predicting that she would love Rose, who showered Ada with kisses; Una, "remarkably developed physically, mentally, and morally" though "inclined to sadness"; and Julian, "a very Hercules in miniature." Ada's words quickly echoed Sophia's, one of the many ways Ada demonstrated that she "wanted to be like" her. "Mrs. H." possessed "all good qualities of Mrs. Mann," Ada wrote Clay, "without those which we do not so much admire, and with a thousand additional graces." No wonder the Hawthorne children and "the handsome Mr. Hawthorne" adored Sophia, "the loveliest woman I ever knew." Ada repeated in one letter after another that no one "could approach perfection more nearly than Mrs. Hawthorne." She could not have been kinder "were I her sister," Ada proclaimed.[4]

And so the Hawthornes welcomed Ada into their company. Bidding Fanny a tearful goodbye, they sailed away from England. A rough crossing on the English Channel was made more unpleasant by cold, rainy weather and the immediate, inevitable evidence that expenses on the Continent would be greater than they had calculated, and Ada quickly proved herself an asset to their company. Her superior knowledge of French permitted her to negotiate lodgings, allaying Sophia's persistent fear of being cheated. But some things Ada could not ameliorate, notably Nathaniel's mood. In Paris, unable to share Sophia's and Ada's limitless enthusiasm for viewing art and architecture, she observed that he was "wearied to death" of galleries. He was also homesick. And his health, which heretofore had been nearly unassailable, showed its very first signs of decline. Nathaniel took ill with a fever and cold that recurred throughout the winter, spring, and into the summer of 1858.[5]

Despite Nathaniel's gloom, a ray of light shone into the Hawthornes' Paris household. Maria Mitchell, the famous astronomer, joined their group. Internationally recognized for her accomplishments—among them her discovery of a comet, now named after her—, she was the first female member of the American Academy of Arts and Sciences. A Quaker turned Unitarian, she was also a friend to many in the women's suffrage movement, her life an emblem of their cause. She had recently been devastated by the death of her companion, the beautiful Ida Russell, whom Sophia had known when they both attended Margaret Fuller's conversations. Nathaniel had even been a tad jealous of Sophia's attentions to Ida, having chided his then fiancée about visiting her "before my return to thine arms!" But Ida's attentions and affections were for Maria alone.[6] As a woman whose primary emotional bonds were with other women, Maria Mitchell embodied alternative possibilities for womanhood.

Having first met the Hawthornes in England, Maria called at their Paris hotel on January 9, inquiring if she might accompany them to Rome. Ada was immediately impressed with this "strong earnest soul whom I should like to know." Nathaniel also liked Maria. Though he quipped that such an emancipated woman should not require an "escort," he realized she would not "fling herself as a burden on our shoulders." It was he who burdened the entourage, at least such was Maria's opinion. His lack of practicality annoyed her, and, because he spoke only English, he relied upon others to translate and transact business. Ada also observed, but without Maria's animus, that Nathaniel did not like to be bothered, particularly with any details of their travels. In Paris, he hemmed and hawed about their itinerary until Maria, Ada, and Una announced that they should proceed directly to Rome. Una's insistence, Maria noted with some relief, finally "decided him."[7]

Maria had been wise to acquire companions for this uncomfortable and perilous journey. Amid cold, rain, and wind, the group made its way to Marseille. There they set sail upon the *Calabrese*, shivering as they headed over the Mediterranean Sea to Civitavecchia. Departing that city after dark, their "vettura"—a large eight-passenger carriage drawn by several horses—trailed a mail carriage in hopes that its armed guards would protect them along their route. Nathaniel, who was feverish with what had become influenza, heeded warnings about notorious bandits and sequestered cash in an umbrella. Skirting danger seemed a mere adventure to the children, made all the more enjoyable because Maria fed them gingerbread—that "perfection of all infantile tastes," as Rose remembered it—and entertained them with information about the stars. Maria Mitchell was thoroughly "delightful and consoling" during their approach to Rome.[8]

They arrived in the Eternal City at midnight during yet another fierce storm—hardly an auspicious welcome. After one night in a hotel, Maria found her own quarters on Via Bocca di Leone close to 37 Via di Porta Pinciana at the Palazzo Laranzani, where the Hawthornes established their residence. This second-floor, ten-room apartment was spacious, but with only two fireplaces, it was cold. Rent was nearly $1,200 per year in addition to the sum paid to a cleaning woman who also prepared breakfast. Restaurants supplied dinner in covered tins, an additional cost. "I have seldom or never spent so wretched a time anywhere," Nathaniel complained in his journal, when he recommenced writing in it. He lacked, so Ada wrote Clay, "patient endurance of small trials" and grumbled constantly about the weather. Dwelling upon Rome's "nastiness, evil smells, narrow lanes between tall, ugly, mean-looking, white-washed houses, sour bread, pavement, most uncomfortable to the feet, enormous prices for poor living, beggars, pickpockets, ancient temples and broken monuments with filth at the base,"[9] Nathaniel was miserable.

Sophia was ecstatic. She was in "Rome, Rome, *Rome*," at long last fulfilling the desire she had expressed more than twenty-six years earlier to live in "the eternal-imperial 'Mother of dead empires'—the retreat of the arts & graces—the garden of Nature." Listing "the illustrious names of what I have all my life long so much desired to see"—the "Baths of Caracalla," "Santa Maria Maggiore"—imparted pleasure to her ceaseless activity: "I have wandered over the Coliseum. . . . I have seen the ruins of the Palace of the Caesars. . . . I have driven under the Arch of Constantine, through the Porta San Sebastiano, to the Appian Way."[10] Yes, Sophia was very happy.

And she loved Rome for the reasons it attracted other American sculptors and painters. Not since her happy days as a resident in Mrs. Clarke's Boston boarding house had she been so immersed in art, so surrounded by artists, many of them New Englanders, who regularly visited the Hawthornes and welcomed Sophia and her husband into their studios. Joseph Mozier, Edward Bartholomew, and Benjamin Paul Akers had moved to Rome after turning to art from other careers, as had George Loring Brown, whom Sophia had met in the United States when they had been Allston's students in Boston. Brown's skilful copies of Claude Lorrain's paintings earned him the moniker, "The American Claude," and he lived in Rome through 1859. Another Massachusetts native, Nicholas Abel, whose Boston studio Sophia had visited two decades earlier, was in Rome and was also acclaimed for his reproductions of Claude Lorrain's landscapes.[11]

Other expatriate artists whom Sophia as well as her husband had initially encountered stateside were William Wetmore Story and Cephas Giovanni Thompson. Story had briefly been a member of the law firm of Charles Sumner and George Hillard: Sumner, that Massachusetts senator so recently bludgeoned for his antislavery views, and Hillard, Sophia's acquaintance since their days at Mrs. Clarke's boarding house and now the Hawthornes' attorney. Story had long since abandoned law to pursue sculpture and in 1851, he had moved to Rome with his wife and three children. The death of Story's two other children perhaps explained a "vein of melancholy" in the man, for Nathaniel thought he lived in "dread that some sorrow would come to counterbalance the prosperity of his present life." The Hawthornes had also met Thompson in Massachusetts when he had painted Nathaniel's portrait two years before departing for Rome with his wife and three children. Julian would tag along with the Thompson boys, becoming more familiar with the Eternal City than he had been with any town in Massachusetts. The Hawthornes, the Storys, the Thompsons were all parents as well as artists and thus did their lives become doubly intertwined.[12]

And there was yet another group of expatriates in Rome, this one composed of women—many of whom were artists, all of whom were dedicated to their professions, none of whom saw the need for heterosexual domestic ties. Sophia delighted in their company as much—or more—than she enjoyed friendships with the conventionally married couples. She had, after all, been a lifelong friend of Sarah Clarke, who never married and devoted her life to art. As young women, Sophia and Sarah had shared the dream of going to Italy, and Sarah had assured Sophia this dream could become reality—that, in fact, Sophia's "children would one day play in the Temple of Peace."[13] Sarah's prophecy was now coming true.

Sophia eagerly sought out independent single women, such as Maria Mitchell, who was as delighted by Sophia as she had been annoyed by Nathaniel. Maria "smiled blissfully" while she and Sophia "ran together like sisters to see the sights of beauty," as Rose later explained, "neither of them ever tired" and "and never disappointed." The astronomer's record of these outings documents how often she was with Sophia, and how frequently Nathaniel was not. Mitchell's biographer, Renée Bergland, concludes that the Hawthornes had "very different Roman experiences." Nathaniel was typically "huddled by the fire" in their apartment "hating the place," his discomfort in large measure because his wife "did not hesitate to leave him behind to wander with [Una] and her women friends. Like Mitchell, Sophia was discovering a happy sisterhood in Rome, and Nathaniel didn't like it. Sophia Hawthorne, Maria Mitchell, Louisa Lander, and Harriet Hosmer among others made a formidable sisterhood."[14]

Louisa Lander and Harriet Hosmer were both sculptors, both originally from Massachussetts, and both central figures in Sophia's Roman experiences. Louisa, like the Hawthornes, hailed from Salem. In 1855, she had arrived in Rome to study with Thomas Crawford and had achieved some success when, barely a month after the Hawthornes' arrival in Rome, she approached Nathaniel about sculpting his bust. He consented, and during the first half of 1858, he went to Louisa's studio where she scrutinized him, and he took "a similar freedom," returning her gaze and taking her "moral likeness." She was living "quite alone, in delightful freedom," he observed, "going fearlessly about these mysterious streets, by night as well as by day, with no household ties, no rule or law but that within her." Nathaniel clearly liked the brash Louisa, as did Sophia and Ada; they all spent hours together. Louisa would dine at the Via Porta Pinciana apartment, and she participated in Una's fourteenth birthday celebration, a family excursion to the Catacombs where she diverted Rose, who was fearful in the Gothic gloom. And there were times when Nathaniel and Sophia met with Louisa separately. "Evening, Miss Lander called after all but me had gone to bed" and "sitting for a bust at Miss Lander's" studio, Nathaniel noted in his pocket diary. Sophia, for her part, would leave Nathaniel in their apartment to tour galleries and ruins with Louisa. When Louisa returned to New England to spend the summer of 1858, Sophia asked her to convey her *Roman Journal* to family and friends—this favor an indication of Sophia's trust in the woman who had sculpted her husband's bust.[15]

And then there was Harriet Hosmer: "I liked her at once," Sophia remarked, responding warmly to Hatty's "most animated gesture to greet us." The trademark smock and cap announced Hatty's profession, her individuality proclaimed by her demeanor and attire: "hands thrust into the pockets of a close-fitting jacket—a collar and cravat like a young man's." This choice of men's clothing was a logical result of her upbringing. After the death of her mother and siblings from tuberculosis, her physician-father sought to toughen his only surviving child with outdoor activities. She became a crack shot and expert with a bow and arrow, a fierce competitor against neighborhood boys, and a daring equestrian who fearlessly performed all manner of stunts. How Dr. Hosmer believed this kind of childhood might prevent untimely death is not clear. But his practices permitted Hatty to take risks—and to succeed— in worlds previously relegated to men. When her passion to become a first-rate sculptor required the study of anatomy, she applied to medical colleges in New England, but was denied admission because she was a woman. Her application to the Missouri Medical College was accepted, however, and she moved to St. Louis in 1850. There she met Cornelia, Emma, and Mary Crow, and their father, Wayman Crow, who became Hatty's patron. Upon returning to the East Coast, she met and became smitten with the renowned actress Charlotte Cushman and her then companion, Matilda Hays. Those women moved to Rome, where Hatty joined them in 1852.[16]

Now twenty-eight years of age, Hatty was already acclaimed for her works in marble, among them *Beatrice Cenci* and *The Clasped Hands of the Brownings* after her good friends Elizabeth Barrett and Robert. In Hatty's studio, Sophia examined "the mischievous mad sprite" *Puck*. Hatty called this statue "the son of her old age," and the women discussed her plans for a massive statue, *Zenobia in Chains*, which Hatty completed the following year. Sophia instinctively enjoyed being with the "frank and cheerful, independent, honest, and sincere—wide awake, energetic, yet not ungentle" Hatty, though others in the Hawthorne household were initially confounded by her. Ada thought Hatty "mannish in her bearing" before determining that she was a "bewitching little person despite her male clothing" and a "great genius" to boot. Nathaniel was also nonplussed by Hatty's "male shirt, collar, and cravat." Though she was "very queer," he quickly realized that "her actual self, nothing affected nor made-up" shone through and "gave her full leave to wear what may suit her best." But other American expatriates refused to accept Hatty, whose solo excursions throughout Rome—demonstrating even more independence than Louisa Lander had shown—provoked William Wetmore Story's derision: "Hatty takes a high hand here," Story informed James Russell Lowell, and "would have the Romans know that a Yankee girl can do anything she pleases, walk alone, ride alone, and laugh at their rules."[17]

Even more transgressive of cultural norms were the circumstances in which Hatty lived. Charlotte Cushman had created a "Sapphic household" (as Lisa Merrill, Cushman's biographer calls it) among the various female artists whom the famous actress supported and promoted, wooed and loved. Nathaniel, who met Charlotte in the United States, had become one of the Hawthornes' friendly acquaintances while they were abroad. An international celebrity, Charlotte was acclaimed for her electrifying portrayals of the ferociously ambitious Lady Macbeth or a wizened Meg Merilies. At five feet, six inches, with a broad forehead and large, square jaw, Charlotte could also play the part of Romeo, a so-called "breeches role" denounced by some as "unnatural" but praised by others as representing that tragic hero's delicate character. Charlotte's sister, Susan, often took the role of Juliet, this casting engineered by Charlotte to help Susan provide for herself and her son Ned. Charlotte dutifully cared for her family that, over the years, included a series of women with whom she had romantic relationships.[18]

Charlotte documented commitment to her first love, the artist Rosalie Sully, in 1844 with one line in her journal: "'R.' Saturday July 6th married." Rosalie had painted a miniature of herself that Charlotte wore on a bracelet and cherished all the more after Rosalie's sudden death. Then Charlotte met Matilda Hays, who abandoned her writing to enter into a "female marriage," as Elizabeth and Robert Browning referred to it. The women dressed alike in tailored clothes and called each other by men's names.

At times, Matilda played Charlotte's Juliet on stage as well as at home. But after they moved to Rome, their relationship became strained when Harriet Hosmer joined their home at 28 Via Corso. Charlotte and Matilda separated, then reunited. But in the spring of 1857, when they were together again in Rome, their relationship ended violently. Charlotte was attracted to Emma Stebbins, an American sculptor recently arrived in Rome and the newest member of their household. Matilda's jealousy of Emma boiled over in Harriet Hosmer's presence, and she recorded the "vulgar" scene that ensued. Charlotte was known to have a temper, and Matilda matched it that day, "beside herself with rage," "attacking" Charlotte with her "fists." The women "fought like two gladiators," and when Hatty intervened, "Max" (as Matilda was called) turned on her, swearing like a "fishwoman." Matilda left Rome on April 20 of 1857, Charlotte paying her a considerable sum of money not to sue over income she had forgone when she suspended her career to be with Charlotte.[19]

The drama of Matilda's departure from 28 Via Corso was over when the Hawthornes arrived in Rome. Charlotte was now living at 38 Via Gregoriana with Emma Stebbins who would remain her lifelong companion and protégée, though another woman—another Emma—became the object of Charlotte's lifelong passion. During an 1858 performance tour in the United States, she had traveled to St. Louis where, thanks to Hatty's letters of introduction, she met the Crows. Wayman Crow assumed the management of Charlotte's finances, and eighteen-year-old Emma Crow immediately became forty-two-year-old Charlotte's "little lover." Her proximity was assured by her marriage to Ned, the nephew whom Charlotte had adopted. Charlotte would later finagle to have Ned appointed consul to Rome so that she could live in the same city with his wife, Charlotte's "little lover," who became simultaneously a "dearest niece" and "darling daughter." By the 1860s, the 38 Via Gregoriana house had become, in the words of Cushman's biographer, the scene of a "tumultuous homoerotic triangle."[20]

But during 1858 and the first half of 1859, while the Hawthornes lived just blocks away on Via di Porta Pinciana, Charlotte and Emma Stebbins with Harriet Hosmer and others, including their visitors from America, Emma Crow and her sisters, would have passed for an enclave of "jolly female bachelors," as Charlotte herself frequently referred to her group. The sensational aspects of her private life remained just that—private. Aware that the physicality of her declarations, particularly to Emma Crow, far exceeded acceptable parameters, Charlotte sedulously guarded her correspondence and controlled the image seen by an adoring public. Victorian assumptions about sexuality further conspired to keep Charlotte's secret. Because women were thought to lack passionate desire or, having it, to refrain from acting upon regrettably unladylike stirrings, Charlotte might appear to be simply a partner in a sexless friendship. Her lack of male companions protected her reputation and elevated her to an apparently irreproachable position of chastity. In a profession where women were automatically suspect because they displayed their bodies on the stage for the delectation of men, Charlotte did not project heterosexual appeal. And if her male impersonations covertly aroused homosexual longings, women would have remained silent about yearnings that then lacked the vocabulary for their expression.[21]

While Charlotte's performances may have been a vehicle for unutterable longings, her relationships with other women would today be recognized as lesbian. Despite past codes of silence surrounding same-sex households, they sometimes provoked questions or raised eyebrows. Hatty felt obliged to explain to Wayman Crow her relationship with her own "little wife," his daughter Mary. She and Hatty were "what we this side of the ocean call 'lovers'." Their "marriage" was "normal," at least in Rome, and Hatty's own father was apparently comfortable with her arrangements. Having accompanied her to Rome when she first moved there, he lived among the "jolly bachelors" who called him "Elizabeth." This sobriquet was a source of amusement for Story, who snidely referred to Charlotte's household as a "harem (scarem) . . . [of] emancipated females who dwell there in a heavenly unit."[22]

Awe. Ignorance. Naïveté. Acceptance. Mockery. Reponses to Charlotte Cushman and her household were filtered through several lenses. Which one did the Hawthornes wear? They had initially encountered the renowned actress in America when Nathaniel—star-struck—had complied with her request to have his likeness taken in a miniature. Charlotte wanted to place it in her pantheon of notable Americans whose portraits decorated her home aboard. When the Hawthornes were living in Liverpool and Charlotte was visiting in the vicinity, she came to their Rock Park home, where the children "liked her prodigiously," Sophia reported. The gems, medals, and miniatures (perhaps one of them painted by Rosalie Sully) dangling from Charlotte's watch chain intrigued Rose. Charlotte was "most amiable . . . so very untheatrical in manner," her "peculiar, square form" aside, and her "eloquent expression" at the piano made Sophia's "blood tingle." Nathaniel, normally so diffident with house guests, was also won over. "Cushman dined and spent the night with me (that is, in my house)," he quipped to Ticknor, a parenthetical clarification about the circumstances of that visit calling attention to his peculiarly suggestive slip of the pen. Throughout the Hawthornes' stay in England, they kept apprised of Charlotte's performances. Coincidence brought them together in Windermere where they all found themselves staying at the same hotel. Charlotte later visited them in Blackheath, arriving with Matilda Hays. And when the Hawthornes had settled in Rome, there was the delightful possibility that Charlotte would produce "private theatricals" in their apartment.[23]

Surely the Hawthornes noticed that Charlotte's domestic arrangements differed from the conventional heterosexual alliance that they so deliberately cultivated and trumpeted to the world. About the nature of these differences, neither Sophia nor Nathaniel commented in any record that survives. What merited their comments was admiration for women with authentic, uncontrived personalities. Maria Mitchell was "a simple, strong, healthy-humored woman"; Hatty Hosmer was "her actual self, nothing affected nor made-up"; even the famous thespian, Charlotte Cushman was "so very untheatrical in manner and bearing." Sophia was understandably drawn to unaffected, professional women, the sort of woman she had been before Nathaniel and her children occupied the emotional space previously allotted to the pursuit of art. But recently, Sophia's appetite for intense personal relationships looked for satisfaction beyond domestic boundaries. Herman Melville had briefly occasioned her own "shock of recognition"; her closeness to John Louis O'Sullivan—a long-term recipient of her affection and adulation—had ever so slightly raised Nathaniel's hackles. Now Sophia delighted in the daily companionship of women who lived independent of men and all the domestic blisses she touted as her own. These were women married to their professions and "married" to other women; their relationships nourished their creativity, drawn together as they were, in Lisa Merrill's words, by an "undercurrent of homoerotic energy."[24]

Did this undercurrent tug at Sophia? Her journals and letters for this period do not directly answer this question, and many others. Perhaps silence about her deepest evaluations of the "jolly bachelors" and their emotional possibilities makes its own statement, as did her refusal to renew her friendship with Caroline Tappan who was in Rome during the winter of 1858. The Hawthornes encountered her on the Corso during Carnival when she pelted them with a handful of lime. Nathaniel calculated Caroline's gesture—was it one of spite or revelry?—as evidence that she was the "one real enemy" they met during the festivities.[25] Whatever her motive, Caroline forced the Hawthornes to acknowledge her presence that day though they ignored the calling card she had left at their residence. Sophia, who espoused kindness and forgiveness, and denounced vengeance and retribution, had closed her heart to Caroline.

But Sophia opened her heart and mind to Maria Mitchell, Louisa Lander, and Harriet Hosmer, who was the "most eminent" member, according to Henry James, of that "strange sisterhood" of "American 'lady sculptors' who at one time settled upon the seven hills in a white, marmorean flock."[26]

Chapter 15

I Am Near You

In her own way, Sophia belonged to this "strange sisterhood." These Roman companions, all professional women, surely called to mind her own past, but now and for various reasons, Sophia did not resume her practice of the visual arts. There was no studio in her apartment on the Via di Porta Pinciana. Family duties as well as her insatiable desire to tour galleries and ruins did not leave the hours to "excurse," as she had so many years ago, when, as a single woman—a single-minded artist—she created original landscapes. And although during her engagement, she had executed two works in the plastic arts, Sophia did not return to sculpting. That art demanded even more space than painting and far more expensive resources than canvases and brushes, oil and watercolor paints. Nor was Sophia inclined to copy the masters, as she had when she was a fledgling artist. In fact, she grew contemptuous of those "Guido machines," her husband's name for copyists who "hide the masterpiece they pretend to repeat."[1]

Sophia did, however, fill a notebook with intricate drawings of Roman columns, facades, and ancient urns. In these minute, precise representations, she unabashedly replicated nude women and men, even though nudity in art typically vexed the puritanical morals of other New Englanders. Their scruples prompted serious American artists to flee to Italy where the display of anatomy was acceptable. There, Harriet Hosmer and William Wetmore Story could bare the bosoms of Beatrice Cenci and Cleopatra.

Nathaniel could tolerate Story's predilection for sculpting ancient subjects in the nude, reasoning that the marble medium—so white and cold— "gave chaste permission to those nudities which would otherwise be licentious." But Nathaniel was shocked by Story's "contempt for the coat and breeches . . . in which he had been required to drape the figure" of George Washington—"Washington naked! It is inconceivable!" Clothing was as "natural" to modern man "as his skin," Nathaniel reasoned, and sculptors had "no more right to undress him than to flay him." Pressing his point with amusing exaggeration, Nathaniel insisted that Washington had been "born with his clothes on and his hair powdered."[2]

When and under what circumstances nudity in sculpture might or might not offend was a topic that did not rise to the level of Sophia's notice. Her extensive commentaries on art, filling nearly six-hundred-fifty pages of five Italian journals, did not register this debate. Her silence on the matter bespeaks an artist's appreciation for the human body—clothed or unclothed, female or male—as a proper object for representation and aesthetic pleasure. Visiting Rome's Capitoline Museum, Sophia felt the "irresistible power" of the naked "The Dying Gladiator," muscles taut, head bowed, legs parted in his fallen position. "The Antinous," a bold, standing nude figure, contrasted markedly with the "infinite bonhommie" of Praxitiles's slouching "Faun" with its decorously placed fig leaf. "The Faun" presented another pleasant possibility for masculinity with its perfect expression of a most unpuritanical sentiment, *"dolce far niente."* In Florence at the Uffizi Museum, the goddess of love and fertility Venus de Medici affirmed her sexuality with one hand touching a breast, the other hovering over her pubic area, indicators of eros coexisting with "a depth and indrawing sweetness." And at the Barbarini Palace, Sophia admired another icon of sensuality, Raphael's portrait of his mistress, the "handsome," bare-breasted "La Fornarina," a "transparent scarf" revealing both her voluptuous belly and long-lost innocence.[3]

"The Dying Gladiator," the "Venus De Medici," and other works of art that Sophia had first encountered as copies did not disappoint in their originals. Such was the case with the portrait of Beatrice Cenci, another painting in the Barbarini Palace and another take on the theme of innocence lost. The historical, sixteenth-century Roman Beatrice was the daughter of brutal Count Francesco Cenci. His incestuous assaults provoked her to participate in his grotesquely violent murder. She was tried, executed, and immediately became an enduring legend whose story permeated nineteenth-century culture and complicated discourse about morality. Percy Shelley's 1819 play, *The Cenci,* dramatized the guilt of vengeance, while Harriet Hosmer's sculpture, "Beatrice Cenci," embodied the repose of innocence. And no one could approach Beatrice's portrait in Barbarini Palace without having passed copies of it clogging the streets of Rome. Nonetheless, Sophia's response to the original "Cenci" was full of fresh appreciation. That masterpiece "baffles words," she concluded, and was "one of the greatest works of man. One could look at it forever and not tire." About the central moral question posed by Beatrice's plight, Sophia judged the "Cenci" painting to represent "virgin innocence and ignorance of all crime."[4]

Sophia demonstrated a range of responses to these eagerly anticipated works of art. The bas-relief of "Endymion" at the Capitoline Museum, the basis of her last oil canvas and the symbolic representation of her first year of marriage, merited only a passing remark that it was the original of Emerson's "water-color painting." Seeing Titian's "miraculous coloring" forced her severe judgments of Washington Allston's "thick and muddy" copies of the master. But whether rapturous, matter-of-fact, or analytical, Sophia's approach to art was layered with transcendent appreciation. Her "goldenest dreams" had become "realities . . . like the ghost of an infinitely precious reality—It is a Has Been even while I see it as a Now." She apprehended Italian art and architecture with "*past-world eyes*" while simultaneously seeing "all the masterpieces of human genius with *actual* eyes—in their own places—in their own settings." Dream and reality. Past and present. These metaphysical paradoxes enhanced rather than hampered her Italian experiences. Her observations in the British Isles, however, had often been burdened by previous knowledge of literature and history, making sites familiar before she saw them. Her record of travel there was further constrained by its genre (letters) and audience (Una). In Italy, Sophia's journal entries were not shackled by maternal propriety or guidebook convention.[5] Rather, onto one after another page she poured candid, astute aesthetic and philosophical analyses of the visual arts. Her accomplishment in Italy was not as a practitioner but as a prescient critic.

Nowhere does Sophia demonstrate greater critical independence than in her critique of religious art, a topic that troubled New Englanders as much, if not more, than did nudity. Puritan settlers in America had imported John Calvin's zeal to eradicate any form of popish idolatry, the art of the Catholic Church being a prime target. Puritan worship was, therefore, devoid of ceremonial embellishments, just as Puritan churches lacked theological symbols or visual representation of biblical narrative. Calvinism had been repudiated by those, like Ralph Waldo Emerson, who had turned Unitarian then left that church to embrace transcendental philosophy. But Calvinists, Unitarians, and transcendentalists shared a cerebral approach to understanding the human relationship to the divine. A founding member of the Brook Farm community, Sophia Ripley, described the "deathlike coldness" of transcendentalism as did another Brook Farm member and Catholic convert Isaac Hecker, who wrote: "A transcendentalist is one who has a keen sight but little warmth of heart. . . . He is all nerve and no blood colourless." By the spring of 1858, Hecker was in Rome; having become a priest, he brought both George Loring Brown and Anna Barker Ward into the Roman Catholic fold.[6]

Like these outliers who abandoned the religion of their New England forebears, Sophia responded positively to certain aspects of Catholicism. While Hecker used "colourless" metaphorically, color was quite literally what Sophia appreciated about Catholic churches. "What were colors made for, if not to use in the worship of God?" she asked. After visiting the chapel of the Palazzo Vecchio where Ghirlandaio's frescoes covered the walls, she asked another rhetorical question: "Must we not go back to this adornment again?" Yes, she affirmed: "If any visible thing can win a soul to Heaven, it is this embodied worship in spirit and in truth," for paintings elicited feelings that transformed the heart. In Domenichino's martyrdom of St. Sebastian, the saint's "triumph over pain" engendered "a peace which passes all understanding." Other kinds of "embodied worship" also evoked emotions conducive to spiritual knowledge. Just as she had been "completely overwhelmed" by that Lenten procession in Portugal, so was she now moved by a child's funeral in a Catholic church. The colorful garments of the priests and the altar boys' robes created a "splendid picture." Organ music produced "tender rapture" heralding the angels "welcoming the young child to heaven."[7]

While these aesthetic effects pleased the artist in Sophia, the mother in her was drawn to a deeper level of Catholic ritual and art. Emphasis upon the sacredness of the child exalted the maternal role—a concept that resonated with Sophia's domestic mythology. "It is a MOTHER," Sophia wrote after seeing Francia's "Holy Family" in Barberini Palace, "with a perfect sense of all a mother's responsibilities,—and a sacred mother." Sodoma's "Madonna" prompted Sophia's speculation—in defiance of Protestant disparagements of Mary's primacy in Catholicism—that if she "symbolizes the Church, it is most appropriate"; "that the sword will pierce her heart" was a painful, inescapable reality. Time and again, Sophia contemplated depictions of the "Deposition," that poignant moment when Christ's dead body is removed from the cross and placed in his mother's arms: "The grief of all the bereaved mothers since Eve is concentrated in her."[8] A child's death and mother's mourning—that all too frequent nineteenth-century occurrence—became the stuff of salvation.

For five months Sophia drank deeply from the well of Roman art, history, and culture, the realization of lifelong dreams made all the more pleasurable in the company of new friends. "Happy and blest am I," she could truly write in her journal. But Nathaniel was neither happy, nor did he feel blessed. He had been persistently unwell, blaming the "Roman atmosphere." Sophia, predictably, thought more kindly of Rome's "mysterious languor," but she worried about her husband's health. As spring crept toward summer, the threat of malaria also approached. "Fever walks arm in arm with you . . . , and Death waits for you at the end of the vista," Nathaniel wrote without exaggeration. Throughout history, this disease had afflicted millions of people with high fever, chills, profuse sweating, and in the worst cases, convulsions, delirium, paralysis, coma, and often death. Those who survived could anticipate recurrent illness and lifelong debility. Though the Hawthornes and their contemporaries believed that *"mal aria"* or "bad air" was the cause, warm summer air did foster the proliferation of mosquitoes; "horribly pungent little particles of Satan," Nathaniel called them, though he did not know their tiny bite could transmit a potentially lethal parasite.[9] Taking temporary refuge in cooler climates, where mosquitoes did not flourish, could, therefore, afford a modicum of protection from malaria, and the Hawthornes, like so many others, fled Rome for the summer.

On May 24, Sophia and Nathaniel with their children and Ada Shepard packed their belongings in a large carriage and headed for Florence. For seven days they traveled first to Spoleto and Foligno, then to Assisi and Perugia, on to Passignano, and Arezzo, each place supplying Sophia with another opportunity to look at paintings by Lo Spagnuolo or Fra Angelico or Perugino. Her thirst for art was unquenchable. "How could the wise and great Mr. E. [Ralph Waldo Emerson] say such a preposterous thing as that it was just as well not to travel as to travel!" she wondered, "and that each man has Europe in him, or something to that effect? No, indeed."[10]

The Hawthornes arrived in Florence on May 31 and quickly sought out Hiram Powers, who "knew everything," so thought Una, for he had lived in that city since 1837. Powers had also become America's most renowned sculptor, and in his studio, Sophia glimpsed his bust of Anna Ward and his "California," the latter sculpture acclaimed for its gently symbolic political implications as much as for its delicate representation of a nude female. To Sophia's delight, Powers suggested a spacious house directly across the street from his own, "the very luxury of comfort" with its flower-filled garden and numerous rooms. Sophia was glad her husband would have a study in this Casa del Bello (Italian for "House of the Beautiful") as she called it, "such as the 'artist of the Beautiful' ought to have, but which till now he has not found." Her husband was glad finally to have discovered a "Paradise of cheapness," the rent being about fifty dollars a month.[11]

Sophia immediately began touring the Uffizi and Pitti palaces and the Accademia, traversing the Ponte Vecchio and Ponte Santa Trinita, and visiting the churches of San Lorenzo and the Duomo. She celebrated the feast of St. John by watching the festivities from the balcony of a villa rented by Harriet Hosmer, who like the Hawthornes, had escaped Rome for the summer.[12] The Hawthornes also paid regular calls upon Elizabeth and Hiram Powers. Nathaniel found Powers to be "fresh, original, and full of bone and muscle." Though his power to summon a human form from marble filled Rose with trepidation, his genius was a source of wonder to both Sophia and Nathaniel.[13]

And it was Powers who accompanied Sophia to meet Elizabeth and Robert Browning to Casa Guidi. "Everything harmonized," Sophia wrote, "Poet, Poetess, child, house, the rich air, the tuneful night." Though light gleamed from Elizabeth's "sapphire eyes," Sophia observed "deep pain furrowed into her face" and recognized that she "lives so ardently that her delicate earthly vesture must soon be burnt up and destroyed by her soul of pure fire."[14] Friendship quickly grew between Sophia and Elizabeth, who was perhaps an extreme version of Sophia herself. Both women possessed finely tuned artistic sensibilities. Both women were less known to contemporaries than their famed writer-husbands. Both women believed their marriages to be supremely intimate, transcendent, happy unions. Both women suffered illnesses that have figured in the fable of their lives. Sophia was, however, robust compared to Elizabeth, who was tethered to earth by great love—Sophia's way of explaining Elizabeth's survival in spite of her fragility. And both women differed with their respective husbands about "spiritism."

Sophia had become aware of this phenomenon, called "spiritualism" in the United States, when Elizabeth Peabody had boldly suggested that Una could act as a medium. Then, Sophia shared neither her sister's enthusiasm nor her husband's condemnation of spiritualism, and now she noted only that "Mr Browning cannot believe, and Mrs. Browning cannot help believing." Nathaniel found the subject "disagreeable" and "wearisome" when it arose during conversation at Casa Guidi. Bryant, also a guest of the Brownings on that occasion, reported James Fennimore Cooper's claim to have communicated with his long-dead sister through a medium. Robert Browning had, however, exposed the chicanery of the medium, a certain "Mr. Hume," who had manipulated—with his feet, no less—the "unearthly hands" that placed a laurel wreath upon Elizabeth's head.[15]

Evenings with the Brownings were lively, and, when they departed for Normandy at the beginning of July, Sophia lamented that there was "nobody in Florence now for us." The Hawthornes quickly determined that they too should leave the confines of the city. On August 1, they moved to the Bellosguardo hill where the Count Montauto, strapped for cash, was willing to rent his estate for a very reasonable price; the Villa Montauto, also called Monte Beni, thereby became the Hawthornes' least expensive as well as their largest dwelling in Italy. With twenty-eight rooms, each member of the household occupied a separate suite. Nathaniel could continue writing the novel he had recently begun, and Ada could sequester herself to pen voluminous letters to Clay. The Villa commanded a view of the Arno as well as Galileo's tower. Glorious sunsets were all the more pleasurable because they could be appreciated outdoors, Sophia believing that the evening air so far north of Rome did not harbor "Italian fever." But the "strange, melancholy hootings" of a pair of owls that inhabited the tower of Villa Montauto made it easy for the children to believe that it harbored a ghost.[16]

The Hawthornes were indebted to Isabella Blagden for finding Villa Montauto, which was near her own Villa Brichieri. This English woman, who had lived in Florence for nearly two decades, was the social hub for Americans and British tourists and expatriates alike. Among her friends were Harriet Hosmer, Charlotte Cushman, and Elizabeth and Robert Browning. Isa and her companion Annette Bracken lived "like enchanted princesses," so Ada thought. A sometime writer, Isa's novel *Agnes Tremone* expressed the "exquisite enjoyments" to be found in "personal intimacy" between women: "There is entire comprehension and knowledge of each other. This is seldom attained, even in the holiest and truest marriage." Sophia often attended Isa's weekly receptions at Villa Brichieri. "I like dearly to go there," Sophia penned in her journal, "because I love her and Annette, and their spheres coalesce with mine."[17]

Shortly after the Hawthornes' arrival at Montauto, Isa brought them to meet Seymour Kirkup in his home, a former residence of the Knights Templar perched above the Arno. He looked "very sprucely," though the man was generally offensively unkempt, as Nathaniel reported in his lively account of their visit that day. This Englishman's extensive antiquarian collection included one of Dante's manuscripts and a plaster cast of his face, taken upon the poet's death. Kirkup claimed to communicate with Dante and other notable dead personages through the agency of a medium. For several years, that medium had been a beautiful if lowbred Florentine woman, Regina. Now dead, she had given birth to a daughter named Imogen. This four-year-old, "pale, large eyed little girl" gamboled about Kirkup's otherwise "shadowy old chambers," and she acted as his medium with any "spirit that may choose to visit." Regina had informed Kirkup that he was the child's father, but, in Robert Browning's words to Isa, he was "as much Imogen's father as I am." Nathaniel even more wryly commented about this paternity question: Kirkup "did not quite know that he had done anything to bring the matter about." Thus did Nathaniel dispose of the oddities surrounding the "somewhat crack-brained" Kirkup.[18]

Although Sophia noted having visited this "antiquary, artist, and magician," she did not record the tawdry, pathetic, and fraudulent incidents in Kirkup's life. Nor did these prevent her from seizing her first-ever opportunity to participate in a "spiritual manifestation." On August 24, Sophia, with Ada, went to Villa Brichieri for Isa's "table turning." For two hours, nothing happened. Then, the tables "trembled," and Ada took up a pencil and "wrote" for Sophia who "discovered" that Ada had been the medium of automatic writing for others in the United States. When someone asked if spirits were present, Ada's hand seemed to be "dragged" across the paper and wrote "mother." "Whose?" another person inquired. "Mrs. Hawthorne," according to Ada's "rapid, agitated" scribblings: "My dear child, I am with you. I wish to speak to you. My dearest child I am *near* you." Thus did Sophia record these events in her journal immediately upon returning to Villa Montauto. The next day, she replicated this information, some of it verbatim, in a long letter to Elizabeth Peabody, adding that the *"soi disant"* declared Lizzy to be quite well despite a cold. But Sophia did not admit to believing—even to this sister who promoted spiritualism—what her eyes had seen: "I kept aloof in my mind, because Mr. Hawthorne has such a repugnance to the whole thing."[19]

But in three short days, Sophia abandoned her "aloof" attitude. On August 27, Ada informed Clay that "Mrs. H. is fully convinced that she talks with her mother and father through me." Despite acting as facilitator of paranormal experiences, Ada questioned whether "a spiritual agency" guided her hand, but she did not question that her hand moved without her "willing it" and that "things are written of which I am not the author, as far as I know." Positing this gap between her conscious and unconscious mind, she concluded that there was "nothing at all satisfactory" about her experiences with spiritism.[20] Ada wrote Clay no more about her newest role in the Hawthorne household, that of medium.

But Nathaniel wrote a good deal about Ada and "her faculties as a spiritual writing medium." By September 1, the Hawthornes' home had become a venue for many conversations with the dead, a phenomenon Nathaniel calmly analyzed, for he had been influenced by the testimony of the Bryants, the Storys, and the Powerses, as well as Isa Blagden, Harriet Hosmer, and Elizabeth Barrett (though not Robert) Browning. In Italy, these acquaintances and friends regularly claimed to have unlocked "the mysteries of life beyond death." Who would dispute Elizabeth Powers's belief that during a "sitting" one of her dead children laid his head in her lap—invisible to all, but known to her when she felt the outline of his face and the texture of his hair? And Hiram Powers claimed to have witnessed an apparition of spectral hands, his vivid account making such appearances as credible as "if I had seen them myself," Nathaniel averred. But Powers's "faith in the verity of spiritual communications" did not answer his questions about "identifying spirits as being what they pretend."[21]

Nathaniel had similar questions about what he had seen. Ada—pencil held loosely, eyes wandering from the paper sometimes anticipating words, sometimes unaware of what was to be written next—transmitted messages purportedly from Sophia's mother and father, her two dead brothers, a sister (who had died within days of her birth), and two unknown persons. Mrs. Peabody "expresses strong affection, and rejoices in the opportunity of conversing with her daughter," Nathaniel noted, and Ada's skepticism about the "the spiritual authenticity of what is communicated through her medium" seemed evidence that her "integrity is absolutely indubitable." But if Ada did not fabricate what she wrote, how might he account for this "communication between my wife and her mother"? Then he hit upon an idea: Ada was not communicating with the dead Mrs. Peabody; she was communicating with the very much alive Mrs. Hawthorne!

> [A]ll the responses are conveyed to her fingers from my wife's mind; for I discern in them much of her beautiful fancy and many of her preconceived ideas, although thinner and weaker than at first hand. They are the echoes of her own voice, returning out the lonely chambers of her heart, and mistaken by her for the tones of her mother.[22]

Nathaniel's "invincible repugnance" for "magnetic phenomena" had been vanquished by Ada Shepard! If a "mesmeric trance" accounted for Ada's ability to echo Sophia's voice, Nathaniel must have found comfort that it was *Ada* who was in that trance; it was *Ada*, not Sophia, who abandoned her will. No longer did he fear the "transfusion of one spirit into another," as he had some seventeen years before when Connie Park had mesmerized Sophia. He had abhorred the prospect that "Mrs. Park's corporeal system" might "bewilder" Sophia, or worse, "contaminate something spiritual and sacred." He had denounced noxious "magnetic miracles" and "revelations" snatched from "the rottenness of the grave." He had "no faith whatever," he had insisted, in "insight into the mysteries of life beyond death, by means of this strange science." And he had sworn to "defy all Hell"—in addition to his sister-in-law—rather than allow Una to be used as a medium.[23] Did he believe that Ada would escape the blight visited upon poor, ruined Alice Pyncheon in *The House of the Seven Gables*?

As Sophia's constant companion and confidante, Ada had assumed a unique position in her life. Ada possessed the energy and desire to "see things thoroughly" when Nathaniel and Una were too unwell or too tired to sightsee. During intimate conversations with Sophia, Ada heard numerous details of the Hawthornes' "marriage scene, their first home, their early married life!"—Ada's exclamation point implying the dramatic content of disclosures not conveyed in her letter to Clay. Sophia had surely grown fond of Ada, showering her with kisses, and dropping the formal "Miss Shepard" in favor of calling her "Ada," or "darling," or "daughter." And Ada worshiped "Mrs. H.," the perfect wife and mother, a woman "utterly without fault" whom Ada strove to imitate and please. No wonder her hand "wrote" words so like those Sophia spoke. No wonder Ada could transmit Mrs. Peabody's consolation and comfort—"I am *oftener with you than any one*," thus demonstrating that Sophia was favored over her sisters. Living in Hawthornes' home "so intimately for a year," Ada had written Clay, she stood "on the borders of this paradise" of domestic bliss. But when she became a conduit to some other world, Ada occupied the center, rather than the periphery, of events in that household.[24]

Ada's good fortune was purchased by prolonged separation from Clay whom she loved passionately. With a mixture of longing and defiance, she recalled their rendezvous in New York before she sailed for Europe, rejecting the "judgment that the world would pronounce upon us, were that last night's scenes known." She would "never, never regret the pure, ecstatic bliss of those interviews in which I came so near to thee and thou to me, that our very beings seemed to coalesce." Although separation had perforce infused a more "spiritual" element into their relationship, she understood the "intentions of God with regard to the exercise of those physical powers" that she discussed with Clay at length; the "normal exercise of these faculties" could never "sully the purity of that love which permits its exercise." Clay contributed to their discourse on sexuality with his disquieting frankness. His "thirteen of April" letter should have commemorated the anniversary of the consummation of their love. Instead, it revealed that he was in "danger of being possessed by an unholy passion." Deeply hurt, Ada extracted some comfort from his resolve to overcome this temptation and conceded that carnal passions were "infinitely stronger in men than in women." She was aware that "deplorably numerous" European men indulged their lust, Maria Mitchell having also alerted her to the "wickedness of men." Ada had been "shocked" to learn from her "how common is the vice of sensuality."[25]

Maria followed closely behind Sophia as Ada's favorite and most frequent companion. So often were they together that people sometimes mistook one woman for the other, calling one by the other's name. Though Maria acknowledged never having "felt the slightest approach of that love which woman feels for man," she responded "as fully as one who has never loved can" to Ada's disclosures about Clay. But Ada did not reveal to others that she was engaged. It was Maria, hoping to avoid embarrassment and "annoyance," who informed men in their circle that Ada was betrothed. Just as Clay provoked Ada's worries about his fidelity, she provoked his by peppering letters with accounts of male companions such as Paul Akers, who piqued Clay's "jealous tendencies." These Ada countered with extreme protestations of her love. Perhaps describing Edward Bartholomew's flaws—he was "uncouth" and spoke "ungrammatically"—rendered her time passed with him less threatening.[26]

Of course, Clay's "jealous tendencies" may have been unfounded and Ada's friendships with men entirely innocent, for she thought of herself as one who attracted friends easily, who was well-liked. Women eagerly sought her friendship, she proudly announced. This confidence about her appeal to others was offset, however, by near despair about her "unworthiness." A "veil," she confessed to Clay, concealed "many imperfections." She begged for his prayers that she might be "worthier of thy love, worthier to be a child of God!" This request was one of Ada's few nods toward religion, her life burdened with problems that were less theological than emotional. She was often "sad and desponding." Then, the "thick mantle that had obscured the light" would fall away, and everything would become once again "bright and joyous" until the curtain would again "shut out the light, without any apparent outward cause." Even happiness could be a troubling, "almost hilarious state of mind."[27]

Ada was a complex woman. She aspired to be a professor of foreign languages, but she emulated Sophia (who had suspended her career as an artist to create paradise in the home) rather than Maria (who had earned her international reputation as an astronomer). Ada was confident and independent, but she was plagued by self-doubt and moodiness. Ada was sexually liberated and somewhat flirtatious, but she reacted with naiveté of a sheltered Victorian woman about her fiancé's temptations and jealousies. And although Ada yearned to return to Clay, she expounded upon the advantages of staying with the Hawthornes until January of 1859, when they planned to leave Italy. When Sophia "invited" the older Thompson children, Cora and Edmond, and little Edith Story to join Una and Julian, Ada was enticed to become director of a veritable school in the Hawthornes' home.[28] She would not return to America, or to Clay, just yet.

When autumn's cooler temperatures rendered Rome safe from the "singular, voiceless curse" of malaria, or so Sophia thought, the Hawthornes, along with Ada, packed their belongings and left Florence, lingering in Siena on their journey back to Rome. On October 16, their arrival "home," as Nathaniel considered the city at that moment, prompted his temporary enthusiasm: "Rome certainly does draw into itself my heart," he wrote, ignoring his oft-recorded misery there. Cephas Thompson had found his friends an apartment at 68 Piazza Poli, a lovely location near the Fountain of Trevi. The small apartment's seven rooms did not include a kitchen, and food had to be delivered in covered tin boxes. Sophia nonetheless quickly settled her children into their new home and immediately established a classroom routine, welcoming the third and youngest Thompson, Hubert, as well as another one of the Storys' children. Ada now had seven "scholars" including Julian and her beloved Una.[29]

At the age of fourteen-and-a-half, Una had shed the vestiges of childhood. Ada was less Una's governess and more her companion, a young woman with whom to enjoy a variety of outings. Such was the case on October 23, as Ada reported in a letter to Clay. The two young women spent a "delightful," "peaceful," "calm" day together at the Coliseum. Sitting among the ruins of the great amphitheater, they sketched and read William Story's poems aloud to each other. So absorbed were they in pleasurable activities that they dallied through the afternoon and past six o'clock, the time prescribed for them to be safely indoors. Surely the evening air posed no threat of illness in the cooler autumn weather.[30]

Three days later, Una was ill. Cold rainy weather, punctuated by an autumn snowfall, and an uncomfortably chilly apartment would have been enough to make anyone unwell. Una's apparently routine illness did not interfere with the Hawthornes' entertaining guests. Hatty visited, as did the cigar-smoking couple Charlotte Cushman and Emma Stebbins— "all extremely interesting people," according to Ada. And Louisa Landers called. She had returned from the United States with a packet of letters for the Hawthornes, who gratefully received these communications from friends and relatives in Massachusetts. But the Hawthornes refused to receive Louisa. Their displeasure with the young sculptor had nothing to do with the unfortunate alteration to her bust of Nathaniel. The Hawthornes had eagerly examined it within days of arrival to Rome, their haste a gauge of hopeful expectations. But the bust looked different from the one Louisa had labored upon during the past winter and spring, the one which Ada had then praised as an "admirable likeness," even if it did make Nathaniel look a bit like a "Roman Senator." During Louisa's summer absence, an American "man of culture" whose identity remains a secret, had ordered alterations. What resulted made Nathaniel resemble an amalgam of Daniel Webster and George Washington.[31]

Louisa's problems were, however, far greater than her altered sculpture. Her reputation had been destroyed. Rumors swirled that, in the words of her cousin John Rogers, she had "lived in uncommonly good terms with a man." Rogers, also a sculptor and also in Rome at the time, did not doubt Louisa had done "some imprudent things." A single woman in Rome "could not have been too careful," but Louisa's behavior had been far from cautious. She had "exposed herself as a model . . . in a way that should astonish all modest Yankees." Rogers questioned her "moral character"; his own mother doubted Louisa's "veracity." If she hoped for support from her family, she would not find it there. Nor would her erstwhile friends in Rome come to her defense. William Wetmore Story appointed himself head of a committee to ferret out the truth. He ordered Louisa to appear before the United States Consul in Rome and testify under oath that she was innocent of these allegations. Louisa refused to comply, claiming that in so doing she would only make a spectacle of herself. Her cousin countered with the obvious; she was already the "talk of the town."[32]

Perhaps Louisa could not, under oath, deny having an affair. Perhaps she rejected Story's self-righteous, self-appointed authority over her moral life. Whatever her motives, her reticence—her defiance—cast her beyond the pale of respectability. That is why the Hawthornes refused to receive her, as a letter from Nathaniel dated November 13 proclaimed. A holograph of this letter exists in Sophia's hand, suggesting that she may have authored what Nathaniel then copied. Lacking salutation or closing signature, and expressing himself in the third person, "Mr. Hawthorne" insisted that Louisa's "full explanation and refutation" of the scandalous charges against her "should have . . . preceded" any visit to his home. After her name had been cleared, then she might make an "attempt at social intercourse with her former friends."[33]

Formality replaced familiarity. Sophia and Nathaniel may have realized that *he* "could not have been too careful" where Louisa was concerned, for her bust exposed him to the world through her eyes as a virile, sensual, youthful, clean-shaven, square-jawed man; hair swept back, eyes gazing toward the heavens, and bare-chested. A viewer might wonder: Was the subject of this bust clothed below its mid-torso termination? Had Nathaniel posed "in a way that should astonish all modest Yankees"? His own disquisition on nudity in art might be applied to such questions. He might claim that the whiteness of Louisa's marble medium elevated him "into a sort of spiritual region, and so gave chaste permission to those nudities which would otherwise be licentious." He might adopt the position of the estimable art critic Anna Jameson that "buttons, breeches, and all other items" of contemporary clothing "degrade the marble and make high sculpture utterly impossible." Sculpture should therefore be "given up" unless, Nathaniel had decided, its purpose be "idealizing the man of the day to himself." And Louisa's bust of Nathaniel surely did just that. The grey-haired, mustachioed, aging Nathaniel (who recently misrepresented his age as fifty-one on his passport application when in fact he had just turned fifty-three, and who remained fifty-one years of age for Ada Shepard's benefit after his fifty-fourth birthday) must have been deeply flattered.[34]

But given Louisa's present predicament, her bust of Nathaniel might degrade more than idealize, embarrass rather than flatter. Never mind some remarks justifying nudity in sculpture, Nathaniel had contradicted himself on that subject with other statements about Story's work. In his current role as moral guardian, Story might recall Nathaniel's volubility over statues of George Washington and Daniel Webster. How foolish Story was, Nathaniel claimed, to propose representing the first president of the United States without clothing. But how wise Story was to have "dressed" Webster "in his actual costume," thereby avoiding the "folly of masquerading our Yankee statesman in a Roman toga, and the indecorousness of presenting him as a brawny nudity." And, Nathaniel continued: "Happy is Webster to have been so truly and adequately sculptured; happy the sculptor in such a subject which no idealization of a demi-god could have supplied him with."[35] Judging from Nathaniel's own statement, he and his sculptor were most foolish, most unhappy.

Louisa's bust of Nathaniel opened the door to another awkward question. If nude sculpture prompted Nathaniel's own, prurient considerations about the sexual dynamic between artist and subject, what might a viewer insinuate about the relationship between Louisa Lander and Nathaniel Hawthorne? Did Nathaniel now regret having gone to Louisa's studio alone, having received her alone when others had retired? And who exactly was that man with whom she was "in uncommonly good terms"? Henceforth the Hawthornes refused Louisa's calls and refused even to "notice her" when they encountered each other on the street. Louisa had become a pariah.[36]

This sordid conclusion to friendship with Louisa Landers did not bode well for Sophia's resumption of a happy, carefree life among her "sisters" in Rome.

Chapter 16

Pungent Little Particles of Satan

Nor did Una's illness. But Nathaniel was not excessively concerned about it, although the family quickly realized that, despite all precautions, Una had contracted Roman fever. From the last week of October, when her symptoms appeared, and into the beginning of November, Una's fever waxed and waned. At her worst moments, she was comatose and delirious, her speech a series of bizarre "rhythmical measures." Una's recovery was entrusted to the city's foremost physician, Dr. Franco, who treated Roman nobility as well as American expatriates. Franco's command of English was one of his assets to the Hawthornes. He was also Rome's premier practitioner of homeopathic medicine, an essential credential for Sophia, even though homeopaths and allopaths concurred about treating malaria with quinine, a medicine that could do as much harm as the disease itself. So with Franco as her doctor and Sophia as her ever-watchful nurse, Una seemed to recover. By mid-January, Sophia reported confidently to her sister Mary that the Roman fever had "faded out" of Una; "she will have it no more forever, I believe."[1]

The small apartment at 68 Piazza Poli was nonetheless a veritable infirmary. Only Julian was immune to bad health. Rose came down with some malady, and Nathaniel was stricken with yet another cold which, he realized, sapped his "life . . . and spirit." For the past twelve months, his healthy intervals had been punctuated by recurring colds, fever, and malaise. Illness was a characteristic feature of his Italian experience. Sophia had developed a cough, her constitution weakened by the cold weather. The temperature dropped to twenty-nine degrees outside, and the apartment could not be warmed above forty degrees. She was also exhausted from caring for her patients; for a time, the sickest among them was Ada Shepard.[2]

During the last week of December, Ada became mortally ill with "gastric fever," what today would probably be diagnosed as typhoid. For more than two weeks, she was bedridden with aches, darting pains, and high fever. She became delirious and cried out, "Oh! Clay!" People were stabbing her, she imagined. Sophia watched vigilantly over Ada, caring for her as if she were her own daughter, doing everything possible to comfort her. But it was Dr. Franco who "alleviated one pain after another & modified" her fever; "no person approached her in that time except myself and the Doctor," Sophia reported to Ada's sister Kate, once the crisis had passed. By January 8, Ada was well enough to write Kate with her own account of grave illness and recovery, thanks to the "skilful" doctor, who had "converted" Ada to homeopathy. He was so very "kind and sympathetic."[3]

But he was also a "raging lion." Ada had painted a very different portrait of Dr. Franco to Clay several weeks before the onset of her illness. With Sophia occupied with Una, and Nathaniel so averse "to seeing anybody," Ada "alone" was required to speak to Franco twice daily about prescriptions for the ailing Hawthornes. The doctor's leering quickly escalated into a "storm of consuming and raging passion." He had "seized" her by her hands to prevent her escape to another room, and she had been "absolutely forced" to listen to this "*married*" man who "*dared*" to declare his love for her. She did not scream for help, neither did she tell the Hawthornes how she was "tormented on their account," convinced that she could end Franco's unwanted advances. Nor did his use of physical force frighten her, for a "virtuous woman"—such as she was—"*can* protect herself by her own virtues." She was not "*afraid* of this pursuing man" but "excessively troubled" that she was "the object of such a persecution. Is it not strange, dear Clay?"[4]

Ada confided in her fiancé reluctantly, so she claimed, and during her illness she longed for a touch of his "dear hand" to relieve her "torturing" headache. But it was Dr. Franco who was at her bedside when "unfortunately" Sophia and Una were asleep in their rooms. Rose, soundly asleep beside Ada, was unaware that Franco "dared to force upon my cheek and lips his hateful, unholy kisses." Weakened by illness, she could barely push him away when Rose awakened, and he ended his assault. Ada begged Clay to forgive her for paining him with these disclosures, insisting that she could not confide in the Hawthornes, for perhaps "all unconsciously" she was to blame for Franco's behavior. If so, Ada could never expose her failing to the pinnacle of virtue, "Mrs. H." Although Ada was "not conscious of having really been wicked," that she had "awakened such a passion" was a possibility that humiliated her. She "longed to die." Amorphous guilt propelled her into a church, where her prayers enabled her to inform Clay: "I am myself again."[5]

Ada wrote Clay that she kept Franco's seduction a secret from the Hawthornes for another reason. Una's health improved—albeit intermittently—under his care. She was well enough to enjoy Carnival with other members of the Hawthorne household, a season made all the merrier by the arrival of Franklin and Jane Pierce, who had just begun an extended stay in Rome. Una could continue being treated by Franco, Ada reasoned, only if Sophia remained ignorant of his rapacious behavior, for "Mrs. H." would "not allow him to come near Una if she knew his character." But, Ada claimed, Una was "too young to excite his terrible passion" and therefore in no danger. Ada refused to "deprive" her of the doctor who might cure the illness for which Ada was, perhaps indirectly, responsible. It was Ada, after all, who had remained with Una in the Coliseum, against Sophia's wishes, into the unsafe evening hours. For this lapse in vigilance, Ada may have borne some guilt.[6]

When Una fell ill once again, her bouts of fever were increasingly severe and frequent. No longer did she enjoy an eight to ten day respite between attacks, as she had when she first showed signs of malaria. As January drew to a close, then through February, and into the first weeks of March, she was wracked with fever every other day. Administering as much quinine as he deemed safe, Franco was satisfied that Una's liver and spleen had not been affected in his attempts to cure her, but she was far from cured. Sophia, exhausted from worry and nonstop vigilance, wrote to her sister Elizabeth that Una's "illnesses nearly destroyed" her. Sophia was relieved, however, that Ada was no longer "wan." For the first time in her life, "she knows how it is to feel well," and Ada's good health permitted her to undertake additional duties while Sophia was absorbed with Una's care.[7] Despite her own past grievous illness and despite now working relentlessly, Ada was "robust." And all the while, she fended off Dr. Franco's importunities.

These Ada continued to recount to Clay, realizing he would be "startled" that, in mid March, Dr. Franco remained a recurring topic in her letters. But Franco's protestations of love persisted, even though Ada had written to him, demanding that he desist. Now worried about Franco's proximity to Una, Ada finally hinted to Sophia about his overtures though she kept Sophia "ignorant of the fact that he has presumed so far." Why trouble the "constantly anxious" Sophia, Ada rationalized, when she "could do nothing, in this case"? With uncharacteristic disapproval of Sophia, Ada declared: "[S]he really annoys me with cautioning me against various things I am perfectly able to do." Clay clearly questioned why Ada did not avoid all private conversation with Franco. Her response: She thought it her "duty to enlighten him a little." After all, "excepting this tendency to indulge his passion whenever he can find an opportunity," Franco was "really a good, kind man." He was "excessively kind" to Una, and to Ada herself when she was ill.[8]

If Ada's convoluted reasoning had not provoked her fiancé s "*jealous* tendencies," her extraordinary analysis of complex feelings for Franco surely did. His presence, she had come to realize, "was not highly repulsive." In fact, it had become "almost a pleasure" to hear his carriage approach and to "see his pleasant smile." During her illness, his hand upon her head was more "soothing" than Sophia's. After he had felt Ada's pulse, he would kiss her hand, which she did not withdraw. To her astonishment, "that physical act was not disagreeable." Could his healing touch be due to "a magnetic influence"? Could her growing pleasure in his company be the result of "some spell" he had cast on her? Or some drug he had inflicted upon her when she was "weakened by disease"? Could she be guilty "of—I know not what"? If she were, then she would exact a most extreme form of expiation: "I should wish to kill myself at this moment."[9]

Pivoting from self-flagellation to disingenuous naiveté, Ada often insisted she knew of circumstances such as hers only from reading novels. In fact, she seemed to be writing one. Her letters resemble Samuel Richardson's epistolary novels, those quintessential eighteenth-century narratives of rape. In Richardson's *Clarissa*, the admirable, innocent heroine eventually succumbs to the machinations of Richard Lovelace, a *bona fide* rake. But unlike the sheltered Clarissa, Ada was a graduate of Antioch College, an experienced traveler, and she knew "how common is the vice of sensuality" among men. So had Maria Mitchell told her; so had Clay admitted to "an unholy passion."[10]

While Ada depicted herself at the center of a drama of lust and seduction, Una was struggling for her life. During the last two weeks of March, she was unable to leave her bed. Malaria had weakened her, and she now exhibited symptoms of typhoid fever. Her immobility seemed "stately" to Sophia, who was heartened that she did not suffer, when in reality, Una was comatose. During the first week of April, Dr. Franco listened to her lungs and diagnosed "rapid consumption," an aggressive form of tuberculosis that would quickly prove fatal. Sophia steeled herself and informed

Nathaniel, who had been, she realized, in a "low state" for months. Unable to sustain the vacillations between "hope and fear. . . he sunk into fear alone." He could not speak to her, nor she to him, about what each one dreaded. "Words," Sophia told her sister Elizabeth, "would have driven us into deserts of dismay."[11]

On that "dim morning" of April 8, Nathaniel scribbled in his pocket diary: "God help us!" Until that day, he had provided a comforting normalcy for Julian and Rose amid the disruptive comings and goings of the doctor and others. For Rose, the greatest misery in the world was sitting still while Cephas Thompson painted her portrait. True, Mamma was unavailable, having sequestered herself with Una, but their sister could not be too seriously ill if Papa could steal a couple hours each day to write and then play games or take walks with the younger children. Even on the day Dr. Franco issued Una's fatal prognosis, Nathaniel began a game of whist, his ritual denial of grim reality. But he could not continue the ruse and put down his hand of cards, saying, "'we won't play any more'."[12]

And on that fateful April 8, Sophia dispelled desolation by writing "My Consolations." Una was a "precious, wondrous gift" whose "baby utterances" had contained "divinest wisdom," her severe judgments, evidence of "burning anger against wrong." "'Wrongness never reigns'," she would chant. But, as a child, she was melancholy: "'I am so tired I wish I could slip into GOD'." Had she wished to renounce life? Did she imagine embracing death, even then? And now, her "hair shorn of its tangled mass," her body emaciated, Una muttered, "'I am going to die now. There is no use in living—Good bye, dear'." Perhaps in death, Una would be as extraordinary as she had been in life. Perhaps Una required "no more mortal life to enter into . . . all wisdom and Love." Should Una die, she would not be separated from Sophia: "Our circles are so large because we have no end of being—no end of relations with all created existences." But even grasping at these consolations, Sophia admitted, "I do not know how I can bear it," should Una die.[13]

Sophia refused to abandon hope, her resilience burning itself into Julian's memory. She "gathered herself up after the blow" of Dr. Franco's horrific pronouncement. She took Elizabeth Story's advice and sought the opinion of another doctor—Dr. Lederer, also a homeopath—who rendered a different diagnosis. Franco was wrong. Una was dangerously ill, but her lungs were not fatally damaged. If her fever broke within forty-eight hours—and it did—she would recover. Sophia maintained a sleepless vigil at her daughter's bedside with "unfaltering strength and devotion." Her determination, Julian believed, saved his sister's life. Even Dr. Franco recognized that "the girl would undoubtedly have died under any other hands but the mother's. There is a sympathy that does by intuition what no medical skill can advise."[14]

The kindness of so many friends—old and new—had sustained Sophia during the thirty days when she slept fitfully in a chair beside Una, spelled only for a couple of hours each morning by Ada. Elizabeth Hoar, in Rome at this very moment, brought the balm of her saintly disposition. Anna Ward—"St. Anna certainly" as far as Sophia was concerned though having so oddly turned Catholic—called for five days in a row. The community of expatriates descended upon the Hawthornes' drawing room like a "cloud of good spirits." Elizabeth Barrett Browning brought broth for Una and compassion for Sophia. Elizabeth Story, who knew the anguish of nursing a dying child, hoped to entice Una to eat some jelly. And the steadfast Franklin Pierce, in Rome when most needed, supplied "palpable" sympathy. Nathaniel was finally beginning to fathom his friend's unfathomable losses and penned in his notebook, "the thing we dreaded did not come to pass," also acknowledging that "Frank" had "neither son nor daughter to keep his heart warm."[15]

Sophia had nearly become a member of another sisterhood, one comprised of women who had lost a child. Jane Pierce, Elizabeth Story. They were typical nineteenth-century women, mothers who grieved when malaria or typhoid or consumption took their children. But Una and Julian and Rose had survived the perils of childhood thanks to Sophia's "carefulness of living," her avoidance of any "danger that could be averted by mortal means."[16] Sophia was an enlightened mother, a wife in an exceptional marriage. Her children were, therefore, exempt from the illnesses and accidents that killed so many others. Or were they?

Once the crisis had passed, Una endured a protracted recovery. Her intermittent fevers became less frequent as April turned into May. Dr. Franco, still in charge of her treatment, demanded that Una "'do *nothing*'" but rest. Sophia quoted his emphatic orders for her sister Elizabeth: "'Do you hear, Miss Una? You shall not knit, you shall not read, you shall not talk. All you shall do is sleep and eat'." Though Sophia now judged Dr. Franco to be somewhat "impulsive" and worried that he might have damaged Una's constitution with too much quinine, Sophia was convinced that her daughter owed her life to homeopathic remedies. Had she been starved or purged in the hands of an allopath, surely she would have died.[17]

Sophia had put aside letter-writing during the months she nursed Una, but Ada continued her voluminous correspondence with Clay. The very week Una began spiraling toward death—that is, the same week Sophia noted how robust Ada had become—Ada wrote Clay not about Una's illness but about her own. Loathe to "trouble" him about her health, Ada nonetheless informed him of a cold in her throat and lungs, and "very happy" she was that this "sickness will probably be consumption," proof that her "tendencies to physical disease" were like Clay's. And then she announced her "duty to enlighten" him about past experiences with "I. A. W.," these initials sufficient to identify the man. Ada belatedly recognized that she had given the "appearance of sin," without actually sinning, by spending so much time alone with him in his study. She was now "convinced" that "I. A. W." harbored feelings for her that "did not resemble those of a brother." She realized only now that she should "have acted more decidedly . . . ." Armed with this new insight, Ada now acted "more decidedly" by treating Dr. Franco "rudely." When this behavior provoked his charge of "cruelty, just as people do in novels," her "conscience smote" her. Again she posed well-worn questions to Clay. Had she been "wicked"? Had Franco exercised a magnetic, "snake-like power" over her? How might she account for "the pleasure" which she "came to feel in his visits"? These queries would undoubtedly "trouble" Clay more than her disclosures about a cold.[18]

Determined to get answers, Ada confronted Franco. She conveyed to Clay a vivid, often verbatim account of her May 8 encounter with the doctor, visiting him, so she claimed, to obtain a prescription for herself and Sophia. Ada decided against taking Rose with her, ignoring the fact that this young "safeguard" had interrupted Franco's assault four months earlier, and ignoring insights so recently gleaned about her experience with "I. A. W." So she should not have been surprised that in the privacy of Franco's office, he "attempted to force his embrace" upon her, but she effectively fought him off, at last threatening to "appeal to Mr. Hawthorne to defend" her. Ada had delivered the *coup de grâce*. Dr. Franco "raved," called her names, and "swore: 'I *hate* you!' " When he composed himself and apologized, Ada demanded to know if she had ever given "him the slightest encouragement to hope I might return his passion." " 'Oh no!' " he responded; only his love had motivated unflagging persistence. Ada was "cleared of blame." No more a long-suffering victim of unwanted advances, she was a triumphant heroine. No one "should ever be able to put an evil construction upon the acts and words of your bride," she assured her fiancé.[19] She would leave Rome, return to Clay, and never inform the Hawthornes of the five-month melodrama of seduction that had transpired before their very eyes, though they failed to see it.

And nothing in Sophia or Nathaniel's written records indicates otherwise. On that fateful May 8—a Sunday—their separate pocket diaries each record that Ada, with Anna Ward, took Rose to Vespers at St. Peter's Cathedral. Neither Sophia nor Nathaniel mentions Ada's going on an errand to Dr. Franco's office. The Hawthornes' notebooks and letters give nary a hint of Franco's declarations and Ada's protestations. Regarding "Miss Shepard," Nathaniel noted only mundane matters, nothing amiss, no whiff of a scandal far greater than the one involving Louisa Landers. And about the doctor, Nathaniel cited his professional calls to the Hawthorne household and a story told by Franco himself: A man vulgarly accosted a woman at Carnival. When he refused to desist, "she drew the bodkin from her hair and stabbed him to the heart."[20] Franco apparently knew that unwanted sexual overtures could have lethal consequences.

And Sophia was also apparently oblivious to all that Ada so laboriously described to Clay. Had Sophia's "beauty making eye" been unable to see this lurid reality? Yes, but the nature of her blindness remains a mystery. Had Sophia been blind to all signs that her "daughter" (as Sophia at times called Ada) was being harassed? Had Sophia seen a "robust," never-healthier young woman when Ada was actually anxious, sick, and preoccupied? Had Sophia been unable to see Franco's lecherous character, placing her real daughter in the hands of a seducer? Or had Sophia been blind to the pathological person she had brought into her home, her heart, and her mind? Had she entrusted her children, confided details of her marriage, and channeled her very thoughts into a woman who was a seductress, deliberately deceptive, the creator of fictions as much the product of imagination as anything Nathaniel ever wrote?

Some elements of Ada's story are clear. Sophia was not alone in her blindness, for Ada's five-month ordeal, if such it was, went unobserved and unheard by the Hawthornes and the numerous daily visitors who crowded into the seven-room Rome apartment at 68 Piazza Poli. And Ada's account becomes credible by believing in her ability to be deceptive. She convincingly played the role of a governess whose only concerns were her duties. She remained mum about anything that might worry Sophia or, more to the point, anything that might lessen Sophia's opinion of her. Ada did not ask Sophia's advice about her potentially "wicked" behavior or request that she never be left alone with Dr. Franco. But by rehearsing her dilemmas with Clay—in many ways an unlikely audience for her troubles—Ada kept herself most coquettishly the focus of his attention during the period when she was erased from Sophia's. No longer did Ada enjoy "Mrs. H.'s" company, as she had when she cavorted with the "sisters" in Italian galleries and ruins. While Sophia's attentions were entirely absorbed by Una, Ada was a little bored, her boredom contributing to the delight she eventually took in Franco's calls, as she admitted to Clay.[21] Perhaps, during her first winter in Rome, her chatter about the Misters Akers, Bartholomew, and others had made Clay sufficiently jealous to confess his temptations to infidelity, thus upping the romantic ante and provoking her to play Dr. Franco as a sordid trump card. A complexly brash yet insecure woman, Ada continuously depicted herself to Clay as an object of desire. As such she remained the center of her narrative, a place that might have been occupied by Una, whose near-fatal illness was in some measure the result of Ada's lax supervision.

On May 25, the Hawthornes left Rome, Ada with them. Sophia was intermittently infirm, and Una remained feeble as the group made its way through Leghorn and Genoa, Marseilles and Avignon, Geneva and Lausanne. Finally, by the twenty-first of June, they arrived in Havre so that Ada might join the Thompsons who were returning to live in America. They all boarded the *Vanderbilt*, and Ada—the young woman who secretly endured, or provoked, or exaggerated, or imagined Dr. Franco's relentless pursuit of her—sailed away from Sophia.

Chapter 17

The Belleslettres Portion of My Being

After Ada and Clay married and joined the faculty at Antioch College, Sophia's assessments of her former governess were modulated by distance and a few months' time. She had eternally "endeared herself" for helping during Una's illness, Sophia wrote Mary, but Ada had been compensated handsomely for her service. She had been included in the Hawthornes' travels throughout Italy and their friends' society. Despite this generosity, Ada had spent too many hours writing to Clay rather than teaching Rose reading and arithmetic. Ada had "no affinity for children," Sophia concluded, aghast that Mary contemplated sending her sons to the college where Ada taught—Ada, who "was not fit to be a professor of anything"; Ada, who was "narrow" and full of "willfulness."[1] Had Sophia silently repressed these harsh judgments while Ada lived under her roof? Had Sophia finally realized things that Ada had concealed?

In years past, Sophia's letters or journals might have yielded answers to many of these questions. Not so while she was in Italy. With the death of her parents, Sophia's impetus to record every nuance of thought and feeling had departed, as had her obligation to inform and entertain with lengthy letters. And in Italy, she was too busy to correspond with her sisters. Her days were occupied with galleries, and churches, and ruins, and—until she put down her pen to nurse Una—writing in her journals. But these five volumes totaling 646 pages contain relatively little personal disclosure.[2] Many of the bits and pieces of Sophia's day-to-day life—her activities, her friends, even her health—must be patched together from the writing of others: Maria Mitchell, Harriet Hosmer, Ada Shepard (if she may be trusted), Julian and Rose (to the degree that their adult reminiscences are reliable), and Nathaniel himself. He had become the King of Journalizers, reigning with Sophia, the Queen.

Under Sophia's influences, Nathaniel had begun and finally mastered the art of insightful, often engaging accounts of daily experience. While abroad, the couple passed many an evening sitting across a table from one another, each spouse writing in her or his separate journal. Nathaniel was both proud and protective of the seven volumes, approximately three hundred thousand words, he had written in England, written with such a "truth-telling a pen" he could "never dare to publish" them in his lifetime. Once in Italy, Nathaniel undertook the "most sustained and detailed journalizing" of his life according to the editor of those notebooks, Thomas Woodson. The results were another seven fulsome volumes. While Nathaniel's journal entries document multiple facets of his life at a particular cultural and historical moment, they also record mean-spirited gossip. Take, for example, Nathaniel's account of a dinner with the artist Joseph Mozier when Margaret Fuller was their topic of conversation. Her "strong and coarse nature" had "always shown such a cruel and bitter scorn of intellectual deficiency," but her lover or husband (no one yet knew which) and father of Margaret's child, Giovanni Angelo Ossoli, was "this boor, this hymen without the intellectual spark."[3] Publishing such entries, he knew, would be impossible.

Sophia took her journals in a different direction, filling them with commentary on art and architecture, exercises in aesthetic criticism and theory that departed from guidebook conventions. The body, naked or clothed, was a proper object for artistic representation. Religious art was not idolatry but "embodied worship." Spiritual values were expressed in the colorful, tangible adornment of churches. The analytic, intellectual nature of these journals recalls the tone—if not the content—of her letters to Una from various points of sightseeing in England. Sophia's restraint may have been occasioned by her desire to cultivate similar emotional decorum in her daughter. But in England as well as in Italy, Sophia's motive for reticence might have been the recurring possibility of publishing her travel writing.

Decades earlier she had rebuffed Elizabeth's efforts to print portions of the *Cuba Journal* in the *American Monthly*, but Sophia permitted those letters from Cuba to circulate (an alternative to publication in the nineteenth century) among friends and strangers until she departed for England. Once there, even though Nathaniel ceded the palm of exceptional travel-writing to her, he insisted that Ticknor not construe this praise as a hint that she might publish her journals. Despite Nathaniel's warning, James T. Fields floated before Sophia, then in Italy, the idea of contributing to the *Atlantic Monthly*. She demurred, and when Fields proffered another invitation at the end of 1859, she refused emphatically: "Nothing less urgent and terrible than the immediate danger of starvation for my husband and children would induce me to put myself in a magazine or a pair of book covers." "Mr. Hawthorne," she insisted, was the "Belleslettres portion of my being." Sophia thereby avoided some domestic friction, for Nathaniel could not "tolerate a literary rival at bed and board," as he told Bennoch.[4]

The spouses had taken divergent paths in journalizing: Sophia's journals had become more impersonal, theoretical, and focused upon art; Nathaniel's, more personal, vivid, detailed and engaging. These differing directions actually converged upon the possibility of bringing private writing before the public. Sophia buried the idea, or rather, Nathaniel buried it for her. And Fields had also advised Nathaniel against contributing to periodicals. He must not jeopardize his career as a writer of fiction that had reached its apotheosis in the years immediately preceding departure for England. But Nathaniel needed money now. The Hawthornes had lived beyond their means in Italy, as Nathaniel knew they would, but he could not have foreseen how Una's illness would prolong that trip, making it far costlier than expected. He must return to "literary labor."[5] He must finish and publish the novel he had begun.

But which one? The "American Claimant," outlined in April of 1855 then laid aside? The "Ancestral Footstep," sketched in the spring of 1858 but a few months later before his interest drifted to a different "romance"? He spent July 14 "principally employed" in plotting it out and began it "in good earnest" twelve days later. Then "journalizing and describing new things" pulled him away from fiction, his writerly energies deriving from real rather than imaginary worlds. In September, he returned to "planning and sketching out a Romance" yet again. At the end of the year, he took stock of his effort: "Since November 25th, I have scribbled more or less of Romance every day; & with interruptions, from Oct. 26." And on January 30, 1859, he claimed to have "finished, to-day, the rough draft of my Romance."[6] This he intended to revise during the first six months of 1859, but Una's illness and the pull of his journal prevented progress. He decided that he would finish this Italian romance after he returned to Concord.

And so, after Ada had departed on the *Vanderbilt*, the Hawthornes boarded the *Alliance* and sailed from Havre to Southampton, planning to leave England in July for the United States and the quiet of the Wayside. But on

June 27, they went to London where they met with James T. Fields and his young, new wife, Annie. The Fieldses had married in 1854 and were now on the first leg of a lengthy trip that would take them to the Continent. Fields happily announced that he had negotiated for Nathaniel 600 from the British publisher Smith and Elder for a three-volume book. That tidy sum, which should preclude Nathaniel's having to draw money from his Barings bank account, was just the beginning of a lucrative arrangement, for Nathaniel could obtain an international copyright if he remained in England until the book was published. But the author did not react as might be expected to his publisher's good news. Rather, Nathaniel "talked nervously about his new romance, the muscles in his face twitching." Then, as Fields noted in his diary, Nathaniel "with a lowered voice" broached a subject that had already been decided: "he thought some time he might print his journal."[7]

Nathaniel had several reasons to be anxious rather than elated. The Hawthornes would incur additional expenses by remaining in England. He may also have been daunted by the obligation to produce a three-volume novel. This British format far better suited Anthony Trollope, whom Nathaniel had grown to admire. Trollope's novels, "written on the strength of beef and through the inspiration of ale," depicted people "going about their daily business, and not suspecting they were made a show of." And Nathaniel's journals were written with just that kind of Trollopean realism. Had such books "ever been tried in America," Nathaniel asked Fields.[8] The journals might earn money immediately while he coaxed the novel from his sluggish imagination. The lightning pace with which he composed his previous novels, published during that remarkably prolific three-year period before departure for England, was irrevocably a thing of the past. And to make matters worse, he had dug himself into a deep financial hole.

Nathaniel had succumbed to John Louis O'Sullivan's latest cockamamie scheme by investing, according to Julian's reminiscences, in Spanish copper mines which "could be bought for a song"—a $10,000 song!—"and would pay a thousand per cent, from the start." Nathaniel continued to be motivated by the desire to "gratify" O'Sullivan and the "hope"—contrary to all experience—"of at least getting his money back." In the fall of 1859, O'Sullivan, still American minister to Portugal, had gone on an expedition to borrow money, traveling first to Paris and then to London. In May of 1860, both men were in London and invited to dine at the home of Robert James Mackintosh.[9]

Perhaps hoping to hasten an account of her beloved "Uncle John," Una supplied her father with the beginnings of a letter about their meeting.

The dateline, salutation, and first paragraph are in Una's hand save for blanks left for her father to fill in: "I have seen Mr O'Sullivan, who went to Paris on _____ & returned on _____ and is going to America from Southampton on _____ & expects to see us there. The mines & floating dock are going on favorably, ..." But Una's wishful thinking about matters related to her godfather did "not quite hit the mark," according to Nathaniel who continued the letter in his own hand. Yes, he had encountered O'Sullivan at the Mackintoshes, but O'Sullivan "has not been to Paris at all," (a curious statement because on October 28, 1859, Nathaniel had noted receipt of a letter from O'Sullivan then in Paris). And about returning to America, O'Sullivan had made no decision. Nathaniel's next trip to London a week later prompted Una to inquire again about her godfather, but this time Nathaniel had even less to report. "I have very little to say on that *subject*," as Nathaniel referred to his business partner and longtime friend. He was not at his hotel when Nathaniel called, and soon thereafter O'Sullivan sent Nathaniel a note announcing his departure for the Continent. "I think you had better intermit writing to him till we hear more," Nathaniel informed Una.[10]

Nathaniel's terse summation of O'Sullivan's whereabouts held something back, but what? He had been unavailable to Nathaniel although they were high-dollar investors together. Their relationship had grown murky, O'Sullivan's actions mysterious. But Nathaniel had been frank with his family about the "mines." However sanguine Una was about them, Sophia, who leaves no record on the matter, would have been troubled, particularly if she knew the amount her husband had "invested," for as Ada had observed to Clay, caution in money matters was "natural to Mrs. H . . . but Mr. H is naturally impulsive." Nathaniel found it bothersome to "think so much about saving in trifling matters," (and also, it appears, in large matters). Sophia, however, was ever on guard dealing with tradespeople; she always feared being cheated, perhaps a Peabody habit for it was one she shared with Mary.[11]

Adding to Sophia's financial concerns during this period was her cherished home in Concord. While the Hawthornes had been abroad, Nat Peabody and his family lived at the Wayside, maintaining it on a day-to-day basis, but they had recently relocated in anticipation of the Hawthornes' return. By mid July, Sophia realized she would be remaining in England for the better part of another year. Her husband must "bury himself" in writing if his book was ever to be completed, Sophia wrote Elizabeth, who might have been the likely person to move into the Wayside, if only she had the resources to care for it. Another option, renting the house, was repugnant to Sophia. Strangers might meddle with her things. Reluctantly, she decided to shutter the house. Bronson Alcott could keep an eye on it.[12]

And then, on August 2, Horace Mann died. Without husband or reason to stay at Antioch College, Mary would move to the Wayside, a comforting place to alight with her sons while she adjusted to widowhood. Horace had left her in "independent in circumstances." With a $58,000 inheritance she had money for upkeep, repairs, and even some improvements. Chairs would be recaned and the roof patched, repairs that Nat with his perennial debts had not been able to afford but which Mary could undertake at her own expense. She proposed buying a lovely oak chair and renovating the space over the library to accommodate a live-in-servant, and Elizabeth could make a temporary home with her. Sophia was delighted to have both sisters together at the Wayside, and she was relieved that Mary could manage daily expenses and supervise inescapable upkeep. But Sophia could not countenance additions or improvements, or anything that smacked of luxury. She was "counting the sixpences," and, she reminded her sisters, the Hawthornes had never been, nor would they ever be, extravagant.[13] Sophia was clearly unaware of the extent of Nathaniel's profligate arrangements with "John."

Even in death, Horace appeared to be the more successful husband, if success is measured by the size of an inheritance. But in dying, Horace had shown himself to be a less than devoted husband to Mary. In Sophia's words, he had been ensnared in the "serpent-folds of R. D.," his niece Rebecca Pennell Dean, the first woman appointed to the Antioch faculty with the same pay and privileges as her male counterparts. She was also "false and cunning" and had wedged herself between Mary and Horace. It was Rebecca, not Mary, who was with him at the end; Rebecca, to whom he spoke his last, intimate words: "you have been to me the kindest, dearest, gentlest, tenderest, faithfulest, daughter, sister, friend, almost wife." Yes, Mary had many reasons to grieve, and knowing that her husband had never ceased mourning his first wife, she had his body buried with Charlotte in Providence, Rhode Island. Ever dutiful and self-effacing, Mary would always believe she was unworthy of Horace's love. And her mourning would not find its solace through belief in an afterlife, however that might be defined. She lacked that "'passport into Elysium' a compensating imagination, which you," she wrote Sophia, "enjoy so richly." Sophia, however, believed that only a veil separated Mary from Horace, and Sophia hoped that her sister might experience the "transparency of that veil." Unable to offer consolation, Sophia's sympathy was infused with her awareness of the loss she had just narrowly escaped. The wall of stoicism Sophia had built around her emotions crumbled. She wept for her sister, for her nephews, and for her own unaccountable good fortune. Luck, not "carefulness of living," had spared Una.[14]

And Sophia also had reason to weep for her husband, who was obviously failing. She attributed his present "low state" to Una's illness, the ordeal having turned his hair white. But he blamed his indispositions, both physical and mental, on the "lassitudinous Roman atmosphere." Nonetheless, he claimed that "no place ever took so strong a hold of my being as Rome," though he had been "miserable" and "languid" there. His attitude toward the Eternal City was inconsistent, if not downright contradictory, as were his thoughts on England. He railed against John Bull yet thought he might like to spend the rest of his life in England. All those years away from his native land had fractured Nathaniel's sense of belonging. By the summer of 1859, he was an unsettled man, unwell and aging, disabled by ennui, as he confessed in his journal: "I lack energy to seek objects of interest, curiosity even so much as to glance at them, heart to enjoy them, intellect to profit by them."[15]

In this condition, revising his very rough draft was nearly impossible, though the pressure to do so was enormous. By the end of July, even though the Hawthornes had moved to Redcar and rented a house with that all-important study, Nathaniel wrote sporadically. He had not "touched the work" for so many months that it now appeared worthless, in need of "many amendments." But by the second half of August and into the beginning of September, he sustained a routine, writing nearly every day until two or three in the afternoon, but making little headway. So he broke with his habit of never discussing a work-in-progress with a friend, and on September 8, solicited Henry Bright's opinion. A *"faun* committing murder"! Bright guffawed at the very premise. Nathaniel then turned to Sophia. On September 10, he handed her what he had completed to date, abandoning another practice, that of seeking her reaction only when a novel was finished, then reading it aloud to her, basking in her effusive praises, and bolstering his confidence before sending it to his publisher. Never before had he solicited her help with a half-finished work, his estimate of these three hundred handwritten pages.[16]

What Sophia read was a story set primarily in Rome and revolving around Nathaniel's typical quartet of two male and two female characters: Kenyon, an American sculptor and Donatello, a youthful descendent of the fading Italian aristocracy; Miriam, an exotic artist with a mysterious past, and Hilda, a naïve young American copyist, her triumph a copy of the Beatrice Cenci portrait. Miriam contemplates confiding her troubled background to Kenyon, before finding him coldly unresponsive. Though her secrets are never fully disclosed, some hints are embodied in her menacing former model, who had "compelled her, as it were, to stain her womanhood with crime" and the subject of her art: women "acting the part of revengeful mischief towards man." And art provides hints about Donatello because he resembles the sculpted faun by Praxitiles in the Museo Capitoline, but the young man keeps his ears covered, refusing to satisfy his friends' curiosity about his nature. A light-hearted, simple, instinctive being, Donatello loves Miriam unquestioningly though she rebuffs his affection. One evening, the foursome ambles to the Tarpeian Rock. Kenyon and Hilda depart, but sensing that Miriam is burdened by "some sorrow or perplexity—which, perhaps it would relieve her to tell me about" Hilda returns to her friend. The "strange persecutor" has meanwhile approached Miriam who issues an unspoken request to Donatello, and Hilda witnesses "the whole quick passage of a deed."[17] Donatello struggles with the model, hurling him off the precipice.

Hilda's weighty secret distances her from Kenyon and dissolves her love for Miriam. Kenyon goes to Florence for the summer where he meets Donatello, now living in his ancestral home. The "Count," as he is known there, has become a somber man, lacking his former familial affinity for Nature and her creatures. Kenyon sculpts Donatello's bust and unwittingly depicts an expression of guilt. The two men then go to Perugia where they meet Miriam. Beneath the statue of Pope Julius III, Kenyon witnesses the duo experience a species of absolution, joined eternally by their complicity in murder. Hilda's knowledge of her friends' crime has become such a burden that she seeks to cast it off in St. Peter's Cathedral. Kenyon, now back in Rome, observes this "daughter of the Puritans" leave a confessional and fears she will become a Catholic. He is in love with her, and though she demonstrates no interest in him, he helps her to acquire compassion for Miriam. The novel reaches its denouement when Hilda remembers an errand to the Cenci Palace she had promised to undertake on Miriam's behalf. Hilda disappears for several days, and at Carnival, Kenyon encounters costumed penitents—Miriam and Donatello—who assure him of Hilda's safe return. When she does, she accepts Kenyon's proposal of marriage; the couple plans to return to the United States.

Amid many references to the art Sophia had seen with her husband in Italy, she would also have discovered in this story his recurring ruminations upon the burdens of a guilty conscience. By placing this story in the Hawthornes' present-day Catholic Italy, Nathaniel could incorporate vehicles for confession and expiation impossible in his fiction set in Puritan New England. Sophia would have recognized that this story-in-progress incorporated their discussions about a religion that, in the words of the narrator, "so marvelously adapts itself to every human need." Her defense of "embodied worship" explains Hilda's devotion to the Virgin: "It was not a Catholic, kneeling at an idolatrous shrine,—but a child, lifting its tear-stained face to seek comfort from a Mother!" Catholic reverence for depictions of a holy child, "Mother," and "Father" meshed with Sophia's exalted domestic values, even though Nathaniel fretted about Una's attraction to "forms and ceremonials, and sanctified places of worship." Kenyon voices a similar concern to Hilda, who retorts: "'Why should I not be a Catholic, if I find there what I need, and what I cannot find elsewhere?'" Her words echo Sophia's rhetorical question: "Must we not go back to this adornment again, since it arose from the demand of the soul, and the soul demands it still?"[18]

Sophia pored over these manuscript pages, so laden with the Hawthornes' recent experiences and acquaintances. Mozier's vicious remarks about Margaret's haughtiness and Ossoli's defects surface in Miriam's attitude toward Donatello, with his "maimed or imperfectly developed intellect. Alternately, she almost admired, or wholly scorned him." William Wetmore Story's "magnificent statue of Cleopatra" is Kenyon's *chef d'oeuvre*. Nathaniel confessed as much in his preface as well as to having "laid felonious hands" upon the work of other expatriate sculptors. Louisa Lander's bust of Nathaniel, distorting him into a virile, more youthful version of himself, suggests, but to opposite effect, Kenyon's bust of Donatello, "spoilt" with the sculptor's errant stroke. Louisa as well as Harriet Hosmer animate Nathaniel's creation of Miriam and Hilda; each is "an example of freedom of life which it is possible for the female artist to enjoy at Rome."[19]

But Hilda and Miriam also resemble Sophia's "sisters"—Hatty, of course, as well as Maria Mitchell, Isa Blagden, Charlotte Cushman, and Emma Stebbins. As Miriam explains to Kenyon,

> It is a mistaken idea which men generally entertain, that Nature has made women especially prone to throw their whole being into what is technically called Love. We have, to say the least, no more necessity for it than your-selves;—only, we have nothing else to do with our hearts. When women have other objects in life, they are not apt to fall in love. I can think of many women, distinguished in art, literature, and science . . .who lead high, lonely lives, and are conscious of no sacrifice, so far as your sex is concerned.

Miriam's statement makes Kenyon despair of winning Hilda's heart. He laments that "'she has no need of love!'" No need of *his* love, for he knows Hilda loves Miriam. To his question about her nature—"'who and what is Miriam?'"— Hilda's retorts, "'I love her dearly . . . and trust her most entirely'." Miriam repeatedly proclaims to Kenyon the depths of her love for Hilda: "'She was all Womanhood to me.'" Separation from Hilda becomes the most devastating consequence of Miriam's crime: "'My lips—my hand—shall never meet Hilda's more!'" This loss affects Miriam to her core: "'I threw away my pride, when Hilda cast me off.'" Never before had Nathaniel portrayed a female character with such passion for another woman. But, where Kenyon is concerned, Hilda "lingered on the hither side of passion," rejecting even his friendship when she "fancied that he sought to be something more!" Her feelings for Kenyon are as cold as her decision to marry him is surprising. But in this story, heterosexual marriage is itself a surprising, if not shocking, institution. Like a clergyman officiating at a wedding ceremony, Kenyon declares to Miriam and Donatello: "'The bond betwixt you, therefore is a true one, and never—except by Heaven's own act should be rent asunder.'" The story draws to a close with a parody of Margaret Fuller's definition of the highest form of marriage as "pilgrimage towards a common goal"; Miriam and Donatello, the "remorseful Man and Woman, linked by a marriage-bond of crime . . . set forth towards an inevitable goal."[20]

While sin and secrecy, guilt and atonement perversely unite this heterosexual couple, no perversions attach to the bond between Hilda and Miriam. The Hawthornes had observed similar relationships among women, some of them Sophia's dear companions during her many a happy day in Rome and Florence. Hatty's masculine appearance prompted Nathaniel's bemused observation: "I never should have imagined that she terminated in a petticoat, any more than in a fish's tail." This mingling of genders and species did not alarm him, although earlier in his career, he had created Beatrice Rappaccini, a character who monstrously, poisonously breeched the boundaries between human and plant life. Although Kenyon—the sometimes author-surrogate—questioned Miriam's nature, Nathaniel's new story was populated with hybrids who were not *ipso facto* monsters. Yes, the model, with his "buffalo hide" and "goat-skin breeches" evokes the "antique Satyrs." But the "Faun of Praxiteles" is neither "man nor animal, and yet no monster, but a being in whom both races meet, on friendly ground." And "Donatello's sympathies . . . linked (and by no monstrous chain) with what we call the inferiour tribes of being." Even Hilda lives high above the street in a Tower among doves; she *is* "The Dove," "as if she were born a sister of their brood."[21] These metaphorical affirmations supply, perhaps, an index to feelings about Sophia's "sisters" and their choices, opinions not explicitly found in the Hawthornes' journals.

Also missing from their personal records were any traces of the ordeal Ada had described to Clay: her misery over Franco's unwanted advances, her doubts about her innocence, and the abyss of self-recrimination that drove her to a Roman church. Absent this knowledge, Nathaniel uncannily reproduced and amplified aspects of Ada's story in his Italian "romance." Miriam is the object of pursuit by two men. "'I wish he would not haunt my footsteps so continually'," she says of the "'amiable and sensual'" Donatello who is the mirror image of the model, the "sinister personage who had dogged her footsteps." She nonetheless feels "'pity'" for this torturer, just as Ada had, oddly, pitied the doctor. "'I would not give you pain,'" Miriam tells the model, whose relentless stalking nearly deranges her: "'I fear I go mad of it! Sometimes, I hope to die of it!'" And Hilda, whose knowledge transforms her expression into that of the enigmatic "Beatrice Cenci" portrait, descends into similar despair: "'It seemed as if I made the awful guilt my own. . . . I grew a fearful thing to myself. I was going mad!'"[22] Hilda's words, Miriam's words—so similar to each other's—seemed ripped from Ada's letters. And Ada, like her fictional counterparts, found comfort through the Catholic Church.

Whether Sophia knew Ada's story, whether she recognized it in her husband's draft will remain mysteries. But Sophia's intervention with Nathaniel's manuscript is indisputable. Her forty-two markings range from trivial spelling corrections to subtle, but significant alterations. Her superior knowledge of Italian, for example, prompted her to correct "con-tadina" to "contadine." In other places, she made her husband's writing more accurately representational. It was "a coat of stucco and yellow-wash" not *white*-wash on a building. She cancelled the more symbolic "black" and inserted the more realistic "iron" as the descriptor for a cross. "Graydon," as Nathaniel had called the sculptor, was crossed out with "Kenyon" inserted in Sophia's hand. Perhaps discarding *Gray*don was also the work of an artist who did not want that righteous character made even duller by coloring him with so drab a hue. By draining these connotations, Sophia's choices ever so gently aligned her husband's story with the ordinary, "daily business" of the real world.[23]

When Sophia returned the manuscript to Nathaniel, he had still not settled upon the book's focus. On the tenth of October, he presented Fields with an array of titles: "Monte Beni; or the Faun. A Romance," and three other variations on that title, each including the words "Monte Beni" and/or "Faun." He also considered four different titles: "Miriam [or Hilda, or Donatello, or The Faun]; a Romance." And then there was "Marble and Life/Man; a Romance." Each title suggested an emphasis on a different character or subject, but on October 14, Nathaniel nonetheless penned the preface to his book, though still uncertain of its direction, claiming the novel was "not yet finished by 60 or 70 pages." Three days later, he sent

Smith and Elder "as far as page 429," this produced by dint of "horrid toil," as Sophia explained to Elizabeth. Finally on November 8, Nathaniel recorded: "Wrote till 5 minutes of 12, & finished the last page of my Romance. 508 manuscript pages." He bundled what he had written and sent it to his English publishers. Taking Fields's advice, he called the book "The Romance of Monte Beni."[24]

The basic elements of this narrative had been established by the time Sophia scattered her emendations throughout forty-nine of its fifty chapters. Though its first three hundred pages were written over the course of fourteen months, after Sophia's intervention, the book moved swiftly toward submission. Nathaniel accepted most of her changes, many of them adjusting his writing to a more accurate representation of the real world, writing more in tune with the journal-writing that was her forte and that had become his strength as well. And thus he fulfilled his contractual obligations for three volumes by larding his "romance" with pages from his Italian notebook.[25]

But Nathaniel feared this was not the kind of book that Smith and Elder wanted. They did not like the title; did they also dislike the book? Would Smith and Elder renege on the promised £600? That worried Nathaniel more than whether he had pleased them. And about the title, when the book appeared in America, it must be called "Saint Hilda's Shrine," or so Nathaniel said in December while he was working on the proofs. That month he conceded to Smith and Elder their choice of title for the English publication, assuming that the publishers knew what drew their readers. Neither Sophia nor Nathaniel would insist on anything that might risk sales. But Sophia was irate when "Transformation; or the Romance of Monte Beni" was published in England on the February 28, 1860: "These stupid people have taken the name 'Transformation' leaving out the 'The'." To her mind, the absence of that article "altered the significance," as she explained to Elizabeth; "we all wanted"—Sophia's "we" emphasizing her understandable sense of ownership over the final work, titled "The Marble Faun, a Romance of Monte Beni." As such it was published on March 7, Nathaniel having tacked an additional chapter on the end of this, his first American edition. He had heeded criticism that too many threads of plot had not been sewn up in "Transformation."[26]

Given its sporadic and unfocused method of composition, no wonder *The Marble Faun* was an unsuccessful novel, according to some reviewers. In addition to complaints that its conclusion was inconclusive, critics thought they had already met Hilda as Phoebe in *The House of the Seven Gables* and Miriam as Zenobia in *The Blithedale Romance*. With proprietary vigor, Sophia led the charge against Henry Chorley, whose review appeared in the *Athenaeum* on March 3: "Why do you run with your fine lance directly into the face of Hilda?" How dare Chorley claim that "Mr. Hawthorne was so absorbed in Italy" that he neglected to tell a good story! And about Chorely's contention that the novel ended "too vaporously," "Mr. Hawthorne had no idea" that Kenyon and Hilda "were destined for each other. Mr. Hawthorne is driven by his Muse, but does not drive her." In truth, Nathaniel's Muse had departed him. In her place was Sophia, who brought her own energies, talents, and proclivities to the task of publishing this book. As Nathaniel told John Lathrop Motley, she "speaks so near to me I cannot tell her voice from my own."[27]

Nathaniel's own judgments of *The Marble Faun* were various and contradictory. He wrote Ticknor, "if I have written anything well, it should be this Romance," but a few days later, he wrote Fields that the book was a "tissue of absurdities." The critics also took opposing sides, but over reasons for the novel's failure. Some complained that *The Marble Faun* contained too much guidebook realism, others that it was too full of fantasy. Motley was among the few who liked "the air of unreality." But Bright persisted in lambasting the "half man, half child, half animal" Donatello. There was "something a little—just a little—*wanting*" in that character, resulting in a "feeling of half development, half idiocy." Bright's wife was annoyed, too, by Nathaniel's "plagiarism if not theft" of a story she had told him: "[Y]ou've stolen the description of Miriam from *her* Jewess," Bright complained. When someone suggested that Nathaniel had based Hilda on his wife, Sophia denied any resemblance. "Mr. H had no idea of portraying me in Hilda," Sophia insisted.[28] Perhaps being equated with a copyist raised Sophia's ire. Copying, after all, had constituted just a fraction of her artistic career. If someone had noticed her resemblance to the original artist, Miriam, Sophia might have been flattered.

During the months preceding publication of *The Marble Faun*, Sophia had rallied every ounce of strength to nurse Una and to help her husband with his book. Nathaniel believed Sophia was "unweariable in sightseeing" while en route to England. But once there, she had begun to crumble; she suffered headaches and coughed persistently. In mid October, upon the advice of Dr. Stuart Sullivan—a homeopath, of course— the Hawthornes moved from Redcar to Leamington, a spa city deemed beneficial for a "delicate person," where she undertook a regimen of walks and cold baths, to little avail. By March 1860, acute bronchitis forced her to remain in bed for seven weeks. Fortunately, Sophia's trusted Fanny Wrigley had returned to the Hawthornes' employ. She was "General of my army," Sophia wrote Elizabeth, and Una, who turned sixteen on March 3, assumed the duties of a nurse. Despite feeling the effects of malaria, she cared for her siblings and mother, even answering Sophia's letters for her. Sophia waxed eloquent to her sister Elizabeth about this daughter's survival of near-fatal illness. Una had "climbed up the Hill of Difficulty and caught sight of the City of the great King." She was now, as ever, "'all my fancy painted her'."[29]

But Una was also "inconsolable," she confided to her Aunt Elizabeth, about the frequent postponements to her family's departure for the United States. Crossing the Atlantic during the late winter fogs was out of the question so the Hawthornes must remain throughout the spring—"the season of dread," as Una called it, when Sophia did become seriously ill once again. In April, now living in Bath, she was bedridden for a week with a high fever and aches. Her health had worsened by May, when Nathaniel regretfully informed Fields that he and Annie could not call on the Hawthornes. Sophia's "housekeeper and factotum," Fanny Wrigley had also become ill "while Mrs. H. herself is in the hospital." Nathaniel had lived through "another winter of shadow and anxiety," this year on account of his wife. He ruefully recognized that there was "no air in England fit for her to breathe." Sophia pegged hope for recovery on the "dry hot . . . and clear cold of America."[30]

Anticipating her return to Concord, Sophia grappled with the Hawthornes' finances. The Wayside would require more repairs and improvements than Mary had undertaken. If there was enough money, the cramped house should be expanded so that Nathaniel would have a study and the children would not be forced to share bedrooms as they had when they were so much younger. But financial reckonings were not forthcoming from Fields. Nathaniel had regularly complained to Ticknor about his partner's unavailability. Fields's failure to respond to Nathaniel's letters was particularly irksome because of pending arrangements for the Fieldses to sail to America with the Hawthornes. In late April, Fields finally wrote Nathaniel, who chidingly responded: "I really began to fear you had been assassinated. . . ." Ticknor was more likely to allay Sophia's financial anxieties, so in mid May, she applied to him for a full accounting: "It is very long since you have told us whether we are bankrupt or not dear sir." Her inquiry conveyed an urgency lacking in her husband's casual request to Ticknor several months earlier: "I should be glad if you could give me some approximate idea of what my investments amount to. But do not put yourself to any trouble about it."[31]

Sophia's financial future was unclear as she readied herself for departure from England. The Hawthornes moved from Bath to Liverpool and into the familiar quarters of Mrs. Blodget's boarding house. They bid a reluctant goodbye to Fanny, and on June 16, 1860, they boarded the Cunard steamer *Europa*. Captain Leiten, who had commanded the *Niagara* seven years earlier, was once again in charge of the ship carrying the Hawthornes across the Atlantic. Also sailing on the *Europa* were James and Annie Fields and Harriet Beecher Stowe.[32] These women, each in different ways, were harbingers of the life Sophia was to find in America.

Chapter 18

He Needs Change Immensely

The lovely Annie, a member of the blue-blood New England Adams family, had been just twenty years old when she married James T. Fields, who was seventeen years her senior. She immediately distinguished herself as the ideal wife for this ambitious man, presiding with aplomb over gatherings of literati in the Fieldses' Boston home while cultivating her own career as a writer. During the twelve-day crossing from Liverpool to Boston, Sophia began to cherish Annie as a dear friend, though Harriet Beecher Stowe never found a place in Sophia's heart. Stowe, one of the "d _____ d mob of scribbling women,"[1] and Sophia remained politely companionable while aboard the *Europa*, their conversations probably avoiding that most volatile topic, abolition.

During Sophia's seven years abroad, slavery had become the flashpoint of American politics. Repatriation to Liberia, an African country founded specifically to welcome slaves from America, was a solution to the problem of slavery for some, a racist sham for others. How could individuals be "*repatriated*" to Africa when they had been born in America? While abolitionists quarreled with one another about the path to their common goal, the discord between Northerners and Southerners became so heated that disunion loomed as an appealing possibility. Establishing the confederate states as a separate nation might avoid violent conflict, but abolitionists recoiled at this expedient. And emancipation was an idealistic though disquieting concept, even among some of William Lloyd Garrison's followers, who foresaw inevitable "amalgamation," the pseudoscientific term for interracial unions. While abolitionists opposed slavery *per se*, they were tethered to their times and to assumptions about racial inferiority or supremacy.[2]

Despite differences over strategy or philosophy, abolitionists recognized that decades of nonviolent action had not improved the lot of the slave. Moral suasion had not prevented renditions. Frederick Douglass's eloquent narratives, Garrison's fiery antislavery *Liberator*, as well as Stowe's own international best seller *Uncle Tom's Cabin* converted many to the abolitionists' cause, but in 1854, the Kansas-Nebraska Act had, nonetheless, become the law of the land. Because settlers might now choose whether or not to permit slavery, many abolitionists as well as so-called proslavery "border ruffians" moved to the new territories, each group hoping to prevail. The result was guerrilla warfare. "Bleeding Kansas" was the grim consequence of failed peaceable means to eradicate, or even contain, slavery, and John Brown became the man around whom antislavery Concordians rallied.

One of the most enigmatic figures in American history, Brown has been venerated as a martyr to the cause of abolition and despised as a violent monomaniac. He possessed genuinely nonracist attitudes, yet he was a dishonest sheep-trader and a failure at business. While he lived his conviction of racial equality in apparent humility on his upstate New York compound, he grandiosely compared himself to Oliver Cromwell. Believing that he was God's instrument in the eradication of slavery, he led the attack against that family in Pottawatomie, Kansas, convinced this unprovoked violence was justifiable, even divinely mandated. Brown then undertook plans to capture a federal arsenal in Harpers Ferry, a city located at that time within the borders of Virginia. He enlisted African Americans in all phases of this raid, assuming, that once weapons were dispersed among slaves, they would rise in rebellion. In order to execute this plan, Brown needed money and other forms of support, both of which he found among New Englanders who perhaps knew about the Pottawatomie massacre. These men were Franklin Sanborn, a recent Harvard graduate who had begun a coeducational school in Concord; Theodore Parker and Thomas Wentworth Higginson, the transcendentalist ministers who had fomented protest against the rendition of Anthony Burns; Samuel Gridley Howe, who agreed to supply Brown with rifles, ammunition, and cash; George Stearns, a wealthy factory owner; and Gerrit Smith. Because William Lloyd Garrison adhered to his pacifist principles, he was not made privy to the plan Brown hatched with The Secret Six, as these abolitionists came to be known.[3]

In May of 1859, Sanborn brought Brown for a second time to Concord. There he addressed Concord's notable citizens, among them Ralph Waldo Emerson, Henry David Thoreau, and Bronson Alcott. Brown discussed the situation in Kansas, hinted about the brewing raid on the Harpers Ferry arsenal, and won over these transcendentalists. They "sanctified," according to Brown's biographer David Reynolds, this man who otherwise might have "remained an obscure, tangential figure—a forgettable oddball." This sea change in attitude among former subscribers to civil disobedience is calculated by Alcott's biographer John Matteson, who notes that Alcott "refused to wear wool for fear of committing an offense against the sheep . . . . And yet, when Brown stood before him at Concord Town Hall not as a defrauder of sheep but as a killer of men, Alcott lauded him as a hero." Brown's listeners saw only the quintessentially self-reliant man who acted upon principles higher than those the law allowed.[4]

On the night of October 16, Brown commenced his raid. He and his band captured the arsenal but did not ignite an uprising of slaves. Among the many ironies of this bloody fiasco, the first man killed by the raiders was a free African American who had the misfortune to be working on a train that crossed paths with Brown's men. The raiders were soon surrounded by a local militia and then by the United States Cavalry, led by Brevet Colonel Robert E. Lee with J. E. B. Stuart as an aide-de-camp. By October 19, Brown had been captured. The casualties included his sons Watson and Oliver, whose agonized dying occurred before their father's steely gaze. Justice was swift, and Brown was hung on December 2.

By then, The Secret Six had fallen into disarray, most of them fearing for their lives as conspirators in treason. Parker, dying from tuberculosis, had departed for Italy even before the raid; there he safely continued to defend Brown's actions. Smith became mentally unhinged and was briefly committed to an asylum. Howe issued a public disclaimer, before fleeing to Canada, as did Stearns. Sanborn hid from federal investigators in the attic of the Wayside, thanks to Mary Mann, before he fled to Canada. Higginson alone among the six remained Brown's highly vocal supporter, as did those who compared his execution to Christ's crucifixion.[5]

But from the Hawthornes' vantage, then on the other side of the Atlantic, John Brown was the frightening herald of a country moving toward full-scale civil war. The Liverpool *Mercury's* coverage of the "so-called Abolitionist invasion of Virginia" announced its implications for "the frightful insecurity of a social condition based on Slavery." Just days before Brown's attack, Nathaniel had mused in his journal about the unnatural bond between the North and the South, wondering why Americans loved the Union at all: "everything falls away except one's native State."[6] And during that fateful fall of 1859, while Brown planned and executed his raid on Harpers Ferry, Sophia helped her husband to complete *The Marble Faun,* its pages bound together thematically by her own abhorrence of vengeance and retaliation, even when redressing a heinous wrong.

For Sophia, John Brown could only personify her opposition to violence as a political strategy. She had excoriated Parker for his role in the Burns' affair, blaming him as the cause, albeit remote, of Burns's death. Abolitionists, Sophia wrote Elizabeth, "tear *each other* to pieces in Boston." They were intolerant of those within their own ranks who espoused different methods. They did not talk "in the spirit of Christian love." And "devoutly believing . . . that not the smallest wrong should be done to arrive at the greatest good," she argued that the "slave holder is really more to be pitied than the slave because his soul is so sunk in sin that it is fearful to think of the ages of suffering he must endure before he can become a child of GOD." But Sophia knew that parsing the slaveholders' ethics would trigger Elizabeth's accusation of indifference to the slaves' suffering.[7]

Sophia would find no sympathy for her ideas with her sisters or with Concord's vocal citizens. But Mary's sequestration of Sanborn at the Wayside—the Wayside, which Sophia had wanted to keep from strangers who might meddle with her things!—was ample demonstration that political tensions were about to invade all corners of her life. Quarrels with Mary about slavery now revealed a reversal in their positions about the possibilities for just war. More than a decade earlier, Mary had withheld from her children fairy tales and myths because they might promote aggression, but at this moment she herself promoted aggression through the persons of Sanborn and his cohort. Discussions with Mary were "marred with a few shots from her political gun," and Sophia returned fire, maintaining that she was not wedded to doctrine, as was Mary. Sophia announced that her objectivity on the subject of slavery derived from experiences abroad. But more than a decade earlier, Sophia had defended aggression as natural and useful in the service of good causes. Then she had exonerated Pierce for his involvement in the Mexican War, claiming if "adjusting differences" peacefully failed, war might be waged "conscientiously."[8] By 1860, she had forgotten or abandoned that theory, or deemed it inapplicable to the current conflict.

Gone was the time in Sophia's life when the most heated arguments with her sisters focused on what to feed little children. Gone, in fact, were Sophia's little children and her assumptions that they were exempt from harm because of her exceptional mothering. Gone was the "imp & angel" Una; she had become a rebellious, volatile sixteen-year-old who distanced herself from her mother. Gone was "Hercules in miniature." There was nothing diminutive about Julian, who had celebrated his fourteenth birthday while crossing the Atlantic; his voracious appetite would soon be diverted from food to girls. Gone was Sophia's "Baby." Nine-year-old Rose could be vocal about her displeasures over the United States, a country that had not yet been her homeland. And gone was the man Sophia had married. The prolific writer with a keen imagination and excellent constitution had been replaced by an unhealthy, sometimes confused, irrevocably unsettled man. The nation's plight was far less important to Sophia than the turmoil in her family.

As soon as the Hawthornes landed in Boston on June 28, 1860, they made their way to Concord. Chaos greeted them at the Wayside. Nathaniel was overwhelmed by the confusion of unpacking, and Sophia took charge, moving "serenely & deliberately," according to Mary, who was there to meet them. Now living in a farmhouse just outside of Concord, Mary had taken far better care of her sister's home during the year she had lived there than had Nat during his six-year residence.[9] But even Sophia's "beauty making eye" could not be blind to the deficiencies of the Wayside, particularly after having lived in *bona fide* palazzos. In August, renovations and expansions began, as did major expenditures.

But more worrisome to Sophia than her decrepit house was her elder daughter. Una now claimed to have been happy "in the midst of Art & Beauty, and the luxurious quiet & seclusion of a European life" but would *"never* feel *perfectly* well" after her "delightful illness," as she oddly referred to malaria in a letter to Aunt Lizzy. During her first weeks at the Wayside, she confided to her cousin Richard Manning that "rebellious feelings" assailed her. She longed to be "out of this killing place" and her doctor concurred: she must be as "free as air." On July 25, Una wrote Richard that she had improved by "keeping away from home (!) . . . but though I appear, & am, perfectly well while I do as I please, (did you ever know such a willful & headstrong young woman as I am?) there is a certain little group of events & sights & sounds that . . . make me faint & sick. . . ."[10] Una was obviously troubled, but what precisely was the root of her problem? Recurring malaria? The aftereffects of quinine? Mental instability, manifested by depressive and manic mood swings? Or the perfectly sane desire to fashion her own identity without scrutiny or expectation? Sophia's anguished speculations must have been multiplied by being excluded from Una's confidence. The sanctuary of domestic bliss had become her daughter's "killing place."

No sooner had the Hawthornes returned to the Wayside than they were fleeing it. Early in August, Nathaniel took Una to Montserrat for a visit with Elizabeth Hawthorne. In September, father and daughter went to Portsmouth to stay with Horatio Bridge for a week. Simply being away from home was not, in fact, a remedy for what ailed Una, who displayed "violent symptoms." There was no hiding or minimizing her condition. Even Franklin Sanborn, now back in Concord, knew that Una's "strange behavior" had escalated into "brain fever," that imprecise but suggestive nineteenth-century term for derangement. Although Nathaniel chose to attribute Una's illness to the consequence of malaria that "physicians foreboded and forewarned," she was not taken to a physician. Neither an allopath nor a homeopath was consulted. Rather, Una was put in the hands of a practitioner of "medical electricity," an early form of electroshock therapy. Nathaniel informed Ticknor that Una's symptoms "yielded at once" to the application of a galvanic battery and "to the incantations of a certain electrical witch," Mrs. Rollins in Beverly, Massachusetts. She diagnosed Una's problem, Nathaniel informed Pierce with some relief, as a complaint of the liver and heart, worsened by Roman fever, and controllable with medical electricity, diet, and exercise. By the end of September, Sanborn announced what the Hawthornes' family, friends, and many Concordians believed: Una had been "cured of her insanity."[11]

Desperate circumstances had required desperate measures. The severity of Una's condition can be calculated by how public her symptoms and how extreme her treatment. Una's "brain fever" or, put less euphemistically, her "insanity" also provides an index to Nathaniel's illness: he, who had nearly succumbed to a "brain fever" after the trauma of his mother's death; he, who exhibited aspects of his daughter's malady, both depressive and, perhaps manic (if one considers his reckless loans and investments). While Una had been devolving in Portsmouth, Sophia had penned her husband—"My beloved" and "My crown of glory"—newsy letters laden with solicitude. She also encouraged Una about her health. It would improve slowly after that "Roman death-struggle," but when Una improved abruptly after Mrs. Rollins's treatment, Nathaniel pronounced that he would "recommend medical electricity for all diseases." So early in October, he too "took the battery" as Sophia put it.[12]

Medical electricity did not, however, restore Nathaniel's health and vigor. While renovations on the Wayside lagged and bills mounted, he remained idle. On December 17, he wrote to his friends in England: to Bennoch, that he was "meditating a new Romance" while his study was being readied; to Bright, that civil war was on the horizon. The "Union is unnatural," he claimed, wondering if England "might be induced to receive the New England States back again."[13] This joke, if such it were, would hardly have passed muster among patriotic Concordians. Three days after Nathaniel wrote these two letters, South Carolina seceded from the Union, as did six more Southern states in January. The Civil War had begun.

The commencement of conflict had a more "beneficial effect" on Nathaniel's mood than had medical electricity. On May 26, he wrote Horatio Bridge that his spirits were no longer "flagging woefully" because "it was delightful to share in the heroic sentiment of the time, and to feel that I had a country—a consciousness which seemed to make me young again." He even regretted being "too old to shoulder a musket," though he was relieved that Julian was too young to do so. Nathaniel's patriotism took him only to the point of personal rejuvenation. He found no cause sufficient for his son to fight, and Sophia thought Julian should not be required to drill at school. Sanborn was readying his male pupils for the possibility of conscription, and Sophia irately asked him to lessen her son's "untimely military discipline," a request that became moot when the boys' weapons were confiscated for Union soldiers. She had mounting reasons to dislike Sanborn, that Wayside trespasser and gossip about Hawthorne family matters whose involvement with the Harpers Ferry carnage was amply signaled by his physiognomy: "sharply cut, small features, and the small head of a cruel person." She had determined that Sanborn, the "much lauded angel is part—well,—the opposite of angel."[14]

Sophia held consistent, albeit unpopular, opinions about the war and some of its heroes. Her husband's judgments vacillated, however, his mood swinging like a pendulum sometimes during the space of a day. In another letter written on May 26, this one to Ticknor, Nathaniel observed that the "invigorating effect" of the war "begins to lose its influence." It was "rather unreasonable," he recognized, "to wish my countrymen to kill one another for the sake of refreshing my palled spirits. . . . ." Two months later, he was again in the doldrums. If he could "catch the infection," he would go off to war himself, he wrote to Bennoch. His depression was obvious, even to Alcott who observed him avoiding others as he walked among the trees behind the Wayside. His isolation "excite[d] a pitying affection" in Alcott, a man so opposed to Nathaniel's politics. Una too saw that her father was "unwell." And Ticknor knew that Nathaniel was "low in tone and spirit," for so did Sophia describe her husband when she asked Ticknor to send a bottle of Madeira. Nathaniel needed some stimulation, but he considered himself too poor to buy the wine.[15]

Sophia was adamant that Nathaniel should indulge himself. Because a change of scene was her panacea for illnesses that were not of the body and could not be cured by homeopathy, she contrived a reason for the first of a series of Nathaniel's trips away from home. *Julian* had been indisposed and needed to recuperate at Pride's Crossing, a farm in Beverly, Massachusetts the town where Nathaniel's sister, Ebe, lived in a boarding house. For a couple of weeks, father and son could visit with Ebe when they were not fishing, swimming, and otherwise escaping the troubles making their way into Concord. Soldiers trickled back after the humiliating Union defeat at Manassas during the First Battle of Bull Run. And tragedy had struck with Fanny Longfellow's gruesome death. A flame had ignited her dress, and she died from burns. Her husband was so badly injured trying to save her that he could not attend the funeral. Sophia was "smitten to the heart," and she sought comfort from her "dearest Peri," one of Sophia's many fond names for Annie Fields. Nathaniel's absence from home freed time for Sophia to write the young woman: "I do no justice to my Love and memory of you, when I remain so long silent. I think of you very often and I am very impatient to see you." Annie provided a charming counterpoint to "all the trials" burdening Sophia. The "heaviest" of these, she candidly admitted to her husband, was seeing him "so apathetic, so indifferent, so hopeless, so unstrung." She urged him to stay away as long as possible, because she had been "weighed to the earth by my sense of your depressed energies." He must restore his spirit, never mind the cost.[16]

Routine expenses and renovations on the Wayside were indeed depleting their funds, and Nathaniel's method of dealing with finances was haphazard, at best. He would submit invoices to Ticknor, requesting that tradespeople, quarterly bills, and taxes be paid from his account, never inquiring about his balance or demanding a reckoning. When he realized that the expenditures for the Wayside would be $2,000 rather than the estimated $500, he admitted he ought to have sold the house rather than renovate it. His fortunes improved slightly when Horatio Bridge made two $500 payments with an additional sum for interest on the $3,000 he had borrowed from Nathaniel in 1854. But Nathaniel still could not resist dispensing money to needy friends and secretly commissioned Ticknor to give Zach Burchmore $50: "I do not wish for my wife to know how I throw away my money." And on the subject of money thrown away, on December 3, 1861, Nathaniel opined to Pierce about O'Sullivan, who was currently hawking artillery to various European heads of state. Though he remained optimistic about those copper mines in Spain, Nathaniel realized this friend and business partner—the man who had been such an important part of Una's life, and Sophia's—was "always on the verge of making a fortune, and always disappointed." Nathaniel concluded, in what would be his last extant comment on John Louis O'Sullivan: "But perhaps I am as much too despondent, as he is too sanguine."[17]

Nathaniel's tower-study, completed by December of 1860, was not the boon to his writing he had banked on. The winter of 1861 turned into spring, and the war, he claimed to Ticknor, interrupted his "literary industry." When summer yielded to fall, he earned a bit here and there by plucking material from his English experiences for publication in the *Atlantic Monthly*. He complied with Fields's "exhortations" to write by beginning to "think seriously" about a story, the war now creating "a happy state of mind," so he wrote Bright. Because Nathaniel could not harness his fleeting energies, he asked Fields to announce the story "conditionally, or hypothetically," for he would submit it only after the last sentence was written. But as the winter of 1862 marched toward spring, Nathaniel admitted to Bridge that he was only "pretending to write a book," for he was "mentally and physically languid."[18]

Nathaniel's depression prompted Sophia to plan another trip for him. Though he denied to Fields the "necessity of going to Washington as Mrs. H supposes," Nathaniel admitted to Bridge that a "change of scene," an excursion to battle sites and the nation's capital "might supply the energy which I lack." On March 6, Nathaniel left Concord equipped with the beginnings of a letter home that Una sketched out for her father. Among the sentences she had prepared were "I feel a good deal better" and "I do not feel any better." Papa could simply cross out the one that did not apply when he was ready to mail it. Nathaniel traveled with Ticknor first to New York, then to Philadelphia, and on to Washington, DC. For the first and only time in his life, Nathaniel adopted the role of a war correspondent, touring and then writing about Harpers Ferry, Fortress Monroe, Newport News, and Manassas. In Washington, he met, and, according to Sophia, influenced Abraham Lincoln. "Thy great presence," she wrote, might convince him to "make a stand against agitators, insane haste, fierce abolitionists, fanatical republicans." After their meeting, the president made a speech containing an "immortal message," that filled Sophia with "unbounded satisfaction," for an "angel"—her husband—had inspired Lincoln.[19]

Inflating the influence of her "dearest Love" upon the president of the United States surely bolstered Nathaniel's confidence, as did Sophia's affectionate letters. "Darling beloved, how I love thee words can never tell," her declaration followed by this advice: "Stay as long as thou canst. . . . I cannot have thee return yet. I am not at all ready—and I have not yet written to thee all I wish to write." Letters from Sophia and her daughters were filled with cheering details of the masquerade and ball that enlivened the Hawthorne household during Nathaniel's absence. Una's costume was well worth the pain it caused Sophia, whose hand ached from sewing it. Una was so fetching that an anonymous "partial individual" considered her the belle of the ball, though she awarded that distinction to her little sister. Wearing a crown and carrying a silver wand, Rose was disguised as Titania, her short dress covered with spangles. Rose dutifully wrote James T. Fields to thank him for "procuring this dress." Fields was also responsible for Julian's costume, and a grand one it was. At not quite sixteen, the five-foot eight-inch Julian cut an impressive figure as the Duke of Buckingham in a rented cloak, lacy doublet, collar and cuffs fastened with sapphire, silk stockings, and buff boots. Una wished her brother owned this costume; in her opinion, he was "really born to be a Duke."[20]

Sophia was delighted to see that her husband was filled with "electrical" energy when he returned to Concord on April 6. His trip had worked wonders on his mood, and he immediately discharged a piece for the *Atlantic Monthly*. On May 7, Sophia listened as he read aloud what he titled "Chiefly about War-Matters, by a Peaceable Man." Later that day, he sent the manuscript to Fields, whose business was interrupted by Henry David Thoreau's funeral on May 9.[21] James and Annie, along with the Hawthornes and many other notables in American letters, paid their respects to a man who had traveled a long political distance between writing "Resistance to Civil Government" in 1849 and "The Last Days of John Brown" in 1860. There was no escaping the bloody cost of abolition as battles raged in the New Mexico territory, Virginia, Arkansas, Tennessee, and Missouri.

Almost two weeks passed before Fields responded with his objections to Nathaniel's article. His sympathy for Southerners would "outrage" the *Atlantic's* readers. References to "Uncle Abe" and description of Lincoln's "awkwardness & general uncouth aspect" should be deleted. Nathaniel made some grudging revisions, ruing this "miserable humbug of a world" that could not bear the "truth" and claiming it was "difficult not to lapse into treason." While he omitted four paragraphs about Lincoln, he retained much that would rile his audience, feigning censure of his own controversial comments by inserting footnotes in the guise of a critical editor.[22] The result was a curious piece of reporting by an author whose private remarks about the war had been mercurial and, at times, insensitive. His remarks now for public consumption were similarly confusing—prescient but obtuse, large-minded but snidely combative.

Nathaniel described, for example, the "atmosphere of the camp and the smoke of the battle-field" to be "morally invigorating." The Union soldiers, he claimed, "enjoy a life of hardship, and the exhilarating sense of danger—to kill men blamelessly, or to be killed gloriously." Yet he pitied the Southern prisoners, young men who did not understand why they were fighting and who were more courteous and respectful than their Northern counterparts. Nathaniel was "struck" by "the immense absurdity that they should fancy us their enemies." His reverence for their humanity seemed misguided at best, willfully ignorant at worst, to Northerners who believed that Confederate soldiers had perpetrated the most heinous atrocities at Bull Run the year before. More shocking was Nathaniel's contemplation of a Confederate victory, which he considered while he lauded (again) those Southern "dynasties" which produced "genial courtesy"; he decried (again) "the awkward frigidity of our Northern manners," here noting specifically "the uncouthness of Uncle Abe." The "editor" (Nathaniel) chastises the "Peaceable Man" (Nathaniel) for being "premature in his kindly feeling towards traitors." The "editor" had earlier noted a "lack *reverence*" in the not-so-flattering description of the president. The "editor" also thought the "Peaceable Man's" fealty to state over nation was "reprehensible." And the "editor" was aghast at condemnation of John Brown: "Can it be a son of old Massachusetts who utters this abominable sentiment? For shame!"[23]

For shame, indeed. After "War-Matters" appeared in July of 1862, Nathaniel was reproached for an "incoherent" piece that "puzzled both friends and foes of human liberty," according to Sanborn, who spoke for many. Attacks upon Nathaniel were met by Sophia's vigorous defenses of him: "I cannot let anyone be saucy about him to me," she warned Elizabeth, who was habitually "saying caustic and disagreeable things" about Nathaniel. And if she persisted, Sophia would cease all correspondence and end all "intercourse" with her. This did not, of course, occur, and when Nathaniel left Concord in August—a vacation with Julian in Gouldsboro, Maine, timed nicely to escape the criticism of his neighbors— Lizzy came to breakfast at the Wayside. She was spending some time in Concord at her other sister's home.[24]

While Nathaniel was away, Sophia also entertained another, far more agreeable and interesting visitor than Elizabeth. Major General Ethan Allen Hitchcock was the grandson of the legendary Revolutionary War hero and member of West Point's class of 1817. During his military career, he had been commandant of cadets at his alma mater, an officer in the Seminole and the Mexican wars, commander of the military division of the Pacific, and the author of a report revealing that the government had defrauded Indian tribes. Hitchcock was also an accomplished amateur musician and collector of music for the flute. But it was Hitchcock's interest in the esoteric that captivated Sophia. In 1846, he published, "The Doctrines of Spinoza and Swedenborg," a work that was well received by Theodore Parker. When Hitchcock resigned from the army in 1855, he immersed himself in literature and mystical studies and published books on alchemy and Christianity. His *Christ the Spirit* appeared in 1861. "Man loves truth instinctively and hates falsehood," Hitchcock wrote. "Give him truth, indeed, and if he understands it, he will drink it as the water of life." When Sophia met him, he had returned to military duty as a special adviser to Abraham Lincoln.[25]

Soldier, philosopher, writer, musician: General Ethan Allen Hitchcock was a veritable Renaissance man, though his esoteric interpretations were dismissed by Sam Ward, Henry Wadsworth Longfellow, and James Russell Lowell, to name a few of his disparagers. But Elizabeth was attracted to any unifying system of thought and to any person who propounded such. Sophia was similarly beguiled and read his *Christ the Spirit* in the beginning of August. On the 14th of that month, she wrote her "dearest husband" about her conversation with this "gentlest and most modest person, with a beautiful dome of a head, with a look of sensibility, delicacy and quiet," a man who agreed "nearly entirely" with her ideas. The next day in another letter, she elaborated on her rapport with Hitchcock: "In this charming apartment I received my general," she wrote Nathaniel:

> We entered upon unspeakable mysteries. . . . the most beautiful light of life beaming from his face at my recognition of his ideas, and at any expression of mine which showed a unity with his—or rather with truth—As the ineffable cannot be spoken except in certain relations, I shall not try to repeat what we said on spiritual subjects.[26]

While Sophia enjoyed these rapturous conversations, she urged her "dearest husband" to find a better, more comfortable place to stay in Gouldsboro. Her "dearest love" should stay away until mid-September.[27]

When Nathaniel returned to the Wayside on the fourth of the month, Sophia proclaimed to her journal, "Oh infinite felicity to have him safe again." Joy at their reunion notwithstanding, she departed with Rose barely two weeks later for an extended trip to Boston. There Sophia dined with that "rose & lily," Annie, and drank "ambrosia" in the comfort of her friend's fine home. Sophia conveyed details of these delightful experiences to her husband, "dearest love," along with Fields's good report about Nathaniel's newest article for the *Atlantic Monthly*. The "world is wild with rapture" about "Leamington Spa," she chirped. Nathaniel must continue to "dig in that mine of gold and jewels," his readily marketable English experiences, while his creative works were gestating slowly, if at all. So Nathaniel started shaping something book-length from his English notebooks while he churned out a couple more articles for Fields, though Nathaniel was "rather despondent about them."[28]

He was, in fact, despondent about most things. He would ascend the stairs to his study, lock the door behind him, and try to write. At dinnertime, he would descend and force himself to eat a bit of potato. Confiding in Annie, Sophia continued to blame her husband's decline upon his fears for Una while they were in Italy. Nathaniel, however, blamed his malaise on the war. But though he wrote Bennoch that it was impossible "to possess one's mind in the midst of a civil war," Nathaniel had claimed to Bright that war "invigorates every man's whole being." Sophia took the latter assertion to be the truth in her husband's case. By the end of 1862, she hoped that another trip to Washington with Ticknor might cheer Nathaniel. Additional exposure to war matters might spark his energies, as it had the year before.[29]

But instead, Nathaniel remained at the Wayside, published two additional articles in the *Atlantic Monthly* and, submitted an edited version of his English notebooks to Fields in April of 1863. During the previous seven months, Nathaniel had received good notices for pieces drawn from his record of life in England, a much safer subject to present American audiences than idiosyncratic impressions of the Civil War. *Our Old Home*, as he immediately titled his new book, should be well received and earn good money, especially since Fields secured the English copyright from Smith and Elder. Nathaniel raised a firestorm of controversy, however, by deciding to dedicate the book to Franklin Pierce, a gesture that might undermine its sales. In mid-July, Fields counseled Nathaniel against this dedication, though he left the decision to his author. While Annie admired this "noble" fidelity to his friend, she knew Nathaniel needed "all that popularity can give him in a pecuniary way for the support of his family."[30]

Then Sophia urged her husband to vacation with Pierce in the White Mountains later that summer. Cost factored into Nathaniel's decision against this trip, and Pierce could not leave Jane, who was mortally ill. Sophia rued Nathaniel's lost opportunity for diversion; "he needs change immensely," she confided in Annie. Nathaniel did take a shorter excursion to visit Pierce in Maine during Independence Day celebrations. Pierce was the featured speaker on the fourth of July, and his anti-Lincoln speech, delivered a day after the hard-won Union victory at Gettysburg, irrevocably rendered him a political pariah. During this speech, Nathaniel sat on the stage beside his old friend, a sign of loyalty that was reaffirmed by refusal to withdraw the dedication of *Our Old Home:* "TO FRANKLIN PIERCE, AS A SLIGHT MEMORIAL OF A COLLEGE FRIENDSHIP, PROLONGED THROUGH MANHOOD, AND RETAINING ALL ITS VITALITY IN OUR AUTUMNAL YEARS, THIS VOLUME IS INSCRIBED." As Nathaniel explained to Fields, there would be no book to dedicate if Pierce had not appointed him consul to Liverpool.

Pierce's current unpopularity was itself reason for Nathaniel to "stand by him. I cannot," Nathaniel declared, "merely on account of pecuniary profit or literary reputation, go back from what I have deliberately felt and thought it right to do." His devotion to Pierce was demonstrated all the more poignantly several months later. On December 2, Jane Pierce died. At her funeral, Nathaniel huddled beneath an umbrella with Pierce, the men attempting futilely to escape a cold New Hampshire rain. That evening they returned to Andover, where Pierce would recall the in-estimable comfort derived from the "unutterable sympathy and sorrow" of his "constant and cherished friend."[31]

Elizabeth Peabody was among the many who saw only profoundly mis-guided values in Nathaniel's allegiances. Her outrage was countered by Nathaniel's lengthy retort. He reviewed the peccadilloes of abolitionists— among them Mary's hiding Sanborn in the Wayside attic and cited, albeit secondhand, "your friend Gen Hitchcock" and his predictions, now real-ized, about the "horrible convulsion" of war. And in a concluding shot, Nathaniel made his own position on Lincoln unmistakable: "I despise the present administration with all my heart." No matter Nathaniel's position on Pierce and the War, *Our Old Home* sold briskly, although—or, perhaps, because—it managed to offend those on the other side of the Atlantic. By the end of 1863, Una saw her father weary of "abusing" mail from people in England and Scotland on account of his portrayals of them. Not all of Nathaniel's descriptions of English life were so biting. There was that touching account of a diseased child who demanded succor from an almshouse visitor. Nathaniel had recorded this incident in his English notebooks and revised it for public consumption by hiding his identity behind the third person. Defending Nathaniel to Elizabeth, who had dared to question his "humanity," Sophia asked, "who was that, do you suppose, who took up in his arms that loathsome disgustful child?" Overcoming his "hatred of touching or being touched" should demonstrate to Elizabeth Nathaniel's capacity for compassion.[32]

Vindicating her husband to her sister, Sophia did not hint at matters that might have turned Elizabeth's censure into pity. These dark worries, Sophia brought to Annie. After mentioning in passing that *Our Old Home* had provoked many "scolding" letters from England, Sophia divulged details of Nathaniel's violent illness one night in late November and his complete inability to write. Sophia trusted Annie to keep "sub rosa" that Nathaniel feared "bedevilment."[33]

Chapter 19

Have I Done My Duty?

For several years, Sophia had lived with signs of Nathaniel's breakdown: his depression punctuated by moments of self-proclaimed "invigoration"; his contradictory, confused statements; his inability to bring forth fiction. Whatever ailed him could not be cured by homeopathy or the battery. A "change of scene" was the only remedy Sophia persistently prescribed for her husband. But travels with Una, and more frequently with Julian, then with Ticknor, and recently to visit Pierce had not staved off Nathaniel's increasing "bedevilment," as they now dared to call his malady. And although Sophia repeatedly suggested and often arranged his change of scene, not once did she accompany him on his quest for vigor. While he was away, she would write solicitous letters to her "dearest husband," addressing him with the archaic "thees" and "thous" of their courtship correspondence. But she did not urge him to return to her arms. She advised him instead to stay away as long as possible, to indulge himself at the shore or in the mountains. Perhaps the specter of his disintegrating mind and body was too painful for her to observe, too ugly for a "beauty making eye" to see.

Coinciding with Nathaniel's steady decline was Sophia's deepening affection for Annie Fields. She was "beautiful," and Sophia told her so without the slightest intention of "flattery." But Sophia was not beautiful, and any attractiveness she may have once possessed was long gone. In Italy, Ada had marveled that "Mr. H.," with his "yearnings for perfection and beauty everywhere," seemed "entirely satisfied" with Sophia who was "particularly plain" and without "a single pretty feature." And some of her features had become downright unsightly. A few teeth had been pulled, and those that remained were discolored from the gallic acid used by the dentist. Sophia was unavoidably aware of her appearance, thanks to a "frightfully unpleasing picture of poor me" that was taken in December of 1861. How she regretted, she told Annie, that she would not be remembered for "a little comeliness."[1]

Annie's good looks, magnificent clothing, and elegant Back Bay home were antidotes to the gloom that hovered over the Wayside. Her visits there were rays of light, and Fields told Nathaniel that Annie thought it "worth twenty visits elsewhere to sojourn under your roof. Long ago she fell in love with Mrs. Hawthorne and it does her a world of good to go to Concord." Sophia and Annie bridged their time apart with letters, Annie's now lost. "Moonlight," "Muse," and "Western Peri" were among Sophia's pet names for her, this last salutation suggesting by way of allusion the nature of their relationship. In ancient Persian mythology, a Peri was a fairy-like creature, angelic or evil, but by the nineteenth century, she signified only a beautiful, spiritual being, and as such, Lord Byron fashioned his Peri in *Childe Harold*. In the prologue to that epic poem, the author-surrogate and title character describes his feelings for her:

> Young Peri of the West!—'tis well for me
> My years already doubly number thine;
> My loveless eye unmoved may gaze on thee,
> And safely view thy ripening beauties shine:
> Happy, I ne'er shall see them in decline;
> Happier, that while all younger hearts shall bleed
> Mine shall escape the doom thine eyes assign
> To those whose admiration shall succeed,
> But mixed with pangs to Love's even loveliest
> hours decreed.[2]

Annie was twenty-nine, when Sophia, twenty-five years her senior, asked "Western Peri": "Can we have too much of true love I should like to know?" In the same letter, Sophia explained that Nathaniel was unable to visit the Fieldses in Boston, his fragility evidence of the ravages of time. At the age of fifty-nine, his body was failing far more precipitously than Sophia's, but her health had been precarious in England, and she had not shaken the pulmonary disorder that had felled her there. At times, she was forced to wear a respirator, which made her look like a "new species of pug dog," as she told Elizabeth. Sophia might take comfort knowing that she "would escape the doom" of witnessing her Western Peri's "beauties" vanish, anguish Sophia was not spared with her husband.[3]

Sophia declared her love for Annie with passionate effusions the likes of which had characterized her correspondence with Nathaniel. "My darling," Sophia wrote her, "how I lose you in the great spaces, and how all I wish to say to you is lost in the silences and—the absences—and how I could not be consoled, if it were not that all eternity is before us." Sophia confided her "sacredest emotions" to Annie, adding coquettishly, "it is your own fault that I can, you know, so do not blame *me*." This "naughty attracting power" distracted Sophia from daily chores as well as contemplation of her dear General Hitchcock's esoteric "truths": "you draw me away from all these, and I am obliged to babble to you" and to scold, when "naughty little invisible Peri" was nowhere to be found. Annie was the recipient of grandly philosophical thoughts as well as trivial observations simply because Sophia loved her "immeasurably."[4]

Sophia's relationship with Annie was as complicated as it was intense. The young woman was, after all, the wife of Nathaniel's publisher, as Sophia coyly acknowledged. Referring to Fields with *his* pet name, Sophia wrote, "My darling [Heart's Ease must not be jealous that I call you so. I do not intrude on his kingdom]." Did Annie keep from James her friend's "[SUB ROSA]" confidences about Nathaniel's "bewilderment"? Did Una, only nine years younger than Annie, intrude on *Sophia's* kingdom? Annie was one of Una's few companions, for she found none at Sanborn's school, where her mother permitted her to participate only in gymnastics and dance, activities beneficial to a young woman's circulatory system. Lacking daily obligations, intellectual challenges, and purposeful activities, Una could only "hope on," as the Reverend Channing had advised her years before, "and not despair" of finding her purpose in life.[5]

But the eighteen-year-old Una had not found her calling. By that age, her mother had already begun cultivating art as her passion and vocation. By that age, Una's neighbor Louisa May Alcott had aspired to a literary career, one she interrupted to nurse Union soldiers. In December of 1862, Sophia had helped Louisa prepare for her departure, and Julian had escorted her to the train that brought her to Washington, DC. Amid unsanitary hospital conditions, Louisa was determined to "make the soldiers jolly," but her service was quickly curtailed when she contracted typhoid fever. In February of 1863, she returned to Concord by train where, by coincidence, she encountered Una. Louisa rested her head upon Una's "shoulder all the way, looking ghastly, and uprolling her eyes, while she was like a sheaf of flames in Una's arms." Once home, Louisa lay mortally ill. She flailed on the floor, plagued by hallucinations, "haunted by scenes and men," as Sophia wrote Annie. When the crisis had passed, Bronson Alcott wrote: "That was our contribution to the war and one we should not have made willingly had we known the danger and the sacrifices."[6]

The heart-wrenching vigil for Louisa surely recalled to Sophia the one she had kept for Una in Rome, but Sophia did not draw that comparison in any written record that survives. Perhaps Sophia did not want to see any likenesses between Louisa May Alcott and Una Hawthorne, anything that might suggest that Una could do more for the war effort than sew for the troops. And Una had been inspired to do much more by Thomas Wentworth Higginson, whose nephew Storrow Higginson was an occasional visitor at the Wayside. Reverend Higginson's lecture about "Cromwell & his Ironsides"—an allusion to John Brown—was "a splendid discourse," Una wrote her Aunt Ebe, for he "showed us what our spirit of action ought to be." But Una did not engage in meaningful activity. Instead, she frittered her time away with frequent trips here and there, to her aunts Ebe or Mary, to the Lorings or the Badgers, and of course, to the Fieldses where she chatted with Annie about clothing and purchases of silk braid for a dress and gray cloth for a jacket. So often was Una a guest in the Back Bay house that, when she left her ivory paper cutter there, she directed Annie to retrieve it from "the little escritoire in *my* room." Sophia recognized that her elder daughter seemed to have two homes, something that created a tiny bit of friction and prompted a request to Annie that they discuss, "in the Palace of Sincerity," Una's numerous defections from the Wayside.[7]

Sophia's younger daughter was also welcomed by the Fieldses and to Rose's great relief. In an early letter to Annie, one of many to come, Rose lamented, "I never have anyone to play with me." Sophia could not resist inserting a postscript to correct Rose's "melancholy cry for companionship" by pointing out that she herself was an available playmate. And no, Rose did not suffer from "chronic nervousness," as Annie erroneously alleged, for the child was obviously relaxed with her, attending the theater—at the age of only nine, as Rose triumphantly wrote her father—and obtaining everything she wanted from the Fieldses.[8] She had them to thank for her Titania costume and for making the masquerade such a gleaming memory.

Julian, too, was indebted to the Fieldses, and not just for renting his Duke of Buckingham costume. Their contributions to his daily wardrobe conspicuously changed his appearance. Sophia gushed to Annie that the ice skates they gave him were "shining blades," veritable "jewels." While Julian came to expect such generosity from Annie and James, Nathaniel worried when his son borrowed ten dollars from Fields. "An Uncle (and your kindness places you in the same position) is a very dangerous member of the family," Nathaniel wrote Fields, who had assumed the avuncular role permanently vacated by O'Sullivan. Julian must never "be a borrower," Nathaniel declared nonetheless abetting his son's ability to borrow by instructing Fields to charge this debt to the Hawthorne account. Julian had become adept at evading responsibility. He absented himself from school on April Fool's Day, as Rose gleefully informed her father. Her "great giant of handsome" maintained his physique with a prodigious appetite that awed and amused his father, who noted that Julian could not keep his "insatiable maw" from Jane Pierce's delectable pies while they were visiting the Pierces.[9]

Sophia considered her son to be "simple hearted and childlike" even after she had evidence to the contrary. She knew he might indulge in "frolic and carelessness" instead of fasting and prayer, as the president had requested on September 26, 1861, after the Union's disastrous loss during the First Battle of Bull Run. Hopes had been dashed that the Civil War would be won quickly; sacrifices would be expected from every citizen. But while the Second Battle of Bull Run raged, Julian vacationed in Gouldsboro "dutifully" honing his epistolary skills for his mother's benefit by recording his pleasures at the shore—swimming, fishing, eating delicious chowder, cavorting with members of the opposite sex. Sophia was delighted that he enhanced his verbal descriptions with minute pictures of sites and people. He was becoming an excellent sketch artist.[10]

Sophia responded to Julian's letters with her own which included edifying details of conversations with General Hitchcock. Sophia did not, however, mention the General's military career or his present worries about Pope's army and McClellan's leadership. She elaborated instead upon Hitchcock's private virtues; he was "as modest as a young girl of spotless purity and as profound as a seer." As the mother of a son approaching adulthood, she seized opportunities to praise propriety and blame others when Julian was deficient in that area. Sanborn and his school had transformed her son into a *cavaliere servente*" who commented "upon flirts and coquettes like an experienced man of the world." Perhaps it was too painful for Sophia to use the English word "lover" in the same sentence with her "sacredly folded bud"—Julian!—who was all innocence before his return to Concord.[11]

While Julian was enjoying himself with his father in Gouldsboro, Samuel Staples—a tailor by trade who had become Concord's sheriff and jailer—was busy acting as a recruiter. He wanted Julian "for the war" and came looking for him at the Wayside. Sophia kept this worrisome fact from her son, but she wailed about it to Nathaniel, adding that Staples had "also enquired for thee!" She was relieved that "[b]oth my treasures are out of his reach," for Staples refused to believe that the strapping Hawthorne lad was really sixteen, two years younger than the legal age for conscription without parental consent. This, the Hawthornes would never give, and Sophia's attitude toward Julian set her apart from many friends and Concord acquaintances, who permitted, even encouraged their sons to enlist, despite the enormous personal costs.[12]

Lidian Emerson, notwithstanding her persistent grief over the loss of little Waldo, would send Eddie to war, but not to preserve the Union. That cause was not worth his life, but abolition—that was another matter. Like other mothers of her ilk, she engaged in an obstructive strategy by withholding permission for an underage son to enlist. If Lincoln hoped to muster troops, he must free the slaves. But by September of 1862, when emancipation was proclaimed, Eddie's health and eyesight were too poor for him to serve. And Eddie had heard sobering words from none other than John Murray Forbes, that longtime abolitionist who deployed his wealth to support John Brown's raid on Harper's Ferry. Forbes's son Will (who would later marry Edward's sister Edith) was then in combat, and Forbes spoke from his heart as a father when he reminded Edward that he was an only son: "I am not half the man I was, since Will went off to war," Forbes confided.[13]

Like the Forbeses, the Hoars were a family with abolitionist *bona fides* reaching back decades. But by September of 1862, they understood the seismic shift in commitment required to move from endorsing abolition in theory to sending one's son, perhaps to his death, in order to free the slaves. When Elizabeth Hoar's nephew Sam wanted to enlist at the age of seventeen, his family did not grant him permission. But that did not stop him. "Sam Hoar has run away to the war," Sophia noted in her diary on September 3. With Bob Higginson, another classmate at Sanborn's school, Sam went to Portland, Maine, where—as luck would have it—they encountered the vacationing Nathaniel Hawthorne who informed the boys' families of their whereabouts. Their plan temporarily foiled, Sam nonetheless soon enlisted with the Massachusetts 48th and served in Louisiana through 1863 when he returned to Concord. Bob became a lieutenant in the 5th Massachusetts (Colored [as it was called]) Cavalry. Their bravery and determination to serve meant nothing to Rose, who was convinced of her brother's superiority to them: "Compare Sam Hoar with Julian Hawthorne. I will not aggravate myself."[14]

Later in the week of Sam's flight from home to enlist, Sophia wrote Nathaniel again. Wedged between other bits of news, she remarked: "Capt

Prescott's troops have typhoid." This captain—George Prescott—was the son of Timothy and Maria Prescott, the Hawthornes' closest neighbors while they lived at The Old Manse, and Maria had assisted Dr. Josiah Bartlett, another ardent abolitionist, when Sophia gave birth to Una. Typhoid would now spell death for a quarter of George's men, and it was a disease that did not discriminate between Union and Confederate soldiers who camped in filth and waste and ate contaminated food. These vile conditions were but one reason why George exclaimed, "I hate war," his parents' long-standing ideals no match for what he witnessed. While on furlough in Concord, he agonized over his duty, and his deliberate decision to return to the front was an act of courage. He would fight at Gettysburg, advance to colonel, and take a fatal bullet leading the Massachusetts 32nd on June 19, 1864. "Have I done my duty?" he asked before dying.[15]

Sophia was in regular contact with the Ripleys, another family to grieve over a son gone to war. Samuel Ripley had been the Hawthornes' landlord at The Old Manse, and during their current period in Concord, the Ripleys' daughter Phoebe came to the Wayside to give Una music lessons. Sophia had much in common with Sarah Alden Bradford Ripley. Both were women of great learning and intellectual acumen. Both abhorred violence and opposed any use of force to achieve an end. "War seems to me to be no better than legalized murder," Sarah Ripley wrote, knowing her sentiments were unpopular in Concord where it was "heresy . . . to be sad about the war." Her son Ezra's plan to enlist—at first thwarted by chronic illness and his age (he was thirty-six)—was a particularly bitter pill to swallow. As a lawyer, he initially obtained the relatively protected position of an aide-de-camp, which he resigned to march with his brigade. He fought in the battle known as "Seven Days before Richmond" becoming so ill that he was returned to Concord to recuperate. Against the advice of his physician and family members, he rejoined his company on the eve of the bloodiest battle of the Civil War, Antietam. Surviving that, he was badly wounded in the Battle of Vicksburg in May 1863, but still rode some seventy miles with his troops before injury and illness combined to fell him. For Sarah Ripley, the Emancipation Proclamation had been some balm for the wounds of war, some hope that Ezra's sacrifice was commensurate with the cause, for she had declared, "I am no Spartan mother."[16]

But another mother, another Sarah was. Sophia's dear, generous friend Sarah Shaw had made many loans and gifts to the Hawthornes. During that idyllic summer of 1843, Sarah was then pregnant with her third child—Josephine, or Effie as she was called—when she visited Sophia at

The Old Manse. In all, Sarah bore five children. The eldest, Robert, born in 1837, attended Mary Peabody's school, but in the fall of 1849, when Sophia was teaching her children at home, Sarah had decided that twelve-year-old Bob needed to be "hardened" by being sent to boarding school. "It almost breaks my heart, & his too," Sarah confessed to Sophia, particularly when the boy begged to return home, but "at last he concluded to 'stand it out' for future good. . . . It is a harder thing than you have any idea of."[17] This mother's resolve to make her son strong and this son's resolve to accept his mother's judgment would be poignant under any circumstance, but this incident is all the more affecting because it was one in a series of mother-son interactions that would culminate on July 18, 1863, when Colonel Robert Gould Shaw, the commander of the Massachusetts 54th, was slaughtered with his men at Fort Wagner.

But Bob's road to Fort Wagner had not been a direct one. In his late teens, he wandered about Europe, enjoying all the pleasure and dissipation that wealth could afford. In a remarkably candid letter he stated: "All I can say is that I have no taste for anything excepting amusing myself. . . . I don't want to become a reformer, Apostle, or anything of that kind, there is no use in doing disagreeable things for nothing." He was, nonetheless, troubled by identification with a nation that permitted slavery, though his distress took the form of embarrassment rather than outrage, his solution to the problem—disunion rather than emancipation. Upon returning to the United States, he enrolled at Harvard but the lackluster student withdrew before graduation and never found his niche. When the Civil War broke out, he enlisted and served honorably at Antietam and Cedar Creek.[18]

Then Governor John A. Andrew asked that he command the Massachusetts 54th Infantry Regiment composed of free black men, a request conveyed through Bob's mother. Even some abolitionists believed that blacks could never acquire the discipline needed to function in battle and lacked the courage to fight. Commanding an all-black regiment was tantamount to suicide, according to many, including Bob, who therefore immediately declined the assignment. Then Sarah exerted her powerful influence: "I feel as if God has called you up to a holy work," she wrote her son, who in turn wrote to his fiancée that he must accept the governor's request otherwise "Mother will think I am shirking my duty." Watching her son march out of Boston with his regiment, Sarah proudly exclaimed: "What have I done, that God has been so good to me!" Her commitment to abolition can be gauged by her words as she glimpsed her son for the last time: "If I never see him again, I shall not feel that he has lived in vain."[19]

War touched the lives of Sophia's acquaintances, friends, and those even closer to her home and heart. Sophia's eighteen-year-old nephew, Horace, was urged to enlist, and by none other than his mother, Mary Mann. Sophia's niece, Ellen Peabody—Nat's daughter—was now married to George Phineas How. He served with the 47th Regiment of Massachusetts Volunteers, rose to the rank of captain, and was among the fortunate men to survive. Sophia's former governess and erstwhile friend, Ada Shepard Badger, saw her brother march off to war as did Annie Fields's brother, and Foster Haven, the son of Sophia's long-deceased friend, Lydia Sears Haven. As a child, Foster had been nurtured and loved by both Sophia and Elizabeth; he had grown up to become a surgeon and served at Antietam before a bullet shattered his leg during the Battle of Fredericksburg in December of 1862. He did not survive the amputation. Foster had believed "his place of duty to be wherever a soldier fell," and at his funeral, he was eulogized as a son and "an only child, inexpressibly dear to his father."[20]

Many of the Hawthornes' literary friends also contended with devastating anxiety and loss. William Ticknor's middle son, Benjamin Holt Ticknor, enlisted with the Massachusetts Volunteers, and survived the war, as did O. Wendell Holmes, Jr., who was shot at Antietam and taken to a field hospital. Because no system existed for identifying soldiers, he pinned to his uniform a scrap of paper with these words scribbled on it: "I am Capt. O. W. Holmes 20th Mass. V Son of Oliver Wendell Holmes, M. D. Boston." Had the younger Holmes died, his father would have been properly informed, a comfort denied to most others whose sons or husbands or fathers or nephews succumbed in battle. And James Russell Lowell, who had suffered the deaths of three children, grieved deeply over his nephews who died during the war. The Battle of Ball's Bluff claimed the life of his sister's only son, William Lowell Powell. During the same battle, the son of his brother Charles Lowell, James Jackson Lowell, was wounded and survived only to be killed at Glendale later that year. Charles Lowell's other son and namesake was the husband of Effie Shaw, Sarah's daughter. By the time she met him in 1862, he had evinced extraordinary bravery in battle. During the Battle of Cedar Creek, Charley was shot in the lung and suffered a broken arm. In spite of these grievous injuries, he was hoisted upon his horse to lead the charge during which a bullet to his spine resulted in his lingering, painful death. Effie could not attend her husband's funeral, for she had just given birth to their daughter.[21]

The mayhem of Civil War touched Julian not at all. In fact, as an adult, he recalled that "there never was and never will be such a genial Concord—for young people at least—as that which existed from 1859 to 1865, or thereabouts." Julian made no personal sacrifices for the Union, nor did he seem to comprehend those made by others, some of them his chums at Sanborn's school. And why would he understand the calculus of wartime woe when his mother reacted to his minor mishaps with near hysteria? She considered his swollen face—the result of something he contacted during a romp in the woods—a "sad tragedy." Julian's features were "completely destroyed," his pain "intolerable to him, though," Sophia admitted to Annie, the situation was "not dangerous." Still, Sophia's worry brought her to the point of "brain fever" and nearly "destroyed" her.[22] Such exaggerated responses are particularly misplaced for a mother who knew well the difference between temporary physical discomfort and mortal illness. She had endured with greater aplomb Una's long struggle with malaria, which was still ongoing. She recounted without undue drama Louisa May's battle against typhoid. She dotted her diaries and letters with fleeting, restrained references to the young men who were departing for, or did not return from war. Perhaps the sturdy Julian—so obviously robust, so evidently out of harm's way—provided a surrogate for genuine and, at the profoundest level, unutterable fears. Her son was in no danger of death or decline, as was her husband, who was daily losing ground.

In the winter of 1863, the Hawthornes began to address their son's prospects for college. Never once did they consider Nathaniel's alma mater, perhaps because Bowdoin's distance from the Wayside would prevent Julian from returning home several days a week. They focused instead on Harvard, where his chances for admission were poor, and Sanborn, of course, was to blame. He did not put a "fellow upon his mettle," Nathaniel claimed when he asked advice of Harvard professor James Russell Lowell. Nathaniel admitted candidly that he was "nervous" although Julian was not "thoroughly alive to the emergency." Lowell arranged for Ephraim Whitman Gurney to tutor Julian, who sat for his entrance exam in July. Nathaniel awaited its result with sardonic humor: "[I]f he succeeds in passing it, I shall think less favorably of the wholesome rigor of the examiners than I do now." The wait, Sophia claimed, "almost destroyed" her. Julian did pass his admission exam, but with a "slight rub" in the area of mathematics, for according to his mother, he had been given insufficient time to answer the questions. His deficiency was actually a mark of his "poetic, aesthetic, philosophic" nature, Sophia explained to Annie, for "[h]is tastes do not lie in the way of Exact Science."[23]

Sophia now found herself in the unenviable position of defending her husband *and* her son. Abba Alcott had "ugly and bitter things" to say about Julian; she did not understand his "aesthetic nature," Sophia lamented to an unsympathetic Elizabeth. Recognizing as Sophia did the "thousands of mothers, wives, sisters, who now hang suspended over an abyss of sorrow," she failed to understand that her position on abolition and Civil War could not be explained by domestic preoccupations. In a blistering counterattack on Elizabeth, Sophia told her that because she had never been a wife and mother, she could not comprehend Sophia's responsibilities and emotional priorities. But at this moment in history, Sophia lacked comprehension of the role she touted as her crowning glory. True, her enlightened "carefulness of living" had displaced the Calvinist mother's resignation to childhood mortality. But she did not understand that a mother could do more than protect her child from harm, more than cling to his life when she might accept—even encourage—his sacrifice of it for the greater good.[24]

At odds more than ever with Elizabeth and Mary, who had been "distanced" by her opinions on slavery and war,[25] Sophia's friends, Hitchcock among them, became all the more important to her. By the end of 1863, Lincoln had appointed him as adviser on the exchange of prisoners of war. Sophia praised the general for his "ideal Christian conduct" in the treatment of Confederate soldiers. He sought no "vengeance for wrong done" to Union soldiers, unlike Sophia's sisters who demanded "instant vengeance over the slave owners." Hitchcock shared Sophia's belief that slavery would have disappeared "without this dreadful convulsive" war, and he echoed Sophia's racist assumptions that the "Negro" was childlike and lazy. Sophia found in Hitchcock a comforting, kindred political spirit and, perhaps, something more. The "chalice of my mind brims over, and I am obliged to tell you," she wrote him. His book *Christ the Spirit* was entirely "transparent," "a rare crystal of glass." Hitchcock became her St. Peter holding the key that unlocked something deep within: "my soul has always responded 'Yes' 'Yes' to every Providence of GOD"—that word underscored three times. The intersection of their metaphysical affirmations signaled to Sophia a deep connection to the general, in whom she confided: "I am sure that for all eternity I hold your hand, that wherever you are I can never lose you." Hitchcock's effect on Sophia was no secret. Sophia wrote Hitchcock that even Una observed how her mother was "perfectly transfigured" by his visits. She appeared to have found a soul mate.[26]

Sophia relayed some of her raptures over Hitchcock to Nathaniel, unseemly disclosures perhaps, to a husband who was becoming weaker by the day. But Hitchcock had become a forceful presence, a vessel into which she poured optimism and cosmic affirmations that Nathaniel had never understood. And Sophia now thought of Nathaniel as "an absolute negation," though she could name "no positive malady"; he was "only negative," Sophia confided to Annie. He would never make a full-length romance out of that story repeatedly discussed with Fields. Nathaniel himself realized that his "literary faculty" had "finally broken down," and he worried, therefore, how Fields would handle his liberal advance: "[Y]ou may publish the first chapter as an insulated fragment, and charge me with $100.00 overpayment. I cannot finish it." Sophia wrote Bridge about this "most sad and serious truth." Nathaniel could no longer write, and he was "lately unable to read."[27]

How such a man might derive benefit from travel is difficult to imagine, but Sophia again insisted upon that useless prescription. He must take another a trip, but not with Pierce, whose bereavement was too fresh, too likely to bring Nathaniel's spirits lower. Sophia therefore enlisted Ticknor, who was cheerful enough to "put soul in the ribs of death"; he would take Nathaniel south, stopping in New York, where a renowned homeopath with "broad comprehension of all remedial powers" might work magic, and perhaps on to Cuba. More than thirty years earlier, Sophia—then plagued by excruciating headaches—had regained marvelous health there. Never mind that Nathaniel could not survive a sea voyage; he had nearly fainted two or three times when she took him by train to Boston. But Sophia chirped to Nathaniel about the wonderful time he would have with Ticknor: "Thou wilt be a thousand times better in heath for such a good time abroad." And after this trip, after Nathaniel finished his book, they would all go to England to secure the copyright.[28]

By the time Sophia had deposited her husband at the Fieldses' Back Bay home to await Ticknor, she was exhausted from pretending to be cheerful. Annie observed how deaf Nathaniel had become, how his limbs were shrunken. He was exceedingly restless and paced constantly, but he managed to depart with Ticknor on March 31. Arriving in Philadelphia, the men checked into the Continental House. Ticknor had come down with a cold, and he and Nathaniel had decided against a sea voyage, fearful of storms. Two days later, on April 9, Nathaniel wrote to Fields that Ticknor had suffered a "billious attack" which came upon him suddenly and grew quickly worse. He had been examined by a doctor, an allopath, whose prescriptions Nathaniel dutifully administered: "I have blistered, and powered, and pilled him, and made my observations on medical science and the sad and comic aspects of human misery." This medical drama had had no apparent adverse effects upon Nathaniel's well-being; in fact, he happily reported, "I am perfectly well."[29]

That night, the men were invited to be guests of honor at the elegant home of Joseph Harrison, but they never arrived, nor did they send word to explain their absence. On the morning of April 10, Harrison sent George William Childs, a newspaper publisher, to the Continental House to inquire about them. Childs arrived at Nathaniel's room, its door ajar, and entered. Nathaniel was pacing about, dazed and barely coherent. Ticknor had died early that morning, and the undertaker had already removed his body. With the help of strangers, Nathaniel oversaw arrangements for Ticknor's corpse and telegraphed his eldest son, who came as quickly as possible. Childs then put Nathaniel in the care of another stranger, who accompanied him to Boston where Nathaniel remained with the Fieldses for several days. They were shocked and grief stricken over Ticknor's death and by the unspoken irony of it: *Ticknor* rather than Nathaniel had died. Annie noted in her diary another irony. Nathaniel seemed inexplicably more clear-minded than when he departed for this trip, though he was paler, exhausted, and could hardly sleep or eat.[30]

Whatever clarity Annie observed in her friend was short-lived. He had rallied to meet the crisis, but the crisis drained almost every ounce of his vital force. He left the Fieldses and took the train to Concord. Because there were no carriages at the station, he walked to the Wayside. His face was streaming with perspiration when he arrived, too weak to mount the stairs, too weak to do anything but sit in silence. Sophia sat beside him for hours. Then she tried to divert him by reading aloud from one of Thackeray's novels—those sturdy works of fiction so grounded in robust life. And finally Nathaniel smiled. But his smile looked ill-suited to his distraught and "infinitely weary" face. Sophia wrote Annie, "the wheels of a small ménage are all stopped."[31]

During the next few days, Sophia pondered the significance of Ticknor's death. She mourned this good friend and trusted publisher, the man more trustworthy than Fields with the Hawthornes' accounts. If any good came from this fateful trip, it might lie in the assurances Ticknor had given before he died. Nathaniel need not worry about providing for himself and his family; if he were to write just one article a month for the *Atlantic*, he could earn a steady stream of income without ever penning another romance. This comforting information did not erase Sophia's thoughts about Mrs. Ticknor and the "inscrutable Providence" that permitted her husband to "die away from her!" "It is well that we have no right to question the Providence of GOD," Sophia wrote Annie, "but know that it must be for all and each—Otherwise—What despair and madness!"[32]

Sophia saw how the ordeal of "nursing and watching and witnessing" Ticknor die had stolen any remnant of her husband's vitality. Nathaniel now expressed his "horror of hotels and rail cars." He was unable to get in or out of a carriage without help. He could not walk for more than ten minutes at a time. His vision, as well as his hearing, became impaired. The cold, wet New England weather removed any chance for improvement, and Sophia dreamed again about taking him to Cuba. Her husband was "ploughed up with care," she wrote Mary, and could not shed the conviction that he would end his days in an almshouse. Sophia asked Pierce to convince Nathaniel this would not happen, and she now considered how Pierce's bereavement might be an asset to her husband, for, as she explained to Annie, Pierce's "love for Mr Hawthorne is the strongest passion of his soul now that his wife is departed." And so, contrary to everything she observed about Nathaniel's fragility, contrary to all evidence that he was approaching his own death, Sophia wanted Pierce to take Nathaniel on a fishing trip.[33]

On May 8, Sophia accompanied Nathaniel to Boston where he awaited Pierce and the commencement of their journey. In so many ways, she ignored the gravity of her husband's condition, but she understood the urgency of finding a remedy, if one could be found. Desperation drove her to seek advice from an allopath, although she knew Nathaniel would succumb to allopathic treatments such as those that had preceded Ticknor's demise. Begging the Fieldses' utmost discretion, Sophia asked them to arrange that their neighbor Dr. Oliver Wendell Holmes examine her husband on the sly. Nathaniel need never know that Holmes had felt his pulse under the guise of greeting him with a warm gesture. Impatient to learn Holmes's diagnosis, Una inquired of Fields, on behalf of her mother. But their hearts surely told them what Holmes withheld from Nathaniel. "[T]he shark's tooth is upon him, but would not have this known," Annie recorded in her diary on May 11, the day Nathaniel departed with Pierce for New Hampshire.[34]

On May 19, Sophia and Una tended to routine matters while Rose prepared to leave for Boston and her thirteenth birthday celebration with Annie the next day. But before Rose could depart, Elizabeth Peabody and Mary Mann arrived at the Wayside and attempted to draw Una aside. Her aunts' solemnity revealed their errand before they could speak. "Papa is gone," cried Una, and thus did Sophia learn of Nathaniel's death. He and Pierce had arrived at the Pemigewasset House in Plymouth, New Hampshire, the day before, their enjoyments muted by Nathaniel's life-weariness. Around nine o'clock, each man retired to his own room. Pierce checked on his friend during the early morning hours, and Nathaniel appeared to be sleeping peacefully. Pierce checked on him again, two hours later. Again, he appeared to be resting tranquilly. But he had not moved at all, a telltale sign that prompted Pierce to place his hand on Nathaniel. At that moment, Pierce realized his friend had "passed from natural slumber to that from which there is no waking." Pierce telegraphed James T. Fields and Elizabeth Peabody with news that could not have come as a surprise to them, or to Sophia. Nathaniel's long decline had finally reached a gentle conclusion.[35]

Chapter 20

Coining His Precious Brain into Gold

Sophia immediately set about a widow's tasks. She commissioned Judge Rockwell Hoar and her eldest children to arrange the funeral. She asked of Annie—via a letter from Una—the great favor of purchasing mourning attire: a bonnet and veil, as well as material for a dress and cloak for herself; suitable clothing for Una, Julian, and Rose, though nothing black for them. Nathaniel would not have wanted that. Another letter, this one to Fields written by both Sophia and Una, contained a very different and far more painful request. Fields must prevent the publication of Holmes's judgment that Nathaniel's mind was failing. Even Sophia's sisters must never know that Dr. Oliver Wendell Holmes had confirmed her husband's secret fear. "The thought that a shadow should fall on his clear mind is an arrow all poison in her heart," wrote Una. Sophia's "agitation" and "sorrow" were evident in her most uncharacteristic pencil-scrawl across the page of her daughter's letter. But in yet another letter, this to Annie, Sophia was entirely serene, her tranquility an amalgam of lifelong, invincible optimism and more recent immersion in Hitchcock's writings on Christianity. "Oh blessed be GOD for so soft a translation—as an infant wakes on its mother's breast so he woke on the bosom of GOD & can never be weary any more." Nathaniel had been the epitome of "tolerance," his "tenderness so infinite—so embracing that GOD's alone could surpass it." Citing that almshouse incident presented anonymously in *Our Old Home*, Sophia revealed to Annie that Nathaniel had been the man who had "folded the loathsome leper in as soft a caress as the child of his home affections—Was not that divine! Was it not Christianity in one action—what a bequest to his children—what a new revelation of Christ to the world was that!"[1]

On May 23, James Freeman Clarke—the man who had performed the Hawthornes' wedding ceremony nearly twenty-two years earlier—officiated during Nathaniel's funeral at Concord's Congregational Church. Sophia and her daughters had decorated the coffin with flowers, and Nathaniel's sixteen distinguished pallbearers comprised a veritable roster of New England's elite and literati: Hillard, the Hawthornes' longtime friend, attorney, and business adviser; Fields, who placed Nathaniel's unfinished manuscript in the coffin for the duration of the service; Alcott, whose presence Nathaniel had so often evaded; Holmes, whose prognosis had proven true sooner than expected; Longfellow, Lowell, and Emerson, each having experienced profound personal losses, each leaving his own indelible mark upon American literature. The staunch abolitionists in the group temporarily stifled their animosity toward Pierce, who accompanied Sophia and her children.[2]

Sophia did not regard the events of that day as "Ceremonies of Death" but as a "Festival of Life" which she described in detail to Elizabeth, who, curiously, absented herself from the funeral. "I do not believe any one understood him better than you except myself," that last word crossed out and "ourselves" inserted above it. "No one appreciated you—as he constantly said—so well as he. 'I am her best friend,' he always said." Did he? In his most gracious moods, Nathaniel thought of Elizabeth as benighted and well-intentioned, but he and Sophia more often considered her to be meddling and overbearing. On more than one occasion, they told her so. Sophia now cited—if she did not actually invent—Nathaniel's "sympathy" with Elizabeth's "great heartedness." And reminding Elizabeth of his kindness to the almshouse child, Sophia crafted this incident into an emblem of his life.[3]

But in letters to Annie immediately after the funeral, Sophia took a different path to consolation. "I seem for these three days to stand on the shore of an endless sapphire sea," with waves lapping "in opaline tints as they turn in the light and spread on the golden sands, I stand hushed into an ineffable Peace." Boundaries between the living and the dead were fluid: "My darling had gone over that Sapphire sea, and these grand soft waves are messages from his Eternal Rest." Sophia's tone was euphoric rather than bereft. Yet even as she solaced herself with grandly poetic, nearly hallucinatory metaphors, she addressed mundane matters, among them her various "debts" to Annie.[4]

Business, particularly the business of her husband's writing, interrupted Sophia's mourning and its consolations. She had been unaware of plans for the unfinished manuscript Fields had carried to the funeral. This story had not jelled at all, as Nathaniel had realized when he returned part of his advance and agreed to publish only its first episode in the *Atlantic*. Sophia was not privy to the plan and objected strenuously when she learned of this exception to the rule against serial publication. "You did not happen to tell me that Mr Hawthorne had decided with you that the chapter should be printed," Sophia scolded Fields. She had not read "one syllable" of this romance and insisted that none of it would be published until she had examined every page. She would not risk the criticism that her husband should have stopped writing after his success with *Our Old Home*.[5]

Sophia sped to complete the daunting task of arranging all manuscript pages, some of which were written on the backs of letters. She then read everything that was legible. Did she notice the conflation of familial relations signaled by the names assigned to the main character's wife—in some places "Bessie," in others "Phoebe"? Or did she wonder why her husband also called that character "Alice," recycling yet another name he had used in *The House of the Seven Gables*? For Fields's benefit Sophia commented only that her husband's "genius" had "never shone more consummately," and she permitted a chapter of *The Dolliver Romance*, as it was to be called, to proceed as planned. It would appear in the July 1864 *Atlantic Monthly*, the very issue that would also carry Holmes's article about Nathaniel. Though Sophia's greatest fear was not realized—Holmes did not betray his judgment about her husband's mental decline—she was nonetheless appalled that a physician would reveal any information about his patient. Holmes's portrayal of Nathaniel during their last meeting was not flattering, though it may have engendered sympathy for a man who "faltered," whose limbs were "shrunken," who suffered from a constant, boring pain in his distended stomach and "obvious depression."[6]

Sophia recoiled from this breech of trust and representation of her husband as a decrepit, old man, a depiction that she had tried to prevent. She forbade Fields from using Whipple's photograph of Nathaniel, for she thought it made her husband's eyes "fail" and lack "speculation." In the midst of her grief—or perhaps as one manifestation of it—Sophia sought to control Nathaniel's image and to vet his writing, a goal that might best be met by authoring a book about him, precisely what the ever-astute Fields invited her to do. She declined, of course, as both James and Annie should have expected. They knew, as did everyone else, of Nathaniel's prejudices against women authors. That Sophia would publish any book, much less one about her husband, was anathema. She would never "act out of opposition to my husband's express wish and opinion," she wrote Annie: "The veil he drew around him no one should lift."[7]

Unless that person be Sophia. Over the next six months, she began to select and copy excerpts from Nathaniel's journals. She could determine later what, if anything, to do with material so ripe with interest and worth $100 per installment, the amount Fields offered to pay. That was the same amount Nathaniel had earned by chopping excerpts out of his English notebooks for the *Atlantic*. And while Sophia considered whether to present Nathaniel's private writing to the public, she was making one after another discovery about the morass that was her husband's financial legacy. Sorting through his papers, she learned about his arrangements for Ebe in the amount of $180 annually. Sophia was, nonetheless surprised when her sister-in-law expected a quarterly payment of $45 in October. Sophia incorrectly assumed that semiannual payments were to be scheduled in May (the month when Nathaniel had died) and November. She scurried to send the money, acting not out of duty but from a desire to honor her husband's wishes and to make her sister-in-law comfortable. Ebe thanked Sophia for her "kind punctuality"; their correspondence was civil, if not cordial. But Nathaniel's failure to inform his wife about his—and now his heirs'—financial obligation to Ebe had added to the tension between women whose relations had been filled with years of misunderstanding.[8]

Sophia discussed this confusion and other financial matters with Pierce. One particularly confounding arrangement involved Nathaniel's murky dealings with John Louis O'Sullivan. How much she knew of these before a packet arrived at the Wayside remains unclear. Addressed to Sophia and her children were four legal documents, "transcripts of a complaint of the National Insurance Company in reference to the estate which Mr. O'Sullivan seemed to secure to Mr. Hawthorne in payment of the debt" of $3,000. Sophia was bewildered by the company's claim of $9,000 upon that "unfortunate property" and could only hope that O'Sullivan's investment in copper mines might yield enough to discharge "his complicated obligations"—and her own, perhaps. Sophia sent these documents to Hillard, who could make nothing of them. She then forwarded them to William Emerson, the attorney to whom Ticknor entrusted all his business. Emerson might be able to explain "the O'Sullivan property and our dues," Sophia told Una.[9]

Hillard's role in Sophia's life also prompted a set of questions. She may have been more savvy than her husband about money matters, more frugal about their spending, more cautious with tradespeople, but she was a product of her era regarding the legalities of inheritance, which is to say she was ignorant of them. Unlike Mary, whose husband had bequeathed her a handsome estate and—perhaps more importantly—clarity about its particulars, Sophia found herself mired in uncertainty. What exactly was an administrator? Was an administrator the same as a trustee? Hillard provided Sophia with clarifications. As administrator, he would pay bills, discharge debts, and take Nathaniel's estate through probate court. After that, he would divide property among the heirs—Sophia, Una, and Julian—and appoint a guardian for "the minor child," Rose. Once these matters were settled, his role as administrator would cease, and he would resume his duties as the Hawthornes' attorney. He had tallied Sophia's income for 1864 and predicted that she might expect roughly the same amount, $2040, the following year. This income derived from the sale of Nathaniel's books, stocks, bonds, mortgages (probably on the O'Sullivan land), and interest held by Ticknor and Fields. And, Hillard warned Sophia, if Julian were to return to college, she would be forced to exercise extreme "economy & self-denial."[10]

When Hillard made this announcement, Julian was in the hands of yet another tutor, having been suspended from Harvard, ostensibly for lack of attendance. Sophia apparently never knew of the macabre coincidence that had occurred during the wee morning hours of May 19. At the very moment Pierce was discovering that Nathaniel lay dead, Julian was lying in a coffin. A blindfold covered his eyes while he participated in a ritual of burial and rebirth that admitted him to Delta Kappa Epsilon. Sophia did know about Julian's association with "societies," as she innocently referred to fraternities. With their "constant demand on his time and care," she blamed them for Julian's poor performance; *they* had "handicapped" her son and "rendered nearly impossible" his academic success. Sam Hoar and Edward Emerson both "besieged Julian with counsel and entreaties about college," but he was indifferent to their advice.[11]

Julian's interests tended toward romantic interludes and the cultivation of his enormous muscles. But even adoring Rose believed his shoulders had grown "improportionally big. " Sophia concurred; "little Ecclesiastica" (Rose) was right about his "'bicepts' as she spells it." And something else Sophia surely did not know: Julian had used his muscles to bloody a Harvard classmate during a fight. His dissipation and lackluster academic performance might be reminiscent of Robert Gould Shaw's Harvard experience had Julian been forced by his mother—as Sarah forced her son—to find purpose outside himself. Instead, Sophia's excuses for Julian had grown legion, and ludicrous. She wrote a note to excuse an absence because his blanket had fallen off during the night, which resulted in his catching a cold. She enlisted Hillard as her ally getting Julian a waiver in mathematics, her son's academic *bête noire*, though to Una, Sophia admitted "consternation" upon discovering that Julian had returned to school—while he was still enrolled there—without his books. All the while Sophia believed that Julian was everyone's great favorite: "General Pierce shares the general furor of love to Julian."[12]

Sophia relied upon Pierce's "truly fatherly interest" in Julian, and "the General" was the only person Julian would "give an ear *what to do*." And what Pierce wanted Julian to do was return to Harvard. If that were to occur, he must be tutored by Ferdinand Hoffman, a man recommended by Professor Gurney. Julian must live in Stockbridge with Hoffman, his wife, and other young men who found themselves in the same predicament. In a letter to Pierce, Sophia calculated costs—$8 per week for provisions, $7 for tuition, another dollar for wood, and 50 cents for laundry—and rued the presence in Hoffman's home of a student "given to whiskey." Julian promised not to associate with him. Julian did, however, accumulate bills for clothing, and these bills he sent to Pierce. Hadn't Pierce told Sophia that Nathaniel would willingly accept his "assistance about Julian"? Sophia's question was somewhat disingenuous, but her efforts to earn money were genuine. She wrote Pierce that she had sold Nathaniel's autographs and was "coining his brain into gold" as she labored on *The Dolliver Romance* to prepare a November installment of it for Fields. This would earn a most welcome $200, the very sum promised to Nathaniel for such a piece in the *Atlantic*. Sophia was also copying sections of his notebooks; Fields had "high expectations for the books" that might result. But if she and her children became "destitute," with her husband's blessing, she would "appeal" to Pierce. And in December, Julian sent him two more bills, one for a $50 coat and the other for $53 owed to a tailor.[13]

Sophia kept her eyes tightly shut to her son's derelictions while she worked diligently copying her husband's writing, but she was forced to see that Nathaniel had deliberately hidden some of it from her. G. W. Curtis published an article for the *North American Review* about Nathaniel's works, among them his earliest called *Fanshawe*. Sophia "stoutly denied there had ever been such," for her husband would have told her about it, if it ever existed. Then she learned the truth; Nathaniel had, indeed, written and published *Fanshawe* at his own expense in 1828. Embarrassed by his youthful foray into fiction, he had enjoined his family and friends "to keep it a profound secret, and of course we did." So did Elizabeth

Hawthorne confirm her brother's authorship of *Fanshawe*. That Ebe kept secrets from Sophia was no surprise, but that Nathaniel did! "It is so wonderful [an odd use of that word] that he never told me even that there was such a book printed," Sophia admitted to Fields.[14]

The months after the funeral had been a season of revelations. Nathaniel had kept secret from her a book he had published. He had kept her in the dark about arrangements for that manuscript he'd been writing when he absconded to his tower. He never told her about the annuity for Ebe, nor had he fully explained his financial entanglements with O'Sullivan. Perhaps she hoped that she could ascertain everything there was to know about him by exploring his notebooks. In December of 1864, she wrote Fields, "I wish to copy, copy, copy. Perhaps nothing will do to print—but I must copy all the same. And," she added, "I also wish to draw."[15]

Her opportunity to do the latter arose early the following year. Mary was writing a biography of Horace and asked Sophia to sketch his picture for it. For the next few months, Sophia spent many exhausting yet happy hours sketching. "It is a tremendous effort to bring a human face out of the past," she wrote Mary: "But here he is!" For a brief moment Sophia's career as an artist seemed to beckon. She executed a small portrait of Posey Loring, hoping that the recently deceased child's "exceeding Peace" would "pass into her mother's heart." But Sophia did not resume her artistic career, and she required Mary to use a daguerreotype of Horace for the book rather than her drawing. "It was drawn from my soul to your soul," she wrote Mary. In June of 1865, the *Life of Horace Mann* appeared, its author identified only as "his Wife." Sophia was "spellbound" by the book. With unsteady penmanship, Sophia wrote Mary, "[y]ou have now fulfilled your part and vindicated him forever."[16]

If Mary could present Horace to the world as she wished him to be remembered, Sophia could similarly "vindicate" Nathaniel. She could erase that image of a feeble old man, incapable of writing stories, and insensitive to the nation's plight. She could show the world the man she had fallen in love with, the writer of acclaimed stories, the husband in an idyllic marriage, the father of remarkable children. Even though *Our Old Home* had demonstrated, and against very heavy odds, a market for Nathaniel's travel writing, Sophia did not mine the "gems" in his French and Italian notebooks. She turned instead to those he had kept before they met and those they maintained together during the first decade of their marriage. Their separate lives thus acquired a symmetry befitting the couple whose existence had been constructed in words. Before Nathaniel had met Sophia, he had read and copied bits of her *Cuban Journal*, thereby imagining the woman he would love. After Nathaniel had died, Sophia read and copied excerpts from his journals, thereby preserving for posterity her image of the man she had loved.[17]

Sophia's task returned her to the profession of copyist, the nineteenth-century métier that demanded much more than slavish imitation of an "original." A copy might be allowed, even expected, to change and thereby improve an original, and according to Elizabeth, Sophia's copy of a Doughty painting had done just that; it was "even better than the original." This kind of creative copying had become a theme in *The Marble Faun*, where Hilda's copies (like Sophia's) captured an ineffable essence and eliminated the distinction between original and reproduction. Though Nathaniel preferred to think of himself as the sole author of his fiction, his composition of that novel clearly demonstrated such was not the case. His request for Sophia's help as well as the cultural values that informed her career in the visual arts sanctioned her "copies" of Nathaniel's notebooks. And of course, she needed no permission to work on what she had co-authored.[18]

With proprietary energy, Sophia looked for "more perfectly finished" pieces that did not require the revisions Nathaniel always undertook before publication. Using the visual arts as her metaphor, she explained to James and Annie that Nathaniel's notebooks contained "very rapid sketches—mere outlines—cartoons of the great pictures he meant to paint fully out." Sophia's own portions of these notebooks particularly challenged her. How might she extract them without compromising the "perfect whole"? The entries she and Nathaniel had composed during "the first year and part of the second of *his* married life" also vexed her. It was, of course, not "*his*" but *their* married life. She might delete herself from the text, but could she extricate herself from the reality? And did she really want to? After all, as she wrote to Fields, while she copied, she lived "all day long with [her] husband." She had found a bridge between her life as wife and widow that destroyed the boundaries of the grave. Like a medium, Sophia became the vehicle for Nathaniel's thoughts. His words flowed through her pen in a collaboration as intimate as the one that had originally produced these journals.[19]

While Sophia's labor created comforting interludes with Nathaniel, editorial dilemmas provoked her anxiety. Should she and Fields retain or eliminate names of friends and neighbors? Perhaps, if these people were still alive, their identities must be hidden. What of the deceased—Jonathan Cilley, for example? Nathaniel's friend from their Bowdoin days had been killed in a duel in 1838, and Nathaniel published a piece about the unfortunate Cilley in the *Democratic Review*. Surely, there would be no breach of propriety in mentioning Cilley's name now. And about the boy who brought milk and flowers to The Old Manse? Should Sophia identify him as George Prescott who had died a hero's death just the year before? And should she reveal the specific sources of Nathaniel's inspiration for his sketches and tales? Anyone interested in Nathaniel would "like to come as near as possible to the full details," she thought. Were not his preliminary scribblings like "the pen and ink and pencil sketches of the pictures of the old masters," she asked, again thinking in terms of the visual arts, "in contemplation of which we come so very near the creative soul of the artist?" Indeed they were, but what if she should "reveal too much"?[20]

By October of 1865, Sophia had made her most important decision. She would proceed with the publication of carefully selected, chronologically organized excerpts from Nathaniel's American notebooks. These would appear in twelve monthly installments in the *Atlantic*, beginning in January. As the publication of the first installment approached, Sophia's task imposed the additional pressure of meeting deadlines. In November, after receiving some copy-edited text, she fired off a late-night letter to Fields with sixteen specific queries. Due to her own mistakes in copying, she noticed some errors in the text and insisted upon changes. Apologetically, she promised to exercise greater care in the future, to work when she was not "excessively agitated." But when might that be? Sophia was in the grip of an "iron necessity to keep copying," or, to put her situation less elegantly, she felt a vise-like pressure to make money.[21]

While Sophia had spent 1865 preparing the American notebooks for publication, Julian had passed the year spending money—hers when she had it, Pierce's when she did not—on tutors and other accoutrements of college life. Sophia had hoped that Julian's association with the highly recommended Professor Hoffman would be positive. Julian told his mother that he was studying as much as his roommate did—an enigmatic statement at best. But Julian was in a foul mood when he arrived in Stockbridge. Mrs. Hoffman "was a damned cuss," a name he refrained from calling his mother though he was also very angry at her. She had charged him with "showering down" over his latest affair of the heart. "Are you not rather exaggerative," he asked, her failure to include five dollars in the trunk she had sent only increasing his ire. After all, he needed trousers! But Julian's unpleasantness and demands did not seep into Sophia's letters to Pierce about her son, who was frugal, she claimed, using his allowance to buy ink, never cigars. He studied twelve hours a day, though she could not tell if that was a joke. But no one was amused by the challenge Julian faced preparing to pass Harvard exams in the spring of 1865, mathematics continuing to be his biggest obstacle to success. Mr. Hoffman had provided

Julian an additional tutor in that area, giving Sophia the confidence to announce in a March 10, 1865 letter to Annie that Julian was "entirely prepared."[22]

Well, perhaps not entirely. Two days later, Sophia reported to Pierce that her son had passed, but with an inevitable condition in algebra, due to Hoffman's choice of an "unamiable tutor." Sophia turned to Professor Gurney, who would find another tutor, because Gurney as well as Pierce continued to believe that Julian's future lay in Cambridge. So Julian went back to Harvard, that is, back to fraternity life, Pierce paying the "fees for societies and such things which it appeared mean to avoid," as Sophia explained. But by the end of April, Julian had retuned to the Wayside, announcing to his mother that he was disgusted by the "beastly drunkenness and dissipation" of students at Harvard. Perhaps "to die is best," he told his mother. His melodrama did not raise Sophia's alarms, for if she knew anything about her son, she knew that his weaknesses were not in the area of melancholy.[23]

According to Sophia, Julian's missteps were due to his "remarkable insight" and lack of "worldly aptitude." Recalling that when he had disguised himself as the Duke of Buckingham, he declared, "I feel much more at home in this dress than I do in common clothes." Sophia explained to Pierce that her son inhabited "an ideal world." He did not "perceive actual facts," especially "financial facts," hardly comforting information for Pierce, who was paying for many of Julian's follies. Sophia nonetheless confided these observations to Pierce, and only Pierce, for he was, besides Sophia, the person who cared most about Julian's "destiny." And so when Gurney announced that neither he nor any one else could make a scholar out of Julian, that it was "IMPOSSIBLE" for Julian to continue at Harvard, Sophia unburdened herself to Pierce. And it was to Pierce she came with the news that in the fall of 1865, Julian was with a new tutor, a Mr. Allen in the nearby town of Northboro, Massachusetts, though once again she withheld from the General Julian's scrawled demands: "Send undershirts. Also more towels." And, he instructed his mother, "when ever you have a dollar bill you don't know what to do with send it down here."[24]

Sophia needed to clarify her earnings, those she was scheduled to receive and the $200 she had already received for the upcoming installments of *Passages from Hawthorne's Note-books*, as the book would be called. On December 3, 1865, she wrote Fields, "I do not quite understand why you are so excessively anxious about the money you pay me for the manuscripts." Fields apparently merited the combative tone Sophia might have leveled at her son. Did Fields think the law required her to render an account of these payments to Hillard? Not so. Having ceased his duties as administrator of Nathaniel's estate, he informed her—by way of a note she would send Fields—that she could spend as she wished without consulting him. Was Fields suggesting that Sophia should account to him? Did Fields think Sophia should take in laundry to fatten her "private purses"? At this juncture, Sophia could not ignore Hillard's pragmatic suggestion that Julian "take up with his connections *now*, and not try to graduate," though Sophia conveyed the idea to Pierce rather than Fields. And at the beginning of 1866, Professor Gurney made it most clear to Sophia that Julian would not succeed with his March exams for he lacked the will to tackle hard work and stick with it. And because of Julian's "indifference" and "want of resolution" about his studies, Gurney declined to be of any further assistance.[25]

But in defiance of Gurney's judgment and Hillard's advice, Sophia wanted her "heavenly baby," as she referred to him just days before his twentieth birthday, to return to Harvard. She somehow cajoled James Russell Lowell, Harvard professor of modern languages, to make an exception to his rule against tutoring. He allowed Julian to come to his office throughout the summer for private recitations, sometimes in the company of his mother. But the wreck of Julian's academic career was beyond repair, and in September, he was permanently dismissed from Harvard. Sophia asked Lowell to intervene, but in this matter, he would make "no exceptions." Julian was unperturbed by his dismissal, an attitude Sophia interpreted as evidence of his "usual serene magnanimity," as she wrote Una. And Hillard greeted news of Julian's expulsion with irony that would have permitted Sophia to remain assured of her son's exceptionality; a prescribed course of study would be "no use to a mind like his," Hillard wrote. And he reminded Sophia about Julian's useful social ties, a benefit that typically required a college degree for other young men. About Sophia's idea that Julian might become a minister, Hillard did not know what to say.[26]

An elaborate construction of Julian's character was but one of the many burdens Sophia shouldered. When she was not intervening on Julian's behalf, she was readying monthly installments of "Passages" for the *Atlantic*, her various decisions more pressing as she faced immediate deadlines. Sophia often accepted Fields's judgments, but sometimes she regretted that he had not steered her course more cautiously. She was profoundly sorry that she had published Cilley's name. Nathaniel's account of his friend's duel and death had drawn fire from Sanborn, and the *Commonwealth* simply took "exception" to naming names. About Hawthorne family matters, Sophia had been "induced" by Fields "to copy more and more of [her husband's] actual life and feeling," despite her reluctance to do so. "I confide in your judgment," Sophia wrote Fields who had pressed her for "fresh matter" from this "exquisite journal" and instructed her "not to strike out anything; or . . . do it o so sparingly." But when the proofs arrived, she made "wild havoc" with them, realizing that "the delicious music must not be piped to all ears." Though Fields was clearly unhappy, she reminded him how "infinitely" sorry she was to have published Cilley's name.[27]

Reluctance and regrets notwithstanding, Sophia did publish ever more personal family material. She knew that her husband's "Photographic study" of Una and Julian would interest readers of the *Atlantic*; written while Nathaniel was composing *The Scarlet Letter*, the "germ of Pearl" was there. And Nathaniel's account of his time with Julian in Lenox during the summer of 1851 had been so deliberately crafted into a self-contained unit that "Twenty Days with Julian and Little Bunny," as Nathaniel himself had titled it, suggested his desire to publish it. Sophia understood the marketable charm of this narrative, but there was no way to disguise her son's identity. Seeking James's and Annie's counsel, Sophia sent them a segment of "Twenty Days"; Fields then passed it to Longfellow for his opinion. Julian's willingness to see his name in print removed only half of Hillard's reservations about the project. But despite Sophia's numerous consultations and almost as many encouragements to publish "Twenty Days," she never did.[28]

Sophia had assumed that anything sent to James and Annie for their review remained with them, that Fields would not circulate copies of Nathaniel's notebooks without her express permission. She was "aghast" therefore that Fields had sent Nathaniel's account of his trip to the Isles of Shoals to Lowell. It should not have been sent to anyone, and *"especially not"* to Lowell, she wrote Fields on September 19, demanding its immediate return. This letter followed upon one from Fields who announced that he might ask Lowell to edit a book-length version of Nathaniel's notebooks. That Lowell might be vested with this honor the very week he had refused to intercede on Julian's behalf was an affront to Sophia. And that anyone but she should edit her husband's writing was preposterous. About this she could not have been more emphatic. "And if you decide to print any thing," she wrote Fields on December 9, 1866, "I could never have more need of the pay for the mss than now—alas me!"[29]

A year had passed since Sophia asked Fields if he thought she should take in laundry to supplement her income. Her pettish tone had turned plaintive.

Chapter 21

My Dear Friend

As soon as the last installment of "Passages" appeared in the December 1866 *Atlantic*, Sophia commenced her most ambitious literary undertaking to date. She—not Lowell, not anyone else—would prepare the book-length *Passages from the American Note-books of Nathaniel Hawthorne*.

By now, she had established procedures for editing her husband's note-books. She made alterations to the physical manuscript, scissoring out passages and pages, chopping sentences into bits, erasing or otherwise rendering words illegible. She also marked the proofs Fields sent her, every word of which she insisted upon reading. Exhaustive examinations of Nathaniel's originals, Sophia's transcriptions, and the Ticknor and Fields copyedited proofs reveal that Sophia's editing practices were impelled by contradictory motives. According to Claude Simpson, the editor of the *Centenary Edition* of Nathaniel's American notebooks, Sophia exhibited a "tenacious desire to be faithful to Hawthorne's every word" while "gentility and propriety" forced her to take many "liberties." Her pen, therefore, transformed Nathaniel into a more abstemious man; she inked out his "two glasses of hot gin-and-water" at bedtime on the Isles of Shoals, this content perhaps explaining her ire that Lowell had seen the account, presumably before she had sanitized it. She transformed Nathaniel from a drinker into an observer in a tavern with a mere shift in pronouns from an inclusive "we" to the anonymous "he"; she turned his "pimp" into an "agent," his "whore" into a "woman"![1]

For these kinds of alterations, Sophia was called a prudish bowdlerizer and thrall to Victorian mores. But if such she had been, she would not have published biographical material at all, an "outrage," according to one of her contemporary reviewers, who castigated her for damaging Nathaniel's reputation with a "conglomerate of odds and ends." Though other reviewers thought the "extracts" enhanced Nathaniel's "reputation as a profound and sagacious thinker, and conscientious artist," still others claimed Sophia had had no right to publish "a selection, not the author's." She had replaced the aura surrounding his romances with revelations about their mundane origins. Negative remarks bruised her deeply. She was afflicted with "awful doubts," knowing that she had violated her husband's wishes. But her need for money and, perhaps, the gratifications derived from finally publishing these journals—albeit not the portion she had authored—propelled her to risk criticisms, those from the public and those she imagined her husband leveling against her.[2]

Fields abetted Sophia's audacity in the literary marketplace, as Randall Stewart, one of Nathaniel's mid-twentieth-century biographers, has noted. Stewart emended his "too sharp, too castigatory" judgment of her editing, having originally dismissed it as an example of "the genteel Victorian female" before understanding that Fields was an "active collaborator" with Sophia. He taught her "how to edit" according to "contemporary standards," and she was "directly influenced by Fields and his wife." Thus Sophia's dealings with Fields grew increasingly more complex. For years he had been her banker of sorts, his firm doling out income from royalties in a most haphazard manner. Now he had become her tutor in the niceties of editing as well as her collaborator. He was also her publisher, determining compensation and establishing deadlines. His many roles inevitably resulted in misunderstandings over large matters and small. If a packet of copies was late, Sophia defensively explained that the courier refused to take them in the rain. When her copy of "Twenty Days with Julian and Little Bunny" was misplaced for several months, Fields and Sophia each blamed the other for its temporary disappearance, and Sophia realized that she must keep careful records in her dealings with Fields.[3]

And further complicating her relationship with Fields was the woman to whom he was married, the recipient of Sophia's passionately effusive letters. Even by nineteenth-century standards, which granted far more latitude to women's declarations of affection for each other, Sophia's outpourings exceeded the boundaries of propriety. She was smitten by Annie's appearance. Having heard that Annie looked particularly striking on one occasion in a sable-trimmed black outfit, Sophia wrote her, "Do not you know I like to see you dressed in your bravest though I love to see you just as well in undress." Contemplating Annie's beauty provoked, as it had on a previous occasion, Sophia's reflection on her own less than comely appearance, and her age: "I do not *feel* old though my hair be stricken white." Because Annie's letters to Sophia do not survive, we cannot know how she responded to these particular outpourings, but letters from Sophia to Annie during 1866 reveal misunderstandings between the women, then Annie's withdrawal, and finally Sophia's disappointment over lost love.[4]

In January, Sophia quoted to Annie her words that "cold winds" were blowing from Concord toward Boston. Sophia, too, had begun to worry about Annie's "faith being immutable—you dear naughty lily." Whatever chill had descended, Sophia continued to write "very inmostly" to Annie. A "true identity of being, a revelation of God's Unity" animated her love for Nathaniel and coexisted with desires for Annie. "What I want now is my beautiful, my rich, my dearest Annie," Sophia wrote her in April. But in May, Sophia lamented that Annie made no effort to visit her while she was in Concord. And in the fall, when Sophia went to Boston, Annie was nowhere to be found. She had, however, written Sophia, requesting her opinion of "Asphodel," a poem Annie had sent without naming its author. On October 1, Sophia penned her candid critique. "Asphodel" was so unpleasantly lacking in "nature, truth, simplicity, vraisemblance" that Sophia could not finish reading it. She hoped Annie did not like the poem "well enough to care whether I like it or not." Was the author someone Annie was promoting? The author was, in fact, Annie who soon published the poem anonymously. Sophia may have never realized her *faux pas* nor understood its significance. Her "Western Peri," the recipient of Sophia's profound thoughts and intimate feelings, was capable of an entirely vapid poem. Perhaps Sophia did not know Annie at all. The next month, when Sophia was again in Boston, James "warned me off you," she wrote Annie, ruing their "endless separation, weeks of non intercourse of all kinds." Casting her sorrow in staccato lines, Sophia wrote:

Annie, I love you.
I wish to see you.
Do you remember me at
all, I wonder?
Am I a tale that is told[5]

By 1867, joyful intimacy with Annie was a thing of the past, and their correspondence became infrequent. Sophia lamented to Fields: "Annie and I have drifted away from the lake of ink." Their friendship evaporated just when Sophia most needed friends, for her children—no longer children at the ages of 23, 21, and 16—continued to be the source of her enormous, if often misplaced concern. And Julian was one of the reasons letters between the women no longer flowed in a comforting stream. When Annie did write, she criticized Julian, and by implication, Sophia. Annie thought Julian had acted irresponsibly regarding his opportunities at Harvard. Not so, was Sophia's retort. Julian had been most dutiful in giving Harvard a try; he thereby fulfilled his father's wishes when all along Julian preferred a more "active" profession. His only flaw was that he did not "assert himself," and Sophia now "transgressed his entreaties" by defending him. "I felt you would be glad to find yourself mistaken in your judgment of him—glad to take a new view," Sophia wrote Annie: "I am right, am I not?"[6] Annie probably did not take the bait of this rhetorical question.

Fields, too, was critical of Julian, alleging that he was responsible for Sophia's financial problems. Not so, Sophia retorted again. Just like his father, Julian wore "tattered" clothing and drew a "veil" around himself. Sophia persisted in thinking about her six-foot tall, now legally independent son as her "own little child forever." One may only guess how the seasoned General Hitchcock received that description in a letter from Sophia where she asserted that Julian had "no affinity for evil," that he obeyed her "instantly," and that he was a source of "inspiration to his sisters." But inspiration to do what? He had moved his rowing machine to his father's tower, thereby converting a study into a gymnasium, a circumstance duly noted by his Aunt Ebe. He briefly succumbed to a "charming Cleopatra," but Sophia could report that he was now rid of this actress who was not born for "domestic happiness." He had also, briefly, considered pursuing a degree in philosophy at a university in Heidelberg and bringing his sisters along with him. But in this instance, Julian faced reality; there was no money for his venture. He bore his disappointment like a "hero," Sophia wrote her sister Elizabeth who, like everyone save Sophia and her daughters, was fatigued by his antics. Then Sophia explained Julian's newest plan to Elizabeth. Acting on Dr. Loring's advice, he would obtain a degree in civil engineering, a practical field that would turn Julian into a wage earner. But before Julian could enroll in the Lawrence Scientific School, he must "burrow" down and master math, a challenge, Sophia surely understood, that was greater than financing his education abroad.[7]

With Sophia's sanguine approach to all that was Julian, Rose understandably held fast to her belief that he was the epitome of manhood. And Rose shared some of her brother's less than noble traits. Like him, she had gained little from her education, desultory as it was until 1866, when

Sophia permitted her to leave home for Diocletian Lewis's Gymnasium in Lexington. During the school's brief existence from 1864 to 1867, one of its instructors was Theodore Weld, the abolitionist with whom Elizabeth Peabody had taught in the early 1850s at his Raritan Bay Union School in New Jersey. If Sophia had put Julian in Sanborn's school during the Civil War, she could surely stomach having her daughter taught by an abolitionist now that the war was over. And Dio Lewis, as he was called, espoused homeopathy, temperance, hygiene, and physical education for young women. He was also a generous man who, revering Nathaniel Hawthorne, had invited Una to attend the Gymnasium without charge. That was in the fall of 1865 when Sophia had enough income to decline becoming indebted to him. She paid for Una's six-month course and an additional expense for the "bloomer dress" Una wore during exercise. Though these trousers would cover Una's legs and never be worn outdoors, Sophia still advised a long skirt over this gym dress to prevent the "gaze of the world." Una did not "appreciate," Sophia told her, that women and men are different. A woman simply cannot do what a man does, and Una was told not to walk from Lexington to Concord.[8]

Una had, nonetheless, blazed the trail from Concord to Lexington for her younger sister. Sophia believed that exercise would cure Rose's "nervousness" (having denied to Annie that Rose suffered that complaint). Dancing, however, was prohibited: "It is so much better to have none of these excitements," she wrote Una. Had Sophia suppressed the memory of her happy waltzing days in Cuba, or remembered all too well the temptations of her youthful infatuation? Whatever her motives, insisting that her daughters seek calm and quiet replicated her own mother's advice to her so many years ago. But Rose was not Sophia, whose rebellions against authority, maternal and otherwise, were unspoken. Rose grumbled about her situation at Mrs. Haskell's, where she boarded with other girls who made her life miserable with their gossip. Rose bristled against rules, particularly the one requiring church attendance, and she wanted Sophia to write a note excusing her from it. Rose chafed at financial constraints, which were tied to her displeasure over churchgoing: "I have nothing to wear, & am in an awful pickl [sic]," she wrote her weary mother, who counseled her to obey rules and realize that she really did not need a new merino jacket to stay warm. By May of 1867, Rose was no longer in Lexington but in Boston with Ada at the school she had established.[9]

Though Rose appeared to emulate Julian with demands about attire and careless attitudes toward study, her adolescent malaise possessed a component of self-scrutiny that never dawned upon her brother. Rose fell short, in her own estimation, for she was not like her mother, who did what was right no matter how difficult or unpleasant. But neither was Rose like her father. She had never really known him while he lived though she now had grown closer to him by reading "his books," she wrote Aunt Ebe; they made Rose "understand his nature." These realizations led to others. Rose confided to Ebe being "pitiably moody & unself controlled" and feared she would "never come off well in the world." Nor would she ever be "loved infinitely," as perhaps she imagined her parents had loved each other. That kind of romantic, transcendental love was "what makes a person the noblest and highest they can dream of." And while she believed her brother to be "the highest man," even he lacked the perfection she sought in the opposite sex. "I hate men as cordially as I love you," she wrote Una. "I think however much they love us they think us inferior."[10]

This vein of what today would be called feminism was cultivated by Mary Betts, a woman in Stanford, Connecticut. She encouraged Rose to be "saucy," and about the "voting question," Betts wrote militantly: "We shall yet see processions of strong minded women, in gymnastic costume, walking on the arms of their husband—meek, dejected men—to the polls." Betts wrote about Rosa Bonheur's triumphs in France and about Thackeray's Becky Sharp, who "crawls and twists" through the pages of *Vanity Fair.* "Don't be content with a frivolous life,—with any life which does not lead to a noble goal," Betts warned Rose. Such inspirational words recall Reverend Channing's exhortations to Una when she was in her teens, and Rose wrote her sister, "I have come to feel the responsibility of my own life—not mine, but given to me in trust." These glimmerings of mature awareness magnified her perceived failures. She was deeply grateful to James Freeman Clarke for his note of encouragement, though she believed she was unworthy of it. Sophia reassured Rose of her sterling character. Yes, at times Rose was "pettish and unreasonable," but, Sophia told her daughter:

> Religious principle and sentiment would surely render you at last gentle and charitable to the shortcomings of your fellow mortals. . . . GOD has given you the perilous gift of genius. With it you are to become greater and lovelier than your less gifted fellow beings.[11]

Sophia's insights into Rose were as prescient as her judgments of Julian were obtuse, and regarding Una, Sophia was cloyingly affectionate on the one hand and censorious about petty matters on the other. "I am hungry for you," Sophia wrote Una, entreating her to return home for an anniversary of Nathaniel's death. But, after leaving the Gymnasium, Una stayed away from Concord, paying long visits to Ebe and others where she did not escape her mother's advice. Una must not wear her hair coiled atop her head; "things must be in *relation*." Una must improve her spelling and avoid redundancy "which makes a statement weaker." Notwithstanding implied criticism of Una's intellect, Sophia insisted that "for a person who has a mind like yours," it would be a "pity" to teach gymnastics. Una's plan, which called for her to live in Dorchester, had provoked a barrage of letters from Sophia over a three-day period in September of 1866. About working to fill that "hole" in her income, Una should realize there would be no "hole" if she only lived at home. If demolishing Una's financial argument did not work, guilt might: "No one can possibly want you so much as I do—and I speak of *heart* want—not help or care." But Una's reply drew Sophia up. "You know I should die outright," she responded, "if I thought you were doing penance by being at home." If the need arose, Sophia would leave Concord and live with her children wherever they might choose to be: "I live in you and not the Wayside."[12]

As the eldest child, Una had borne the brunt of expectations that she often dutifully fulfilled. When Sophia had been ill for several months during 1866, and when influenza completely felled her in December, she did require Una's "help" and "care." Sophia was generally debilitated by worry and by work, her hand was often lame from copying, and pulmonary problems had become chronic. As Sophia's problems mounted and her health declined, she told Annie about a "kind of desperation of the nerves, which made me wish to *die*." But Sophia claimed that her children kept her from uttering "'nunc dimittis'." This was the "Euthanasia" Sophia referred to when writing to Elizabeth. By January of 1867, Sophia's exhaustion was so profound that "earthly existence became intolerable." She was not "*sad*," Sophia insisted, countering Elizabeth's use of that word, though "sometimes outward life oppresses me, and I think of the 'nunc dimittis' with rapture." But her life's work was not yet complete. Sophia was not ready to be dismissed until her children were settled.[13]

And barely five months later, it appeared that Una would be settled. She became engaged to Samuel Storrow Higginson, her choice of a spouse announcing values Sophia did not share. Una had been stirred when Storrow's "Uncle Wentworth," as she too now called him, roused Concordians to a "spirit of action" at the beginning of the Civil War. Of the Secret Six, only Higginson had taken his commitment to abolition into battle as colonel in charge of the first federally sponsored regiment of freed African Americans. Living among these troops had broadened Higginson's views, and after the war, he became an ardent supporter of Negro enfranchisement as well as other liberal causes, including women's rights. These postwar campaigns were further evidence to Sophia of Higginson's "fanaticism," for she considered the Negro to be "utterly unfit" to vote. She hoped Mary would stop haranguing her on that subject and forbade her to take Rose to lectures by Higginson and George William Curtis, the latter having had the temerity to expose *Fanshawe* to the world. Both Higginson and Curtis skewed issues with their "one sidedness" and "artificiality," Sophia claimed. Though the Civil War had ended, the country had entered "a season of political animosities, national tournaments, and swift harsh human decisions, in which there is often neither justice, love, nor truth." Sophia intended to protect her children from all such "transient disturbance," to keep them "folded up till the fullness of time."[14]

Storrow was, therefore, an unlikely candidate for marriage to a Hawthorne, though he was a fine representative of Higginson family values. He had served the Union forces as chaplain to the 9th Regiment of the Massachusetts Colored Infantry. Immediately after the war ended, while he was attached to the 1st Division Army of the James, Storrow went to Salisbury, Maryland, his errand, delivering letters from his troops. There he met the African American Charles Pollitt, a revered preacher who had begun a school, and Storrow published their encounter in a letter to the *Freedman's Report* in July of 1865. He was taken with the reverend, so "noble" and "Princely in his step," and marveled that "[w]ithout the aid of a single white person," Pollitt's school "brought the children to proficiency" in reading and arithmetic. More remarkable still was Pollitt's complete lack of rancor over the injustices he and his people had suffered: "The fires that had burned up into his life had left only ashes of forgiveness."[15] Respect imbued Storrow's observations; they entirely lacked the prejudices found even among some of his most enlightened contemporaries.

There were many sides to Storrow Higginson, whom Sophia had come to know not as army chaplain or as proponent of Negro enfranchisement but as the son of her friend in "maidenhood"; a Harvard graduate slightly older than Julian; a casual visitor to the Wayside over the past seven years; and a courier of sorts who brought Sophia a book from General Hitchcock. When Storrow's visits had grown frequent, his intentions toward Una became apparent with his gift to her on her twenty-third birthday, a three-volume set of Shelley's poems. The young couple was "wildly happy" in a "profound, radiant, blazing adoration of each other," Sophia wrote Rose. Everyone seemed to rejoice in Una's good fortune. Even Ebe was pleased with Storrow because he had fought in the war and he held very "correct notions," among them disdain for Sophia's treatment of Julian. Congratulations on the engagement came from all quarters, family as well as friends like Hitchcock and Pierce. "We shall have no more heartachs [sic] about Una's health and happiness," Sophia predicted because "GOD has established her joy forever." On May 19, 1867, Sophia conveyed her entirely positive judgment of Storrow to Thomas Wentworth Higginson. "I did not think the earth contained a man to whom without a misgiving, I could confide Una," she wrote him: "So delicate, high, noble and large a soul as Storrow's can never disappoint."[16]

Little more than a week later, Una was "quiet as a lake" when Storrow sailed for South America: his purpose, to improve his fortunes. He left Una with three letters, to be opened while he was at sea. Over the course of several months, she received more letters from her fiancé, some of which she read to Ebe. But during the couple's increasingly long separation, Ebe and all others, except Julian, changed their opinion of Storrow. He had not been quite candid about his motives for travel. His plan, it now seemed, was to perfect his foreign languages in order to become a professor, an occupation that would "perpetuate poverty in our family," according to Ebe. And worse, he "got into his old groove." That was how Julian characterized what Ebe explained to the Manning relatives, what Storrow's own mother finally admitted, and what the Higginsons had known all along. Though they had hoped Una would be his "salvation," he was never going to marry anyone. Julian alone remained willing to defend Storrow's "integrity as far as adherence to his principles goes," according to Ebe, but Julian had to admit, "they are very bad principles." By April of 1868, Sophia announced that Una had written Storrow with his "dismissal."[17]

Sophia was relieved that the "utterly selfish, self righteous fanatic," as she now characterized him, was out of her daughter's life. Una handled the breakup well, claiming that she was "inexpressibly relieved" for she had never really loved Storrow. She confided as much to Ebe, who was pleased that her own letters had become "indispensable" to her niece. Ebe knew Sophia would be "utterly astounded" by the topics discussed in correspondence with Una. When she had differed with Storrow over Negro enfranchisement, Ebe told her "she was a Copperhead." Though Ebe believed women's privileges were more valuable than any rights they might acquire, she scoffed at Una's notion that "women would vote as well as most men," "a herd of mediocre men" at that. From the confines of her boardinghouse room, Ebe kept abreast of national movements, and she delivered reasoned judgments about them. When the war was winding down, she asked Una, "Do you not exult at Jeff's capture." Ebe was as flip in referring to the president of the confederacy, Jefferson Davis, as she was respectful of President Lincoln's "common sense" and "shrewd" policies. In Aunt Ebe, Una had found a correspondent with whom she could confide personal matters and debate national and world issues.[18]

Reconstruction-era politics and reformist ideas were not Sophia's concerns, however. The North's victory over the South, the assassination of President Lincoln, and the enfranchisement of all Americans rarely found their way into her letters or journals. Sophia briefly alluded to Lincoln's death in a letter to Nat only because his grandson's christening robes prompted her to think of the deceased president now wearing "the white robes of the saint." Even in letters to Hitchcock, who had been Lincoln's special adviser on the exchange of prisoners, Sophia did not address the nation's plight. Hitchcock's political and military accomplishments did not interest her, but his esoteric philosophy did. She thought him to be an ideal confidant, now that her husband, "That 'Essence Royal' has returned to Court from his visit to the country," Nathaniel's death couched in language she had lifted from Hitchcock's own *Swedenborg, A Hermetic Philosopher*. His books were her "infinite" joy, and she concurred with his idea that every work of true art was a symbol of divine love. Her "Dear, priceless friend," as she addressed him, made her "dim dreams . . . realities." Her flattery might have appeared self-serving or facetious, but not to Hitchcock, who wrote on the envelope of her August 4, 1867, letter: "She is sincere and does not mean to jest with me."[19]

Sophia sang Hitchcock's praises to family and friends. She directed Rose to his commentary on the *Arabian Nights*, and Eliza Thayer Clapp, the author of *Studies in Religion*, to his remarks on the "Sonnets of Shakespeare (Lord Bacon)." Like Delia Bacon, whom Sophia had met in England, Hitchcock did not think Shakespeare was the author of the works attributed to him. Sophia told Elizabeth Peabody that Hitchcock, "Lord Bacon," and Plato were her "Counselors," as were the truths she found in the *Bhagavad Gita*. So many of Sophia's ideas "chime[d]," she wrote her other sister, with the concept of "sattwa," or goodness, adduced in that ancient Hindu text. Sophia strove to interpret her life—which daily grew more burdened with worry—through all-encompassing, highly eclectic, and somewhat idiosyncratic philosophies. She also sought solace in friends— Hitchcock now, Annie earlier—whom she deemed equal to her intimate, elevated discourse.[20]

With Sarah Clarke, however, Sophia enjoyed the ease of decades-long, mutual affection. Sophia preferred her company above all others, so Sophia claimed while spending restful weeks with her in Newport, Rhode Island. Sophia also grew fond of Mary Hemenway, a woman unlike Sophia and Sarah in so many ways. Though Mary Porter Tileston Hemenway was a member of James Freeman Clarke's Church of the Disciples, she was also married to Edward Augustus Holyoke Hemenway, the richest man in the United States for a period of time. Despite their vast wealth, the

Hemenways could do nothing to save their daughter's life, and Lotty died in 1865. Sophia had become "so closely bound" to Mary that she felt this loss as if it were her own. Mary was, Sophia explained to General Hitchcock, in tune "with the highest thought I am capable of." Sophia could "unburthen" herself to Mary who took an interest in Julian, invited Una to her mountain retreat, and proffered advice to Rose when she complained about her "shabby" attire: "simplicity" was most becoming. Like Sophia's friend Sarah Shaw, the "divine" "Mrs. H." shared her wealth. A vacation at Mary's home at the shore "cured" Sophia, when she had been ill on-and-off for months. And Mary's generosity—like Sarah Shaw's—went beyond kindness to personal friends. Mary became a philanthropist and advocate for women's suffrage; she founded the Boston Normal schools for cookery and gymnastics and funded archaeological expeditions in the far west. Mary Hemenway was a visionary as well as being Sophia's "intimate and dear" friend.[21]

Sophia's friendships were as eclectic as her philosophies, and she added to her "counselors" Mary Abigail Dodge, or Gail Hamilton as she was known through her writing and as Sophia always referred to her. The women met at the Fieldses' home on March 28, 1866. By that time, Gail had written essays for the *Atlantic* and published six books with Ticknor and Fields, among them a volume of travel writing. A protofeminist on the order of some of the other women in Sophia's circle, Gail's topics ranged from the profession of authorship in America to the roles of women and men. Sophia immediately liked her and invited her to spend several days at the Wayside in May of 1866.[22] These two women soon discovered they had much in common, in particular, the cost of doing business with a friend.

John Louis O'Sullivan should have already taught Sophia that painful lesson, though she may have never learned all facts about his financial entanglements with Nathaniel. These are not entirely illuminated by extant correspondence, and O'Sullivan's last known letter on the matter was dated February of 1866. In it, he expressed his regrets about the "land," presumably his wife's property in New York state that Nathaniel had purchased in lieu of lending him $3,000. Unfortunately, it had depreciated in value, and O'Sullivan wished to know the exact date of its conveyance to Nathaniel as well as the amount realized from its foreclosure sale. Despite this financial debacle, O'Sullivan was confident that his "relation [so] well established" with Sophia would survive any misunderstanding.[23]

Sophia's once-admired friend O'Sullivan had lost her thousands of dollars by the time she asked Fields in the fall of 1866, "Did not you say to me that you would be 'very near me' in my widowhood?" Sophia penned this letter after receiving Hillard's warning to expect less from Nathaniel's copyrights and "$1,200 less income from Fields," exactly what she had earned from publishing installments of "Passages." By January of 1867, for the first time in her life, she was afraid she would not have the income to pay her bills, and earnings from her book-length *Passages* would be delayed. Copying it had made her hand "lame" and progress was stalled. Again she looked to Fields, asking about income from her husband's copyrights. In March, she wrote that she had no money to pay for coal or to discharge debts with tradesmen or to pay Dio Lewis what she owed for Rose's tuition and board. She was nearly bankrupt, she claimed. Then Hillard delivered more bad news. Her dividends would be less than expected because of "some swindling transactions" at the bank. An advance on *Passages* would prevent her from asking her cousin George Peabody to "save her." In May, her situation was no better. Fearing that she would be arrested for debt, she asked if any money might be expected from Ticknor and Fields during the summer. And in June, upon receipt of an unexpected bill of $60 for cemetery expenses, Sophia again asked Fields if he owed her any money. In the same letter, she remarked that James and Annie no longer visited her. There must be "far grander landscapes where you are," she wrote Fields.[24]

Sophia was now forced to consider renting or selling the Wayside. "ON NO ACCOUNT sell the Wayside," Hillard told Sophia, who conveyed his opinion with her own emphasis to Elizabeth Peabody, adding that "Mr. Hawthorne pleased himself with the idea of a permanent homestead for his family." Sophia, therefore, devised another plan. She eliminated some expenses by dismissing her maids and shuttering the house. With the children, she then made prolonged visits to friends. In August they stayed with Pierce in New Hampshire. There, Una diverted herself riding horses while Sophia had no escape from thoughts about selling the Wayside. She wrote Fields that her family could move into a "shanty" and "bear it, as becomes the children and widow of the noblest of men." In September, Sophia with Julian and Rose stayed with Eliza Clapp in her Dorchester home, while Una went to Lexington.[25]

When Sophia reopened the Wayside in late September, she immediately wrote Eliza that she was "practicing ferocious economy." Una and Rose tended to household chores previously relegated to maids. Una hoped to teach gymnastics at Miss Wiley's school. Rose, whose artistic talent Sophia happily cultivated, sold her paintings at Childs and Jenks. And for the briefest moment, Sophia toyed with returning to art. She could paint and "ask what I please . . . then get what I can," she explained to

Fields, immediately realizing she was much too busy copying to entertain that fantasy.[26]

Sophia's letters to Fields continually mingled business questions to her publisher with emotional disclosures to her friend. His promise, to be "very near" her throughout the trials of widowhood, if she recalled his somewhat vague words accurately, led to expectations—equally vague— that Fields might not have intended. When her questions about being owed anything from Ticknor and Fields were answered with money, she accepted it without scrutinizing the source. An advance? Some royalties? Disbursements from that indeterminate sum kept on account for the Hawthornes at the firm? Perhaps relief over having kept those "hounds" temporarily at bay stifled her desire for clarification. And Fields did not offer it, just as he had never given Nathaniel statements about his assets and liabilities with the firm. Sophia was, therefore, "aghast" when, in October of 1867, Hillard informed her that she was overdrawn by $700. The "beginning of our ruin is at hand," she responded; the firm would have to be repaid from her principal. And about that money she had received in April? It was not, as she had thought, from Nathaniel's copy-rights but a loan from Fields. "I never asked you to lend me a penny in my life," she wrote Fields indignantly. Perhaps she had not, but her pitiful prediction about leaving the Wayside for a "shanty" may have leveraged money out of his pockets.[27]

A year of toil and worry ended in severe illness that worsened during the first months of 1868. Sophia wrote Elizabeth, who was then in Germany beginning her investigation of kindergarten education, that the doctor had for a time given up hope for her recovery. She was diagnosed with pneu-monia and pleurisy, "lung fever" as Julian called it when he wrote to Hitchcock on his mother's behalf. The "angelic" Una put aside her pre-occupations over her then dissolving engagement to Storrow to nurse her mother. For nearly three months, she was bedridden. In April, and only with her daughter's assistance, could she venture downstairs for a few minutes. Ebe commiserated with Una, knowing she had a "dull time." Caring for Sophia chipped away at Una's own health. She managed bravely with the help of a maid who returned to the Wayside for an interval, but Una refused the assistance of her Aunt Mary. She had sold her home in Concord two years before and was living in Cambridge in a house purchased from John Forbes for $1,200. Mary's financial resources assured her the comfort and security that eluded Sophia who hoped that once *Passages* was published "we shall get along very well." By May, she was healthy enough to conclude work on that book and to make the difficult, inevitable decision that the Wayside must be sold, a decision she would not reverse.[28]

Sophia began to plan her next book composed of excerpts from Nathaniel's English notebooks, and Fields, having just returned from a six-month tour with Charles Dickens, was available for negotiations. But before entering into another arrangement with Fields, she wanted an accurate reckoning of her "liabilities and resources." Her request disingenuously deflected responsibility for omissions in bookkeeping from Fields to Ticknor. *He* would never give "Mr Hawthorne his account. . . . Not all my efforts could persuade him to add up the sum, and Mr. Hawthorne himself would not ask, though he wished exceedingly to know." When she received this "account" some two weeks later, she assumed a clerk had made an error. But no, Sophia had been overdrawn at the firm for months, and royalties from Nathaniel's books were insufficient to repay her debts. Reeling, she inquired about another asset: "Have I then swallowed up all the [rest] of the 10,000 dollars in your hands for the last year as well as the copy right income?" Fields answered her question with one of his own. What $10,000? The $10,000, Sophia shot back, that Hillard had deposited with Ticknor and Fields. Again she refrained from accusing Fields and asked, could *Hillard* have made so "huge a mistake, or has he now disposed of that sum in another way?" Fields's reply made Sophia all the more distraught: Hillard knew nothing of it, Fields insisted, repeating that his firm "never" had it in their hands.[29]

During this flurry of May 1868 correspondence, Sophia remained civil, even cordial. She needed to stay on good terms with her publisher, her letters filled with questions about the proofs (there were errors and omissions that must be addressed) and decisions about who would create its index (she was too ill to do it herself). But she pressed for clarifications about her finances, flabbergasted that Fields continued to deny the "amount due from Ticknor and Fields $9,569." This asset was documented on a paper from Hillard that she was looking at when she wrote Fields on June 2, the day her outrage boiled over. Did he and Hillard think she was an "idiot"? "I cannot believe my senses when I see on one paper his record of this fact, and in your note a denial of such a thing!" Dancing around the truth, Fields acknowledged that the money in question had been held by the firm, but at an earlier date. Sophia responded to Fields that had he only said "'We *once* had' rather than 'we *never* had,'" she would have understood immediately. Apparently mollified, she returned to the business of getting *Passages* printed and agreed to do the index herself. Perhaps this acquiescence was calculated. She had lost a battle, but she might still win a war, and she immediately broached the subject of payment for future publications with Ticknor and Fields. Hillard had not drawn up a contract, and Sophia asked if her royalties would be calculated as Nathaniel's had been. There was no simple answer to this question, as she was to discover.[30]

In 1860, 1861, and 1862, Nathaniel's fiction—that is, his novels and collected stories—earned royalties of between 10 and 15 *percent* per volume. *Our Old Home* earned fifteen *cents* per volume (a 12% royalty when the book sold at $1.25). But the cost books of Ticknor and Fields reveal that in 1863 calculations changed and no evidence exists that Nathaniel knew anything about this. He had been earning 15% per volume on *The Scarlet Letter* when it sold at 75 cents, but in 1863 the book earned 15 *cents* when it sold for $1.25 (a 12% royalty), and in 1864, it earned 11.25 *cents* when the book sold for $1.50 (a 7.5% royalty). Payments for a particular title were inconsistent from one year to the next, and payments for different titles were inconsistent with each other. For example, in 1863, *The Blithedale Romance* earned 11.25 cents on a book that sold for $1.00 (an 11.25% royalty); in 1864, the novel continued to earn 11.25 cents per book when it sold at $1.50 (yielding a royalty of 7.5%). Some consistent patterns do emerge: the selling price of books had risen, the remuneration to the author had fallen, and profits to the firm had increased three- and fourfold during the years immediately after the Civil War. As Rosemary Mims Fisk points out in her thorough study of Nathaniel's relationship with James T. Fields, postwar inflation drove up the cost of producing books, and the "only cost which Fields had any hope of controlling was the author's copyright." He did so by changing a percentage royalty to a flat fee. Emerson, Holmes, and others received 20 cents per copy, but according to Fisk, "Hawthorne did not fare so well. . . . Fields either intentionally or neglectfully failed to increase the copyright payment as retail prices rose."[31]

Why was Nathaniel treated differently? Perhaps Fields believed that his largesse toward the Hawthorne children informally compensated for lower royalty payments. But a more cynical explanation is probable. Nathaniel was an easy dupe. Unlike Emerson, who was attentive to his financial arrangements with Ticknor and Fields, Nathaniel had been unwilling to inquire about these details, even during his most robust period of activity with the firm in the early 1850s. By 1862, having begun his descent into "bewilderment," Nathaniel was unable to manage his affairs. If Fields had been oblivious to his friend's failings that year or the following, he was fully aware of the Hawthornes' debts and liabilities. Annie knew about these and about Nathaniel's mental and physical decline, Sophia having confided in her. And Fields saw that wreck of a man who returned to Charles Street after the fatal trip with Ticknor, yet Fields withheld from Nathaniel what he paid to some other authors.

Sophia knew nothing about the disadvantageous shift in copyright calculations that had begun in 1863 when, in June of 1868, she asked Fields if her own books would earn 15% as had Nathaniel's. She was ignorant about the shift from a percentage to a flat rate when determining royalties. And she did not know that Ticknor and Fields had two categories of payment, one for Nathaniel's fiction and another for *Our Old Home*, a book based on his travel writing. But even before getting a clear answer to her June 12 question—would she be paid as was her husband for *Our Old Home?*—she began preparing excerpts from Nathaniel's English notebooks to publish with Fields's firm, and he agreed to give her a $500 advance, which she gratefully accepted so that she could pay her bills.[32]

Cordial correspondence about the advance was punctuated by other business. Sophia insisted upon corrections to the proofs of *Passages from the American Note-Books*. Nathaniel's "style must always be retained" no matter the delay caused by corrections. And Sophia turned to discussion of her advance from Smith and Elder, which she expected to be on a par with the British publisher's payment for the copyright to *Our Old Home*. Fields thought the amount was £100, his uncertainty sending Sophia to review letters from Ticknor on the matter, and on August 2, she confidently asserted her right to £250, adding that surely her projected *two* volumes was worth what Smith and Elder had paid for Nathaniel's single-volume *Our Old Home*. But when Fields insisted that sum was £100, Sophia returned to the subject of royalties. On August 2, she wrote "My dear friend," her salutation perhaps an attempt to forfend against his growing annoyance: "[W]ill you tell me *why* your house *now* gives 12 per cent instead of fifteen per cent for the books? For I supposed the price of the book being higher, the percentage should keep up to the former mark. But I need to be instructed." Fields's supply of cordiality had been exhausted. Hadn't he already explained the "percentage"? She would get, he wrote her, "all that a publisher can afford."[33]

His explanation of the "percentage" remained cloaked in obscurity, and Sophia was not alone in her perplexity about bookkeeping at Ticknor and Fields. Gail Hamilton, who had also considered Fields her friend, had become suspicious about payments from the firm, and she discovered that they were indeed inequitable. During the summer of 1868, she and Sophia caused such a stir over their demands for clarity, and equity, that Fields asked Hillard to step in. He wrote Sophia that, while the issues she raised with Ticknor and Fields were "substantially like" Gail Hamilton's, neither woman had grounds for complaint. Only then did Hillard reveal that, in

December of 1864, he had made a verbal agreement on Sophia's behalf with Howard M. Ticknor, his father's successor, to change Nathaniel's royalties from a percentage to a flat fee. "It was suggested to me," Hillard's passive voice obscuring responsibility, that this arrangement would be more "convenient" for the firm and yield a more "liberal" payment to Sophia. Given Sophia's "intimacy" with Fields, Hillard told her, "I drew the inference that you were aware of the terms of the contract, and executed it without consulting you. This I now see I should not have done." Gail immediately decried this additional evidence of corrupt practices at the firm. "If Mr. Meadows" she wrote Sophia, calling him by their pet synonym for fields, had "been the Soul of honor," he had conducted matters "so bunglingly as to make them seem dishonest."[34]

Several months before this appalling revelation, Sophia had dreamed about going to the Fieldses' elegant Back Bay home only to discover that it was under renovation. Numerous rooms had been added. Sophia walked throughout a veritable "city of chambers all fair and orderly." But not one room was for her. She was wearing muddy shoes and did not belong inside that house.[35]

Chapter 22

Starve Her into Compliance

There was no room for Sophia in Annie's home, at the publishing house of Ticknor and Fields, at the Wayside, in Concord, or in America.

"Having conjured up a fancied wrong, she nurses it well," Annie penned in her diary, dismissing Sophia as "disloyal." But it was Fields who was disloyal, something Sophia may have sensed more than ten years earlier when she declined his invitation to publish in the *Atlantic*. Only the "danger of starvation" would induce her to do so, she had joked, but her refusal foretold the inevitable collision of their personalities:

> I am still glad that I have not to combat any of your arguments upon this subject viva voce; . . . I should find it painful to oppose you. Yet I *should* oppose you with as steady and immovable pertinacity as the biggest created rock would resist the raging sea or the sweet lapsing tide. You have no idea how inexorable I am.

Nathaniel had immediately followed her letter to Fields with one of his own, lauding his wife's "narrative and descriptive epistles." Fields was "quite right to want Mrs. Hawthorne for contributress; and perhaps I may yet starve her into compliance." Nathaniel's bantering hyperbole had actually been grim foreshadowing. He had escaped ending his days in an alms-house, a fate that loomed over his wife. His foolish loans, bad investments, expenditures beyond his means, and willful ignorance about accounts with Ticknor and Fields had conspired to "starve" Sophia into publishing her "Cathedral Letters" and "Italian Journal." But not with Ticknor and Fields. By the fall of 1868, her trust in Fields destroyed, she took her "treasures" to her cousin, the publisher George Palmer Putnam.[1]

Sophia was, indeed, "inexorable," and opposing Fields was painful. As a single woman fighting a large, prestigious firm for financial disclosures and compensation equal to that paid a man, she had entered an entirely new arena. Lacking a precedent for her struggle, her strategies sometimes ineptly relied upon pathos as much as logic. Cloaking threats in maternal sentiment, she had warned Fields, "[y]ou see how fiercely sharp I am getting—as a lioness over her cubs—." Sophia's "tone of martyrdom is unpleasant, and some of her appeals for sympathy will strike the reader as surprisingly indelicate," Randall Stewart writes, but he forgives any "lapses in dignity and taste" in light of the "acuteness" of her financial distress and her otherwise "rigorous inquiry." Playing the card of the poor widow to "Heart's Ease" (another pet name for Fields) was partially Fields's fault for, as Gail reminded Sophia, he had cultivated a "friendly and familiar style of doing business." Gail would prefer "hostile and formal accuracy" any day, if only her accounts could be tallied without error, and she counseled Sophia about how to frame her accusations and modulate her tone. She should claim only that she had never *received* an accounting because she could not truly assert that Fields had never *sent* one. She should not accuse Fields of bad intentions but cry loudly about bad consequences. While Gail's letters advised restraint, elsewhere she vented her spleen about that "jackal" Fields with his "mean face and ophidian eyes and puny voice."[2]

Sophia leaves no record of similarly venomous judgments. She was too unwell, too weary with relentless copying and editing and proofreading, too preoccupied with her children's troubles, too oppressed by an onslaught of bills and debts, and much too disappointed by former friends to muster such ire. She turned her problems with Fields over to Elizabeth, who had just returned from an extended trip in Europe, and a most productive trip it had been. She had traveled to Germany, first to Heidelberg, then to Berlin, Hamburg, and Dresden, where she furthered her study of early childhood development. In Neufchatel, Switzerland, she met with Thomas Wentworth Higginson, and in Rome, thanks to Sophia's interventions, Elizabeth spent the winter and spring of 1868 in Charlotte Cushman's home. Back in the United States, Elizabeth was beginning her most important contribution to American education, the establishment of the kindergarten system. She could also resume her role as Sophia's advocate, now also functioning as her "business advisor." With Elizabeth willing to tackle the mess at Ticknor and Fields, Sophia freed herself to confront the next phase of her life.[3]

Reports about Germany had made the possibility of living there plausible and enticing. Because Julian's career ostensibly lay in engineering, Elizabeth promoted Dresden's "Polytecknik," where tuition was far less than in America. Everything cost less in Dresden. Instead of spending $4,000 annually to live in the United States, Sophia and her three children could make do with only $1,200. This information came by way of Mary Vandervoort, a longtime Dresden resident who had made the Hawthornes' acquaintance in Italy. She assured Sophia that a genteel, inexpensive life beckoned in this city with its galleries and cathedrals and concert halls, one of many reasons to forsake Concord, so lacking in cultural opportunities. Better to leave now than have all recollection of marital bliss erased by an ugly new reality, a gang of burglars who roamed through the town. Better to leave the Wayside, the symbol of her domestic achievement, before she lost it to her debts. The Wayside had become a "hateful" place for Una, the scene of her mother's recent "struggle for life" and Una's "sorrow" over her failed engagement. Her "faith in everything earthly" was "forever shaken," she wrote Higginson, whose affection was her great solace. Both Sophia and her daughter needed a change of scene; Sophia, in particular, craved a new "*land* and *people*," though she admitted that she would miss a few friends. Eliza Clapp was among these six, so Sophia wrote her. Una hoped to see "Uncle Wentworth" "across the water." But Sarah Shaw, despite having traveled so much at an earlier point in her life, doubted she would ever see Sophia again and wistfully recalled how Sophia had amused little Bob by drawing horses for him. Such innocently happy moments were irrevocably past.[4]

"*Nothing*" was left in Concord for Sophia, or so she had convinced herself by September of 1868. She also convinced herself that conducting every aspect of life in a foreign tongue would pose no problem; "we shall soon be adept" at speaking enough German to converse with porters and servants, she wrote Mary Vandervoort. But Sophia did not have the luxury of deluding herself about finding money for her voyage. She turned to Franklin Pierce asking him "frankly and fairly" for $500, perhaps even $1000: "Can you spare so much to the family of your dearest friend?" He did not immediately reply, perhaps because he was seriously ill with erysipelas and had little more than a year to live. When he did reply, it was to announce that he could "neither advise nor help me!" Sophia wrote Mrs. Vandervoort: "We have lost him!" But even without a parting gift from Pierce, Sophia scraped together the money to book four, first-class passages for the price of three on the *Deutschland*. She also arranged to transport some furniture, including Hawthorne family tables, as well as trunks and "heaps of boxes," many heavy with Nathaniel's English notebooks and "Continental Journal," her "Cathedral letters," and "Italian journals," his love letters, and her *Cuba Journal*.[5]

Her plans in place, Sophia began her farewells, some of them fraught with the awareness that a friendship had already vanished. There would be no goodbye at all to Annie. Pierce was "lost" to Sophia, as was her other general, Ethan Allen Hitchcock. He had recently married and had not answered Sophia's letter congratulating him on the "happy change in your relations." Sophia feared that this and other letters had fallen into the hands of that "babylonish woman," as she called his wife when writing to Mrs. Vandervoort, confiding that she could "weep over him for very pity and sorrow for him and me." Had Sophia wanted more than friendship, if "friendship" defines a relationship that may not have been mutual?[6]

Sophia also said farewell to her sisters and sister-in-law. Goodbyes to Elizabeth Peabody were brightened by the hope that she might well be among those to appear in Dresden some day, though leaving the Manns at this moment was terribly difficult, for Horace Jr. was mortally ill. Parting from Elizabeth Hawthorne must have stirred altogether different emotions, one of which was surely Sophia's relief that a vast ocean would separate her from Ebe's relentless displeasure. And the idea of foreign travel displeased Ebe immensely. Permanently relocating to another country indicated a character flaw that occasioned her biting criticism, which she conveyed to her cousin Richard Manning. Blaming Nathaniel's decline on "one of Mrs. Hawthorne's absurdities"—specifically, her desire to be in Italy—Ebe now claimed Sophia compelled Julian to accompany her to Dresden because she could not "dispense with his society," never mind his alleged plan to further his education abroad. And Sophia's influence on Una had been consistently "hurtful," according to Ebe, who ignored the many sources of that young woman's pain. Ebe would miss Una terribly; Sophia would not miss Ebe at all.[7]

Just days before Sophia sailed, Elizabeth Peabody wrote Fields "to beg" that he "make all bright & clear" so that her sister would not "fret herself to death at Dresden with this miserable doubt in your good faith," a doubt Elizabeth herself shared. She was appalled to discover that Nathaniel's works had earned a measly $17,000 during the seventeen years of their publication by Ticknor and Fields. During that same period, Washington Irving's books had made a whopping $150,000 with George Putnam, who abetted his cousins' suspicions. He told them about Fields's underhanded dealings with fellow publishers; one particularly "base transaction" might have wiped George out. But Elizabeth did not bring her cousin into the argument about her sister's treatment. Rather, she penned a very long, carefully worded letter appealing first to Fields's self-interest: "[I]t is of *immense importance* to *you* that you should not be suspected of not dealing—I will not say *justly* but *generously* with the widow and orphans of *your dearest friend.*" Elizabeth's convoluted syntax pulled the strings of emotion with impunity, "considering that it was faith *in your friendship* that has led to the most *unbusinesslike* (let me say) deficiency of written contracts, it seems to me that an appeal *to sentiment* is in place here." And in the ensuing pages, she laid out multiple disturbing facts about secretly changed percentages confirmed by "young Mr. T's statement," now in Sophia's possession, about this *"verbal arrangement"* and another receipt showing the true amount paid by Smith and Elder for *Our Old Home.* "When an *infinite confidence* is disturbed," Elizabeth wrote with a grandiloquent flourish, "the doubt partakes of the infinity."[8] Surely Fields would provide a satisfactory response.

He did not. Sophia put the matter in the hands of an attorney, but *not* George Hillard, who claimed her mind was "ulcerated." On October 14, she left Boston; the next day she was in New York, where she met with George Putnam and discussed taking Nathaniel's "Continental Journal" (as she called his French and Italian notebooks) from Ticknor and Fields; she could let Putnam publish them. On October 22, she sailed away from the United States. But she was no longer in the spring of womanhood, as she had been when she voyaged to Cuba for eighteen pleasurable months. Nor was she in the summer of marriage and motherhood, as she had been when she traveled to Europe as a consul's wife. She was now in the autumn of poverty and infirmity, a bereft widow leaving her homeland forever. Nonetheless, she mustered her perennial optimism, notwithstanding the rough sea and inevitable seasickness. She reveled in the "boundless spaces of celestial blue above and sapphire below." She waxed rhapsodic about the "salads served under a golden foam of egg" in the dining room and the exquisite bird's-eye maple and rosewood furnishings in the saloon. The burdens of bills and housekeeping were lifted; her spirits were as light as "a plume in the south wind." She felt like a sixteen-year-old girl, she wrote Elizabeth: "I know that my husband is glad that we are on our way to the old world." Una was at "peace *at last.*" Rose was in "ecstasy." And Julian, well, Julian had begun his own journal aboard ship. One of his entries noted: "I capture a young lady, and elope with her to the bows, or behind the Pilot-House."[9]

Sophia's respite from trouble was brief. After landing in Bremen, the Hawthornes obtained inelegant, second-class accommodations on a train that deposited them in Dresden on November 5. There, they acquired a third-floor apartment in a large stone house where the annual rent would be $150. Sophia immediately began recording each expense in an account book, calculating that they could live on $2 a day. Boxes and trunks were barely unpacked when they learned that Horace Mann Jr., had died on November 11. Though the news came as no surprise, it made Sophia physically ill, and she immediately located a physician. The "dear, old wise" Dr. Elb informed her that "clear cold would be more salubrious" than Dresden's damp December. Sophia was ill for weeks, disappointed that she was unable to hear the magnificent Christmas music in the cathedrals. By January, she was in the grip of bronchitis. She had stayed out of bed in her nightdress, she wrote Elizabeth, "just one minute too long" before the fire was kindled, as if one minute might be time enough to change the course of failing health.[10]

The new year had not brought a satisfactory conclusion to questions about Fields, though Elizabeth had pressed him for nearly four months in letters citing one after another irregularity, from trivial miscalculations by a clerk to Mr. Ticknor Jr.'s scandalous retirement in 1868 with a rumored "*200,000 dollars.*" Could he and the firm have grown so rich on its best author's books while that author's family became so poor? And then the answer came. Though Ticknor and Fields had not acted ethically, though Fields had not behaved as a friend, there was nothing illegal in that verbal agreement executed on behalf of the author's estate by his attorney. Elizabeth was forced to concede, as she wrote to Fields, that the "business transactions between your firm and the Hawthornes are legally righteous." Sophia swallowed this bitter pill and made the unpalatable though astute decision to continue with Ticknor and Fields as publisher of her husband's works. She knew they had become "classics." People everywhere wanted to display them on their shelves, and Fields had the widest means of distribution.[11]

Sophia now embarked upon eighteen months of prodigious work. She wrote a preface for the second edition of *Passages from the American Notebooks of Nathaniel Hawthorne.* Then she turned her attentions to Nathaniel's English notebooks, working despite influenza, a debilitating cough, and discouragement, for Ticknor and Fields decided to postpone publication of those notebooks until the following year, thus delaying Sophia's income from them. And there would be no money from Smith and Elder. Sophia suspected that Fields had influenced that firm's refusal to publish a British edition of these notebooks, which she dispatched to Fields, preface and all, by the end of July. Her relentless work made her back ache and her hand lame. When treatments with steam baths relieved her pain, she began work in earnest on Nathaniel's "Continental Journal," reading it in its entirety for the first time. And what a revelation! She had believed that *The Marble Faun* "absorbed it all," she wrote Elizabeth, but not so. Sophia also saw that she and her husband "often speak of the same things" in their separate notebooks and feared people might think she had "plagiarized—alas!"[12]

Sophia had not copied from Nathaniel, nor had he copied from her, though they both copied "nature," as nineteenth-century writers and artists conceived of the world they sought to represent. Comparisons between their texts would be inevitable; hints about "literary rivalry" made Sophia cringe. And Nathaniel's published writing benefited from Sophia's effort to present him "in as cheerful and dignified an attitude as possible" and to "embellish" his descriptions, according to Thomas Woodson, the editor of these notebooks. Sophia lavished more time and care editing her husband's writing than her own. But motivated by her immediate need for money, in June and July, she finished work on selections from her own "Cathedral letters" and "Italian journal." In August, she penned a preface and dedication and sent everything to Putnam. Then, in October, she received not proofs, as she had expected, but her stereotyped "poor book." She was "much harassed" by its defects, some of them attributable to her.[13]

Notes in England and Italy, the title chosen by Putnam and displeasing to Sophia, suffered from its hasty preparation. Had she more leisure, she might have thought to make her letters to Una more accessible to a wider audience. Too infrequently Sophia failed to anticipate her readers' perplexity. They might infer the identity of "Papa" or "J___," but what would they know about "Miss Shepard"? Nor does Sophia flesh out the interesting public personalities in her narrative: Powers, Story, Hosmer, Mitchell, and others. And her sequencing of entries is, at times, confusing; for example, the June 27, 1858, entry precedes the one for June 19. Exercising insufficient control over her book, she ended it with this enigmatic postscript: "My journal was suddenly interrupted by illness—even in the midst of a sentence, and was never resumed; which will account for the abruptness of the close."[14]

Sophia was profoundly disappointed that her "illumination of the vignettes" had to be omitted. These magnificent sketches, so marvelously wedding verbal and visual representation of travel, were prohibitively expensive to print, so had Putnam informed her early in their discussions about the book. And Sophia was even more unhappy about other, unexpected deletions. "I groan in spirit at the cutting up of the text," she wrote Elizabeth, for Putnam had trimmed words and lopped off parts of sentences, making them "clumsy" and "destroying the cadences." Whole sections had been truncated, causing Sophia to feel as if she had "fallen off a precipice into some dreary vacuum." She grew to "to hate & despise" her own writing and disparage Putnam's judgment and taste. He was "not a cultivated man," and she wanted him to print an errata. Sophia conveyed these complaints to Elizabeth, who claimed that she might have intervened with their cousin, if only Sophia had consulted her about the book. "You do not seem to observe," Sophia shot back, "that I dedicated the book to you."[15]

While Sophia was in Dresden, her efforts to earn money through publication were not limited to *Notes in England and Italy*, or the two-volume *Passages from the English Notebooks of Nathaniel Hawthorne*, which finally appeared in the summer of 1870, or to "First Impressions of France and Italy," which Strahan and Company published serially in 1871. Sophia delved into the boxes of notebooks and letters she had brought with her from America, pulled out Nathaniel's love letters and her *Cuba Journal*, and re-read them. These artifacts of her maiden life had been precious cargo indeed. On May 2, she noted in her diary that she had been copying her husband's letters and when she reread them, she wrote, "never were such letters written before nor ever will be again." Was she considering coining Nathaniel's heart into gold just as she had his brain? On that question, her diary is mute, but it does reveal that she wondered if her own letters from Cuba "would do to print." She pored over them for two days then rejected the idea. "There is so much about people in them," she penned in her diary. And by "people" was she referring to the Zayas family? They had been on her mind recently, for among Sophia's visitors in Dresden was a Mrs. Von Plato, the daughter of Carolina Fernandez, Sophia's friend from her days in Cuba. Mrs. Von Plato informed Sophia: "Fernando & Manuel Zayas are dead." There is no further comment in Sophia's diary about the death of these brothers, one of whom had been the object of her youthful infatuation.[16]

Sophia's 1869 diary comprised more than terse comments about visitors and events. Many entries were crafted with a care that suggests they were composed with publication in mind. Several entries early in the year were embellished with illuminations; these do not recur after George informed Sophia he would not publish her sketches in *Notes*. The January 20 entry is an example of particularly charming description. Sophia sets the scene: On a "scrupulously clean" street, a man carries a basket of faggots laced to his back, that person sketched in the center of her page. All citizens, even the poor, wear fur, an observation also illustrated with a sketch. Small carts are pulled by "patient" dogs; when at rest, their owners kindly provide the animals with woolen covers. Children on their way to school—and all children were obliged by law to go to school in Germany—carry books on their backs "exactly as soldiers take their knapsacks."[17]

Later in the year, Sophia described regular morning cavalry exercises: some soldiers riding horses, others leading riderless horses, all walking at a very fast clip. She failed to note, however, that this civil order was purchased at tremendous human cost, one that her sister Elizabeth had not ignored. The discipline of the Prussian Army was so brutal that some soldiers chose suicide in order to escape it. When Elizabeth had been in Dresden during the fall of 1867, she wrote: "I passed the drilling ground, and saw some of the exercises. They were terrible to witness." But Sophia was as oblivious to this oppression and the coming political upheaval as she was to Julian's behavior, although she knew that by the end of January, he had left the Polytechnik. The other scholars were "execrable" and the classroom filthy, he declared. And his command of German was inadequate to the study of scientific subjects. This should have come as no surprise to Sophia who had witnessed Julian's inability to master mathematics in his native tongue. From afar, Elizabeth Hawthorne held Sophia solely responsible for this miscalculation, when, in fact, she had been only partially to blame. Elizabeth Peabody had misled Sophia about the ease with which they might all learn German. In the future, Sophia informed Lizzy, she should advise only those fluent in that language to attempt studies in Dresden. Even the business of daily life in a foreign tongue was most "inconvenient," Sophia had immediately discovered.[18]

But Sophia did not abandon the notion that Julian would resume classes at the Polytechnik, and she hired a "walking & talking tutor" in whose company Julian could learn German. But this tutor, like those before him, had little influence upon Julian who much preferred the company of others. Their escapades became the stuff of several journal entries where Julian describes his life as a dissolute young American male taking full advantage of freedoms unavailable at home. The Masked Ball he attended on January 29, for example, was a far cry from the innocent affair in Concord seven years earlier that he had attended disguised as Duke of Buckingham. The Dresden version of a masquerade was a "night of alternate dancing, drinking, fighting and love making," a scene of "legalized . . . debauchery and excess" which went on until four in the morning. Billiards, cigars, and beer kept him well occupied, as did a visit to his friend, a "Mr. W.," who fortified himself with a glass of beer while, of a morning, he wandered about his room—cigars, pipes, trousers, and stockings strewn over the floor.[19]

May 19, 1869, the fifth anniversary of Nathaniel Hawthorne's death, occasioned Julian's regret over his "sins," but he deflected responsibility for these: "I had no one to guide and instruct me at the most critical period of my life," he wrote in his journal. Apparently the former president of the United States was "no one" to Julian. But his life had taken a decisive turn two months earlier. He had met the nineteen-year-old "M. A. A.," May Albertina Amelung, or Minne as everyone called her, an American living in Dresden with her mother and two brothers. Her great-grandfather had been a German immigrant to Maryland, where he had founded a highly successful family business, a glassworks factory. The Amelungs were among those post–Civil War expatriates enjoying all the culture and amusement to be found in Dresden. According to Julian, this "very singular young lady" was, by her own admission, "wicked." She had learned how to smoke and told men what to do. Julian knew he had met his match.[20]

In short order, he was in love and inspired to produce a "more honorable record" during the next twenty-three years, so he confided to his journal on his twenty-third birthday. He had found the person who would "elevate and purify" his life. Sophia enthusiastically approved of Minne, a young woman "full of talent and fine character and deep warm heart— she is a treasure" and "beyond words exquisite." When Minne and her family returned to the United States in mid-July, she and Julian were engaged. He determined that "with the help of God," he would "leave off forever *all bad habits*," and he dedicated his regimen of weightlifting to Minne. He would be her "marvel of muscle" because he had nothing "mentally & intellectually" to give her, nor had he the money to begin married life. Any expectation of a substantial inheritance from Pierce, who had died in October, was dashed because Pierce had bequeathed the Hawthorne children just $500. Whatever Julian's deficits, he remained Sophia's "glorious child," the epitome of all things "moral, intellectual, spiritual, physical."[21]

If Julian's Dresden journal suggests *A Rake's Progress*, then Una's resembles *The Way of Perfection*. The contrast between these siblings' lives was stark. Una wistfully recalled other times and places and a "happy enthusiastic girl-hood" in England and Italy. Her memory, embellished by more than a decade's absence, added to her current melancholy. She took refuge from "the Dutch animals," as she referred to Germans in a letter to Ebe, by reading former family friend Herman Melville's *Moby Dick* and Henry David Thoreau's *Walden*, her Concord neighbor's reflection on his year of solitude. The Bible was always close at hand, for Una found her most abundant comfort in religion. She marked her days according to the liturgical calendar—the conversion of St. Paul, the purification of the Blessed Virgin Mary, and on April 23, her journey to the

Anglican Church reached its destination. The bishop of Ross baptized her in the Wassenhaus Kirche. Sophia, seeking to soften the blow dealt Elizabeth Peabody by her niece's "Episcopalian phase," praised the Bishop's sermon; it was "so practical, so high, so holy, so available." Several months later, Sophia made another effort to mitigate Elizabeth's shock over Una's conversion: "I more and more feel that doctrine is of small account, if the life be true & religious." But Ebe, with her maverick opinions, needed no coaxing to "heartily approve" of her niece's choice.[22]

The Hawthornes had been in Dresden nearly a year when the Lathrop brothers became regular callers. Ten years earlier, Sophia's brief acquaintance with their father, Dr. George Alfred Lathrop, had convinced her that she did "not quite like" him. Nor did Henry Bright, with whom Sophia shared her judgment that Dr. Lathrop was "not only earthly, but earthy." During roughly the same period that Nathaniel was the United States consul in Liverpool, Lathrop had served as consul in Honolulu, where Francis and George had been born. They and their mother moved to Dresden in 1867, having just spent time in America when Rose may have first met George, if that "friend" in Mary Betts's May 21, 1868 letter refers to him. "Not tell me about your friend in Germany?" she quizzed Rose, who was then living in Salem, a distance sufficient to prevent her mother and siblings from knowing what she confided to Miss Betts. "I should like to know all about him. What joy for you, little Rose, to know yourself so beloved! . . . with that heart of yours beating so fast with his over the seas." No other trace of Rose's "friend" in Germany survives in any of the Hawthornes' letters or journals for that period. Perhaps, during the spring of 1868, she sedulously guarded her secret out of kindness, unwilling to flaunt happiness so recently lost by Una. Perhaps Rose sought to protect herself from the family drama that attached to Una's engagement and its dissolution. Or perhaps Rose was defending herself against her mother's harsh criticism of her friend's father, if indeed he was Dr. Lathrop.[23]

Whatever Sophia's initial reaction to this man, by the end of 1869 and the beginning of 1870, his younger son's name appears frequently in all four of the Hawthornes' journals. The Lathrop brothers, like Julian and many others, were in Dresden to further their education, and Rose took another stab at being a student. She boarded at a school run by a hot-tempered headmistress whose treatment so angered Rose that she left after just a month. She then spent her days without regular study, save for her lessons in art. Unlike the retiring, pensive Una, Rose happily pursued social opportunities with other young people in the American colony. And unlike the self-indulgent Julian, dissatisfaction with an "idle life" gnawed at Rose. Poised to find some purpose, she was attracted to George who gave her a carved napkin ring and had her fan mended, innocent gestures perhaps, but hinting his special interest in her. She, along with her brother and sister, spent Christmas Day 1869 at the Lathrops' home, and at the dawn of the new year, Rose confided to her diary that George "looked so *good*." But his academic future lay in the United States, and in April of 1870, George Lathrop left Dresden to study law at Columbia University in New York City.[24]

Rose missed the attentions of her suitor, Julian was adrift without his fiancée. And Una increasingly loathed the "stolid, dirty Germans, who disenchant one of all ideas of beauty," as she wrote "Uncle Wentworth," though her mood was occasionally lifted by American visitors, one in particular. While Una's piano teacher from Concord, Phoebe Ripley was in Dresden, Una stayed with her for many days and nights, thereby temporarily living apart from her mother. On October 29, this freedom and companionship ended. Forlorn, Una noted in her journal: "My dear Miss Ripley left Dresden." Her departure hit hard, for, as Una explained to "Uncle Wentworth": "The doors of my heart are shut I believe, on the short and precious number already inside." She confided to "Uncle Wentworth" that she hoped to be "gayer by and by."[25]

How different might Una's life have become if, like Higginson's other young female correspondent, she had accepted his invitation to contribute to the *Atlantic*. But Una Hawthorne was no Emily Dickinson. "I shall never be able to write anything worth putting in your paper," she wrote him. And adding to her depressed mood were poor health and worry. She was unwell with endless colds, and her mother had contracted erysipelas, the infectious disease that had precipitated Pierce's demise. Sophia's constitution, weakened by near-fatal illness the previous winter, had been further eroded by nonstop work, fatigue, and inescapable concerns about money. Everything was costlier than she had expected and prices were rising. War with France loomed, and Prussian soldiers were being quartered all over Dresden, pushing up the cost of rent. It was time for Sophia to find another home.[26]

On May 11, Sophia went to England where she proofread Nathaniel's *Passages from the English Note-books* and awaited its publication, thereby securing English as well as American copyrights. She also laid plans to move there with her daughters. She had left Rose with Julian in Dresden; it was the "hardest thing" Sophia had ever done, she told Rose, who would surely cement the bonds of affection with her brother before he returned to the United States, and to Minne. Una, who had accompanied her mother, was overjoyed to be back in England, but being *"too glad,"* Sophia wrote Elizabeth Peabody, was "as disastrous for Una's nerves as *too sorry*."

Una needed to look forward to something and that, Sophia believed, would be found in England.[27]

Sophia and Una sampled the life that was about to be theirs while staying with the Bennochs, who received them warmly into their home at Blackheath. So grateful was Sophia for Bennoch's present and past kindnesses that she dedicated *Passages from The English Note-books* to this "dear and valued friend, who, by his generous and genial hospitality and unfailing sympathy, contributed so largely . . . to render Mr. Hawthorne's residence in England agreeable and homelike." During moments when Sophia was not working, she visited the National Gallery and attended a magnificent concert. Flowers were in late-spring, gorgeous bloom. If these descriptions of culture and nature did not entice Rose, Sophia knew her daughter would be interested that clothing was less expensive in England. Rose would also be pleased that Francis Lathrop and his mother were living in Kensington. Rose could attend art school with Frank. "It is *life* here," Sophia exclaimed: "It is the very centre of the world!" Friends such as dear "Fancy," now Fanny Arnold, a wife and mother, eagerly awaited their arrival. No one, not even the Bennochs' maid Ellen, had forgotten them. Sophia was all optimism proclaiming: "Oh we shall have real bona fide friends in Our dear Old Home."[28]

Chapter 23

Stillness and Silence

I had an extraordinary dream. . . . My husband wanted me to make an excursion to a wonderful lake. He said it was sheer down unfathomable depths from the very edge and he seemed to wish me to have a plunging bath with him—a kind of diving. We drove over a sort of wilderness and saw a good deal of water—suddenly we came close on the margin of the lake. It was glittering silver white—and I had hardly time to take one glance before my husband had lifted me and plunged down down down into the depths. It was not cold nor even wet, but there was a sense of infinite comfort, snugness warmth and softness . . . . We rose to the surface and I was safe on the shore.[1]

Such a dream might portend good things at this juncture in Sophia's life when she contemplated crossing yet another body of water to create yet another new life. A memory of this dream should remove any reluctance about moving with her daughters to England. Once there, they would find the warmth of kind friends.

Sophia and Una returned to Dresden on June 18 for a hectic month of packing and another round of goodbyes. Just a few days after their arrival, Julian departed. When or if Sophia would see her son again, she did not know. The expense and difficulty of crossing the Atlantic created an enormous obstacle to future reunion. But Sophia greeted separation from Julian with an equanimity that would have been unthinkable in the past. She could take heart that he seemed, finally, to have found his way. He had begun to write and publish poetry, and Minne would be at his side, helping to steer his course aright. While Sophia prepared for her own departure, she learned that the Wayside had been sold for $3000, half the sum Nathaniel had paid for it but enough to help her make a fresh start.[2]

There would be no reluctance about this move to England, no hesitation about leaving Dresden because, on July 19, the first shots of the Franco-Prusssian War had been fired. Elizabeth Hawthorne had warned Una that Dresden—whatever its allure to Americans flocking there—was politically unstable. But Sophia and her daughters could not have predicted on August 2, when they fled in all haste, that Dresden would escape invasion by the vast French forces. Though the Prussian army was smaller, it was highly disciplined as both Sophia (in all admiration) and Elizabeth Peabody (with great disgust) had observed. In a few short months, Paris would fall to the Prussian forces, and the war would end. This brief war, which planted the seeds of the "Great" one, created only inconvenience and minor adventure for the Hawthorne women. "We rushed for our lives, leaving Dresden with delight," Rose wrote a friend, "plunging headlong into whatever dangers were brewing on our road."[3]

Sophia equaled Rose's youthful excitement in her descriptions of their exodus from Germany. Forced to take a circuitous route to Rotterdam through the north of Prussia, their train was frequently delayed by others filled with troops. Sophia undertook the protection of a young French girl in their compartment. This Gertrude, with her large frame, "long, manly step," and "peculiar aquiline nose" was suspected of being a male spy disguised in female attire. She was quizzed mercilessly by German soldiers until they were "convinced of her sex" by her blush and confusion. Sophia wrote Elizabeth: "This was our only adventure, and amounted to nothing, except my heartquake." The placid sea voyage to Harwick was followed by the last leg of their journey, a train to London filled with raucous drunks. Finally, at midnight they arrived in London.[4]

Sophia and her daughters took temporary quarters at 25 Eldon Road in Kensington where Frank Lathrop and his mother had established themselves. Frank, the brother of Julian's "adoring friend" George, as Sophia identified the young artist, immediately escorted Rose on a tour of London. Rose was quickly won over by the city and all it offered her. A month later, neither the Lathrops nor the Hawthornes were living on Eldon Road. Mrs. Lathrop and Frank had departed for New York City to join George, and Sophia had secured a permanent place to reside with her daughters. Number 4 Shaftsbury Terrace on Allen Street, also in Kensington, was "small," she admitted to Julian, but big enough for "people who cannot afford to receive dinner parties." Sophia enthusiastically described each detail of her new home for her son: the oak woodwork, the gold-spangled wallpaper, and the glass conservatory on a sunny landing where potted plants would thrive. Her own grand bedroom had two large windows. She was "lost in astonishment" at her good fortune and with the conviction that she would roam no more.[5]

Another source of Sophia's contentment came from her children. Julian and Minne were married on November 15. Sophia conveyed gleeful good wishes to them, never once lamenting her inability to attend the wedding, though the Lathrops had the good fortune to do so. Frank regaled Una with a description of the ceremony and the handsome groom who made the bride the envy of every young woman in the church. Rose was taking classes at the Kensington Art Museum and had begun her first original painting. As a suddenly sage nineteen-year-old, she wrote her Aunt Mary that, "after all, the earth bears some gladness for us on its maternal bosom, even if one does begin to doubt the fact in one's teens." If Rose attributed any of her growing "gladness" to George Lathrop, she did not say, though she did make note of seeing a tintype of the handsome young man. And Una was finding happiness in the renewal of English acquaintances. Attending the Reverend Channing's lectures was, once again, a deeply satisfying activity to her.[6]

Life in England seemed to have fulfilled its promises for Rose, Una, and Sophia, who was at leisure for the first time since her husband's death nearly seven years ago. She was also gratified by good reviews of her most recent publication, *Passages from the English Note-books of Nathaniel Hawthorne*, and unperturbed by the harsh ones, having long since leveled at herself all imaginable criticisms. As she had feared, some reviewers charged her with indecorously exposing what should remain private, and worse, with presenting an unflattering portrait of her husband. "It s to be regretted that the editor [as Sophia had identified herself] did not exclude all passages that showed lack of charity, good feeling, and common sense," wrote the reviewer for the *Athenaeum* who judged that "the work is detrimental to Mr. Hawthorne's character." Such an opinion was balanced by another, quite opposite one held by the reviewer for the *Literary World*: "These volumes afford almost the only record" of a "wonderful man," "sensitive, retiring, content to be known by his works only, and secluding himself within the circle of a few close friendships."[7] These last words might now apply to Sophia whose comfortable, retiring, somewhat circumscribed life had been purchased with her own pen.

On February 11, Sophia accompanied Una to hear Channing's lecture. His talk was disappointing, probably all the more so for the speaker, because so few people were in attendance. And for that very reason,

Sophia went to hear Channing again on February 13; she did not want him to become discouraged by a skimpy audience. Although such outings made her terribly weary, she forged ahead with the business of daily life. She accepted an invitation to tea where she encountered Robert Browning who was delighted to see her and eager to call, as soon as she gave word that she was ready for callers. To that end, she continued to spruce up her home and hired a man to hang pictures according to her specifications, a minor task but one that thoroughly exhausted her. That night she told Una, "I have a sort of defenceless [sic] feeling, as if I have no refuge." These had been her words, Una recalled, two years earlier when Sophia had been stricken terribly ill.

During the night of February 14 and into the next morning, Sophia became violently nauseous and ran a fever. Throughout the following week, she spat blood constantly, her head ached, and she was unable to take any nourishment but milk diluted with water. Her lips and tongue became so parched that she could hardly speak. She could not tolerate being touched or hearing the nearby church bells toll. Relentless coughing prevented her from sleeping. Did she recall her husband's observation, now a dire prediction, "there is no air in England fit for her to breathe"? Congestion of the lung and pleurisy were the diagnoses given by Dr. Wyld, who, despite the severity of her condition held out hope for her recovery. And indeed, she rallied from time to time, after receiving a letter from Mary Hemenway or when Una relayed information about Julian.

Five days of nonstop nursing began to crush Una, and Bennoch kindly sent Ellen to assist her. Together they devised ways to warm Sophia with a hot water bottle and prop her into a more comfortable position with an air pillow; their ministrations had temporary beneficial effect. Sophia became well enough to notice Una's dreary dressing gown and to ask her to replace it with her purple merino wool dress. This colorful transformation made her look very pretty, so Sophia told her daughter. A mundane observation such as this might confirm the doctor's most optimistic prognosis, and on the night of February 23, Una allowed herself to go to bed, leaving her mother in Ellen's care.

But Una had hardly fallen asleep when Ellen roused her. Sophia's pain was "excruciating." She thrashed about the bed. Death rattled every breath that came from her throat. Still Una hoped, allowing herself to be deceived by Sophia's occasional lucid moment. "I think I must understand something of the agony of love with which a mother would rush to her child, for our positions seemed reversed," Una wrote in her long account for Julian of their mother's dying days. No longer the girl snatched from death by her mother's steely will, Una was a woman who might outwit death, if only she could help her mother to rest. If only Una could entice her to eat. But Sophia refused food. In the late hours of February 25, she asked, "Why do you wait? Can't you give me anything?" Una then administered what Dr. Wyld had prescribed; the chloroform that eased Sophia's pain would hasten her death. Ellen, Rose, and Una stoked the fire and opened the window, and "the cold air from the starless night rushed in." Throughout the remainder of this long, cold night and into Sunday morning, the twenty-sixth of February, Sophia made her tortured departure from life. Then "a breathless stillness and silence" descended on the room. Sophia had been enveloped in the "infinite comfort, snugness warmth and softness" of her dream.

When Sophia's life of sixty-one years had ended, Una slipped her mother's wedding ring off her finger and put it on her own. The following day, she and Rose adorned Sophia's bed with fresh flowers, and thus her body lay throughout the week. Friday March 3 was Una's birthday; even in death her mother was a comforting presence. The following day, without much ceremony or many mourners, the sisters accompanied Sophia's body to Kensal Green. In this grassy garden of a Kensington cemetery, her body remained until 2006, when it was re-interred beside her husband's in Concord's Sleepy Hollow Cemetery.[8]

"Sophia, wife of Nathaniel Hawthorne": Una and Rose chose these words to inscribe the headstone marking their mother's original resting place, paring her life into one sliver of her identity. In the years immediately preceding her death, these daughters had witnessed their mother pour herself into wifely duties. She had spared no effort to present the best possible version of her husband to the world. His "mood was always cheerful and equal, and his mind peculiarly healthful," Sophia proclaimed in the preface to *Passages from the English Note-books;* "the airy splendor of his wit and humor was the light of his home." But Sophia had dared to be more than Nathaniel's spouse when she became his editor and his biographer. She drew away the veil of privacy that surrounded him, perhaps inadvertently exposing his flaws while deliberately revealing the sources of his creative genius. When she announced that his journals were "an open sesame to the artistic works," she legitimated future biographical study of her husband's fiction.[9]

Sophia would not have touted these accomplishments, nor would Una and Rose have proclaimed that their mother had unwittingly become a model for women's rights. Just months before her death, she had railed against women who "thrust themselves in to the market place," her long letter to Elizabeth a screed against those "unveiled," "foolish, brawling women" who dare to walk "the street of life, instead of keeping their appointed retreats." But had Sophia looked hard into a mirror, she would have seen reflected a "brawling" woman, wrangling with her publisher about fair pay and accurate accounts. She had "thrust" her husband's writing as well as her own *Notes in England and Italy* into the literary marketplace. Yet she remained "rabid" in her defense of the "noblest vocation of a human being," that of a mother.[10]

Julian knew that his mother's "every act and thought had reference to her children." She believed them capable of an exacting moral code, of pursuing good for its own sake. But Julian acknowledged that to be "the object of such limitless devotion and affection" was "almost appalling." Neither he nor his sisters found the extraordinary marital love their mother had created in her home or in her words, or, perhaps, in both. Julian fathered nine children with Minne and two more outside of that marriage.[11] After Minne's death, he married Edith Garrigues. He died in 1934, having committed many indiscretions during his eighty-eight years of life, including the sale of worthless stock in Canadian mines. For this crime, he was incarcerated in a federal prison for a year. Una never married, her second engagement ending when another fiancé, Albert Webster, sailed away in search of health, only to die in the Sandwich Islands. Una then retired to an Anglican nunnery in Clewer, England. In 1877, at thirty-three years of age, she died. Her remains, along with Sophia's, have now been reinterred in Sleepy Hollow Cemetery. Rose married George Parsons Lathrop six months after her mother's death, but in the 1890s, she abandoned the religion of her forebears as well as married life. After converting to Roman Catholicism, she left her husband and founded an order of nuns to care for indigent, dying cancer patients in New York City. She was seventy-five when she died in 1926. The hospice work she founded survives to this day.

Perhaps Sophia—again unwittingly—had sown the seeds of her children's unconventional choices, be they good or ill. Perhaps Julian, Una, and Rose were simply enacting various motifs in their mother's own narrative of individuality. The range of Sophia's emotional life had extended well beyond the circumference of the domestic circle; her appetite for intimacy was voracious. Though her decision to become an expatriate can be seen as the conclusion of a downward trajectory of poverty and loss, leaving the United States forever also signifies an exquisite act of self-reliance. An intrepid traveler, she was propelled beyond her New England roots by the transcendental nourishment she had drawn from its soil. Having made her contribution to American arts and literature, she became a citizen of the wider world.

Notes

Abbreviations

AAF	Annie Adams Fields
AS	Ada Shepard
Dr. P.	Nathaniel Peabody (Sophia's father)
EMH	Elizabeth Manning Hawthorne (Nathaniel's sister) aka Ebe
EPP	Elizabeth Palmer Peabody (Sophia's sister) aka Lizzy
FP	Franklin Pierce
JH	Julian Hawthorne
JTF	James T. Fields
HM	Herman Melville
MP/MPM	Mary Peabody / Mary Peabody Mann
Mrs. P.	Elizabeth Palmer Peabody (Sophia's mother)
NH	Nathaniel Hawthorne
RH/RHL	Rose Hawthorne/ Rose Hawthorne Lathrop
SP/SPH	Sophia Peabody / Sophia Peabody Hawthorne

CE	*The Centenary Edition of the Works of Nathaniel Hawthorne.*

When material from the *Centenary Edition* is cited, endnotes will include the following information: author (if known), title (which may at times be the name of the volume itself) or letter description, *CE*, volume number, and page(s).

MS/S	manuscript/manuscripts
TS/S	transcript/transcripts

Endnotes cite sources of all information in paragraphs as well as quotations.

Preface

1. R. W. Emerson to SP, January 20, 1836, MS The Henry W. and Albert A. Berg Collection of English and American Literature, The New York Public Library, Astor, Lenox, and Tilden Foundations, hereafter cited as MS Berg. "[B]eauty making eye" is printed as Emerson wrote it, without a hyphen.

Chapter 1. Carefulness of Living

1. SPH to Mrs. P., August 17 and September 7, 1845, and R. W. Emerson to SP, January 20, 1836, MSS Berg.

2. O'Sullivan to NH, March 21, 1845, quoted in JH, *Hawthorne and His Wife*, I:285.

3. James R. Mellow, *Hawthorne in His Times*, 264; NH to Bridge, September 28, 1845, *CE*,16:120; information about royalties is found in *CE*, 16:140, fn 5; and O'Sullivan to Bancroft, May 10, 1845, quoted in *CE*, 16:93, fn 2; E. Haviland Miller, *Salem Is My Dwelling Place*, 239–240.

4. SPH to Mrs. P., May n.d., 1845, MS Berg; SPH to Bridge, ca. June 10, July 4, 1845, rpt in *CE*, 16:100, 110; SPH to MPM, August 14, 1845, MS Berg; Bridge quoted in fn 8, *CE*, 16: 111.

5. NH to Duyckinck, October 10, 1845, and NH to SPH, November 10, 1845, *CE*, 16:126, 129–130. NH, "Lost Notebook," *CE*, 23:152.

6. NH to SPH, January 19, 1846, *CE*, 16:137.

7. See references to the Herbert Street house as "Castle Dismal" in NH to SPH, November 10 and 13, 1845, *CE*, 16:129,133; SPH to LH, June 12, 1846, May 3, 1846, and SPH to Mrs. P., March 23, September 9–10, 1847, March 16, 1846, MSS Berg.

8. Sarah Shaw to SPH, [1846], March 3, 1846, MSS Berg; April Selley, "Francis George Shaw," 235-236.

9. NH in a postscript to SPH to LH, June 21, 1846, rpt in *CE*, 16:171–173.

10. Taylor Stoehr, *Hawthorne's Mad Scientists*, 105–107, 113, Hahnemann quoted on 104; EPP, *Memorial of William Wesselhoeft*, 656, 659.

11. SPH to Mrs. P., November 12, 1846, and Mrs. P. to SPH, January 8,1847, July 26, 1849, MSS Berg; NH to C. W. Weber, December 18, 1849, *CE*, 16:301; SPH to MPM, April 6, [1845], MS Berg.

12. NH to SPH, July 1, 1848, *CE*, 16: 231; Charles Rosenberg, *The Cholera Years*, 121.

13. SPH to MPM, March 18, 1849, October 15, 1848, MSS Berg; JH, *Hawthorne and His Wife*, I:328.

14. SPH to LH, June 21, 1846, rpt in *CE*, 16:171; SPH to MPM, October 15, 1848, and SPH to Mrs. P., August 17, December [9], 1845, MSS Berg.

15. SPH to Mrs. P., April 6, December [9], 1845, MSS Berg; NH to SPH, July 13,1847, *CE*, 16:213; SPH to LH, ca. July 15,1845, MS Berg and rpt in *CE*, 16:112.

16. SPH to Mrs. P., January n.d., 1845, August 30, 1846; SPH to MPM, February

2, 1845, October 15, 1848, May 14 [1848], June 12, [1848] & March 18, 1849, August 30, 1849, MSS Berg.

17. Gillian Avery, *Behold the Child*, especially chapter 4, "Doctrine and Virtuous Twaddle: Religious Education and Sunday School Fiction," 93–120.

18. Charles Rosenberg, "Bitter Fruit," 190–194, 197–201.

19. SPH to Mrs. P., February 5, 1847, MS Berg.

20. Jonathan Messerli, *Horace Mann*, 147, 180, 114, 382.

21. Messerli, *Horace Mann*, 382; Mann's journal entry for April 30, 1843, quoted on 384.

22. Mrs. P. to SPH [April] 17, 1848, MS Berg; Messerli, *Horace Mann*, 350–352.

23. SPH to Mrs P., February 4, 1844, August 17, 1845, MSS Berg.

24. JH, *Hawthorne and His Wife*: I, 275, 51–56, 79; SPH to Mrs. P., January, n.d., 1846, MS Berg.

25. Messerli, *Horace Mann*, 430–431; on Frank Shaw's payment of rent, see *CE*, 16:217–217, fn 3.

26. Messerli, *Horace Mann*, 446–448; SPH to MPM, January 14, 1848, MS Berg. See Jean Fagan Yellin, "Hawthorne and the Slavery Question," 140–150 for discussion of Sophia's attitude toward race and her lack of abolitionist sentiments. Yellin cites Nathaniel's inclusion, while he was editor of the *Atlantic Monthly Magazine* in 1836, of three pieces on skin color, one of which asserted that "Africans' adaptation to heat . . . causes 'the peculiar odour of the coloured race'" (150).

27. On Julian's scarlet fever, see *CE*, 16:236, fn 3 and SPH to MPM, July 16, 1848, MS Berg.

28. Messerli, *Horace Mann*, 426.

29. SPH to MPM, [August 1848], July 16, 1848, MSS Berg.

Chapter 2. Imp and Angel

1. SPH to Mrs. P., January 12, [1845], August 8, [1846], and [May 1847], MSS Berg; SPH, "Sophia Hawthorne's *American Notebooks*," 151.

2. SPH, "Sophia Hawthorne's *American Notebooks*," 155; SPH to Mrs. P., March 6, 1845, April 23, 1847, MSS Berg.

3. SPH to Mrs. P., November 12, 1846, [spring 1849], MSS Berg. (Mrs.) Elizabeth Palmer Peabody, *Holiness; or the Legend of St. George: A Tale from Spenser's "Faerie Queene,"* 125; SPH, "Sophia Peabody Hawthorne's *American Notebooks*," 149.

4. SPH to Mrs. P., August 30, [1846], MS Berg.

5. Mrs. P. to SPH, March 20, 1848, and SPH to Mrs. P., March 26, November 5, 1848, July 17, 1849, MSS Berg; NH, *The American Notebook*, *CE*, 8:434.

6. SPH to Mrs. P., October 5, 1846, MS Berg; NH to Bridge, November 9, 1846, and SPH to Bridge, December 20, 1846, *CE*, 16:190, 193.

7. NH in a postscript to SPH's letter to LH, June 21, 1846, rpt in *CE*, 16:171–173; NH to LH, March 3, 1844, 16:15; NH, *The American Notebooks*, *CE*, 8:399–403.

8. NH, *The American Notebooks, CE,* 8:399, 403–420 passim.

9. NH, *The American Notebooks, CE,* 8:415, 420, 402, 406, 407.

10. NH to SPH, July 13, 1847, *CE,* 16:212–213.

11. SPH to NH, July n.d., 1847, MS Berg.

12. JH, *Nathaniel Hawthorne and His Wife,* I:314; SPH to Mrs. P., September 10, 1847, MS Berg.

13. SPH to Mrs. P., September 9–10, 1847, March 6, 1846, and SPH to LH, June 12, 1846, MSS Berg.

14. NH, *The American Notebooks, CE,* 8:430, 424, 425, 426, 431.

15. NH, *The American Notebooks, CE,* 8:430.

16. SPH to MPM, July 16, 1848, MS Berg; NH, *The American Notebooks, CE,* 8:429, 430–431.

17. NH, *The American Notebooks, CE,* 8:318–320; SPH, "Sophia Peabody Hawthorne's *American Notebooks,*" 130.

Chapter 3. The Gods Prefer Integrity to Charity

1. SPH to MPM, November 12, 1847, MS Berg.

2. SPH to NH, July n.d., 1847, November 16, 1846; SPH to Mrs. P., December 19, 1847; SPH to MPM, November 12, 1847, MSS Berg. See Rita Gollin's portrait of Dora Golden in "The Hawthornes' 'Golden Dora,'" 393–401, and about household help more generally see Faye E. Dudden's *Serving Women: Household Service in Nineteenth-Century America.*

3. JH, *Hawthorne and His Wife,* I:341; SPH to Mrs. P., August 1, 1849, and SPH to MPM, August 12, 1849, MSS Berg.

4. SPH to Mrs. P., August 1, 1849, and SPH to MPM, August 12, 1849, MSS Berg.

5. NH to G. S. Hillard, March 5, 1849, and NH to H. W. Longfellow, June 5, 1849, *CE,* 16:263–265, 269–272; Mellow, *Nathaniel Hawthorne,* 292–294, 300–302.

6. NH to G. S. Hillard, June 8, 1849, and SPH to MPM, June 9, 1849, *CE,* 16:273, 275.

7. NH to HM, June 26, 1849, *CE,* 16:284–285; JH, *Hawthorne and His Wife,* I:340.

8. EPP to MP, June 21,1836, MS Berg.

9. SP to EPP, May 2, 7–8, 1838, MS Berg. Parts of this journal-letter correspondence have been copied by an unknown hand and are found in both the Bancroft Library at Berkeley and the Berg Collection.

10. Emerson, "Self-Reliance," 265; EPP to SP, July 31, 1838, EPP, *The Letters,* 204–205.

11. Catalogued as Sophia Hawthorne to _____ n.d, Salutation: "My dearest Lizzie," MS Barrett.

12. Caroline Dall, years later, asserted that Elizabeth had confided she had been engaged to Nathaniel. Dall's credibility is undermined by several erroneous statements about Elizabeth and has been contested by Nathaniel's various biographers. Bruce Ronda, in *Elizabeth Palmer Peabody,* 174, says: "There is no evidence

to substantiate [Dall's] claim." See also Norman Holmes Pearson, *Hawthorne's Two Engagements*, 12, and Megan Marshall, *The Peabody Sisters*, 357, as well as Marshall's article "The Other Sister: Was Nathaniel Hawthorne a Cad?" Marshall relies for her evidence upon a 1904 biography of Elizabeth by her erstwhile disciple Mary Van Wyck Church based on late-in-life conversations with Elizabeth and no longer extant Peabody Mann papers. Marshall's article supplies evidence of a close connection between Elizabeth and Nathaniel before he met and while he wooed Sophia, but that evidence points to Nathaniel's calculating use of his future sister-in-law to advance his career. Marshall does not claim they were engaged. Brenda Wineapple (*Hawthorne*, 130, 417) surmises, without offering proof, that the Peabody and Hawthorne clans *assumed* that Nathaniel and Elizabeth were engaged: "Word of this engagement remained part of Boston scuttlebutt for many years."

13. SP to EPP, June 28, July [after the 4th] 1839, MS Stanford.

14. Helen R. Deese, in "A New England Women's Network" describes a similar pattern of rejection when Elizabeth's patronage of Dall ceased to be welcome. Peabody's criticism of Dall grew in tandem with Dall's independence and perceived lack of feminine decorum. "Serious conflict" between the two ensued when Dall's "development . . . outstripped, or at least diverged from, that of her mentor" (80).

15. E. Haviland Miller's "Calendar of the Letters of Sophia Hawthorne," 224–232, identifies no extant letters from SP/H to EPP for the following years: 1840, 1842, 1843, 1844, 1845, 1846, 1847, and 1848. In 1841, only four of SP's letters to EPP survive. And during this same period, very few letters from Elizabeth to Sophia survive.

16. MPM to SPH, spring 1845, MS Berg.

17. NH to O'Sullivan, April 19, May 19, 1839, *CE*, 15:272, fn 4, 273, and 313, fn 4, 314, and Miller, *Salem Is My Dwelling Place*, 224. These publications appeared under Elizabeth's imprint as follows: *Grandfather's Chair: A History for Youth*. E. P. Peabody. New York: Wiley & Putnam, 1841; *Famous Old People: Being the Second Epoch of Grandfather's Chair*. Boston: E. P. Peabody, 1841; *Liberty Tree: With the Last Words of Grandfather's Chair*. Boston: E. P. Peabody, 1841.

18. See NH, *CE*, 15:547, fn 2; NH to EPP, February 19, 1842, *CE*, 15:609, fn 1, 610; Mellow, *Nathaniel Hawthorne*, 192; Ronda, *Elizabeth Palmer Peabody*, 206.

19. NH to SPH, June 27, 1848, *CE*, 16:228–229.

Chapter 4. An Art That Sufficed

1. SPH to Mrs. P., September 2, 1849, and SPH to MPM, August 12, 1849, MSS Berg; NH to Hillard, January 20, 1850, *CE*, 16:309, fn 1, 310; Sarah Shaw to SPH, September 10, 1849, MS Berg.

2. SPH to MPM, September 12, 1849, MS Berg; JH, *Hawthorne and His Wife*, I:340.

3. SPH to Mrs. P., September 2, 1849, SPH to EPP, November 11 and 25, 1849, MSS Berg.

4. SPH to EPP, November 30, December 3, 1849, MSS Berg.

5. NH to C. W. Webber, December 18, 1849, *CE*, 16:300–301; SPH to MPM, November 4, 1849, and SPH to EPP, November 11, December 30, 1849, MSS Berg.

6. SPH to EPP, January 16, January n.d., 1850, MSS Berg.

7. SPH to EPP, November 30, 1849, MS Berg; Ronda, *Elizabeth Palmer Peabody*, 132–136, quotation from letter on 133; EPP to MPM, [May 1836], MS Berg. For Elizabeth's later published reflections on this child, see her "A Psychological Observation," 109, 111.

8. Ronda, *Elizabeth Palmer Peabody*, 7, 211–213, 218, 225–227; SPH to Mrs. P., March 8–9, 1849, and Mrs. P. to SPH, [January or February 1849], MMS Berg; JH, *Hawthorne and His Circle*, 11.

9. SPH, "Sophia Peabody Hawthorne's *American Notebooks*," 155, 158.

10. The Reverend Francis Wayland's comments in his 1831 letter to the editor of *The American Baptist Magazine* are quoted in William G. McLoughlin, "Evangelical Childrearing in the Age of Jackson," 23, 35–36.

11. SPH to MPM, October 21, November 4, 1849, and SPH to Mrs. P., September 2, 1849, MSS Berg; NH to JTF, January 15, 1850, *CE*, 16:305. In *Salem Is My Dwelling Place*, 278, Miller writes that during this period, Nathaniel's "emotional-intellectual state vibrated as intensely as the scarlet letter on Hester's bosom."

12. NH, *The Scarlet Letter*, *CE*, 1:10, 26, 34–35, 38–39; Charles Rosenberg, "Sexuality, Class, and Race in 19th-Century America," 146.

13. See T. Walter Herbert's *Dearest Beloved*, xvii, and his "Nathaniel Hawthorne, Una Hawthorne, and *The Scarlet Letter*: Interactive Selfhoods and the Cultural Construction of Gender." Sophia definitively confirms this link in her letter to JTF, August 19, 1866, MS courtesy of the Trustees of the Boston Public Library/Rare Books, hereafter cited as BPL. Sophia misdates the writing of *The Scarlet Letter* as occurring in 1848. See Chapter 20, "Coining His Precious Brain into Gold" for a full discussion of this issue.

14. Nathaniel referred to Sophia as a "ministering angel" while she cared for her brother George when he was dying. NH to SP, November 20, 1839, *CE*, 15:369; NH, *The Scarlet Letter, CE*, 1:161, 100,110, 81, 82.

15. Among scholars who have addressed the autobiographical disclosures and obfuscations in "The Custom-House" and *The Scarlet Letter* are Michael Ragussis in "Family Discourse and Fiction in *The Scarlet Letter*": "both sections of this text are alloys: can we distinguish between the truth of autobiography and the fiction of the tale . . . ?" (880); Claudia Johnson in "Impotence and Omnipotence in *The Scarlet Letter*": "the subject of impotence is profoundly intrinsic" to the novella and "amplifies and enriches the subjects of literary dysfunction and ontological disappointment" announced in the sketch (595); T. Walter Herbert in Chapter 11 of *Dearest Beloved*, "Double Marriage, Double Adultery": "discrepant marriages subject [Hester] to an internally divided masculinity, to Roger and Arthur as fragments of a divided manhood" (187–188). Neither Ragussis nor Johnson ground their interpretation in the Hawthornes' domestic circumstances, and Herbert attributes

Nathaniel's masculine vulnerabilities to wider cultural forces, not to the strengths of his wife.

16. NH, *The Scarlet Letter*, CE, 1:125. Carol M. Bensick in "Dimmesdale and His Bachelorhood" writes: "No precedent in the historical record for an unmarried young minister in the 1640's in the churches near Boston is to be found" (103–104). Puritans considered lawful exercise of sexuality within marriage to be the preferred, safer state for man and minister. See Edmund S. Morgan's "The Puritans and Sex," 591–607.

17. NH, *The American Notebooks*, CE, 8:431.

18. NH, *The Lost Notebook*, CE, 23:152; NH to SP, August 16, 1841, CE, 15:560. Sophia's words are dated April 28, 1840, and found in a commonplace book she used more than two decades later. SPH, *Commonplace Book*, Volume III, 1862–69, MS Berg. This quotation exemplifies her occasional practice of using commonplace books to copy or draft letters.

19. NH, *The Scarlet Letter*, CE, 1:198, 34.

20. NH to Bridge, February 4, 1850, CE, 16:311–312; SPH to EPP, February 2, 1850, MS Berg.

Chapter 5. Keep Thee Like a Lady

1. SPH to EPP, February 3–4, 1850, MS Berg; Warren S. Tyron and William Charvat, "Introduction," *The Cost Books of Ticknor and Fields*, xiv–xviii; Mellow, *Hawthorne*, 309–310.

2. NH to Ticknor, January 19, 1855, CE, 17:304; NH to Bridge, February, 4 1850, CE, 16:311. Gary Scharnhorst's *The Critical Response to Nathaniel Hawthorne's* The Scarlet Letter provides convenient access to numerous contemporary reviews, including excerpts from reviews by Orestes Brownson and Arthur Cleveland Coxe.

3. NH to HM, August 8, 1849, CE, 16:293 and CE, 16:339, fn 2.

4. NH to John Jay, August 22, 1849, CE, 16:296; Horatio Bridge to NH, August 1, 1849, MS Berg; Mellow, *Hawthorne*, 317; SPH to Mrs. P., May 23, 1849, and February 14, 1850, SPH to MPM, February 12, 1850, MSS Berg; NH to Horatio Bridge, April 13, 1850, and SPH to EPP, July 21,1850, CE, 16:329–330, 350.

5. NH to SPH, April 26, 1850, CE, 16:334; NH to Margaret Fuller, August 25, 1842, CE, 15:646; NH to Horatio Bridge, August 18, 1850, CE, 16:357.

6. SPH to MPM, October 21, 1849, MS Berg.

7. Wendy Gamber, *The Boarding House in Nineteenth-Century America*, 3, 7.

8. Gamber, *The Boarding House in Nineteenth-Century America*, 3; NH to SPH, April 26, 1850, CE, 16:332–333.

9. NH, *The American Notebooks*, CE, 8:499, 493. See Gamber, *The Boarding House*, particularly chapter 1, "Away from Home," and chapter 6, "Will They Board, or Keep House?"

10. SPH to Mrs. P., June 9, 1850, and Caroline Tappan to SPH [spring 1850], MSS Berg.

11. NH to Zachary Burchmore, June 9, 1850, *CE*, 16:340.

12. Barbara Downs Wojtusik, "Anna Hazard Barker Ward," 264, "Samuel Gray Ward," 264–265; Eleanor Tilton, "The True Romance of Anna Barker Hazard Ward and Samuel Gray Ward," 53-72; Charles Capper, *Margaret Fuller*, 1:281. Thomas R. Mitchell, in *Hawthorne's Fuller Mystery* (79–80), contends that by dispatching Sam and Sophia, Margaret manipulated an opportunity to be alone with Nathaniel, who was attracted to her. The incident suggests to me, however, that dynamic among those four that day was charged by Margaret's past emotional history with Sam and Anna, and Margaret's awareness that Sam was now a conspicuously happy married man.

13. Cornelia Brooke Gilder, *Hawthorne's Lenox*, 20–26; SPH to Mrs. P., September 12, 1849, MS Berg.

14. Gilder, *Hawthorne's Lenox*, 91; Capper, *Margaret Fuller*, I:191, 272.

15. Gilder, *Hawthorne's Lenox*, "Tanglewood and the Tappans," 35–43.

16. F. E. Parker to E. D. Sedgwick, July 24, 1850, quoted Gilder, *Hawthorne's Lenox*, 19.

17. NH, *The House of the Seven Gables*, CE, 2:25.

18. NH, *The House of the Seven Gables*, CE, 2:10, 7, 11, 17, 33, 22, 24.

19. NH, *The House of the Seven Gables*, CE, 2:38, 39.

20. NH, *The House of the Seven Gables*, CE, 2:34, 24, 50, 51, 43.

21. NH, *The House of the Seven Gables*, CE, 2:31–32, 105.

22. NH, *The House of the Seven Gables*, CE, 2:74, 79, 71–72.

23. NH, *The House of the Seven Gables*, CE, 2:81, 39, 80.

24. RHL, *Memories of Hawthorne*, 474; Cecile Anne De Rocher, "Introduction," *Elizabeth Manning Hawthorne: A Life in Letters*, 15–17; JH, *Hawthorne and His Wife*, I:353.

25. NH, *The House of the Seven Gables*, CE, 2:80.

26. NH, *The House of the Seven Gables*, CE, 2:258. Teresa Goddu's "The Circulation of Women in *The House of the Seven Gables*" addresses similar points about the relationship between Clifford and Hepzibah, though Goddu concludes that "Hebzibah's incestuous feelings for Clifford . . . symbolize a restrictive social posture more than sexual attraction" (121). About the conclusion of the book, Goddu observes how Nathaniel abandons his original interrogations, turning "a story of class conflict into a family feud when he retreats from the radical economic alternative of the book, the generalized exchange of business, and chooses instead another inheritance model, the restricted exchange of alliance" (125).

Chapter 6. The Paradise of Children

1. Fuller's dream quoted in Bell Gale Chevigny, *The Woman and the Myth*, 393; Sarah Clarke to Margaret Fuller, March 5, 1850, quoted in Capper, *Margaret Fuller*, II:473.

2. See Capper, *Margaret Fuller*, II, chapter 14, "Dark Passages," for a complete analysis of the Ossolis' fateful Atlantic crossing.

3. Gilder, *Hawthorne's Lenox*, 73. Fuller's last words are quoted in Chevigny, *The Woman and the Myth*, 397, and in Capper, *Margaret Fuller*, II:510. For analysis of Margaret's motivations, see Capper, *Margaret Fuller*, II:509.

4. SPH to Mrs. P., August 1, 1850, and SPH to MPM, September 9, 1850, MSS Berg.

5. MPM to SPH, [n.d., n.y.], and SPH to Mrs. P., September 29, 1850, MSS Berg.

6. Quoted in Chevigny, *The Woman and the Myth*, 256–257; SPH to Mrs. P., September 29, 1850, and SPH to MPM, February 3, 1851, MSS Berg.

7. SPH to EPP, April 3, 17, 1851, and SPH to MPM, October 9, 1851, MSS Berg; NH to EPP, April 3, 1851, *CE*, 16:414, fn 2, 491.

8. SPH to Mrs. P., January 27, April 13, 1851, and SPH to EPP, February 3, 1851, MSS Berg.

9. SPH to MPM, June 22, 1951, MS Berg.

10. NH to LH, May 20, 1851, NH to EPP, May 25, 1851, *CE*, 16:433, 440–441; SPH to Mrs. P., April 13, 1851, MS Berg.

11. SPH to Mrs. P., April 13, 1851, September 7, 1851, MSS Berg; SPH quoted in JH, *Hawthorne and His Wife*, I:375–376, 383; NH, *The American Notebooks*, *CE*, 8:339–400.

12. SPH to Mrs. P., September 9, 1850, MS Berg, SPH, March 13–14, *1851 Journal*, MS Berg. RHL, *Memories of Hawthorne*, 161–162.

13. SPH to Grace Greenwood, February 7, 1851, and SPH to MTM, July 16, 1848, MSS Berg; NH, *The American Notebooks*, *CE*, 8:403.

14. Larry R. Long, "Samuel Griswold Goodrich," 158–159; Samuel Griswold Goodrich, *Recollections of a Lifetime*, 1:166–167.

15. NH, *The American Notebooks*, *CE*, 8: 399, 414, 419, 418–420; SPH, March 13, *1851 Journal*, and SPH to Mrs. P., [15] January 1850, MSS Berg.

16. "Pandora Brought to Epimetheus" is one of six sketches in a booklet titled "The Legend of Pandora" housed at the House of the Seven Gables and catalogued as follows: "A series of six pencil tracings of the Theogany [sic] 1817 [Flaxman] by Sophia Hawthorne with a specially illuminated cover in watercolor and pen by Una for the Concord Fair." No more is known of the provenance of this booklet. These exact tracings may actually have been produced by Una or Rose, rather than their mother, for one of the fairs held in Concord during the Civil War. Whoever executed "The Legend of Pandora," it demonstrates the centrality of this myth in the Hawthorne household for over fifteen years. For further references to Pandora, see SPH to EPP, November 11, 1849, SPH to Mrs. P., [fall 1849], November 18, 1849, and RH to Patty, n.d, n.m., 1862, MSS Berg; SPH, "Sophia Peabody Hawthorne's *American Notebooks*," 158.

17. Mrs. P. to SPH, March 20, 1848, and SPH to Mrs. P., March 26, 1848, MSS Berg; NH, *The American Notebooks*, *CE*, 8:445.

18. Mary's letter quoted in Alexander Kern, "A Note on Hawthorne's Juveniles," 245; NH to SP, August 22, 1841, *CE*, 15:563. For a full analysis of the impact of

Nathaniel's domestic circumstances upon his writing for children, see Patricia Dunlavy Valenti, "'None but Imaginative Authority,'" 1–27.

19. Fredson Bowers, "Textual Introduction," *CE*, 6:332; NH, "Samuel Johnson," *CE*, 6:241, 6.

20. NH to JTF, May 23, 1851, *CE*, 16:436–437.

21. NH, "The Chimaera," *CE*, 7:150, 165; SPH, "The American Notebooks," 174. The American edition of *A Wonder Book* quickly sold out and was followed by seven separate printings, constituting the sale of well over fourteen thousand books, during the 1850s. To these sales must be added books sold in England as well as the American and British total sales of *Tanglewood Tales*.

22. On Marygold as "emblem of [the] excessive importance placed on children by their parents," see Gillian Brown, "Hawthorne and Children in the Nineteenth Century," 90. Brown sees the origin of Marigold in both Hawthornes' "ideas about the upbringing of children, which included home-schooling and intensive parental attention to every aspect of their children's lives" (89).

23. "The Pomegranate Seeds" appeared in the later *Tanglewood Tales*, *CE*, 7:306, 325; SPH to Mrs. P., July 15, 1851, MS Berg.

24. NH, "The Paradise of Children," *CE*, 7:66, 71, 79, 77.

25. SPH, February 14, March 3, January 8, and *passim 1851 Journal*; SPH to EPP, April 27, 1851, and SPH to Mrs. P., February 12, 1851, MSS Berg.

26. NH to Mrs. Tappan, September 5, 1851, *CE*, 16:481–484.

27. SPH to EPP, September 4, 1851, October 2, 1851, MSS Berg.

Chapter 7. Shock of Recognition

1. NH to LH, July 10, 1851, *CE*, 16:454; SPH to MPM, July 4, 1851, and SPH to EPP, July 10, 1851, MSS Berg; NH, *The American Notebooks*, *CE*, 8:439.

2. NH to Pike, July 24, 1851, *CE*, 16:465.

3. SPH to L. W. Mansfield, January 8, 1851, MS Berg. See also NH's earlier letter to Mansfield, December 26, 1849, *CE*, 16:302–303.

4. Rebecca R. Saulsbury, "Catharine Maria Sedgwick (1789–1867)," 351–360; SPH to Mrs. P., October 27, 1850, December 25, 1850, MSS Berg.

5. SPH to EPP, September 4, 1851, MS Berg.

6. SPH to EPP, August 8, 1850, MS Berg, see also *CE*, 16:423, fn 7; SPH to Mrs. P., September 3, 4, 1850, MS Berg.

7. HM, "Hawthorne and His Mosses," 2393; SPH and NH to E. A. Duyckinck, August 29, 1850, *CE*, 16:361–362.

8. HM, "Hawthorne and His Mosses," 2301, 2294, 2300; Miller, *Salem Is My Dwelling Place*, 314.

9. SPH, December 26, *1843 Diary*, MS Berg; SPH, "A Sophia Hawthorne Journal, 1843–44," 16; SPH, January 14, *Lenox Diary 1851*, MS Berg. See Miller's similar observations about Sophia's reaction to Melville in *Salem Is My Dwelling Place*, 314–315. HM, "Hawthorne and His Mosses," 2295–2296.

10. Hershel Parker, *Herman Melville: A Biography, Vol. 2, 1851–1891*, 2, 3. SPH to EPP, August 5, 1850, MS Berg; NH to Bridge, August 7, 1850, *CE*, 16:355.

11. SPH to Mrs. P., October 24, [1852], MS courtesy of the Department of Special Collections and University Archives, Stanford University Library, hereafter cited as Stanford. References to *Typee* and *Omoo* and lack of reference to *Moby-Dick* suggest that this letter was probably written in 1851.

12. Wineapple, *Hawthorne*, 224; Miller, *Salem Is My Dwelling Place*, 314.

13. JH, *Hawthorne and His Wife*, I:396–397, 407, 415, 397, 377; NH, *The American Notebooks*, *CE*, 8:447, 448.

14. HM to NH, June 29, 1851, quoted in JH, *Hawthorne and His Wife*, I:400, and in HM, *The Writings of Herman Melville*, 196; NH, *The American Notebooks*, *CE*, 8:464.

15. NH, *The American Notebooks*, *CE*, 8:464–468.

16. HM to NH, November [17], 1851, *Correspondence*, 212, 213.

17. HM to NH, n.d., *Correspondence*, 190, and quoted in JH, Hawthorne and His Wife, 1:400. HM, *Correspondence*, 212. Miller, *Salem Is My Dwelling Place*, 351; NH, *The American Notebooks*, *CE*, 8:464; For a more tempered assessment of the decline of Nathaniel's friendship with Melville, see Wineapple, *Hawthorne*, 227–228.

18. HM to SPH, January 8, 1852, HM, *Correspondence*, 219.

19. NH to SH, October 18, 1841, *CE*, 15:588-590.

20. Ann Braude, *Radical Spirits*, 10–16.

21. Braude, *Radical Spirits*, 85; Mrs. P. to SPH, December 28, [1850], MS Berg; Ronda, *Elizabeth Palmer Peabody*, 247, 248.

22. Banner of Light quoted in Braude, *Radical Spirits*, 85; EPP to SPH, March 23, 1851, quoted in Ronda, *Elizabeth Palmer Peabody*, 249.

23. Mrs. P. to EPP, January 12, 1851; SPH to EPP, February 3, March 15, 1851, MSS Berg.

24. Braude, *Radical Spirits*, 16; Barbara Weisberg, *Kate and Maggie Fox and the Rise of Spiritualism*, 55.

25. Samuel Chase Coale, *Mesmerism and Hawthorne*, 4.

26. NH to SPH, August 8, 1851, *CE*, 16:470; SPH to Mrs. P., August 19, 1851, MS Berg.

Chapter 8. The Deeper Her Cry

1. JH, *Hawthorne and His Wife*, 1:429–431.

2. NH to SPH, September 19, 1851, *CE*, 16:490; SPH to EPP, October 2, 1851, and SPH to MPM, [February 19-20], 1851, MSS Berg.

3. NH to Caroline Tappan, September 5, 1851, *CE*, 16:481; NH to SPH, September 23, 1851, *CE*, 16:492; SPH to MPM, September 23, October 11, 1851, MSS Berg.

4. SPH to LH, December 1, 1851, MS Berg.

5. NH, *The Blithedale Romance*, *CE*, 3:2, 3; NH to Ticknor, January 19, 1855, 17:304.

6. NH, *The Blithedale Romance, CE,* 3:63, 13, 17, 46.

7. SP, *Cuba Journal,* May 16, 1834, I:117, MS Berg; NH, *The Blithedale Romance, CE,* 3:21.

8. NH, *The Blithedale Romance, CE,* 3:28, 42, 41, 70, 133, 134, 194; HM to NH, November [17], 1851, *Correspondence,* 213. Messerli in *Horace Mann* (504) also notes the "striking psychological and ideological similarities between Hollingsworth, the compulsive and egocentric prison reformer, and the personality and career of Horace Mann." Miller in *Salem Is My Dwelling Place* (353–359) suggests that the Coverdale-Hollingsworth relationship represents Nathaniel's exorcism of the discomfort he experienced with the too-intense attention that Melville exhibited.

9. NH, *The Blithedale Romance, CE,* 3:27, 73, 59, 60.

10. NH, *The Blithedale Romance, CE,* 3:179, 182, 183, 48.

11. NH, *The Blithedale Romance, CE,* 3:125. About the suspicions that women in trances became sexually tainted, see Adam Crabtree, *From Mesmerism to Freud,* 100, and Stoehr, *Hawthorne's Mad Scientists,* 47.

12. NH, *The Blithedale Romance, CE,* 3:77, 78; NH, *The House of the Seven Gables, CE,* 2:188, 204, 206, 209.

13. Others have commented upon the similarities between Zenobia and Priscilla and the paradoxical cultural phenomena they represent. Angela Mills in "'The Sweet Word,' Sister," sees the novel as a "tale about America reformism— a tale about sisterhood and its overlapping incarnations as personal and political relationship (114). In *Culture of Letters,* Richard H. Brodhead's analysis of Priscilla may be applied to mediums in general: "Produced as a creature of physical invisibility, the Veiled Lady nevertheless leads a life of pure exhibitionism" (51).

14. NH, *The Blithedale Romance, CE,* 3:217, 103; NH, *The American Notebooks, CE,* 8:262–263; SPH to MPM, February 3, 1851, MS Berg.

15. NH to Whipple, May 2, 1852, *CE,* 16:536; SPH, January 13, 14, *1851 Diary,* MS Berg; NH, *The Blithedale Romance, CE,* 3:222, 223.

16. SPH to LH, July 17, 1852, SPH to Mrs. P., June 6, 13, 1852, MSS Berg; Mrs. P. to EPP, June 3,1852, MS Morgan (misattributed to Elizabeth Manning Hawthorne); JH, *Hawthorne and His Wife,* I:453; RHL, *Memories of Hawthorne,* 178; NH to G. W. Curtis, July 14, 1852, *CE,* 16:567, 568.

17. SPH to Mrs. P., July 4, 1852, MS Stanford; NH to G. W. Curtis, July 14, 1852, NH to G. P. Putnam, July 16, 1852, *CE,* 16:567–569, 572.

Chapter 9. The Revulsion of Joy

1. Mellow, *Nathaniel Hawthorne,* 410–411; Wineapple, *Hawthorne,* 260.

2. SPH to Mrs. P., August 13, 1852, MS Berg.

3. SPH to LH, July 17, February 2, 1852, MSS Berg; JH, *Hawthorne and His Wife,* I:452; SPH to Mrs. P., August 13, 5, 1852, MSS Berg.

4. SPH to Mrs. P., August 5, December 26, 1852, MSS Berg.

5. NH, *The American Notebooks*, *CE*, 8:538, 521, 513, 543, 512; "Explanatory Notes," *CE*, 8:665, 667; NH to Ticknor, September 7, 1852, *CE*, 16:595 and fn 1.

6. SPH, "Sophia Peabody Hawthorne's *American Notebooks*," 164, 162, 161, 167, 160, 162.

7. SPH,"Sophia Peabody Hawthornes's *American Notebooks*," 161, 162.

8. SPH, "Sophia Peabody Hawthorne's *American Notebooks*,"165, 171.

9. SPH, "Sophia Peabody Hawthorne's *American Notebooks*,"165; EPP, "Reminiscences" in JH's hand, *Autograph Notebook signed 1892*, MS Morgan. Miller in *Salem Is My Dwelling Place* (397) asserts, without citing a source, that Nathaniel Hawthorne "pledged himself to chastity at forty-seven."

10. NH to SPH, September 3, 1852, *CE*, 16:593.

11. SPH, "Sophia Peabody Hawthorne's *American Notebooks*," 173; SPH to Mrs. P., January 21, 1844, MS Berg; NH to Phoebe, September 3, 1852, and NH to Una, September 8, 1852, *CE*, 16:593, 596.

12. SPH, "Sophia Peabody Hawthorne's *American Notebooks*," 168, 171,173; Ebe to NH, September 23, 1852, MS Berg; SPH to Mrs. P., August 13, September 10, 1852, MSS Berg; SPH to Mrs. P., September 19, 1852, MS Stanford.

13. NH, "Preface," to *The Whole History of Grandfather's Chair*, *CE*, 6:6; NH to Bridge, October 13, 1852, NH, *CE*, 16:605. For a full discussion of Pierce's background and analysis of Nathaniel's composition of the *Life of Franklin Pierce*, see "Historical and Textual Commentary," section VII, *Biography*, *CE*, 23:636–643.

14. Larry Reynolds in *Devils and Rebels* analyzes O'Sullivan's stance on "Manifest Destiny" and the war with Mexico (27–28, 151–152).

15. HM to MPM, July 26, 1852, MHS; Mrs. P. to SPH, March 20, 1848, MS Berg; "Franklin Pierce's Mexican Diary" rpt in *CE*, 23:493. For analysis of Pierce's nuanced attitude toward war, the Mexican War in particular, see Reynolds, *Devils and Rebels*, 155–157.

16. SPH to Mrs. P., March 26,1848, MS Berg; NH, *Life of Franklin Pierce*, *CE*, 23:352.

17. Quoted in Sandra Harbert Petrulionis, *To Set This World Right*, 20.

18. SPH to Mrs. P., November 15, 1843, January 21, 1844, MSS Berg. Yellin, in "Hawthorne and the Slavery Question" (40), claims that Sophia's remarks reveal her disdain for the abolitionist movement. Petrulionis, in *To Set This World Right* (34), asserts: "Sophia bragged to her mother about exploiting the female society."

19. NH, *Life of Franklin Pierce*, *CE*, 23:350.

20. SPH to Mrs. P., [August 13, 1852], MS Stanford. Quotations from Webster's "Seventh of March Speech" taken from Petrulionis, *To Set This World Right*, 75, and Robert Remini, *Daniel Webster*, 669. Petrulionis says that "this consummate politician miscalculated the extent to which [the people of Massachusetts] would resent a federal law authorizing slave owners to invade their state and reenslave their black neighbors and friends" (75). For reaction to Webster's "Seventh of March Speech," see Remini, 676–677, who notes that Webster was a "passionate, romantic man," rumored to have fathered a son with a mulatto woman and

charged with attempted rape (306, 307, 569). SPH to Mrs. P., October 31, 1852, MS Berg.

21. SPH to Mrs. P., October 31, 1852, MS Berg, portions rpt. in JH, *Hawthorne and His Wife*, I:478 ff.

22. SPH to Mary Mann, July 16, 1848, MS Berg; SPH to Mrs. P., October 31, 1852, MS Berg.

23. Sophia, quoting Proverbs 15:1, in SPH to Una [New Year's Eve 1852], and SPH to MPM, December [17] 1852, MSS Berg.

Chapter 10. All Partings in This World Are Final

1. EPP to SPH, January 11, 1853, *Letters of EPP*, 277–279; SPH to MPM, December [17, 1852], SPH to Dr. P., February 13, 1852, MSS Berg; Dr. P. to SPH, February 6, 1853, MS Berg.

2. Mrs. P. quoted in Ronda, *Elizabeth Palmer Peabody*, 242.

3. NH to Ticknor, January 21, 1853, 16:631; SPH to Dr. P., February 3, 1853, and SPH to MPM, February 10, 1853, MSS Berg; EPP, *The Letters*, 278.

4. SP to Mrs. P., June 6, May 11, 1834, *Cuba Journal*, I:154, 111, and SPH to Dr. P., February 20 and 27, March 3, 1853; Una to Dr. P., March 13, 1853, MSS Berg.

5. NH to JTF, June 17, 1852, NH to Bridge, October 13, 1852, *CE*, 16:550–551, 605; SPH to Dr. P., March 20, 1853, MS Berg.

6. Betty Boyd Caroli, *First Ladies*, 52–53; Mellow, *Nathaniel Hawthorne*, 419.

7. SPH to Dr. P., March 20, 1853, MS Berg; Caroli, *First Ladies*, 53–54.

8. Raymona E. Hull, *The English Experience*, 20; Mellow, *Nathaniel Hawthorne*, 415, 428; NH to Charlotte Bridge, May 18, 1853, *CE*, 16:685.

9. SPH, April 29, *1853 Journal*, MS Stanford; SPH to MPM, February 7, 1853, and May 2, 1852, MSS Berg; NH to "Gentlemen" July 5, 1853, *CE*, 16:702; Dr. P., to SPH, February 3, 6, 1853, MSS Berg; SPH to EPP, n.d., MS Morgan; SPH to Dr. P., April 14, 1853, MS Barrett.

10. SPH, April 14 and 29, *1853 Journal*, MS Stanford; SPH to Dr. P., February 3, 13, 20, 27, March 6, 1853, MSS Berg; Una to Dr. P., March 13, 1853, MS Morgan; Una to Dr. P., February 27, 1853, MS courtesy of Dominican Sisters of Hawthorne Archives, Rose Hawthorne Lathrop Papers, formerly known as Archives of the Sisters of Relief for Incurable Cancer, ASRIC hereafter cited as DSHA; NH to Ticknor, January 19, 1855, *CE*, 17:304.

11. SPH, April 29 and May 8, *1853 Journal*, MS Stanford; NH to SPH, April 17, 19, cont'd 21, 1853, *CE*, 16:675, 677–678; NH to Bridge, December 21, 1854, *CE*, 17:298.

12. SPH to Dr. P., May 8, 1853, MS Berg; NH to C. W. Hackley, June 22, 1853, *CE*, 16:693; NH, *The American Notebooks*, *CE*, 8:552.

13. Warren S. Tyron quoted in "Introduction," *CE*, 17:15, fn 27. The maids' last name appears variously as "Herne" and "Hearne."

14. Elizabeth Barrett Browning and Mary Russell Mitford quoted in Thomas Woodson, "Introduction," *CE*, 17:18, 19.

15. Hull, *The English Experience*, 6; SPH to Dr. P., March 27, 1853, July 17, MSS Berg.

16. SPH to Dr. P., July 7, 1853, and SPH to [Dr. P.], July 1853, MSS Berg; SPH quoted Hull, *The English Experience*, 10.

17. JH, *Hawthorne and His Wife*, II:11.

Chapter 11. Sick to Death

1. SPH to Dr. P., July 17 through 21, 1853, printed in RHL, *Memories of Hawthorne*, 222–224; SPH to Dr. P., August 9, 1853, MS Berg; Hull, *The English Experience*, 17–18; JH, *Hawthorne and His Wife*, II:18–19. For information on Mrs. Blodget's establishment, see *CE*, 17:102, fn 3.

2. SPH to Dr. P., August 9 and 5, 1853, MSS Berg. JH, *Hawthorne and His Wife*, II:21; RHL, *Memories of Hawthorne*, 225.

3. SPH to Dr. P., August 5, 26, 1853, MSS Berg; NH to Ticknor, August 6, 1853, *CE*, 17:106, and fn 5 for Nathaniel's desire not to accept invitations.

4. SPH to Dr. P., August 26, September 2, 14, 1853, MSS Berg; Hull, *The English Experience*, 33–35.

5. SPH to Dr. P., October 4, 1853, MS Berg.

6. NH to Pike [September 13, 1853], NH to Ticknor, December 8, 1853, May 27, 1855, *CE*, 17:118, 151, 347.

7. NH to Caleb Foote, January 17, 1842, *CE*, 15:604; NH to Louisa, March 15, 1844, NH to Hillard, May 14, August 19, 1844, *CE*, 16:21, 35, 63. Robert E. Metzdorf, "Hawthorne's Suit again Dana and Ripley," 235–241; NH to Ticknor, March 30, 1854, *CE*, 17:191.

8. NH to O'Sullivan [April 20, 1840], *CE*, 15:447. For an account of the relationship among Nathaniel Hawthorne, Mary Silsbee, and John Louis O'Sullivan, see Patricia Dunlavy Valenti, *Sophia Peabody Hawthorne: A Life*, 1:113–115. Nathaniel Hawthorne's biographers have accepted Elizabeth Peabody's late-in-life account, conveyed to Julian, of Nathaniel's thwarted duel with O'Sullivan. Because she offered no documentation or corroboration about a circumstance so uncharacteristic of her brother-in-law, Brenda Wineapple postulates that Nathaniel's "near duel seems a Peabodyesque fanstasia" (*Hawthorne*, 104). But while Elizabeth was prone to exaggerate, she was unlikely to invent incidents whole-cloth. Nathaniel's mention of Mary Silsbee Sparks in this same letter offering a generous loan supports speculation about her peculiar, though unspoken, past connection to both men. Finally, Sheldon Howard Harris, in his unpublished 1958 dissertation, "The Public Career of John Louis O'Sullivan" (78–79)—still the best source of information on O'Sullivan—believes that Nathaniel challenged O'Sullivan to duel, citing Julian's December 27, 1882, letter to Bridge as corroboration for Elizabeth's account. NH to SPH, March 16, 1843, *CE*, 15:678; SPH to Mrs. P., January 12, 1843, MS Berg.

9. Harris, "The Public Career of John Louis O'Sullivan," 275–278.

10. Harris, "The Public Career of John Louis O'Sullivan," 309, 311–312, 321, 346.

11. NH to Ticknor, March 30, December 8, March 16, April 26, October 26, 1855, *CE*, 17:289, 318, 334, 395.

12. Hull, *The English Experience*, 33; NH to Bridge, April 17, 1854, *CE*, 17:203.

13. SPH to MPM, October 9, 1853, SPH to EPP, September 29, 1853, SPH to Dr. P., March 30, 1854, MSS Berg. For information about printings of *Tanglewood Tales*, see *CE*, 17:139, fn 3.

14. SPH to Ticknor, December 2, 1856; SPH to Dr. P., August 9, 17, September 14, 29, 1853, MSS Berg; NH to Ticknor, July 22, 1853, *CE*, 17:101.

15. SPH to EPP, September 29, October 25, 1853; Una to EPP, October 25, 1953; SPH to Dr. P., September 29, October 20, 1853; January 5, November 14, 1854; SPH to MPM, October 9, 1853, MSS Berg.

16. Ronda, *Elizabeth Palmer Peabody*, 250–251; SPH to Dr. P., March 29, April 3, 1853, SPH to EPP, September 29, 1853, MSS Berg; NH to Ticknor, December 8, 1854, *CE*, 17:289.

17. SPH to EPP, October 31, 1854, MS Berg; Ronda, *Elizabeth Palmer Peabody*, 251.

18. SPH to EPP, November 14, 1854, February 8, 1855, SPH to Dr. P., [January 1], 1855, MSS Berg; NH to EPP, April 20, 1855, *CE*, 17:330.

19. Sophia's comments about the girls' faces suggest her departure from phrenological assumptions that character was signaled by the structure of the head. That theory met another challenge some months later when Sophia encountered the "phrenological wonder" of a certain Mrs. Holland, a particularly pleasant dinner table companion whose exceptionally low forehead should have predicted a disagreeable person. SPH to Dr. P., August 7, 1853, October 20, 1853, [November] 23 [1853], January 5, 1854, MSS Berg.

20. NH, *The English Notebooks*, 1853–1856, *CE*, 21:285, 399, 26, 412.

21. NH to Pike, [September 13, 1853], 17:119; SPH to Dr. P., [November] 23, 1853, May 12, 28, 1854, MSS Berg; Harris, "The Public Career of John Louis O'Sullivan," 357; Hull, *The English Experience*, 48.

22. NH, *The English Notebooks 1853–1856*, *CE*, 21:92, 93.

23. SPH to Dr. P., July 4, 1854, MS Berg.

24. SPH to Dr. P., July 4, 1854, MS Berg; Petrulionis, *To Set This World Right*, 98–100; Larry Reynolds, *Devils and Rebels*, 196–198.

25. Harris, "The Public Career of John Louis O'Sullivan," 346–348; SPH to MPM, July 3, 1854, MS Berg.

26. SPH to Dr. P., July 4, 1854, MS Berg; NH to Bridge, April 13, 1855, *CE*, 17:327.

27. Una to Richard Manning, June 7, 1855, quoted in Hull, *The English Experience*, 246.

28. Hull, *The English Experience*, 58.

29. SPH to EPP, June 8, 1855, Una to EPP, July 1, September 12, 1855; SPH fragment to NH, September 20, [1855], MSS Berg.

Chapter 12. At the Turning Tide

1. SPH to MPM, April 13, 1856, MS Berg.

2. SPH to MPM, July 16, 1848, MS Berg; Una to EPP, August 23, 1853, TS Berg; Una to MPM, October 31, 1855, MS Berg.

3. SPH to EPP, October 31, 1854, SPH to Dr. P., August 18, January 19, 1854, MSS Berg.

4. Una to Dr. P., March 23, 1853, June 22, October 26, 1854, MSS Berg. Sophia's cross-written comment is found on the October 26 letter.

5. SPH to MPM, December 30, 1856; SPH to EPP, April 19, 1855; Una to EPP, July 1, 1855, June 3, [1857, misdated as 1856], December 4, September 23 [1857, misdated as 1856], MSS Berg.

6. Miller's "A Calendar of the Letters of Sophia Peabody Hawthorne" (247) lists as Sophia's extant letters from Portugal only the following: two to Elizabeth Peabody, two to Mary Mann, three to Julian, and one to Nathaniel. Some others, now lost, were transcribed by Una and are housed at the Stanford University Library among Rose Hawthorne Lathrop's papers. Catalogued as Rose's editing of "Sophia Hawthorne's *Madeira Journal*," this "journal" is comprised of chapters XV and XVI, numbered as pages 659 through 721 and 722 through 771 respectively. Chapter XV begins with Rose's words in her hand: "In Portugal. The following letters were written from Portugal, to which my mother, sister, & I went for a visit to the O'Sullivans, while my father remained at the Consulate in Liverpool. I concluded not to let the foreign scene break in upon the English one; waiting till that had passed." This last sentence together with Rose's obvious emendations and additions suggest that she anticipated using this material in her *Memories of Hawthorne*. No holographs or additional transcript letters of these chapters of this so-called *Madeira Journal* have been located, and none were published in *Memories*. Although some of the letters were written from Lisbon, citations to this transcription will refer to it as the Hawthornes did, *Madeira Journal*, and employ pagination presumably inserted in Rose's hand. Una to EPP June 3, [1857, misdated as 1856], MS Berg.

7. Harris,"The Public Career of John Louis O'Sullivan," 372.

8. SPH, *Madeira Journal*, 660, 665–668, 675, 689, 712, 720, 721, MS Stanford.

9. SPH, *Madeira Journal*, 670–672, 721, 707, MS Stanford.

10. Harris, "The Public Career of John Louis O'Sullivan," 365, 356–359, 368; SPH, *Madeira Journal*, 685, 720, MS Stanford.

11. SPH to JH, November 13, 1855, October 27, 1855, MSS Berg; SPH, *Madeira Journal*, 708, MS Stanford.

12. SPH, *Madeira Journal*, 718–719, 692, MS Stanford.

13. SPH, *Madeira Journal*, 687, 674, 691, 717, 669, MS Stanford.

14. SPH, *Madeira Journal*, 678, 670, 714, MS Stanford; Una to MPM, December [28], 1855, MS Berg. "Extract: Description of Madeira Visit Feb 1856 Written Later," p. 1792, is undoubtedly by Una although it is catalogued with the Louise Deming

and Aretta Stevens Project Papers among the letters of Sophia Peabody Hawthorne, Manuscripts, Archives, and Special Collections, Washington State University Libraries.

15. SPH, *Madeira Journal,* 679, MS Stanford; NH to SPH, November 24, 1855, *CE,* 17:410; Una to MPM, December 28, 1855, MS Berg.

16. SPH, *Madeira Journal,* 684, 680, 679, 715, MS Stanford; SPH to NH, n.d., n.y., and SPH to JH, October 12, 1855, MSS DSHA. NH to RH, March 14, 1856, *CE,* 17:451. In the transcript of *Madeira Journal,* Rose copies "John" as her mother had written the word, then strikes through "~~ohn~~" to minimize the familiarity with which her mother referred to O'Sullivan.

17. SPH, *Madeira Journal,* 668, MS Stanford; SPH to JH, January 22, 1856, MS Berg; NH to SPH, November 14, 1855, *CE,* 17:410.

18. SPH to JH, January 22, 1856, in JH, *Hawthorne and His Wife,* II:84–101; NH to SPH, November 3, 1856, *CE,* 17:398.

19. SPH, *Madeira Journal,* 673, 682, MS Stanford; NH to SPH, February 7, 1856, 17:436; Una to NH, December 18, 1855, MS DSHA.

20. Una to NH, February 3, 1856, MS Berg; NH to SPH, April 7, February 7, 1856, *CE,* 17:463, 437–438.

21. NH to O'Sullivan, November 13, 1855, NH to SPH, February 7, 1856, *CE,* 17:404, 437–438; SPH to MPM, April 13, 1856, MS Berg.

22. SPH, *Madeira Journal,* 684, 660, MS Stanford; SPH to JH, October 27, 1855, January 22, 1856, MSS Berg.

23. SPH, *Madeira Journal,* 721, 726–727, MS Stanford.

24. SPH, *Madeira Journal,* 727, 728, 722, 740, 730, 736, 750, MS Stanford; NH to Ticknor, November 9, 1855, NH to SPH, March 18, 1856, *CE,* 17:401–402, 457.

25. Regarding Welsh, see *CE,* 17:459 fn 3; SPH, *Madeira Journal,* 728, 722, 738, 732–734, 724, 741–44, 758, 760, MS Stanford.

26. SPH, *Madeira Journal,* 745–746, MS Stanford.

27. SPH, *Madeira Journal,* 764–771, MS Stanford.

28. SPH to MPM, April 13, 1856, MS Berg.

Chapter 13. The Most Perfect Pictures

1. JH quoted in Hull, *The English Experience,* 70, 69; NH, *The English Notebooks, 1853–1856, CE,* 21:406–407.

2. Woodson, "Introduction," *CE,* 17:24–30; NH quoted in JH, *Hawthorne and His Wife,* I:127–128; Hull, *The English Experience,* 88.

3. SPH to EPP, May 7, 1857, September 23, 1856; SPH to NH, July 22, 1856; Una to EPP, September 20, 1856, MSS Berg.

4. SPH to MPM, December 30, 1856; SPH to EPP, October 23, November 19, December 16, [August 6–7, 1856]; Una to EPP, December 31, August 26, 1856, MSS Berg; Una to EPP, October 20, 1857, TS Berg.

5. Una to EPP, November 30, 1856, MS Berg.

6. SPH to Una, May 23, 1857, MS Morgan; Una to EPP, August 26, September 20, 1856, MSS Berg.

7. SPH to Una, May 24, June 30, 1857, MSS Morgan; SPH to Una, May 22, 1857, MSS Morgan. Sophia's journal letters to Una were written (here listed in chronological order) from Lincoln, Boston, Peterboro, Nottingham, Carlisle, Dunfries, Ayr, Glasgow, Dumbarton, Inversaid, Inverannan, Bridge of Alain, and Linlithgow. The original holographs are housed at the Morgan Library, catalogued as MA1220. Sophia made her own copies of these original holograph letters that she used as the printer's copies when she published them in *Notes in England and Italy*. These copies are housed at the Berg Collection. In this chapter, references to Sophia's "Cathedral letters," as she would later call them, are drawn from MA1220.

8. SPH to Una, May 28, 23, 26, 22, and 24, 1857, MSS Morgan.

9. SPH to EPP, April 22, 1857, MS Berg. Analyzing Sophia's published version of her "Cathedral letters" in *Notes in England and Italy*, Mary Suzanne Schriber claims in *Writing Home* that Sophia attempts "to conceal, ignore, and destroy the trace of another voice, another self-possibility" (110). Annamaria Formichella Elsden in "Watery Angels" (132) recaps published appraisals of Sophia's tone and voice in *Notes* by Schriber and by Julie Hall ("'Coming to Europe,' Coming to Authorship: Sophia Hawthorne and Her Notes in England and Italy") before arguing that Sophia nonetheless articulates a "philosophical and political commentary on the world around her, specifically its gender ideology and humanitarianism." Claude Simpson less kindly labels Sophia's letters "guidebook puffery" ("Introduction," *CE*, 5:xl). While each interpretation of Sophia's conventional tone and impersonal voice varies, each addresses Sophia's conspicuous personal detachment from her descriptions.

10. SPH, *Madeira Journal*, 712, 668, MS Stanford; SPH to Una, June 30, July 2, 1857, MSS Morgan; SPH to JH, October 27, 1855, MS Berg. See, for example, Sophia's July 2, 1857, letter to Una about looking at the waterfall in Glenfallock through the lens of Wordsworth's "The Highland Girl," and her response to Gothic architecture as informed by John Ruskin.

11. NH to Ticknor, June 5, 1857, NH to EPP, August 13, 1857, *CE*, 18:63–64, 90; NH to SPH, November 3, 24, 1855, *CE*, 17:398, 400, fn 8, 410. Although Thomas Woodson wonders "how much husband and wife shared . . . as they sat down to write each evening" ("Historical Commentary" *CE*, 21:725), Nathaniel was sufficiently aware of his wife's letters in England and Scotland to discuss them with Ticknor and Elizabeth as publishable possibilities.

12. NH to Bridge, February 13, 1857, and NH to Ticknor, March 13, 1857, *CE*, 18:18, 37.

13. NH to Bridge, February 13, 1857, NH to Ticknor, March 13, 1857, 18:19–20, fn 4, *CE*, 18:37, fn 5, 18:40; Harris, "The Public Career of John Louis O'Sullivan," 378–379.

14. JH, *Hawthorne and His Circle*, 68–69; Una to EPP, February 22, 1857, TS Berg; Una to EPP, March 9, 1857, MS Berg.

15. Una to EPP, January 14 and December 9, 1857, TS Berg.

16. Una to EPP, October 30, May 20, 1857, TS Berg; William Reenan, *Nathaniel Hawthorne Diary 1859*, Appendix, 128, Berg; Reenan's transcription, housed at the Berg, contains extensive, valuable annotations in its appendix. NH to SPH, December 13, 1855, 17:419.

17. Una to EPP, January 1, 1857, MS DSHA; Una to EPP, November 30, December 9, 1857, TSS Berg; Una to EPP, September 20, November 6, October 8, 1856, MSS Berg.

18. SPH to Ticknor, December 2, [1857, misdated as 1856], SPH to EPP [1857], SPH to MPM, December 30, 1856, MSS Berg.

19. SPH to MPM, December 30, 1856, and SPH to EPP, May 7, 1857, MSS Berg; UNA to EPP, February 22, 1857, TS Berg; NH, *The English Notebooks, 1856–1860*, CE, 22:180–181.

20. SPH to MPM, September n.d., June 16, 1857, and SPH to EPP [May 1857], May 7, 1857, June 4, 1857, MSS Berg.

21. NH to EPP, August 13, October 8, 1857, *CE*, 18:89, 115; SPH to MPM, September, n.d., 1857, and SPH to EPP, August 7, 1857, MSS Berg.

22. NH to Bright, September 21, 1857, and NH to Fields, September 15, 1857, *CE*, 18:105, 96.

Chapter 14. Like Sisters

1. Una to EPP, September 20, October 8, 1856, MSS Berg, and January 27, TS Berg; JH quoted in Hull, *The English Experience*, 53–54. On Fanny Wrigley, see also Patricia Dunlavy Valenti, *To Myself a Stranger*, 8–9, and SPH to EPP, January 27, 1857, MS Berg.

2. SPH to EPP, October 23, November 23, December 11, 16, 1856; Una to EPP, October 1856; SPH to MPM, December 30, 1856, January 2, 1857, MSS Berg; Hull, *The English Experience*, 108–109; NH to Bennoch, November 21, 1856, *CE*, 17:577–578; Tharp, *Until Victory*, 270, 280.

3. Ada Shepard's holograph letters have only recently been discovered, according to her great niece and literary heir, Susan Abele. Cited in this book with permission from Ms. Abele are the typescript transcriptions of Ada's letters housed in the Norman Holmes Pearson Collection of the Beinecke Library, Yale University. The vast majority of these typescript letters are addressed to Clay Badger with fewer addressed to Ada's sisters Kate and Lucy Shepard. The transcription comprises nearly fourteen hundred pages and is organized chronologically with Clay's letters preceding those to the other recipients. Each letter is dated and several pages in length. For ease in locating sources, citations employ page numbers, not dates. When a particular date of correspondence or name of correspondent is necessary for clarification, that information is supplied in the chapter, rather than in endnotes. AS, *Letters*, 91, 119, 125, TS Beinecke.

4. AS, *Letters*, 113, 119, 168, 124, 119, 361 121, 125, 112, TS Beinecke.

5. JH, *Hawthorne and His Wife*, II:169, 175–77; Hull, *The English Experience*, 140, 145.

6. NH to SP, November 27, 1841, *CE*, 15:597; Renée Bergland, *Maria Mitchell*, 87, 121.

7. NH, *The French and Italian Notebooks, CE*, 14:17; Maria Mitchell's journal quoted in "Explanatory Notes," *CE*, 14:728, 729, 731; AS, *Letters*, 296, 237, 289, TS Beinecke.

8. JH, *Hawthorne and His Wife*, II:174–176; RHL, *Memories of Hawthorne*, 365; Bergland, *Maria Mitchell*, 122.

9. Hull, *The English Experience*, 147; AS, *Letters*, 413, TS Beinecke; NH, *The French and Italian Notebooks, CE*, 14:53, 54.

10. SP to EPP, September 5, 1832, SPH to EPP n.d., [1858], MSS Berg; SPH, *Notes in England and Italy*, 198.

11. For biographical notes on Mozier, Akers, and Brown, see Hull, *The English Experience*, 288, 271, 269–270, 276; on Mozier, Akers, Brown, and Abel, see "Explanatory Notes," *CE*, 14:765, 778, 773–774, 777–778, 780.

12. For biographical information on Story and Thompson, see "Explanatory Notes," *CE*, 14:737–739; JH, *Hawthorne and His Wife*, II:18; NH, *The French and Italian Notebooks, CE*, 14:229.

13. For a full account of Sarah Clarke, see Joel Myerson's "'A True and High Minded Person': Transcendentalist Sarah Clarke"; SPH, *Notes in England and Italy*, 293.

14. RHL, *Memories of Hawthorne*, 365; Bergland, *Maria Mitchell*, 131–132.

15. On Lander and Crawford, see "Explanatory Notes," *CE*, 14:740–742, 757 respectively; NH, *The French and Italian Notebooks, CE*, 14:77–78. For dates in January, February, March, and April when NH visited Louisa's studio, see NH's *1858 Pocket Diary, CE*, 14:575–594, especially March 2 and April 13; *CE*, 14:585, 591. Lander's name does not appear in RHL's *Memories of Hawthorne* or Henry James's *William Wetmore Story and His Friends*. Sophia purged Louisa's name from *Notes in England and Italy* but referred to her in the original holograph of the *Roman Journal* on March 3, 1858, MS Berg. Citations to Sophia's holograph Roman or Florence journals occur only when these contain information she deleted for publication in *Notes in England and Italy*. All other citations are to this published version. SPH to MPM, May 16, 1858, MS Berg; AS, *Letters*, 379, TS Beinecke.

16. Dolly Sherwood, *Harriet Hosmer*, 12, 23.

17. Sherwood, *Harriet Hosmer*, 142; SPH, *Notes in England and Italy*, 265–266; NH, *The French and Italian Notebooks, CE*, 14:158–159; AS, *Letters*, 400, 1143, TS Beinecke; Story to J. R. Lowell, February 11, 1853, quoted in James, *William Wetmore Story*, I:255.

18. Lisa Merrill, *When Romeo Was a Woman*, 198, 235, 47, 127, 128, 44.

19. Merrill, *When Romeo Was a Woman*, 9–12, 176, 159, Hatty Hosmer quoted on 183–185.

20. Merrill, *When Romeo Was a Woman*, 211–219. Cushman quoted on 220; Merrill concludes that "[b]y marrying Emma Crow to her nephew and adopted son, Cushman could subsume her passion for and maintain the lifelong connection she desired with Emma Crow."

21. Merrill, *When Romeo Was a Woman*, 169, 35, 38, 39, 53, 126; Merrill is an invaluable source on Cushman and the dynamics of "lesbian" relationships in the nineteenth century.

22. Harriet Hosmer quoted in Merrill, *When Romeo Was a Woman*, 171, 173; William Wetmore Story to JR Lowell, quoted in James, *William Wetmore Story and His Friends*, I:258–259.

23. SPH to Dr. P., [January 1854], quoted in RHL, *Memories of Hawthorne*, 261–262; NH to Grace Greenwood, April 17, 1852, *CE*, 16:532; NH to Ticknor, January 6, 1854, NH to Ephraim F. Miller, March 3, 1854, NH to Ticknor, August 31, 1855, NH to SPH, April 7, 1856, NH to Ticknor, August 15, 1856, *CE*, 17:161, 184–185, 379, 464, 532; AS, *Letters*, 1314, TS Beinecke.

24. Merrill, *When Romeo Was a Woman*, 171.

25. NH, *The French and Italian Notebooks, CE*, 14:68–69.

26. James, *William Wetmore Story*, I:257.

Chapter 15. I Am Near You

1. SP to MP, November 20, 1832, MS Berg; SPH, *Notes in England and Italy*, 260.

2. NH, *The French and Italian Notebooks, CE*, 14:293, 281, 177, 281. Regarding the "chaste permission" to look upon nudity granted by marble, Nathaniel is concurring with Hiram Powers's ideas.

3. SPH, *Notes in England and Italy*, 225, 226, 349, 351, 116; SPH, March 15, *Roman Journal 1858*, MS Berg. Perhaps Sophia's influence caused Nathaniel to render a similar judgment of the Venus de Medici which represented "all womankind," her nudity somehow "modest," "tender and chaste" (*CE*, 14:298).

4. SPH, *Notes in England and Italy*, 212, 213, 214.

5. SPH, *Notes in England and Italy*, 224, 263, 264, 229; "a Has Been," etc., found in SPH, July 19, *2nd Florence Journal 1858*, 75, MS Berg. Schriber in *Writing Home* (123, 118) points out, Sophia sheds the "straitjacket" of convention in her Italian journals and writes from a "a different version of self . . . the energetic and responsive artist."

6. See Elsden, "Watery Angels," for a similar interpretation of Sophia's critique of Catholic religious art. Sophia Ripley quoted in Jenny Franchot, *Roads to Rome*, 314, 312; Isaac Hecker, *Isaac T. Hecker: The Diary*, 206; Joseph McSorley, *Isaac Hecker and His Friends*, 63.

7. SPH, *Notes in England and Italy*, 416, 312, 205; SPH, *Madeira Journal*, 745, MS Stanford. RHL, *Memories of Hawthorne* (390), wrote that her mother would not have been so moved by "pettiness of a brief burial service in a private parlor or in a meager meeting-house."

8. SPH, *Notes in England and Italy*, 113, 509, 235, 379, 208; SPH, July 13, *2nd Florence Journal 1858*, 53, MS Berg.

9. SPH to MPM, June 7, 1858, MS Berg; NH, *The French and Italian Notebooks, CE*, 14:148, 426; Frederick L. Dunn, "Malaria," 855–862.

10. SPH, *Notes in England and Italy*, 326.

11. NH to Powers, May 16, 1858, *CE*, 18:144; SPH, *Notes in England and Italy*, 338; SPH, June 5, 12, *1st Florence Journal 1858*, and Una to MPM [July 19, 1858], MSS Berg; NH, *The French and Italian Notebooks, CE*, 14:283.

12. SPH, *Notes in England and Italy*, 338–395, passim.

13. RHL, *Memories of Hawthorne*, 384; NH, *The French and Italian Notebooks, CE*, 14:314, 365; SPH, *Notes in England and Italy*, 363.

14. SPH, June 8, *1st Florence Journal 1858*, MS Berg.

15. SPH, June 25, *1st Florence Journal 1858*, 98, MS Berg; SPH, *Notes in England and Italy*, 346; NH, *The French and Italian Notebooks, CE*, 14:302. Nathaniel spelled Daniel Dunglas Home's name as it was commonly pronounced: "Hume."

16. SPH, July 2, *1st Florence Journal 1858*, 136; SPH to MPM, n.d., and SPH to EPP, August 15, 1858, MSS Berg; JH, *Hawthorne and His Wife*, II:190,198.

17. Hull, *The English Experience*, 272; AS, *Letters*, 1283, TS Beinecke. For dates of Sophia's activities with Isa and Annette in Florence June through September, see NH, *Pocket Diary 1858, CE*, 14:598–612 passim, and "Explanatory Notes," *CE*, 14:820–821, for information about Isabella Blagden and Annette Bracken; *Agnes Tremone* quoted in Merrill, *When Romeo Was a Woman*, 195–196; SPH, September 11, *2nd Florence Journal 1858*, 113, MS Berg.

18. NH, *The French and Italian Notebooks, CE*, 14:392–394; Browning quoted in "Explanatory Notes," *CE*, 14:837.

19. SPH, September 11, August 24, *2nd Florence Journal 1858*, MS Berg; SPH to EPP, August 25, 1858, MS Berg.

20. AS, *Letters*, 758, TS Beinecke. Also dated August 27, 1858, is an account of these events in Ada's letter to her sister Kate, *Letters*, 728, TS Beinecke.

21. NH, *The French and Italian Notebooks, CE*, 14:398, 417.

22. NH, *The French and Italian Notebooks, CE*, 14:396–400.

23. NH to SP, October 18, 1841, *CE*, 15:588–590; SPH to EPP, February 3, 1851, MS Berg.

24. AS, *Letters*, 810, 119, 171, 227, 165, 173, 140, 344, TS Beinecke.

25. AS, *Letters*, 445–446, 577–579, 465, TS Beinecke.

26. AS, *Letters*, 391, 454, 366, 580, 409, 442, 543, 425, TS Beinecke.

27. AS, *Letters*, 135, 231, 445, TS Beinecke.

28. AS, *Letters*, 834, 978, TS Beinecke.

29. In NH, *Pocket Diary 1858, CE*, 14:615, NH records the date of the Hawthornes' return to Rome on October 16, while SPH records it as October 18 in *Notes in England and Italy*, 542; AS, *Letters*, 884, TS Beinecke; JH, *Hawthorne and His Wife*, II:203–205; NH, *The French and Italian Notebooks, CE*, 14:488, 491.

30. AS, *Letters*, 840, TS Beinecke; NH, *The French and Italian Notebooks, CE*, 14:405. Both Ada and Nathaniel record the fateful venue as the Coliseum on the very day Una and Ada sketched there. In *Notes in England and Italy*, Sophia changed Coliseum to Palace of the Caesars, an error that was picked up by JH in *Hawthorne and His Wife*, II:206.

31. Nathaniel and Una record separately that the first signs of her malaria appeared on October 26, 1858. See NH, *Pocket Diary 1858, CE,* 14:616, and Una to EPP, February 1859, MS Berg. John Rogers to Henry, January 19, 1859, MS, New-York Historical Society. AS, *Letters,* 437, TS Beinecke; JH, *Hawthorne and His Wife,* II:183.

32. John Rogers to [his mother], [n.y., n.d., 1858], John Rogers to his father, December 16, 1858, MSS, New-York Historical Society.

33. NH to Louisa Lander, November 13, 1858, *CE,* 18:158 and holograph in Sophia's hand, MS Morgan.

34. NH, *The French and Italian Notebooks, CE,* 14:293, 209; AS, *Letters,* 750, TS Beinecke.

35. NH, *The French and Italian Notebooks, CE,* 14:281, 433.

36. John Rogers to Henry, [n.d., n.m., 1858], New-York Historical Society.

Chapter 16. Pungent Little Particles of Satan

1. NH, *The French and Italian Notebooks, CE,* 14:495; on Dr. Franco see "Explanatory Notes," *CE,* 14:853–854; Hull, *The English Experience,* 280; SPH to MPM, January [1859], MS Berg.

2. NH, *The French and Italian Notebooks, CE,* 14:493; SPH to MPM, January 15, [1859], MS Berg.

3. AS, *Letters,* 993, TS Beinecke; SPH to Kate Shepard, January 8, 1859, TS Beinecke; NH, January 3, 5, *Pocket Diary 1859, CE,* 14:633, 634; SPH to MPM, January 15 [1859], MS Berg; AS, *Letters,* 1326, TS Beinecke.

4. AS, *Letters,* 910–913, TS Beinecke.

5. AS, *Letters,* 919, 920, 928, TS Beinecke.

6. AS, *Letters,* 920, TS Beinecke.

7. In the nineteenth century, the massive doses of quinine prescribed for malaria sometimes caused yet another illness, Blackwater fever, from which Una may have now been suffering. See Dunn, "Malaria," 855–862. SPH to EPP, March 29, 21, 1859, and Una to EPP, May 11, 1859, MSS Berg.

8. AS, *Letters,* 973–974, 1016, TS Beinecke.

9. AS, *Letters,* 1015–1020, 1016, TS Beinecke.

10. AS, *Letters,* 465, 577–579, TS Beinecke.

11. SPH to EPP, March 29, July 3, 1859, Una to EPP, May 11, 1859, MSS Berg.

12. NH, *The French and Italian Notebooks, CE,* 14:657; RHL, *Memories of Hawthorne,* 352, 361, 373; NH quoted in JH, *Hawthorne and His Wife,* II:207–208.

13. Probably miscatalogued as SPH to MPM, April 8, 1859, this MS lacks a salutation and is titled "My Consolations"; and SPH to EPP, July 3, 1859, MSS Berg.

14. Una to EPP, May 11, 1859, MS Berg; JH, *Hawthorne and His Wife,* II:203–209. To date, Herbert in *Dearest Beloved* is the only scholar to examine at length Sophia's response to Una's illness. Herbert seems to explain Sophia's behavior as an example of "Munchausen by Proxy," that rare psychological disorder wherein a mother pathologically feeds her own ego by the attention she receives during her child's

illness, be it fabricated or inflicted by the mother herself: "Sophia took center stage in the drama of her daughter's illness. Now as before, she cannibalizes Una's emotional life in dramatizing her own struggle with the dilemmas of womanhood" (250). Labeling Sophia's care for Una "obsessive fascination" and her "absorption in the psychic vagaries of her increasingly emaciated daughter . . . one side of a morbid intercourse" (252), Herbert ignores entirely both the parasitic etiology of malaria, which had killed millions of people in the course of history, and the fearful realities of childhood mortality in the nineteenth century. Julian is undoubtedly more valid than Herbert in assessing the nature and effect of Sophia's care for Una.

15. SPH to EPP, April 24, [1859], July 3, 1859, MSS Berg; RHL, *Memories of Hawthorne,* 370–371; JH, *Hawthorne and His Wife,* II:212; NH, *The French and Italian Notebooks, CE,* 14:508, 518. On other reactions to Anna's conversion to Catholicism, see Richard D. Birdsall's "Emerson and the Church of Rome," 273–281.

16. SPH to Mrs. P., January 1845, and SPH to MPM, March 18, 1849, MSS Berg.

17. SPH to EPP, March 21, 1859, MS Berg.

18. AS, *Letters,* 1010, 1018, 1019, 1042, 1041, 1035, 1059, TS Beinecke.

19. AS, *Letters,* 1059, 1060,1061, TS Beinecke.

20. SPH, May 8, *Pocket Diary 1859,* MS Berg; NH, May 8, March 13, *Pocket Diary 1859, CE,* 14:665, 503.

21. AS, *Letters,* 1041, TS Beinecke.

Chapter 17. The Belleslettres Portion of My Being

1. SPH to MPM, April 8, 1860, MS Berg. Una and Ada each present different perspectives on two issues. Writing to EPP on February 24, 1858, MS Berg, Una gave a positive assessment of Ada's instruction of Rose. And Ada, writing to Clay, *Letters,* 350, TS Beinecke, believed Sophia's interruption of her late-night letter-writing a sign of concern.

2. SPH to MPM, August 8, 1858, MS Berg. The Berg Collection houses Sophia's holograph Italian journals for 1858 comprised of vol. I, including the *1st Rome Journal,* February 14 through March 15 (93 pages) and the *2nd Rome Journal,* March 17 through March 31, (48 pages); vol. II, May 24 through the following eight days of travel from Rome to Florence (91 pages); vol. III, June 8 through July 3, the *1st Florence Journal* (155 pages); vol. IV, July 3 though October 8, the *2nd Florence Journal,* (153 pages); and vol. V, October 9 through 21, the return to Rome, ending abruptly when Una fell ill (106 pages). Also housed at the Berg is Sophia's *Pocket Diary for 1859.*

3. NH to EPP, August 13, 1857, *CE,* 18:90. Thomas Woodson, "Historical Commentary," *CE,* 14:903, 913. In England, Nathaniel produced seven holograph journals between August 4, 1853, and his departure for the continent, July 3, 1857. He also kept a pocket diary in England in 1856, and two others in Italy for 1858 and 1859 where he produced another seven holograph journals with accounts of travel through France and in Italy beginning in Paris on January 6, 1858, and

ending in Havre on June 22, 1859. There is a lacuna in his journal (though not in the pocket diaries) between November 2, 1858, and February 27, 1859. See "Textual Commentary," *CE,* 21:749–750, and Neal L. Smith, "Textual Commentary," *CE,* 14:938–940; NH, *The French and Italian Notebooks, CE,* 14:155.

4. NH to Ticknor, June 5, 1857, and NH to Bennoch, November 29, 1859, *CE,* 18:63–64, 204; Ticknor to SPH, March 25, 1859, MS Berg; SPH to Fields, November 28, 1859, MS BPL.

5. NH to Bridge, February 13, 1857, *CE,* 18:18; NH *The French and Italian Notebooks, CE,* 14:570. By November 25, 1859, Fields had reversed his opinion that Nathaniel should not "contribute to any periodical sound and clear at that time. Now circumstances render those reasons void," *CE,* 18:203, fn 2.

6. "A Chronology of Nathaniel Hawthorne's Life from 1853," *CE,* 17:88, 92, 93; NH, December 31, *The Pocket Diary 1858,* January 30, *The Pocket Diary 1859, CE,* 14:628, 640; NH, *The French and Italian Notebooks,* July 27, September 1, 1858, *CE,* 14:375, 396.

7. NH, June 27, *Pocket Diary 1859, CE,* 14:677; Fields quoted in "Explanatory Notes," *CE,*14:889. NH to Ticknor, October 6, 1859, *CE,* 18:191; on the arrangements with Smith and Elder, see *CE,* 18:181, fn 2.

8. NH to Fields, February 11, 1860, *CE,* 18:229.

9. JH, in *Hawthorne and His Circle,* 69, recalls that his father invested with O'Sullivan in late 1858 or 1859. See Harris, "The Public Career of John Louis O'Sullivan" (386–390) on O'Sullivan's desire to borrow from George Peabody and John Bigelow.

10. NH to Una, May 14, 16, 25 [emphasis added], 1860, *CE,* 18:279, 282–283, fn 3, 293; NH, October 28, *Pocket Diary 1859, CE,* 14:698.

11. AS, *Letters,* 532, 697, 723, TS Beinecke.

12. SPH to EPP, July 15, 31, 1859, MSS Berg; "Explanatory Notes," *CE,* 14:887.

13. SPH to EPP, July 31, 15, October 2, 1859, February 28, 1860, and MPM to SPH, [after August 2], 1859, MSS Berg.

14. Louisa Hall Tharp, *Until Victory,* 308, 282, 312–313, Mann's last words to Rebecca quoted on 313; SPH to MPM, April 4, [1859] and undated fragment, TSS Antioch 4422-A, 4422-B; MPM to SPH, [n.d. 1859], March 30, 1860, and SPH to MPM, August 24, 27, 28, October, 1859, MSS Berg.

15. SPH to EPP, July 3, 1859, MS Berg; NH, *1858 Pocket Diary, CE,* 14:642; NH *The French and Italian Notebooks, CE,* 14:524, 488, 551.

16. NH to Fields, August 6, 1859, *CE,* 18:189; Bright quoted in *CE,* 18:193, fn 1; NH, September 10, *Pocket Diary 1859, CE,* 14:691.

17. NH, *The Marble Faun, CE,* 4:190,169, 44, 171.

18. NH, *The Marble Faun, CE,* 4:344, 332 316, 323; NH to SPH, December 13, 1855, *CE,* 17:418; NH, *The Marble Faun, CE,* 4:368, compare with SPH, *Notes in England and Italy,* 416, 312.

19. NH, *The Marble Faun, CE,* 4:80, 4, 54, compare with NH, *The French and Italian Notebooks, CE,* 14:155.

20. NH, *The Marble Faun*, *CE*, 4:121, 108, 109, 287, 204, 317, 374, 174, 321, 435.

21. NH, *The Marble Faun*, *CE*, 4:30, 71, 10, 56; NH, *The French and Italian Notebooks*, *CE*, 14:229. Simpson, in his "Introduction" to *The Marble Faun*, *CE*, 4:xxxiii–xxxvii, notes that Nathaniel frequently allows Kenyon to voice ideas "closely paraphrased from journal entries."

22. NH, *The Marble Faun*, *CE*, 4:18, 92, 96, 94, 359, 128.

23. See Fredson Bowers, "Textual Introduction" to *The Marble Faun*, *CE*, 4:lxv–lxx, and "Alterations in the Manuscript," *CE*, 4:529–576, where Sophia's suggestions for changes are indicated by a dagger. Claude L. Simpson, "Introduction," *CE*, 4:xxv fn 18, finds it "tantalizing to think" that Sophia may have assigned the name of a major character. And Bowers, "Textual Introduction," *CE*, 4:lxvi, lxxix, claims that Sophia "was not content to be the simple handmaiden" but offered "corrections and suggestions," some of which "must be assumed to have Hawthorne's approval and as much authority as if he had written them in himself."

24. NH to Fields, October 10, and NH to Ticknor, December 1, 1859, *CE*, 18:196, 206; NH, October 14, 17, *Pocket Diary 1859*, *CE*, 14:696–697, 700; SPH to EPP, October 20, [1859], MS Berg.

25. Rosemary Mims Fisk, in her dissertation "The Profession of Authorship: Nathaniel Hawthorne and His Publisher, James T. Fields" (225–226), claims that pressured to supply the contractually agreed upon three volumes, Nathaniel added "novelistic description" from *The French and Italian Notebooks* to the manuscript he had completed in January of 1859. The editors of *The Letters, 1857–1864* (*CE*, 18:193 fn 2) take this speculation further by suggesting that between February and May of 1859, Nathaniel may have written in his journals with the intention of harvesting them in his novel then in progress. Simpson, "Introduction," *CE*, 4:xxxiii–xxxv, states plainly that Nathaniel drew upon his "journal savings bank," particularly in Chapters XVI–XVIII of *The Marble Faun*.

26. NH to Fields, November 17, NH to Ticknor, December 1 and 22, 1859, *CE*, 18:200, 206, 211; SPH to EPP, February 27, 1860, quoted in *CE*, 18:224–225. For all dates pertaining to the composition and publication of *The Marble Faun*, see SPH *Pocket Diary for 1859*, MS Berg; "Chronology," *CE*, 17:92–94; and NH, *Pocket Diary for 1859*, *CE*, 14:686–700.

27. SPH to Henry F. Chorley, *CE*, 18:238–240. On these pages, Sophia's letter and Nathaniel's postscript are printed in their entirety along with sections of Chorley's review in fn 1 and 4 and portions of Chorley's response to Sophia in fn 2 and 5; NH to John Lothrop Motley, April 1, 1860, *CE*, 18:256.

28. NH to Ticknor, April 6, NH to JTF, April 26, 1860, *CE*, 18:262, 271; Bright quoted in JH, *Hawthorne and His Wife*, II:239–240; Motley quoted in *CE*, 18, fn 1 257–258; SPH to EPP [frag 1860, misdated 1858 or 1859], MS Berg.

29. NH, *The French and Italian Notebooks*, *CE*, 14:539; SPH to MPM, February 29, 1860, October 28, cont'd 31, 1859, MS Berg; Una to Richard Manning, [April], quoted in *CE*, 18:219, fn 2.; Una to MPM, January 25, 1860, MS Berg; SPH to EPP, February 27, 1860, July 15, 1859, January 1860, MSS Berg.

30. Una to EPP, August 13,1859, TS Berg; NH to JTF, May 13, NH to John Lothrop Motley, April 1, NH to Bright, March 10, 1860, *CE*, 18:274, 256, 248; SPH to MPM, April 27, March 14, 1860, MSS Berg.

31. NH to Ticknor, April 6, 1860, NH to JTF, April 26, and NH to Ticknor, January 26, 1860, *CE*, 18:271, 216; SPH to Ticknor, May 16, 1860, MS Berg. For NH's complaints about Fields, see NH to Ticknor, April 6 and 19, 1860, *CE*, 18:262, 266.

32. Judith A. Roman, *Annie Adams Fields*, 18.

Chapter 18. He Needs Change Immensely

1. NH to Ticknor, January 19, 1855, *CE*, 17:304.

2. Petrulionis, *To Set This World Right*, 8–9, 12–13, 123–124.

3. David Reynolds, *John Brown, Abolitionist*, 222, 208, 212, 209, 214.

4. John Matteson, *Eden's Outcasts*, 51; David Reynolds, *John Brown, Abolitionist*, 215, 290.

5. David Reynolds, *John Brown, Abolitionist*, 215, 291, 216, 218.

6. Quoted in David Reynolds, *John Brown, Abolitionist*, 411; NH, October 11, 1858, *The French and Italian Notebooks*, *CE*, 14:463.

7. SPH to EPP, n.d., MS Morgan.

8. SPH to Mrs. P., March 26, 1848, SPH to EPP, [1858 or1859], MSS Berg.

9. On Mary Mann and Nat Peabody at the Wayside, see *CE*, 18:309 fn 1.

10. Una to EPP, February 28, 1859, MS Berg; Una to Richard Manning, July 20, July 25, 1860, *CE*, 18:309 fn 2, 310 fn 2.

11. Sanborn to Benjamin Smith Lyman, September 18, September 30, quoted in *CE*, 18:317 fn 1 and 324 fn 3; NH to JTF, September 21, 27, NH to Pierce, October 9, 1860, *CE*, 18:319, 323; 18:327.

12. SPH to NH, September 8, 9, 1860, MSS Morgan; SPH to Una, September 9, [early October 1860] 1860, MSS Berg; NH to Ticknor, October 3, 1860, *CE*, 18:325, SPH quoted in fn 2.

13. NH to Bennoch, December 17, NH to Bright, December 17, 1860, *CE*, 18:352, 355.

14. NH to Bridge, May 26, 1861, *CE*, 18:380–381; SPH to Sanborn, n.d., MS Berg; Una to EPP, June 5, 1861, MS Berg; SPH to NH, September 9–10, 13, 1860, MSS Morgan.

15. NH to Ticknor, May 26, 1861, NH to Bennoch, [July, 1861], *CE*, 18:382, 388; Bronson Alcott Journal, February 17, 1861, quoted in fn 1, *CE*, 18:363–364; Una to EPP, April 4, 1861, MS DSHA; SPH to Ticknor, May 15, 1861, MS Berg.

16. SPH to NH, July 25, 1861, quoted in JH, *Hawthorne and His Wife*, II:283, and in *CE*, 18:394 fn 1; SPH to NH, August 13 [1861], August 2, 1861, [1861] MSS Morgan; RH to Papa, July 31, 1861, MS Berg; SPH to AAF, August 4, 1861, MS BPL.

17. Requests for specific sums of money were made in NH to Ticknor, September 27, October 3, 29, December 8, 1860, *CE*, 18:323, 325, 333, 343; January 30, 1861,

CE, 18:361; NH to JTF, July 14 and 16, October 6, 1861, *CE*, 18:391, 393, 408. On bills submitted for payment, see NH to Ticknor, November 17, 1860, February 16, 1861, *CE*, 18:338, 363; on expenses for renovation, NH to Ticknor, December 28, 1860, *CE*, 18:358; on Bridge's repayment of loan, NH to Ticknor, May 26, October 7, 1861, *CE*, 18:382, 410; on the gift to Burchmore, NH to Ticknor, November 23, 1860, *CE*, 18:340; on O'Sullivan, NH to Pierce, December 3, 1861, *CE*, 18:425 and fn 1.

18. NH to Ticknor, May 16, 1861, *CE*, 18:379. "Some of the Haunts of Burns" appeared in the *Atlantic* in October of 1860, "Near Oxford" the following October, and "A Pilgrimage to Old Boston" in January of 1862. NH to Fields, October 6, November 6, 1861, *CE*, 18:408, 418; NH to Bright, November 14, 1861, *CE*, 18:421; NH to Bridge, February 13, 1862, *CE*, 18:427.

19. NH to Bridge, February 13, 1862, *CE*, 18:427; SPH to JTF, February 20, [1862], and P.S. in NH's hand, *CE*, 18:431. SPH to NH, n.d. [pre-March 13, 1862], March 15, 1862, MSS Morgan; for information about Una's preparation of her father's letters, see *CE*, 18:436, fn 1.

20. SPH to NH, March 15, 1862, and Una to NH [March 15, 1862], MSS Morgan; Una to Ebie, March 16, 1862, MS DSHA; RH to JTF, March 17, 1862, BPL; SPH to JTF, February 20, [1862], *CE*, 18:431.

21. SPH to AAF, April 1862, BPL; SPH, May 6 through 9, *1862 Diary*, MS Morgan. This diary was edited by Thomas Woodson and published under the title "With Hawthorne in Wartime Concord: Sophia Hawthorne's 1862 Diary" in *Studies in the American Renaissance* (1988).

22. JTF to NH, May 21, 1862, quoted in fn 4, *CE*, 18:458; NH to JTF, May 7, 23, 1862, *CE*, 18:455, 461; see also fn 3, *CE*, 18:439.

23. NH, "Chiefly about War-Matters, by a Peaceable Man," *CE*, 23:421, 431, 441–442, 415, 417, 427; Thomas Woodson, Claude Simpson, and Neal L. Smith, "Historical and Textual Commentary," *CE*, 23:683–684. Larry J. Reynolds, in *Devils and Rebels*, "posits that a Christian pacifism, not unlike that of the Quakers, serves as the foundation of [Hawthorne's] politics, which, though characterized as thoughtless and benighted, actually possess a depth and subtlety comparable to those of his literary works themselves" (xvi). Although Reynolds does not present a detailed analysis of "War-Matters," he notes that the "detached and ironic speculations" found in it "can seem hostile and treasonous" (24) to a nation at war. I believe that Nathaniel's inconsistencies and inappropriate remarks regarding the war did not reflect pacifism but a mental disintegration which coincided with the war and which Sophia observed, to her mounting alarm.

24. Sanborn quoted in Larry J. Reynolds (4 and 7), who states that the "most hostile criticism received during [Nathaniel's] lifetime came in response to his public comments on the Civil War in 'Chiefly about War-Matters.'" SPH to EPP, [1861], MS Berg; based on the content of this letter, it was more likely to have been written in 1862. SPH, August 10, *1862 Diary*, MS Morgan.

25. Ronda, *The Letters of EPP*, 310. Ethan Allen Hitchcock, *Christ the Spirit: being an Attempt to state the Primitive View of Christianity.*

26. About Hitchcock in Concord during August of 1862, see Ronda, *The Letters of EPP*, 310. About EPP's reaction to Hitchcock, see Ronda, *Elizabeth Palmer Peabody*, 289–290: "Anything that suggested nature as a kind of vast symbol system made Elizabeth just weak at the knees," Ronda writes. SPH, August 3, *1862 Diary*, SPH to NH, August 13, 1862, and SPH to "my dearest," August 14, 1862, MSS Morgan.

27. SPH to NH, August 13, 19, 1862, MSS Morgan.

28. SPH, September 4, *1862 Diary* and SPH to NH, September 25, 1862, MSS MA 3400; NH to JTF, December 6, *CE*, 18:508.

29. SPH to Una, December 11, 1862, MS Berg; SPH to AAF, December 14, 1862, MS BPL; NH to Bennoch, October 12, 1862, *CE*, 18:501.

30. JTF to NH, July 15, 1863, quoted in fn 1, *CE*, 18:584; AAF, July 26, 1863 quoted in M. A. De Wolfe Howe, *Memories of a Hostess*, 13 and 14.

31. SPH to AAF, [early July 1863], BPL; NH to Pierce, July 24, 1863, and NH to JTF, May 3, July 18, 1863, *CE*, 18:595, 567, 586–587; FP to Sarah Morris Fish Webster, March 18, 1868, quoted in fn 2, *CE*, 18:610.

32. NH to EPP, July 20, 1863, *CE*, 18:589–591; JTF to NH, n.d. [post September 16, 1863] quoted in fn 1, *CE*, 18:599; Una to Ebe, November 22, 1863, MS DSHA; SPH to EEP, January 31, [1864], MS Berg.

33. SPH to AAF, November 29, [1863], MS BPL, brackets in original.

Chapter 19. Have I Done My Duty?

1. SPH to AAF, August 2, 1863, December 8, 1861, MSS BPL; SPH to MPM, February 29, 1860, MS Berg; AS, *Letters*, 173, 685, TS Beinecke.

2. JTF to NH, ca. July 12, 1862, quoted in fn 1, *CE*, 18:467. Later in this letter, Fields refers to Nathaniel as "Childe Hawthorne," furthering the supposition that this poem may have been part of conversations between the Hawthornes and the Fieldses. Lord George Gordon Byron, *Childe Harold's Pilgrimage*, 10.

3. SPH to AAF, [January], 1864, BPL; SPH to EPP, [n.d. 1861], MS Berg.

4. SPH to AAF, October 11, 1863, January 25, 1864, August 2, 1863, MSS BPL.

5. SPH to AAF, February 28, [1864], and November 29, [1863], MS BPL.

6. SPH to Una, December 11, 1862, MSS Berg; SPH to AAF, February 20, 1863, MS BPL; Bronson Alcott quoted in Matteson, *Eden's Outcasts*, 291.

7. SPH, June 28, *1862 Diary*, MS Morgan; Una to EMH, December 9, 1861, MS DSHA; Una to AAF, April 9, 1862 [emphasis added], March 5, 1863, February 20, 1863, December 17, 1862, June 14, 1863, MSS BPL; SPH to Una, 5 [September, 1863], MS Berg.

8. RH to Mary Ellen Bull, n.d., MS Morgan; SPH to AAF, c. June, 1864, MSS BPL; RH to NH, ca. May 20, 1861, MS DSHA; Valenti, *To Myself a Stranger*, 23.

9. SPH to AAF, December 14, 1862, and February 20, 1863, MSS BPL; NH to JTF, December 6, 1862, October 18, 1863, *CE*, 18:508, 603; RH to NH, April 2, 1862, MS Morgan; RH to JH, [1863 or '64?], MS Berg; NH to RH, August 5, 1861, *CE*, 18:400.

10. SPH to AAF, December 14, 1862, MS BPL; SPH to Una, September 25, 1862, MS Berg, partially rpt in *CE*, 18:407 where the recipient is misidentified as Nathaniel. JH to SPH, August 10, 21–23, 25, MSS Berg.

11. SPH to JH, August 18, 22, 1862, MSS Berg; SPH to Sanborn quoted in fn 8, *CE*, 18:481.

12. For information about Staples, see Thomas Woodson's "Index of Names," in "With Hawthorne in Wartime Concord," 345; SPH to NH, [August] 29, 1862, MS Morgan. W. J. Rorabaugh presents a thorough investigation of conscription practices in "Who Fought for the North in the Civil War? Concord, Massachusetts, Enlistments," 695–701.

13. Joan Goodwin, *The Remarkable Mrs. Ripley*, 512; Forbes quoted in Robert D. Richardson, *Emerson: The Mind on Fire*, 550.

14. Petrulionis, *To Set This World Right*, 47–50; SPH, September 3 1862 *Diary*, MS Morgan; Woodson, "Index of Names" in "With Hawthorne in Wartime Concord: Sophia Hawthorne's *1862 Diary*," 351, 350; RH to JH, [1863 or 1864], MS Berg.

15. SPH to NH, August 6, 1862, MS Morgan; George Ripley quoted in Goodwin, *The Remarkable Mrs. Ripley*, 506; Townsend Scudder, *Concord: American Town*, 242, 256, Prescott quoted on 260. In *The American Notebooks, CE*, 8:316, Nathaniel remarks about the then eleven-year old George's habit of dropping by The Old Manse: he "has not yet grown earthly enough, I suppose, to be debarred from occasional visits to Paradise."

16. See SPH, *1862 Diary*, MS Morgan passim for Pheobe's numerous visits to the Wayside to give Una music lessons. Sarah Ripley quoted in Goodwin, *The Remarkable Mrs. Ripley*, 522, 508, 516, 505.

17. Russell Duncan, "Robert Gould Shaw: A Biographical Essay" in *Blue-Eyed Child of Fortune: The Civil War Letters of Colonel Robert Gould Shaw*, 2; Sarah Shaw to SPH, September 10, 1849, MS Berg.

18. Robert Gould Shaw quoted in Joan Waugh, "The Shaw Family and the Fifty-Fourth Massachusetts Regiment," 64.

19. Robert Gould Shaw quoted in Duncan, "Robert Gould Shaw: A Biographical Essay" in *Blue-Eyed Child of Fortune: The Civil War Letters of Colonel Robert Gould Shaw*, 24; Sarah Shaw quoted on 37.

20. SPH, July 21, *1862 Diary*, MS Morgan; SPH to NH, August 8, 1862, and June [1862], MS Morgan; Woodson, "Index of Names" in "With Hawthorne in Wartime Concord: Sophia Hawthorne's *1862 Diary*," 351. Haven quoted in Andrew Elmer Ford, *The Story of the Fifteenth Regiment Massachusetts Volunteer Infantry in the Civil War 1861–1864*, 229–231.

21. Drew Gilpin Faust, *This Republic of Suffering*, 121–122; for information about Lowell's nephews, see *CE*, 18:423 fn 5; Joan Waugh, *Unsentimental Reformer: The Life of Josephine Shaw Lowell*, especially Chapter 3, pages 62 ff.

22. JH, *Hawthorne and His Wife*, II:267; SPH to AAF, [July 1862], MS BPL.

23. NH to Lowell, February 22, 1863, *CE*, 18:540–542, and fn 1 for Lowell's response on February 26, 1863; NH to Ephraim Whitman Gurney, March 13, 1863,

CE, 18:548; NH to JTF, July 14, and NH to FP, July 24, 1863, *CE*, 18:583, 595 and fn 1, 584; SPH to AAF, [July 24, 1863], MS BPL.

24. SPH to EPP, [1863], MS Berg; SPH to AAF, July 5, 1862, MS BPL; SPH to EPP, [1861], MS Berg. For the Hawthornes' problems with the Alcotts, see Claudia Johnson's "Discord in Concord" in *Hawthorne and Women*, 104–120.

25. SPH to Una, September 17, 1864, MS Berg.

26. SPH to Hitchcock, November [13? or 18?], August 9, 1863, November 30, and December 7, 1862, MSS Barrett; SPH to NH, August 14, 1862, MS Morgan.

27. SPH to AAF, January 2, 25, 1864, MSS BPL; NH to JTF, February 25, 1864, *CE*, 18:640–641; SPH to Bridge, April 5, 1864, quoted in *CE*, 18:641.

28. SPH to Ticknor, March 10, 14, 17, 21, 1864, MSS Berg; Una to EMH, March 20, 1864, MS DSHA; SPH to NH, March 24, [1864], TS fragment DSHA.

29. SPH to AAF, March 31, [1864], MS BPL; *AAF Diary* March 28, 1864, rpt. in fn 1, 18:650; RHL to Papa, April 4, 1864, MS Morgan; NH to JTF, April 9, 1864, *CE*, 18:651, fn 1 18:652.

30. For an account of Nathaniel after Ticknor's death see *CE*, fn 2 18:653–654; *AAF Diary* rpt. in fn 3 *CE*, 18:653.

31. SPH to AAF, [ca. April 18, 1864], MS BPL.

32. MPM to Horace Mann Jr., April 24, 1864, fn 3 *CE*, 18:653; SPH to AAF, April 13 [1864], MS BPL.

33. SPH to FP, April 20 and May 6, 1864, TS, Beinecke; SPH to MPM [ca. April 18, 1864], MS Berg; SPH to AAF, [April 18, 1864], [April 22, 1864], MSS BPL.

34. SPH to JTF [May 7, 1864], MS BPL; Una to JTF, May 8 and ca. May 8, 1864, MSS BPL. AAF quotes Holmes in her May 11, 1864 Diary which is found in M. A. De Wolfe Howe, *Memories of a Hostess*, 27.

35. FP quoted in *CE*, fn 2, 18:656. See Roy Franklin Nichols, *Franklin Pierce*, 525, for a brief account of Nathaniel's death. MPM to Horace Mann Jr., May 22, 1864, quoted in *CE*, 18:563; Ronda, *EEP*, 283.

Chapter 20. Coining His Precious Brain into Gold

1. Miller, *Salem Is My Dwelling Place*, 518–519; Una to AAF [May 19, 1864], SPH and Una to JTF [May 21, 1864], SPH to AAF, May 20, 1864, MSS BPL.

2. JH, *Hawthorne and His Wife*, 347–348; SPH to Anne O'Gara, September 4, 1864, MS. Bancroft; Claude Simpson and Edward H. Davidson, "Historical Commentary," *CE*, 13:582, fn 46.

3. Ronda, *Elizabeth Palmer Peabody*, 283 concludes that Sophia's detailed description of Nathaniel's funeral in her letter to Elizabeth on May 25 indicates that Elizabeth did not attend the funeral. SPH to EPP, May 25, 1864, MS Berg.

4. SPH to AAF [May 30, 1864], MS BPL.

5. SPH to JTF, June 6, [1864], and June 9, 1864, MSS BPL.

6. Simpson and Davidson, "Historical Commentary," *CE*, 13:573–574, 580; SPH to JTF, June 9, 1864, MS Berg; SPH to Una, June 24, 1864, MS Berg; Oliver Wendell Holmes, "Hawthorne," 98–101.

7. SPH to JTF, June 11, 1864, and SPH to AAF, [ca. July 1864], MSS BPL.

8. SPH to AAF, August 2, 1864, MS BPL; Claude Simpson, "Historical Commentary," *CE*, 8:682–683; SPH to EMH, October 30, 1864, March 4, 1865, and EMH to SPH, November 24, [1864] MSS Berg.

9. SPH to FP, September 30, 1864, TS Beinecke; SPH to Una, August 10, 1865, MS Berg.

10. Hillard to SPH, March 7, 1865, MS Berg; Hillard to SPH, February 9, 1865, MS Morgan.

11. SPH to FP, September 30, 1864, TS Beinecke; SPH to Una, October 3, MS Berg; Maurice Bassan, *Hawthorne's Son*, 3.

12. RH to JH, December 22, 1864, January 18, 1865, MSS Berg; SPH to JH, January 19, 1865, MS St. Lawrence University; SPH to EPP, November 14, 1863, MS Berg; SPH to Una, October 7, September 12, 1864, MSS Berg; Bassan, *Hawthorne's Son*, 31; SPH to Hillard, September 7, 1864, MS Berg.

13. SPH to Una, October 7, September 17, 1864, MSS Berg; SPH to FP, October 3, 17, 27, November 22, December 27, 1864, TS Beinecke; SPH to JTF, November 9, December 5, 1864, MSS Berg The second installment of *Dolliver* appeared in *The Atlantic Monthly* in January of 1865. Simpson and Davidson in "Historical Commentary" remark that Sophia's transcription of *The Dolliver Romance*, which was never "offered for publication during Sophia's life-time . . . was far more faithful to Hawthorne's manuscript than was the text published in 1876" (*CE*, 13:582–583).

14. EMH quoted in JH, *Hawthorne and His Wife*, I:124; Fredson Bowers, "Introduction" to *Fanshawe* 3:312–313; SPH to JTF, October 3, 1864, MS BPL.

15. SPH to JTF, December 5, 1864, MS Berg.

16. SPH to MPM, February 26, March 12 and 31, June 25, 1865, and n.d., MSS Barrett.

17. After Sophia had copied a portion of Nathaniel's earliest notebook, she informed Fields that upon Nathaniel's return from a three-month trip in 1838, she and her future husband "first met personally, though he had before known of me through E. and my Cuban letters and others which E. unknown to me had showed him." It was then the fire "kindled" between them. SPH to JTF, November 6, 1865, MS BPL.

18. For an analysis of the mid-nineteenth-century cultural understanding of copying and its application to Sophia's art and editing, see Patricia Dunlavy Valenti's "Sophia Peabody Hawthorne and 'The—What?'" 48–72. For discussion of Sophia and Nathaniel's collaborative American notebooks, see Valenti's "Introduction" to "Sophia Peabody Hawthorne's American Notebooks," 115–127, and *Sophia Peabody Hawthorne: A Life, Volume I*, chapter 17, "The Power of Counter-Forces," 182–194.

19. According to Simpson's "Historical Commentary" *CE*, 8:686–687, Sophia took many "liberties" with the text, although she did not destroy the "considerable fraction of her journalizing," an understated description of the extant 30,000 words Sophia contributed to the spouses' collaborative journal. SPH to JTF, April 14, October 4 and 13, 1865, MSS BPL, emphasis added; SPH to AAF, April 18, 1865, MS BPL. In "This Is His—This Is My Mystery," Marta Werner and Nicholas

Lawrence state that Sophia's work on *The American Notebooks* exhibits a "play of invisibility and visibility" with "Sophia's shifting between the desire to efface herself in order to serve her husband's spirit and the conflicting desire to inscribe herself in a text she had coauthored" (15). Werner and Lawrence also offer an interesting hypothesis by situating the "psychology of Sophia's copying" within the spiritualist movement: "the cultural phenomena of mesmerism and automatic writing—both . . . involve logical, if extreme, extensions of the collaborative ethos." Through copying, Sophia might "identify absolutely with the absent beloved" (11).

20. Nathaniel's account of Cilley, *CE*, 8:61; Simpson, "Explanatory Notes," *CE*, 8:579, 580 and "Historical Commentary," *CE*, 8:683–684; Valenti, *Sophia Peabody Hawthorne, A Life*, I:115; SPH to JTF, October 8, 14, 20, 1865, MSS BPL.

21. SPH to JTF, [November 1865], MS BPL.

22. JH to SPH, N[ovember], 8 [1864], MS Berg; SPH to JTF, October 20, 1865, MS BPL; SPH to FP, February 15, 20, 1865, TS Beinecke; SPH to AAF, March 10, 1865, MS BPL.

23. SPH to FP, March 12, 27, 28, 31, April 28, 1865, TSS Beinecke.

24. SPH to FP, March 31, May 20, 1865, TS Beinecke; JH to SPH, November 28, [1865], MS Berg.

25. SPH to JTF, December 3, 5, 1865, MSS BPL. See also Simpson, "Historical Commentary," *CE*, 8:683 regarding Sophia's pay per installment; SPH to FP, December 14, 1865, TS Beinecke; E. W. Gurney to SPH, February 9, 1866, MS Berg.

26. SPH to EEP, June 15, 1866, MS Berg; SPH to AAF, July 8, 1866, MS BPL; SPH, September *1866 Diary*, MS DSHA; SPH to Una, September 13, 1866, MS Berg; Hillard to SPH, September 20, 1866, MS Berg.

27. SPH to JTF, March 8, 19, February 18, July 24, 27, 1866, MSS BPL; JTF to SPH, July 22, 1866, MS Berg.

28. SPH to JTF, August 19, 1866, MS BPL. In this letter, Sophia incorrectly gives the date of Nathaniel's account of the children as 1848; it occurred during the summer and fall of 1849, while he was writing *The Scarlet Letter*. JTF to SPH, August 23, September 17, 1866, MSS Berg; SPH to JTF, September 5, 19, October 14, 1866, MSS Berg. "Twenty Days with Julian and Little Bunny" was first printed privately in 1904, and nearly a century later, in 2003, Paul Auster published *Twenty Days with Julian and Little Bunny* making Nathaniel's account widely available.

29. SPH to JTF, September 19, 1866, MS BPL; JTF to SPH September 17, December 9, 1866, MSS BPL.

Chapter 21. My Dear Friend

1. Simpson, "Historical Commentary," *CE*, 8:685–690. Sophia's edition of *Passages* provided evidence that Nathaniel's earliest American notebook, presumed lost for many years, had existed. For a full discussion of its discovery in the 1970s, see Hyatt Howe Waggoner's "A Hawthorne Discovery: The Lost Notebook, 1835-1841," among his two other publications on this subject.

2. Reviews quoted in Simpson, "Historical Commentary," *CE*, 8:691, 692; SPH to AAF, July 4, 1866, MS BPL.

3. Randall Stewart, "Editing *The American Notebooks*," 278; Simpson, "Historical Commentary," *CE*, 8:682. Claire M. Badaracco in "Pitfalls and Rewards of the Solo Editor" claims that the "Widow Hawthorne, produced the 1868 edition out of financial necessity rather than excessive love" and that it "was not only typical of the day, it might have been produced by any number of other Victorian editors" (96, 99). SPH to JTF, September 4, 1866, October 9, 1867, MSS BPL; SPH to JTF, [1866], MS Berg.

4. SPH to AAF, January 4, 1866, March 16, 1865, MSS BPL.

5. SPH to AAF, January 4, April 25, May 28, October 1, November 24, 1866, MSS BPL. AAF's biographer Judith Roman concurs with Sophia's criticism of "Asphodel" (35).

6. SPH to JTF, June 16, 1867, SPH to AAF, [August 1867], MSS BPL.

7. SPH to JTF, August 4, 1867, MS BPL; EMH to Rebecca Manning, April 9, [1867, misdated as 1868], De Rocher, ed. *EMH, A Life in Letters*, 113; SPH to Hitchcock, October 20, 1867, MS Barrett; SPH to RH, March 8, 24, 1867, MS DSHA; SPH to EPP, September 28, October 13, 1867, MSS Berg. Bassan, *Hawthorne's Son*, 43–44.

8. SPH Diary October 22, 1866, MS DSHA; SPH to Augustine, October 27, 1866, MS Barrett; SPH to Una, July 27, October 12, 18, 1865, Feb 25, 1866, MSS Berg. For Julian's awestruck description of Dio Lewis's physique, see JH, *Memoirs of Julian Hawthorne*, 138–141.

9. SPH to Una, February 1, 6, 1866, MSS Berg; RH to SPH, November 4, 1866, MS Berg; SPH to RH, November 13, 1866, MS Morgan; SPH to RH, January 14, 1867, MS Berg; SPH to "My dear little Pet," May 12, 1867, MS Barrett.

10. RH to EMH, February 1, 1868, MS DSHA; RH to Una, July 15, January 13, 1866, MSS Berg.

11. Mary Betts to RH, August 2, 1867, MS DSHA; RH to Una, July 21, 1867, MS Berg; RH to James Freeman Clarke, June 16, 1867, MS MHS; SPH to RH, May 20, 1868, MS Morgan.

12. SPH to Una May 3, March 15 and 29, 1866, September 20, 21, 22, 1866, MSS Berg.

13. SPH to AAF, June 13, 1866, MS BPL; SPH to EPP, May 13, June 15, 1866, and January 20, 1867, MSS Berg.

14. Una to EMH, December 9, 1861, and February 19, 1865, MS DSHA; for information on Higginson, see Tilden G. Edelstein, *Strange Enthusiasm*, 286–287, 298–299; SPH to Una, June 26, 1865, MS Berg; SPH to MPM, November 26, 1865, MS Barrett.

15. Letter from Storrow Higginson, in "Extracts from Teachers' Letters," n.p.

16. SPH to EPP, February 11, 1867, MS Berg; SPH to RH, March 3, May 10, 16, and n.d. 1867, MSS DSHA; SPH to RH, April 19, May 3, 13, 1867, MSS Morgan; SPH to "My dear little Pet," May 12, 1867, Barrett; EMH to Robert Manning, [May 1867], in De Rocher, *Elizabeth Manning Hawthorne*, 107; SPH to T. W. Higginson, May 19, 1867, MS Huntington.

17. SPH to EPP, May 29, 1867, April 19, 1868, MSS Berg; EMH to Rebecca Manning, February 23, [1868], April 26, [1868], and EMH to Maria Manning, February 20, 1868, in De Rocher, *Elizabeth Manning Hawthorne*, 11, 114, 110–111.

18. SPH to AAF, May 10, 1868, MS BPL; EMH to Rebecca Manning, February 23, [1868], April 26, [1868], March 3, 1865, in De Rocher, *Elizabeth Manning Hawthorne*, 111–112, 114, 94–95; EMH to Una, May 24 and March 3, 1865, May 11, March 4, 1869, De Rocher, *Elizabeth Manning Hawthorne*, 102–103, 97, 94.

19. SPH to Nat Peabody, May 23, 1865, TS owned by Bradford Johnson; SPH to Hitchcock, March 16, 1867, February 14, 1866, September 30, [1867], June 2, 1867, August 4, 1867, MSS Barrett; Hitchcock, *Swedenborg, A Hermetic Philosopher*, 106.

20. Hitchcock, *The Red Book of Appin; a Story of the Middle Ages with other Hermetical Stories and Allegorical Tales*; SPH to RH, January 26, 1867, MS Morgan; SPH to Eliza Clapp, September 26, 1867, MS Morgan; SPH to MPM, March 20, 1866, MS Berg; SPH to EPP, January 20, 1867, MS Berg.

21. SPH to Una, September 10, June 8, 1865, MSS Berg; SPH to Hitchcock, March 16, 1867, and SPH to MPM, May 8, 1865, MSS Barrett; SPH to RH [winter '67], [August 24, 1866], MSS Morgan; SPH to Una, August 24, 1866, MS Berg. Biographical information and archival material pertaining to Mary Hemenway can be found at the Peabody Essex Museum: http://www.pem.org/library/finding_aids/MH122_HemenwayFamily.pdf.

22. Robert E. Kantor, "Gail Hamilton (Mary Abigail Dodge) (1833–1896)," 199–205; SPH, March 28, *1866 Diary*, MS DSHA; SPH to Una, March 29, 1866, and SPH to EPP, May 13, 1866, MSS Berg.

23. O'Sullivan to William Prichard, February 14, 1866, MS Berg.

24. SPH to Una, October 7, 1866, MS Berg; SPH to EPP, October 13, 1867, MS Berg; SPH to JTF, October 14, 1866, January 2, March 28, May 31, June 10, 1867, MSS BPL; SPH to RH, June 10, 1867, MS Morgan.

25. SPH to EPP, March 3, 1867, MS Berg; SPH to EPP, May 17, 1867, MS Morgan; SPH to JTF, October 8, 1867, MS BPL; SPH to AAF, [August 1867], MS BPL.

26. SPH to Eliza Clapp, September 26, 1867, MS Morgan; Bassan, *Hawthorne's Son*, 44.

27. SPH to JTF, October 27, November 3, 18, 1867, MSS BPL.

28. SPH to EPP, April 19, 1868, MS Berg; JH to Hitchcock, February 7, 1868, MS Barrett; EMH to Rebecca Manning, April 26, 1868, De Rocher, *Elizabeth Manning Hawthorne*, 115; Una to MPM, February 2, 26, 1868, MSS DSHA; SPH to RH, April 4, 1868, MS Morgan. About Mary's relocation to Cambridge, see SPH to Una, February 1, 6, and March 19, 1866, MSS Berg; SPH to RH, April 23, 1868, MS Morgan; SPH to Frederick Goddard Tuckerman, April 5, 1868, MS Bancroft.

29. SPH to JTF, May 2, 20, 24, 1868, MSS BPL; JTF to SPH, May 22, 29, 1868, MSS Morgan; Fiske, "The Profession of Authorship," 327.

30. JTF to SPH, May 22, 1868, MS Morgan; JTF to SPH, May 20, 29, 1868, MSS BPL; SPH to JTF, May 24, June 2, 7, 12, 1868, MSS BPL.

31. Fisk, "The Profession of Authorship," 319, 321–322, and Appendix B, "A Chronology of Hawthorne's Royalties from Ticknor & Fields, 1860–1866, Drawn from the Cost Books of Ticknor and Fields Volumes 3 and 4 in the Houghton Library." Fisk's dissertation is an invaluable resource because Tryon and Charvat's *The Cost Books of Ticknor and Fields and Their Predecessors: 1832–1858* does not include the period in question.

32. JTF to SPH, July 14, 1868, MS Berg; SPH to JTF, July 15, 16, 1868, MSS BPL.

33. SPH to JTF, July 1, 14, 15, 16, 28, August 2, 1868, MSS BPL; JTF to SPH, July 27, August 6, 1868, MSS Berg. EPP to Moncure Conway, [1868], in Ronda, *Letters of Elizabeth Palmer Peabody*, 344, provides evidence of Sophia's contention about Nathaniel's payment from Smith and Elder for *Our Old Home*. EPP writes Conway that Sophia "did have in her possession the letter that enclosed £250 for *that* in the handwriting of either Ticknor or Fields."

34. Hillard to SPH, August 10, 1868, MS Morgan; EPP to JTF, October 1868, Stewart, "Mrs. Hawthorne's Quarrel," 257; Gail Hamilton to SPH, August 11, 1868, MS Morgan. According to Coultrap-McQuin, in *Doing Literary Business*, 134, Hamilton "exposed the Gentleman Publisher's market for what it really was: a relationship based on power, even when conducted as friendship."

35. SPH to AAF, October 16, 1867, MS BPL.

Chapter 22. Starve Her into Compliance

1. AAF quoted in Warren S. Tyron, *Parnassus Corner*, 344–345; SPH to JTF, March 6, 1851, July 29, 1864, MSS BPL; SPH to JTF, November 28, 1859, MS BPL; and in *CE*, 18:202, followed by NH to JTF, November 28, 1859, *CE*, 18:203; SPH to EPP, January 29, 1869, MS Berg.

2. SPH to JTF, August 2, 1868, MS BPL. Randall Stewart, "Mrs. Hawthorne's Financial Difficulties," 52, 47, and Stewart, "Mrs. Hawthorne's Quarrel with James T. Fields," 255. Though Stewart is generally sympathetic to Sophia and her demands, he becomes "impatient with her management of affairs" and "pampered" children ("Financial Difficulties," 51). Gail Hamilton to SPH, September 2, 1868, MS Berg; Hamilton on Fields quoted on 121 of Susan Coultrap-McQuin, *Doing Literary Business*, who also makes the point that Hamilton was an early standard bearer of "equal pay for equal work," 129.

3. Ronda, *Elizabeth Palmer Peabody*, 296–300; EPP to Moncure Conway, fall [1868], *Letters*, 344–345.

4. SPH to Eliza Clapp, August 16, 1868, and SPH to EPP, autumn [1868], MS Morgan; SPH to EPP, October 13, 1867, June 13, 1868, MSS Berg; Una to TWH, June 15, [n.y.], MS BPL; SPH to Mary Vandervoort, September 6, 1868, MS Berg; Sarah Shaw to SPH, March 1 [1867, more probably 1868], MS Berg.

5. SPH to Mary Hemenway September 6, 29, 1868, MSS Berg; SPH to FP, September 15, 1868, TS Yale.

6. SPH to Hitchcock, June 7, 1868, MS Barrett; SPH to Mary [Vandervoort], September 6, 1868, MS Berg.

7. SPH to EPP, n.d. [fall 1868], MS Berg; EMH to Richard Manning, March 6, 1870, De Rocher, *Elizabeth Manning Hawthorne*, 128–131.

8. EPP to JTF, .n.d, October, 1868, in Stewart, "Mrs. Hawthorne's Quarrel with Fields," 256–259.

9. SPH to EPP, 19 n.m. [predeparture for Germany 1868], MS Berg; SPH to EPP, Friday, October 26, 1868, aboard the *Deutchland*, MS Morgan. JH, *October 14, 1868–November 1869 Diary*, 17, MS Berg, hereafter cited simply as JH, *Dresden Diary*, MS Berg. According to that diary, the family departed Boston on October 14 and spent two days in New York before sailing. But Una's October 22 entry in her 1869 *Dresden Diary*, MS Berg, reads, "It is a year today since we sailed from New York."

10. Una's entry for November 5 in her *1869 Dresden Diary*, MS Berg, gives the date of the Hawthornes' arrival in Dresden the year before; SPH to EPP, [first letter from Dresden November 1868], fragment n.d.[November or December 1868], January 27, 1869, MSS Morgan.

11. EPP to JTF, January 4, 1869, Stewart, "Mrs. Hawthorne's Quarrel with James T. Fields," 262; SPH to EPP, January 27, 1869, MS Morgan; SPH to EPP, n.d., Dresden, MS Morgan. As Fisk in "The Profession of Authorship," 329–330, makes clear, "argument that a fixed rate protected both author and publisher in a time of fluctuating prices was specious because prices were only fluctuating one way, upward, and Fields knew it. In this instance, he had sacrificed his guiding principle of generosity as a friend and patron of authors to the cold principles of the businessman."

12. Woodson, "Historical Commentary," *CE*, 21:736; SPH, June 13, July 20, 22 [1869, misdated as 1868], Diary, MS Berg; SPH to EPP, February 16, July 18, December 3, 1869, MS Morgan.

13. Woodson, "Historical Commentary," *CE*, 21:733; Woodson, "Historical Commentary," *CE*, 14:923, 925, 927; SPH, June passim, August 18, October 7–17, *Dresden Diary [1869, misdated 1868]*, MS Berg; SPH to EPP, December 3, 1869, MS Morgan.

14. SPH, *Notes in England and Italy*, 386, 549.

15. SPH to EPP, February 16, October 17, December 3, 1869, MSS Morgan.

16. SPH, May 2, June 26, 27, February 14, *[1869] Dresden Journal*, MS Berg.

17. SPH to EPP, February 16, 1868, MS Morgan; SPH January 20, December 29, *[1869] Dresden Journal*, MS Berg.

18. EPP quoted in Ronda, *Elizabeth Palmer Peabody*, 296; SPH, January 19, *1869 Journal*, MS Berg; EMH to Richard Manning, March 6, 1870, in De Rocher, *Elizabeth Manning Hawthorne*, 129; SPH to EPP, n.d., January 27, 1869, MSS Morgan; JH, *Dresden Diary*, 110, 111; SPH December 29, *[1869] Dresden Diary*, MS Berg.

19. SPH to EPP, January 27, 1869, MS Morgan; JH, *Dresden Journal*, 116, 117, 146, 165–167, MS Berg.

20. JH, May 19, April 15, 27, June 22, *Dresden Journal*, MS Berg; Bassan, *Hawthorne's Son*, 50–51.

21. JH, June 22, July 25, November 2, 9, *Dresden Journal*, MS Berg; SPH, July 6, 13, *1869 Dresden Journal*, MS Berg; SPH to EPP, October 17, 1869, MS Morgan.

22. Una to EMH, October 13, 1869, MS DSHA; SPH to EPP, n.d. frag, October 17, MS Morgan; EMH to Una, March 4, 1869, MS Bancroft.

23. SPH to Henry Bright, September 12, 1859, MS Beinecke; Mary Betts to RH, May 21, 1868, MS DSHA.

24. Valenti, *To Myself A Stranger*, 40–42; RH to Miss Clapp, November 28, 1869, MS DSHA; SPH, November 25, *1869 Dresden Diary*, MS Berg; RH, January 10, April *1870 Diary*, MS DSHA.

25. Una to Aunt Mary, October 13, 1869, MS DSHA; Una to TWH, April 19, 1869, MS BPL. On the Ripleys' visit to Dresden, see RH to Miss Clapp, March 23, 1869, MS Morgan; Una, October passim, *1869 Dresden Diary* and SPH, June and July passim, *1869 Dresden Journal*, MSS Berg.

26. Una to TWH, January 28, 1870, MS BPL; SPH to EPP, n.d. [1869], January 27, 1869, MS Morgan.

27. SPH to EPP, February 16, 1870, MS Morgan; RH, March 12, May 11, June 18, *1870 Diary*, MS DSHA; SPH to RH, June 11, 5, 1870, MS DSHA.

28. Woodson, "Historical Commentary," *CE*, 21:721; NH, *Passages from The English Note-Books By Nathaniel Hawthorne*. SPH to RH, May 22, 1870, MS Morgan; SPH to RH, June 11, 5, May 25, 1870, MSS DSHA.

Chapter 23. Stillness and Silence

1. SPH, February 23, *1869 Dresden Journal*, MS Berg.

2. SPH to RH, May 30, June 3, 11, 1870, and n.d., [1870] MS DSHA; SPH to EPP, June 28, 1870, MS Morgan.

3. RH to Mattie, August 10, 1870, MS Berg.

4. SPH to EPP, September 2, and SPH to Hillard, August 24, [1870], MSS Morgan.

5. SPH to EPP, September 2, 1870, MS Morgan; SPH to JH, November 9, 1870, MS Berg.

6. SPH to JH, November 9, 1870, MS Berg; RH to MPM, August 26, 1870, MS Berg; Frank Lathrop to Una, November 25, 1870, MS Bancroft.

7. For reviews of *Passages from the English Note-books*, see Woodson, "Historical Commentary," *CE*, 21:744–748, the *Athenaeum* quoted on 744 and the *Literary World* on 748.

8. Una's narrative of the last days of her mother's life is found in JH, *Hawthorne and His Wife*, II:353–371.

9. SPH, "Preface," *Passages from the English Note-books by Nathaniel Hawthorne*, http://www.gutenberg.org.

10. SPH to EPP, February 16, 1870, MS Morgan.

11. Gary Scharnhorst, *Julian Hawthorne: The Life of a Prodigal Son*, 160–163.

Bibliography

Manuscript Sources

I am grateful to Bradford Johnson for his permission to quote from a transcript of a letter in his possession written by his great-great-aunt, Sophia Peabody Hawthorne. I thank Susan Abele, Ada Shepard's literary heir, for permission to quote from transcripts of Ada's letters in the Beinecke Library. I also wish to express my gratitude to curators at the manuscripts collections and archives below for granting permission, when needed, to quote or cite portions of holograph letters and journals.

Antioch: Robert L. Straker Transcription Peabody and Mann Letters, Antiochiana, Antioch University, Yellow Springs, Ohio.

Bancroft: The Bancroft Library, Hawthorne Family Papers, Papers of Sophia Amelia (Peabody) Hawthorne, University of California at Berkeley, Berkeley, California.

Barrett: Clifton Waller Barrett Library of American Literature, Sophia Peabody Hawthorne Collection, University of Virginia, Charlottesville, Virginia.

Berg: Henry W. and Albert A. Berg Collection, New York Public Library, Astor, Lenox, and Tilden Foundations, New York City, New York.

Bienecke: The Norman Holmes Pearson Collection, Bienecke Library, Yale University, New Haven, Connecticut.

BPL: The Boston Public Library/Rare Books, Boston, Massachusetts.

DSHA: Dominican Sisters of Hawthorne Archives, Hawthorne, New York.

Huntington: The Huntington Library, San Marino, California.

MHS: Massachusetts Historical Society, the Horace Mann Papers, Boston, Massachusetts

Morgan: The Pierpont Morgan Library, Hawthorne Family Papers, New York City, New York.

New-York Historical Society, New York City, New York.

Stanford: Green Library, Department of Special Collections and University Archives, Hawthorne Family Papers, Stanford University, Stanford, California.

St. Lawrence University: The Ulysses S. Milburn Collection of the Owen D. Young Library, St. Lawrence University, Canton, New York.

Washington State University Libraries: Louise Deming and Aretta Stevens Project Papers among the letters of Sophia Peabody Hawthorne, Manuscripts, Archives, and Special Collections, Pullman, Washington.

Unpublished Sources

Fisk, Rosemary Mims. "The Profession of Authorship: Nathaniel Hawthorne and His Publisher, James T. Fields." PhD diss, Rice University, 1984. http://scholarship.rice.edu/bitstream/handle/1911/15897/8517196.PDF?sequence=1, date of access, June 26, 2013.

Harris, Sheldon Howard. "The Public Career of John Louis O'Sullivan." PhD diss., Columbia University, 1958.

Reenan, William, ed. *Nathaniel Hawthorne Diary of 1859* with Appendix. Privately printed, Freelands, TS Berg.

Published Sources

Auster, Paul. *Twenty Days with Julian and Little Bunny.* New York: New York Review of Books, 2003.

Avery, Gillian. *Behold the Child: American Children and Their Books 1621–1922.* Baltimore: Johns Hopkins University Press, 1994.

Badaracco, Claire M. "Pitfalls and Rewards of the Solo Editor: Sophia Peabody Hawthorne." *Resources for American Literary Study* 11:3 (Spring 1981): 91–100.

Bassan, Maurice. *Hawthorne's Son: The Life and Literary Career of Julian Hawthorne.* Columbus, Ohio: Ohio State University Press, 1970.

Bensick, Carol M. "Dimmesdale and His Bachelorhood: 'Priestly Celibacy' in *The Scarlet Letter.*" *Studies in American Fiction* 21:1 (1993): 103–110.

Bergland, Renée. *Maria Mitchell and the Sexing of Science: An Astronomer among the American Romantics.* Boston: Beacon Press, 2008.

Birdsall, Richard D. "Emerson and the Church of Rome." *American Literature* 23:1 (1959): 273–281.

Bowers, Fredson. "Introduction to *Fanshawe*." *The Blithedale Romance* and *Fanshawe*. Vol. 3 of *The Centenary Edition of The Works of Nathaniel Hawthorne*, edited by William Charvat, Roy Harvey Pearce, and Claude M. Simpson. Columbus: Ohio State University Press, 1964: 301–330.

————. "Textual Introduction" and "Alterations in the Manuscript." *The Marble Faun*. Vol. 4 of *The Centenary Edition of The Works of Nathaniel Hawthorne*, edited by William Charvat, Roy Harvey Pearce, and Claude M. Simpson. Columbus: Ohio State University Press, 1968: xlvcxxxiii; 529–576.

————. "Textual Introduction." *True Stories*. Vol. 6 of *The Centenary Edition of The Works of Nathaniel Hawthorne*, edited by William Charvat, Roy Harvey Pearce, and Claude M. Simpson. Columbus: Ohio State University Press, 1972: 313–336.

Braude, Ann. *Radical Spirits: Spiritualism and Women's Rights in Nineteenth-Century America*. Boston: Beacon Press, 1989.

Brodhead, Richard. *Culture of Letters: Scenes of Reading and Writing in Nineteenth-Century America*. Chicago: University of Chicago Press, 1993.

Brown, Gillian. "Hawthorne and Children in the Nineteenth Century: Daughters, Flowers, Stories." In *A Historical Guide to Nathaniel Hawthorne*, edited by Larry J. Reynolds, 79–108. New York: Oxford University Press, 2001.

Byron, Lord George Gordon. *Childe Harold's Pilgrimage*. New York: The F. M. Lupton Publishing Company, n.d.

Capper, Charles. *Margaret Fuller: An American Romantic Life*, Vol. 1, *The Private Years*. New York: Oxford University Press, 1992.

————. *Margaret Fuller: An American Romantic Life*, Vol. 2, *The Public Years*. New York: Oxford University Press, 2007.

Caroli, Betty Boyd. *First Ladies*. Expanded Edition. New York: Oxford University Press, 1995.

Chevigny, Bell Gale. *The Woman and the Myth: Margaret Fuller's Life and Writings*. Revised and Expanded. Boston: Northeastern University Press, 1994.

Coale, Samuel Chase. *Mesmerism and Hawthorne: Mediums of American Romance*. Tuscaloosa and London: University of Alabama Press, 1998.

Cost Books of Ticknor and Fields and Their Predecessors: 1832–1858. Edited with an introduction and notes by Warren S. Tryon and William Charvat. New York: The Bibliographical Society of America, 1949.

Coultrap-McQuin, Susan. *Doing Literary Business: American Women Writers in the Nineteenth Century*. Chapel Hill: University of North Carolina Press, 1990.

Crabtree, Adam. *From Mesmerism to Freud: Magnetic Sleep and the Roots of Psychological Healing*. New Haven: Yale University Press, 1993.

Deese, Helen R. "A New England Women's Network: Elizabeth Palmer Peabody, Caroline Healey Dall, and Delia S. Bacon." *Legacy: A Journal of American Women Writers* 8:2 (1991): 77–91.

De Rocher, Cecile Anne. Introduction to *Elizabeth Manning Hawthorne: A Life in Letters*. Tuscaloosa: University of Alabama Press, 2006.

Dudden, Faye E. *Serving Women: Household Service in Nineteenth-Century America*. Middletown: Wesleyan University Press, 1983.

Duncan, Russell. "Robert Gould Shaw: A Biographical Essay." In *Blue-Eyed Child of Fortune: The Civil War Letters of Colonel Robert Gould Shaw*, edited by Russell Duncan. Athens: University of Georgia Press, 1992: 1–68.

Dunn, Frederick L. "Malaria." In *The Cambridge World History of Human Disease*, edited by Kenneth Kiple. New York: Cambridge University Press, 1993: 855–860.

Edelstein, Tilden G. *Strange Enthusiasm: The Life of Thomas Wentworth Higginson*. New York: Athenaeum, 1970.

Elsden, Annamaria Formichella. "Watery Angels: Sophia Peabody Hawthorne's Artistic Argument in *Notes in England and Italy*." In *Reinventing the Peabody Sisters*, edited by Monika Elbert, Julie E. Hall, and Katharine Rodier. Iowa City: University of Iowa Press, 2006: 129–145.

Emerson, Ralph Waldo. *Essays & Lectures*. Edited by Joel Porte. New York: Library of America, 1983.

Faust, Drew Gilpin. *This Republic of Suffering: Death and the American Civil War*. New York: Random House, 2008.

Ford, Andrew Elmer. *The Story of the Fifteenth Regiment Massachusetts Volunteer Infantry in the Civil War 1861–1864*. Clinton: Press of W. J. Coulter Courant Office, 1898, http://books.google.com.

Franchot, Jenny. *Roads to Rome: The Antebellum Protestant Encounter with Catholicism*. Berkeley: University of California Press, 1994.

Gamber, Wendy. *The Boarding House in Nineteenth-Century America*. Baltimore: Johns Hopkins University Press, 2007.

Gilder, Cornelia Brooke with Julia Conklin Peters. *Hawthorne's Lenox: The Tanglewood Circle*. Charleston: The History Press, 2008.

Goddu, Teresa. "The Circulation of Women in *The House of the Seven Gables*." *Studies in the Novel* 23:1 (1991): 119–128.

Gollin, Rita. "The Hawthornes' 'Golden Dora'." *Studies in the American Renaissance* (1981), ed. Joel Myerson. Charlottesville: University Press of Virginia: 393–401.

Goodrich, Samuel Griswold. *Recollections of a Lifetime, or, Men and Things I Have Seen: in a Series of Familiar Letters to a Friend, Historical, Biographical, Anecdotal, and Descriptive.* 2 vols. New York and Auburn: Miller, Orton & Co., 1857.

Goodwin, Joan. *The Remarkable Mrs. Ripley: The Life of Sarah Alden Bradford Ripley.* Boston: Northeastern University Press, 1998.

Hall, Julie E. "'Coming to Europe,' Coming to Authorship: Sophia Hawthorne and Her *Notes in England and Italy." Legacy: A Journal of American Women Writers* 19 (2002): 137–151.

————. "Writing at the Crossroads: Sophia Hawthorne's Civil War Letters to Annie Fields." *Legacy: A Journal of American Women Writers* 25:2 (2008) 251–261.

Hamilton, Gail. *The Battle of the Books, Recorded by an Unknown Writer, for the Use of Authors and Publishers.* Cambridge: Riverside Press, 1870.

Hawthorne, Elizabeth Manning. *Elizabeth Manning Hawthorne, A Life in Letters.* Edited by Cecile De Rocher. Athens: University of Georgia Press, 2006.

Hawthorne, Julian. *Hawthorne and His Wife.* 2 vols. Boston: Houghton Mifflin, 1884.

————. *Hawthorne and His Circle.* Lexington: Filiquarian Publishing, 2010.

————. *Memoirs of Julian Hawthorne.* Edited by Edith Garrigues Hawthorne. New York: Macmillan, 1938.

Hawthorne, Nathaniel. *Centenary Edition of the Works of Nathaniel Hawthorne.* Edited by William Charvat et al. 23 vols. Columbus: Ohio State University Press, 1962–1997.

————. *Passages from the American Note-books.* Boston: Ticknor and Fields, 1868.

————. Preface to *The Gentle Boy: A Thrice Told Tale.* Boston: Weeks, Jordan & Co.; New York & London: Wiley & Putnam, 1839.

Hawthorne, Sophia Peabody. *Notes in England and Italy.* New York: Putnam & Son, 1869.

————. *Ordinary Mysteries: The Common Journal of Nathaniel and Sophia Hawthorne, 1842–1843.* Edited with an introduction by Nicholas R. Lawrence and Marta L. Werner. Philadelphia: American Philosophical Society, 2005.

————. "Preface," *Passages from the English Note-books by Nathaniel Hawthorne, 1868.* http://www.gutenberg.org.

———. "Sophia Peabody Hawthorne's *American Notebooks*." Edited with an introduction by Patricia Dunlavy Valenti. *Studies in the American Renaissance* (1996), ed. Joel Myerson. Charlottesville: University of Press of Virginia: 115–185.

———. "A Sophia Hawthorne Journal, 1843–44." Edited by John McDonald. *Nathaniel Hawthorne Journal* (1974): 1–30.

———. "With Hawthorne in Wartime Concord: Sophia Hawthorne's 1862 Diary." Edited with an introduction and "Index of Names" by Thomas Woodson, James A. Rubino, and Jamie Barlowe Kayes. *Studies in the American Renaissance* (1988), ed. Joel Myerson. Charlottesville: University Press of Virginia: 281–359.

Hecker, Isaac T. *Isaac T. Hecker: The Diary: Romantic Religion in Ante-Bellum America.* New York: Paulist Press, 1988.

Herbert, T. Walter. *Dearest Beloved: The Hawthornes and the Makings of the Middle-Class Family.* Berkeley: University of California Press, 1993.

———. "Nathaniel Hawthorne, Una Hawthorne, and *The Scarlet Letter*: Interactive Selfhoods and the Cultural Construction of Gender." *Publications of the Modern Language Association* 103 (1988): 285–297.

Higginson, Storrow. "Extracts from Teachers' Letters," *The Freedmen's Record*, July 1865, http://mac110.assumption.edu/aas/reports/freedrechig.html. An American Antiquarian Society Online Exhibition, Curated by Lucia Z. Knoles, Professor of English, Assumption College. Date of access December 18, 2008 (no longer available).

Hitchcock, Ethan Allen. *A Traveler in Indian Territory: The Journal of Ethan Allen Hitchcock.* Edited by Grant Foreman. *Oklahoma Historical Society's Encyclopedia of Oklahoma History and Culture.* http://digital.library.okstate.edu.

———. *Christ the Spirit: being an Attempt to state the Primitive View of Christianity.* http://www.cclibraries.com.

———. *Swedenborg, A Hermetic Philosopher, Being a Sequel to Remarks on Alchemy and the Alchemist.* New York: D. Appleton and Co., 1858, http://books.google.com.

———. *The Red Book of Appin; a Story of the Middle Ages with other Hermetical Stories and Allegorical Tales . . . and Remarks upon The Arabian Nights' Entertainments.* New York: James Miller Publishers, 1866.

Holmes, Oliver Wendell. "Hawthorne." *The Atlantic Monthly* 14:81 (July 1864): 98–101.

Howe, M. A. De Wolfe. *Memories of a Hostess, A Chronicle of Eminent Friendships, Drawn Chiefly from the Diaries of Mrs. James T. Fields.* Boston: The Atlantic Monthly Press, 1922.

Hull, Raymona E. *Nathaniel Hawthorne: The English Experience, 1853–1864.* Pittsburgh: University of Pittsburgh Press, 1980.

James, Henry. *William Wetmore Story and His Friends.* 2 vols. Boston: Houghton Mifflin, 1904. http://books.google.com/books?id=t9eY44fvPyIC &printsec=frontcover&source=gbs_ge_summary_r&cad=0#v=onepage&q&f=false.

Johnson, Claudia. "Discord in Concord." In *Hawthorne and Women: Engendering and Expanding the Hawthorne Tradition,* edited by John L. Idol Jr. and Melinda M. Ponder, Boston: University of Massachusetts Press, 1999: 104–120.

———. "Impotence and Omnipotence in *The Scarlet Letter.*" *New England Quarterly* 66:4 (1993): 594–612.

Kantor, Robert E. "Gail Hamilton (Mary Abigail Dodge) (1833–1896)." In *Nineteenth-Century American Women Writers: A Bio-Bibliographical Critical Sourcebook,* edited by Denise D. Knight. Westport: Greenwood Press, 1997: 199–205.

Keats, John. "Endymion." *The Poems of John Keats.* Edited by Jack Stillinger. Cambridge: Harvard University Press, 1978.

Kern, Alexander. "A Note on Hawthorne's Juveniles." *Philological Quarterly* 39 (1960): 242–246.

Kissan, Richard. *The Nurses Manual and Young Mother's Guide.* Hartford: 1834.

Lathrop, Rose Hawthorne. *Memories of Hawthorne.* Boston: Houghton Mifflin, 1897.

Loggins, Vernon. *The Hawthornes: The Story of Seven Generations of an American Family.* New York: Columbia University Press, 1951; rpt. New York: Greenwood Press, 1968.

Long, Larry R. "Samuel Griswold Goodrich (Peter Parley)." In *The Dictionary of Literary Biography,* edited by Wesley T. Mott, Vol. 243. Farmington Hills: Gale Group, 2001: 156–163.

Mann, Mary. *Life of Horace Mann by his Wife.* Boston: Walker Fuller and Co., 1865.

Marshall, Megan. *The Peabody Sisters: Three Women Who Ignited American Romanticism.* Boston: Houghton Mifflin, 2005.

———. "The Other Sister." *The New Yorker* (March 21, 2005): 40–47.

Matteson, John. *Eden's Outcasts: The Story of Louisa May Alcott and Her Father.* New York: Norton, 2007.

McLoughlin, William G. "Evangelical Childrearing in the Age of Jackson: Francis Wayland's View on When and How to Subdue the Willfulness of Children." *Journal of Social History* 9:1 (1975): 20–43.

McSorley, Joseph. *Isaac Hecker and His Friends.* New York: Paulist Press, 1972.

Mellow, James R. *Nathaniel Hawthorne and His Times*. Boston: Houghton Mifflin, 1980.

Melville, Herman. *The Writings of Herman Melville*. Vol. 14, *Correspondence*. Edited by Lynn Horth. The Northwestern-Newberry Edition. Evanston and Chicago: Northwestern University Press and Newberry Library, 1993.

———. "Hawthorne and His Mosses." In *The Norton Anthology of American Literature, 1820–1865*. Vol. B, Sixth Edition. Nina Baym, General Editor. New York: Norton, 2003: 2292–2304.

Merrill, Lisa. *When Romeo Was a Woman: Charlotte Cushman and Her Circle of Female Spectators*. Ann Arbor: University of Michigan Press, 1999.

Messerli, Jonathan. *Horace Mann: A Biography*. New York: Knopf, 1972.

Metzdorf, Robert F. "Hawthorne's Suit against Dana and Ripley." *American Literature* 12 (1940): 235–241.

Miller, Edwin Haviland. "A Calendar of the Letters of Sophia Peabody Hawthorne." In *Studies in the American Renaissance* (1986), ed. Joel Myerson. Charlottesville: University Press of Virginia: 199–281.

———. *Salem Is My Dwelling Place*. Iowa City: University of Iowa Press, 1991.

Mills, Angela. "'The Sweet Word,' Sister: The Transformative Threat of Sisterhood and *The Blithedale Romance*." *American Transcendental Quarterly* 17:2 (2003): 97–121.

Mitchell, Thomas R. *Hawthorne's Fuller Mystery*. Amherst: University of Massachusetts Press, 1998.

Morgan, Edmund S. "The Puritans and Sex." *New England Quarterly* 15 (1942): 591–607.

Mott, Wesley T., ed. *Encyclopedia of Transcendentalism*. Westport: Greenwood Press, 1996.

Myerson, Joel. "'A True and High Minded Person': Transcendentalist Sarah Clarke." *Southwest Review* 59 (Spring 1974): 163–172.

Nichols, Roy Franklin. *Franklin Pierce: Young Hickory of Granite Hills*. Philadelphia: University of Pennsylvania Press, 1958.

Parker, Hershel. *Herman Melville: A Biography* Vol. 2, *1851–1891*. Baltimore: Johns Hopkins University Press, 2002.

Peabody, Elizabeth Palmer. *The Letters of Elizabeth Palmer Peabody: American Renaissance Woman*. Edited with an introduction by Bruce Ronda. Middletown: Wesleyan University Press, 1984.

———. *Memorial of William Wesselhoeft*. Boston: N. C. Cranch, 1859; rpt. in Bradford, Thomas Lindsley. *The Pioneers of Homeopathy*. Philadelphia: Boericke & Tafel, 1897: 644–62.

———. "A Psychological Observation." In *Lectures in the Training Schools for Kindergartners*. Boston: D. C. Heath, 1888.

Peabody, Elizabeth Palmer (Mrs.). *Holiness; or the Legend of St. George: A Tale from Spencer's Faerie Queene*, by a mother. Boston: E. R. Broaders, 1836.

Pearson, Norman Holmes. *Hawthorne's Two Engagements*. Northampton: Smith College, 1963.

———. "Elizabeth Peabody on Hawthorne." *Essex Institute Historical Collections* 94 (July 1958): 256–276.

———. "Hawthorne's Duel." *Essex Institute Historical Collections* 94 (July 1958): 229–242.

Petrulionis, Sandra Harbert. *To Set This World Right: The Anti-Slavery Movement in Thoreau's Concord*. Ithaca: Cornell University Press, 2006.

Ragussis, Michael. "Family Discourse and Fiction in *The Scarlet Letter*." *English Literary History* 49:1 (1982): 863–888.

Remini, Robert. *Daniel Webster: The Man and His Times*. New York: Norton, 1997.

Reynolds, David. *John Brown, Abolitionist: The Man Who Killed Slavery, Sparked the Civil War, and Seeded Civil Rights*. New York: Knopf, 2005.

Reynolds, Larry J. *Devils and Rebels: The Making of Hawthorne's Damned Politics*. Ann Arbor: University of Michigan Press, 2008.

———. *A Historical Guide to Nathaniel Hawthorne*. New York: Oxford University Press, 2001.

Richardson, Robert D., Jr. *Emerson: The Mind on Fire, A Biography*. Berkeley and Los Angeles: University of California Press, 1995.

Roman, Judith A. *Annie Adams Fields: The Spirit of Charles Street*. Bloomington: Indiana University Press, 1990.

Romero, Mary. "Sisterhood and Domestic Service: Race, Class and Gender in the Mistress-Maid Relationship." *Humanity and Society* 12:4 (1988): 318–346.

Ronda, Bruce. *Elizabeth Palmer Peabody: A Reformer on Her Own Terms*. Cambridge: Harvard University Press, 1999.

Rorabaugh, W. J. "Who Fought for the North in the Civil War? Concord, Massachusetts, Enlistments." *Journal of American History* 73:3 (December 1986): 695–701.

Rosenberg, Charles. "Bitter Fruit: Heredity, Disease and Social Thought in Nineteenth-Century America." *Perspectives in American History* 8 (1974): 189–235.

———. *The Cholera Years: The United States in 1832, 1849, and 1866*. Chicago: University of Chicago Press, 1962.

————. "Sexuality, Class, and Race in 19th-Century America." *American Quarterly* 25 (1973):121–153.

————. "The Therapeutic Revolution: Medicine, Meaning, and Social Change in Nineteenth-Century America." In *The Therapeutic Revolution: Essays in the Social History of American Medicine*, edited by Morris J. Vogel and Charles Rosenberg. Philadelphia: University of Pennsylvania Press, 1979: 3–25.

Saulsbury, Rebecca R. "Catharine Maria Sedgwick (1789–1867)." In *Nineteenth-Century American Women Writers: A Bio-Bibliographical Critical Sourcebook*, edited by Denise K. Knight. Westport: Greenwood Press, 1997: 351–360.

Sampson, Robert D. *John L. O'Sullivan and His Times*. Kent: Kent State University Press, 2003.

Scharnhorst, Gary. *The Critical Responses to Nathaniel Hawthorne's* The Scarlet Letter. New York: Greenwood Press, 1992.

————. *Julian Hawthorne: The Life of a Prodigal Son*. Urbana: University of Illinois Press, 2014.

Schriber, Mary Suzanne. *Writing Home: American Women Abroad, 1830–1920*. Charlottesville: University Press of Virginia, 1997.

Scudder, Townsend. *Concord: American Town*. Boston: Little Brown, 1947.

Selley, April. "Francis George Shaw." In *Biographical Dictionary of Transcendentalism*, edited by Wesley T. Mott. Westport: Greenwood Press, 1996: 235–236.

Sherwood, Dolly. *Harriet Hosmer, American Sculptor, 1830–1908*. Columbia: University of Missouri Press, 1991.

Simpson, Claude. "Historical Commentary." *The American Notebooks*. Vol. 8 of *The Centenary Edition of the Works of Nathaniel Hawthorne*, edited by William Charvat, Roy Harvey Pearce and Claude M. Simpson. Columbus: Ohio State University Press, 1972.

————. With Edward H. Davidson. "Historical Commentary." *The Elixir of Life Manuscripts*, Vol. 13 of *The Centenary Edition of the Works of Nathaniel Hawthorne*, edited by Edward H. Davidson, Claude M. Simpson, and L. Neal Smith. Columbus, Ohio: Ohio State University Press, 1994: 557–590.

————. "Introduction." *The Marble Faun*. Vol. 4 of *The Centenary Edition of The Works of Nathaniel Hawthorne*, edited by William Charvat, Roy Harvey Pearce, and Claude M. Simpson. Columbus: Ohio State University Press, 1968: xix–xliv.

————. "Introduction." *Our Old Home*. Vol. 5 of *The Centenary Edition of the Works of Nathaniel Hawthorne*, edited by William Charvat, Roy Harvey Pearce, Claude M. Simpson, Matthew J. Bruccoli. Columbus: Ohio State University Press, 1970: xiii–xli.

Smith, L. Neal. "Textual Commentary." *The French and Italian Notebooks*. Vol. 14 of *The Centenary Edition of the Works of Nathaniel Hawthorne*, edited by William Charvat, Roy Harvey Pearce, Claude M. Simpson, and Thomas Woodson. Columbus: Ohio State University Press, 1980: 937–942.

Stewart, Randall. *Nathaniel Hawthorne: A Biography*. New Haven: Yale University Press, 1948.

———. "Editing *The American Notebooks*." *The Essex Institute Historical Collections* 94 (1958): 277–281.

———. "Mrs. Hawthorne's Financial Difficulties: Letters to Fields 1865–1868." *More Books: Bulletin of the Boston Public Library* 21 (1946): 43–52.

———. "Mrs. Hawthorne's Quarrel with James T. Fields. Selections of the Letters to Fields by Mrs. Hawthorne and Elizabeth Peabody." *More Books: Bulletin of the Boston Public Library* 21 (1946): 254–263.

———. "Editing Hawthorne's Notebooks: Selections from Mrs. Hawthorne's Letters to Mr. and Mrs. Fields, 1864–68." *More Books: Bulletin of the Boston Public Library* 21 (September 1945): 299–315.

Stoehr, Taylor. *Hawthorne's Mad Scientists: Pseudoscience and Social Science in Nineteenth-Century Life and Letters*. Hamden: Shoe String Press, 1978.

Tharp, Louisa Hall. *The Peabody Sisters of Salem*. Boston: Little, Brown, 1950.

———. *Until Victory: Horace Mann and Mary Peabody*. Reprint. Westport: Greenwood Press, 1953/1977.

Tilton, Eleanor. "The True Romance of Anna Hazard Barker and Samuel Gray Ward." *Studies in the American Renaissance* (1987), ed. Joel Myerson. Charlottesville: University Press of Virginia: 53–72.

Tyron, Warren S. and William Charvat. Introduction and Notes to *The Cost Books of Ticknor and Fields and Their Predecessors: 1832–1858*. Edited by Warren S. Tyron and William Charvat. New York: The Bibliographical Society of America, 1949.

Tyron, Warren S. *Parnassus Corner: A Life of James T. Fields*. Boston: Houghton Mifflin, 1963.

Valenti, Patricia D. "Editing Sophia Peabody Hawthorne's Travel Writing and the Conundrum of Copies." *Documentary Editing* 32 (2011): 1–11.

———. Introduction to "Sophia Peabody Hawthorne's American Notebooks." *Studies in the American Renaissance* (1996), ed. Joel Myerson. Charlottesville: University Press of Virginia: 115–128.

————. " 'None but Imaginative Authority': Nathaniel Hawthorne and the Progress of Nineteenth-Century (Juvenile) Literature in America." *Nathaniel Hawthorne Review* 36:1 (Spring 2010): 1–27.

————. *Sophia Peabody Hawthorne, A Life,* Vol. 1, *1809–1847.* Columbia: University of Missouri Press, 2004.

————. "Sophia Peabody Hawthorne: A Study of Artistic Influence." *Studies in the American Renaissance* (1990), ed. Joel Myerson. Charlottesville: University Press of Virginia: 1-21.

————. "Sophia Peabody Hawthorne and 'The—What?': Creative Copies in Art and Literature." *Nathaniel Hawthorne Review* 37:2 (Fall 2011): 48–72.

————. *To Myself a Stranger: A Biography of Rose Hawthorne Lathrop.* Baton Rouge: Lousiana State University Press, 1991.

Waggoner, Hyatt Howe. Introduction. *Hawthorne's Lost Notebook: 1835–1841.* University Park: Pennsylvania State University Press, 1978.

————. "The New Hawthorne Notebook: Further Reflections on the Life and Work." *Novel* 11 (September 1978): 218–226.

————. "A Hawthorne Discovery: The Lost Notebook, 1835–1841." *New England Quarterly* 49 (December 1976): 618–626.

Waugh, Joan. "The Shaw Family and the Fifty-Fourth Massachusetts Regiment." In *Hope and Glory: Essays on the Legacy of the Fifty-Fourth Massachusetts Regiment,* edited by Martin H. Blatt, Thomas J. Brown, and Donald Yacovone. Amherst: University of Massachusetts Press, 2001: 52–78.

————. *Unsentimental Reformer: The Life of Josephine Shaw Lowell.* Cambridge: Harvard University Press, 1997.

Weisberg, Barbara. *Talking to the Dead: Kate and Maggie Fox and the Rise of Spiritualism.* San Francisco: Harper, 2004.

Werner, Marta, and Nicholas Lawrence. "This Is His—This Is My Mystery: The Common Journal of Nathaniel and Sophia Hawthorne, 1842–1843." In *Reinventing the Peabody Sisters,* edited by Monika M. Elbert, Julie E. Hall, and Katharine Rodier. Iowa City: University of Iowa Press, 2006.

Wineapple, Brenda. *Hawthorne.* New York: Knopf, 2002.

Wojtusik, Barbara Downs. "Anna Hazard Barker Ward" and "Samuel Gray Ward." In *The Biographical Dictionary of Transcendentalism,* edited by Wesley T. Mott, Westport: Greenwood Press: 264–265.

Woodson, Thomas. "Introduction." *The Letters, 1853–1856.* Vol. 17 of *The Centenary Edition of the Works of Nathaniel Hawthorne,* edited by Thomas Woodson, James Rubino, L. Neal Smith, and Norman

Holmes Pearson. Columbus: Ohio State University Press, 1987: 3–85.

———. "Historical Commentary." *The English Notebooks 1853–1856*. Vol. 21 of *The Centenary Edition of the Works of Nathaniel Hawthorne*, edited by William Charvat, Roy Harvey Pearce, Claude M. Simpson, and Thomas Woodson. Columbus: Ohio State University Press, 1997: 709–748.

———. "Historical Commentary." *The French and Italian Notebooks*. Vol. 14 of *The Centenary Edition of the Works of Nathaniel Hawthorne*, edited by William Charvat, Roy Harvey Pearce, Claude M. Simpson, and Thomas Woodson. Columbus: Ohio State University Press, 1980: 903–935.

———. "Historical and Textual Commentary." *Miscellaneous Prose and Verse*. Vol. 23 of *The Centenary Edition of the Works of Nathaniel Hawthorne*, edited by Thomas Woodson, Claude M. Simpson, and L. Neal Smith. Columbus: Ohio State University Press, 1994: 551–705.

———. "With Hawthorne in Wartime Concord: Sophia Hawthorne's 1862 Diary." Edited with an introduction and "Index of Names" by Thomas Woodson, James A. Rubino, Jamie Barlowe Kayes. *Studies in the American Renaissance* (1988), ed. Joel Myerson. Charlottesville: University Press of Virginia: 281–359.

Yellin, Jean Fagan. "Hawthorne and the Slavery Question." In *A Historical Guide to Nathaniel Hawthorne*, edited by Larry J. Reynolds. New York: Oxford University Press, 2001: 135–164.

Index